"Life is amazing. And then it's awful. And then it's amazing again. And in between the amazing and awful it's ordinary and mundane and routine. Breath in the amazing, hold on through the awful, and relax and exhale during the ordinary. That's just living heartbreaking, soul-healing, amazing, awful, ordinary life.
And it's breathtakingly beautiful."

L.R. Knost

Joseph,
I have always had great respect for you as a leader and a friend. You were truly the glue that held the Occupational Medicine Division together for all these years. I wish for you and Leilani a wonderful and adventurous retirement. Please feel free to reach out to me anytime.
Take care,
Jeff

# THE
# BUCKET
# LIST

First published in the United States of America in 2017 by
Universe Publishing, a division of
Rizzoli International Publications, Inc.
300 Park Avenue South
New York, NY 10010
www.rizzoliusa.com

Fifteenth printing, 2019
2019 2020 2021 2022 / 15

ISBN: 978-0-7893-3269-1

Library of Congress Control Number: 2016955479

The Bright Press, an imprint of The Quarto Group
The Old Brewery
6 Blundell Street
London N7 9BH
United Kingdom
**T** (0)20 7700 6700
**www.QuartoKnows.com**

Managing Editor: Rica Dearman
General Editor: Kath Stathers
Senior Editor: Caroline Elliker
Designer: Maru Studio
Jacket design: Linda Pricci
Picture Researcher: Lauren Azor
Art Director: Michael Charles
Associate Publisher: Emma Bastow
Publisher: Mark Searle

Manufactured in Hong Kong

EDITED BY KATH STATHERS

# THE
# BUCKET
# LIST

*1000 Adventures*
*Big & Small*

**UNIVERSE**

# CONTENTS

 Micro adventure

Cultural discoveries

 Feast for the senses

The Casa del Arbol swing, in Baños, Ecuador (see page 400)

# INTRODUCTION

At every point of our lives we have things we really want to do … whether it's to perform on stage with Katy Perry when we're seven or to walk under cherry trees in Kyoto when we're seventy. We've come to refer to these wish lists as "Bucket Lists," even though we make them at any age and not just when kicking the bucket is a more imminent concern.

Often the wishes are travel related, but they don't have to be. In fact, the term "Bucket List" only came into popular use after the 2007 movie *The Bucket List* made it big, and guess what was on screenwriter Justin Zackham's list? "Get a movie made by a major studio."

Bucket list entries take many forms: they can be personal goals, such as writing a novel, or epic adventures, such as taking a road trip. They can be a big deal, such as scaling every mountain on every continent, or gentle achievements, such as selling something you made with your own hands.

Some people's bucket lists are about doing something in a certain time, such as James Asquith, who wanted to visit every sovereign country in the world before he was twenty-five. He completed it, earning himself a spot in *Guinness World Records* in the process.

Other entries can reflect more on the simple pleasures of life. In *The Bucket List* movie,

number three on Jack Nicholson and Morgan Freeman's list was "Laugh until I cry."

What makes a goal worthy of appearing on a bucket list is that it's something you've never done before; you'll get a deep personal satisfaction from doing it; and you'll remember the experience for the rest of your life.

In this book we have brought together 1,000 different ideas for a bucket list. We start at the North Pole and work our way down the planet by latitude until we arrive at the South Pole. There are ideas that are definitely destination based, such as climbing to the top of Sigiriya in Sri Lanka, and others that could act as an inspiration to add an activity to your list, such as taking a cue from Memory Lane in Syracuse, in the US, to write your memoirs. To easily find the locations of the bucket list entries in this book, simply visit **www.quartoknows.com/page/bucket-list**

Before you write your list, browse through the book for inspiration and see what really speaks to you. There is no set amount of entries that a list should have, and no rules about how often you can add to it. It is your personal creation to reflect where you want to go, and what you want to see and do in your life. So start dreaming, start planning, and get going!

One of the picture-perfect fjords
in the west of Norway (see page 14)

# CHAPTER 1
# NORTHERN
# HEMISPHERE

from 90° north to 60° north

## 1. Soar over the wilderness of the North Pole

**When:** Planned trips run June and July

**Latitude:** 90°N **Longitude:** 0°

The Polar Route, or "Santa's Shortcut," has been open to many long-haul twin-jet flights since 2011, so technically, you could be flying over the North Pole as you head off on your summer holiday. To get closer to the "Top of the World," though—the only place on Earth you can look only south—you need to take an icebreaker ship and then a helicopter or a tethered hot-air balloon.

If the weather allows, you can soar high over the sculpted snow and ice of the Arctic Ocean, a pristine, white-and-blue wilderness that stretches for miles in every southerly direction.

## 2. Do the "Grand Slam" of mountain climbing

**When:** All year

**Latitude:** 90°N **Longitude:** 0°

To join the exclusive Explorers Grand Slam club, you must summit the highest peak on each of the seven continents, and walk unsupported to the geographic North and South Poles.

The highest peaks are: Africa's Kilimanjaro; Mount Elbrus in Russia; the Carstensz Pyramid, also known as Puncak Jaya, in Asia; Mount Aconcagua in South America; Alaska's Denali; Mount Vinson in Antarctica; and Everest. Then you have the North and South Poles to contend with.

Fancy giving the Grand Slam a go? You'd better get training; only forty-six people have ever done it.

## 3. Bird-watch at the extremes of the Earth

**When:** All year (weather permitting)

**Latitude:** 78.2167°N

**Longitude:** 15.5500°E

Visit the world's most northerly and most southerly towns—especially if you are a keen twitcher. In Longyearbyen, in Norway, a ban on cats keeps the region's Arctic seabird population thriving, while Argentina's Ushuaia offers the chance to walk with penguins.

## 4. Dare to stare from the edge of a cliff

**When:** April to October (to avoid snow and ice)

**Latitude:** 69.9225°N

**Longitude:** 22.0925°E

Make your way up the glacially formed, vast granite plateau of "Pulpit Rock," which rises 1,982 ft (604 m) above Lysefjorden ("Light Fjord"), and you'll be rewarded with jaw-dropping views over the lush, green valleys of the Ryfylke region. It's steep, but such a worthwhile walk to the top.

## 5. Howl at the moon in the company of wolves

**When:** All year

**Latitude:** 68.6917°N

**Longitude:** 18.1098°E

The wolves at Norway's Polar Park are socialized with humans, which means you can get up close and personal with them. Play with them, cuddle them—even spend the night, howling beneath the moon with them.

## 6. Search for the world's last polar bears

**When:** June to September
**Latitude:** 78.2167°N **Longitude:** 15.5500°E

As the world's sea ice melts due to rising temperatures, polar bears are losing their natural habitat and have been listed as a "vulnerable" species—meaning its numbers are expected to decline by more than 30 percent in the next thirty years.

Seek them out in northern Norway, where during summer, the waters surrounding the Svalbard islands melt enough for boats to take visitors out through the islands. There are up to 3,500 polar bears in the region, according to the Norwegian Polar Institute.

## 7. Explore the whalebone Stonehenge

**When:** All year
**Latitude:** 64.5833°N
**Longitude:** 172.4500°W

It was only in the 1970s that archaeologists discovered the dozens of 600-year-old whalebones that jut out of the Siberian tundra to make up Whale Bone Alley on Yttygran island. Explore the site, which is believed to be an ancient place of worship.

KOMI REPUBLIC, RUSSIA
## 8. Tread in Europe's ancient woodland
**When:** All year (weather permitting)
**Latitude:** 62.4167°N
**Longitude:** 58.7833°E (Yugud-Va National Park)

Russia's first UNESCO World Heritage-protected site, the Virgin Komi Forests are the largest, oldest forests in Europe. Discover vast swathes of untouched conifers and aspens, rivers, and lakes in the 8.10 m ac (3.28 m ha) forests that are home to wolves, mink, otters, and beavers, among others.

JOSTEDAL, NORWAY
## 9. Walk on a glacier
**When:** July to August
**Latitude:** 61.7106°N
**Longitude:** 6.9241°E

Jostedalsbreen is the largest glacier in Europe, at over 37 mi (60 km) long. Take a guided walk in the summer and set foot on this slow-moving piece of geological history as you trek through spectacular scenery and blue-ice formations.

BERGEN, NORWAY
## 10. Create a Christmas tree decoration
**When:** December
**Latitude:** 60.3894°N
**Longitude:** 5.3300°E

There's no time like Christmas for inventing traditions, and filling a Norwegian heart-shaped basket with sweets is a fine tradition for any family to create. Learn how to make your own basket—they are traditionally made of woven red and green paper, but with creation, improvisation is key.

LOFOTEN, NORWAY
## 11. Watch puffins fish for their supper
**When:** June to August
**Latitude:** 68.3333°N
**Longitude:** 14.6667°E

The cliffs and bays of Norway's Lofoten archipelago are home to one of the world's most unique seabirds, the Atlantic puffin. Watch this hardy breed of auk—known as the sea parrot because of its colorful bill—emerge from its underground burrow and dive to scoop up beakfuls of schooling fish from the Arctic-chilled water.

GEILO, NORWAY
## 12. Step back in time for a white Christmas
**When:** December 25
**Latitude:** 60.5167°N
**Longitude:** 8.2000°E

Everybody should see snow at Christmastime—at least once. Take the scenic Bergen Railway line from Oslo to the picturesque mountain village of Geilo in Norway. Traditional festive celebrations, horse sleigh rides, and plenty of *glögg* (mulled wine) and cheer will make this a Christmas to remember.

Å, LOFOTEN, NORWAY
## 13. Visit a town called Å
**When:** All year
**Latitude:** 67.8792°N
**Longitude:** 12.9831°E

As the Old Norse word for "small river," *Å* (pronounced "*aw*") is actually a name that is shared among several villages dotted throughout Norway. Visit the one nestled in the Lofoten archipelago in the north of the country for stunning scenery, glorious mountains, and quaint fishing villages.

NORWAY'S WEST COAST

## 14. Voyage along Norway's picture-perfect west coast

**When:** All year (June to August for the midnight sun)
**Latitude:** 69.7269°N **Longitude:** 30.0456°E (Kirkenes, the most northerly port)

The rewards for voyagers along Norway's craggy, water-festooned coastline are immense: UNESCO World Heritage Sites, fishing ports, fjords surrounded by sheer cliffs, waterfalls, and in summer, endless sunshine.

Board a vessel that is nimble enough to sail all the way up the fjords. But before departing from Bergen, meander through the alleyways of the Bryggen wharf, a UNESCO World Heritage site, which will help set the scene for the seafaring journey before you. Ahead lie Norway's fjords—inlets created by Ice Age glaciers, where the water can get as deep as 4,265 ft (1,300 m). These waterways are fringed by fertile soil, surrounded by imposing 6,560 ft (2,000 m) tall mountains.

Of all the picturesque fjords on the journey, there is one that best captures the blue water and fairy-tale landscape of snow-covered mountains and cascading

waterfalls: Geirangerfjord, one of the two Norwegian fjords to secure UNESCO World Heritage status. These waterways are the only way to navigate western Norway, and the voyage follows the route of the original vessels that delivered supplies along this coast.

Head north beyond the Arctic Circle, and the Lofoten islands display unique architecture among idyllic scenery and some of the world's most northerly surfing beaches. Farther north lies Tromsø, where you can visit the stunning Arctic Cathedral. Overlooked by the 3,937 ft (1,200 m) tall Tromsdalstinden peak, the cathedral boasts one of Europe's largest stained-glass windows.

As the cruise reaches its most northerly point, Kirkenes, you will find yourself farther east than Istanbul and St. Petersburg. From here, during winter, you can take a husky-pulled sled across the frozen landscape to a snow hotel. Summertime excursions include hunting for king crab, fishing in the Barents Sea, or heading out in the chilled Arctic waters for a boat ride under the midnight sun.

But whatever the season, as the ship starts its voyage south, you must head out on deck for one final panoramic view of the Arctic wilderness.

Norway's picture-perfect west coast

## 15. Bathe in the magic of the northern lights

**When:** September to March
**Latitude:** 68.3354°N **Longitude:** 27.3345°E

Almost no other image of a natural phenomenon evokes such wonder as that of the northern lights, or aurora borealis. In person, they are even more incomparable, a mysterious dancing mass of color. In Finnish Lapland, the northern lights are visible on roughly 200 nights a year; in southern Finland, it's ten to twenty nights a year. Either way, that's a great chance of seeing the world's greatest natural light show.

Traditional ways to spot them are snowshoeing, cross-country skiing, snowmobile, or sled-dog touring. You can also sleep under the rainbow glow in a 360-degree-view glass igloo located far from artificial light, so you can watch them all night while safely tucked in bed.

▶ RUKA, KUUSAMO, FINLAND
## 16. Safari in the snow on a trip to Finland's wilderness
**When:** December to March
**Latitude:** 66.1651°N **Longitude:** 29.1550°E

North of the metropolitan capital Helsinki and below Lapland lies Kuusamo. In this world of pristine lakes, picturesque fells, and abundant forests, you'll discover the perfect place for a journey into the winter wilderness.

Setting out from the fell Ruka, you'll leave civilization (and cellular phone signals) far behind as you embark on a snowmobile safari. You'll glide through breathtaking landscapes of untouched snowy woodland, and speed across vast frozen lakes. At some of the lakes, holes have been bored through the thick ice, where would-be anglers can drop a line in the hope of hooking a fish. The trail then heads for one of Kuusamo's wilderness huts for you to enjoy a campsite picnic.

A full snow safari experience should also include an ascent to the top of the 1,578 ft (481 m) high Kuntivaara fell, where Finland borders its imposing neighbor, Russia.

For the weary returning to Ruka, you can indulge in a restorative and traditional Finnish sauna. Then feast upon a local dinner inside a candlelit, snow-covered lodge, alongside a roaring fire. The perfect ending to a

Fishing in Finland's wilderness, in Kuusamo

trip in the snow-covered wilderness is a starlit sleigh ride over the Ruka fell.

KVARKEN ARCHIPELAGO, FINLAND
## 17. Watch Earth move in Finland
**When:** All year
**Latitude:** 63.4096°N **Longitude:** 20.9489°E

In the Kvarken Archipelago—the stretch of the Gulf of Bothnia between Finland and Sweden—view the land that is quite literally "growing" out of the sea, as Ice Age glaciers melt in a rare geological process of land uplift called isostasy.

As the bands and ridges (De Geer moraines) of Kvarken's emerging land rise, sheltered, shallow pools form between them, creating havens for bird and marine wildlife. Kvarken's human residents are also drawn together as the uplift advances the shorelines of already inhabited islands and the mainland on either side of the gulf.

Explore Kvarken by boat to experience the space, serenity, and sense of timelessness of the place.

LAPLAND, FINLAND
## 18. Run with a herd of reindeer
**When:** All year (sledding and skiing November to April)
**Latitude:** 67.8402°N
**Longitude:** 25.2835°E

The reindeer of Lapland are semi-domesticated, so spotting a herd of them should be straightforward. The only choice you need to make is whether you choose reindeer sledding, lending a hand on one of the biannual reindeer roundups, or simply skiing past them.

▼ RAUHANIEMI BEACH, TAMPERE, AND ACROSS FINLAND
### 19. Feel the fire and ice of a Finnish lake sauna
**When:** Winter
**Latitude:** 60.3642°N **Longitude:** 24.0038°E

The Finns reign supreme when it comes to the art of the sauna: when the World Sauna Championship was a thing between 1999 and 2010, a Finn won every year, and there's even a Finnish Sauna Society dedicated to keeping up standards across the board. There's only one way to do it properly, and that involves a frozen lake.

It's not for the fainthearted, plunging into icy water after emerging from a hotbox, but the levels of invigoration, the energy boost, and the newfound sense of courage acquired afterwards—once the momentary loss of all feeling to the legs and the screaming has stopped—are spine-tingling. Rauhaniemi Beach is a mecca for this, but you can visit similar versions across Finland.

HELSINKI, FINLAND
### 20. Celebrate springtime in Helsinki
**When:** April 30 to May 1
**Latitude:** 60.1708°N
**Longitude:** 24.9375°E

Vappu, the arrival of spring, sees Helsinkians ditch their hardworking reputation and celebrate with a citywide festival of food and music. Join thousands of local inhabitants as they head to Kaivopuisto (one of the city's oldest parks), clutching bottles of *sima* (Finnish mead), for an indulgent picnic.

An icy dip in a freezing Finnish lake follows a fiery sauna

START IN QAANAAQ, GREENLAND

## 21. Dip your toes in every ocean on the planet

**When:** Location dependent (check for calmest waters)
**Latitude:** 77.4670°N **Longitude:** 69.2222°W

More than 71 percent of Earth is covered in water that has, for the sake of human navigation, been divided into five major oceans: the Arctic, Atlantic, Indian, Pacific, and Southern (Antarctic). That's a lot of water to choose your top five dipping spots from, so why not start at the top?

Dip your toes in the freezing Arctic Ocean in Qaanaaq in Greenland—glaciers are less than an hour's walk from town. Then head over to the warm waters of the Bahamas, for a toe-dipping salute to Christopher Columbus, the first man to cross the Atlantic Ocean.

It was Portuguese explorer Vasco da Gama who "discovered" Asia on a voyage to what is now known as the Indian Ocean. With soft, sandy beaches and tranquil, turquoise sea for most of the year, it would be wrong not to go for a paddle.

For the penultimate toe-dip, it doesn't get any wilder than the Galápagos Islands. Dip your toes in warm waters between December and May when sea turtles are nesting. Then, for the final toe-testing experience, venture down to Albany on Australia's "Rainbow Coast" for a wet and windy dip in the Antarctic-circling Southern Ocean—some 8,261 nm (15,299 km) from where you first began.

ILULISSAT, GREENLAND

## 22. Go hiking in snowshoes

**When:** All year
**Latitude:** 69.2167°N
**Longitude:** 51.1000°W

Snowshoeing may not be the fastest method of travel, but it is an easy, fun, and traditional way to get close to the enigmatic Arctic landscape. So strap on some snowshoes to savor every last bit of its beauty.

SKAFTAFELL, ICELAND

## 23. Trek to Iceland's "Black Falls"

**When:** All year
**Latitude:** 64.0230°N
**Longitude:** 16.9750°W

At the southern end of Europe's second-largest national park, Vatnajökull, lies the Svartifoss ("Black Falls"), a dramatic 65 ft (20 m) waterfall. Trek the 3.5 mi (5.5 km) trail to the heart-shaped falls, which takes you across a rugged landscape of glaciers, volcanoes, and black sand.

ICELAND

## 24. Ride high in a monster truck

**When:** All year
**Latitude:** 64.1333°N
**Longitude:** 21.9333°W

With wheels a few feet tall, monster trucks just shout adventure. Hop aboard one in Iceland, and they will take you up impossible mountain paths and across frozen crusts of ice.

VIÐEY ISLAND, ICELAND

## 25. Feel the love at the Imagine Peace Tower

**When:** October to March (various dates)
**Latitude:** 64.1643°N
**Longitude:** 21.8529°W

Stop over at Yoko Ono's skyscraping, geothermal-powered pillar of light on the island of Viðey. It serves as a loving memorial to late husband John Lennon and also a mesmerizing reminder of the ultimate wish—that we can all imagine peace if we try.

## 26. See a whale's tail in the ocean waves

**When:** April to September
**Latitude:** 66.0500°N **Longitude:** 17.3167°W

Few sights in the natural world can equal watching the pristine waters of the Greenland Sea break as a leviathan of the deep breaches the surface. Being in the presence of creatures so powerful, and yet so gentle, is inspiring and humbling.

During the summer whale-watching season, you can head out in a boat from the fishing port at Húsavík and enter the waters of Skjálfandi Bay, the whale-watching capital of Europe—the Icelandic waters are home to some twenty-four species. Winter whale-watching tours depart less frequently, but come with the chance to see the Northern Lights.

► REYKJAVIK, ICELAND

## 27. Wonder at the uniqueness of Reykjavik

**When:** All year (but best in summer)
**Latitude:** 64.1333°N
**Longitude:** 21.9333°W

Reykjavik is a city of quirks. It's a capital city, yet view it from the top of the rocket-like tower of Reykjavik's Hallgrímskirkja church, and all its edges can be seen at once. When you look down at the city center below, the view is a curious patchwork of colorful roofs.

The unique Hallgrímskirkja church in Reykjavik, Iceland

COASTLINE OF ICELAND

## 28. Drive around Iceland's coastline

**When:** Summer
**Latitude:** 64.1333°N  **Longitude:** 21.9333°W

Nowhere is quite like Iceland. It is full of hot geysers, steaming natural baths, lava fields, waterfalls, volcanoes, and glaciers. There is also a ring road that navigates 832 mi (1,340 km) around its coastline. Travel round it to see awe-inspiring scenery. Some people will say you need a 4x4 on this road, but a family car is fine—as long as you're happy to slow down where the paved road gives way to a dirt track. It can be a little difficult to predict.

The ring road will take you through rock-strewn Arctic desert and pass by green tussocked fields. It winds its way around natural harbors and deeply gouged fjords, peninsulas, and islands, many deserted, except for flocks of seabirds.

With so much to marvel at from the main road, it's tough not to stop off at every site marked on the map, as there's little like these anywhere else in the world. You'll be itching to head off on other adventures—caving through volcanic tubes, bird-watching on the fjords, whale-watching out at sea, or *tölt*-ing an Icelandic horse across the tundra. It's lucky that in the summer months the sun barely dips below the horizon, as you need all the daylight you can get to fit everything in.

► ICELAND

## 29. Bask in the beautiful Blue Lagoon

**When:** All year (but most fun in winter)
**Latitude:** 63.8441°N
**Longitude:** 22.4383°W

Essentially the greatest bath on the planet, a day at the Blue Lagoon is like no other pampering experience. A massive, man-made geothermal spa located on the Reykjanes Peninsula, 24 mi (39 km) outside Reykjavik, it is fueled by a nearby power plant and surrounded by enigmatic volcanic rocks. The blue hue is created from the silica contained in the water and the way it reflects sunlight. Slip into the 102°F (39°C) water temperature for an absolute treat.

Iceland's beautiful
Blue Lagoon

SKAFTAFELL, ICELAND
## 30. Experience fifty shades of blue
**When:** Winter only
**Latitude:** 64.0160°N
**Longitude:** 16.9720°W

One of Europe's largest glaciers outside the Arctic, Vatnajökull conceals a number of mountain valleys, and when the glacial rivers retract in winter you can marvel at the new ice caves that are formed each year. Admire their breathtaking hues of blue light that pass through the glacial ice.

▼ JUKKASJÄRVI, SWEDEN
## 31. Stay in a hotel that will melt when the season ends
**When:** December to April
**Latitude:** 67.8497°N **Longitude:** 20.5944°E

Every year, the Icehotel in northern Sweden takes two months to build from snow and blocks of ice harvested from the Torne River, and every year it melts back into the same river five months later. Everything in the hotel is made from ice—or the mixture of snow and ice, which is called, simply, "snice." No two rooms are the same, as each year artists submit their imaginative designs for suites, which are judged and chosen.

For more than twenty-five years, the Icehotel has been as much an art exhibition as it is a quirky place to stay. Temperatures have to stay below 32°F (0°C)—they hover around 23°F (-5°C)—but you'll have reindeer furs and polar-tested sleeping bags to keep you warm.

The Art Suite in the Icehotel in Jukkasjärvi, Sweden, was made by artists Lotta Lampa and Julia Gamborg Nielsen, and was inspired by Michael Ende's novel, *Momo*

TREEHOTEL, HARADS, SWEDEN
## 32. Sleep up in a tree
**When:** All year
**Latitude:** 66.0667°N
**Longitude:** 20.9833°E

Sweden's Treehotel offers stunning, sustainable, and contemporary accommodation high amid the pine forest of the Lule River valley. Glass-fronted "tree rooms" look out over forest and the river—or opt for the Mirrorcube room for a 360-degree view.

ABISKO TO HEMAVAN, SWEDEN
## 33. Ski cross-country in the Arctic Circle
**When:** Winter
**Latitude:** 69.3500°N
**Longitude:** 18.8167°E (Abisko)

Enter the Arctic Circle to ski some of north Sweden's Kungsleden or "King's Trail"—a 270 mi (435 km) long hiking trail linking Abisko to Hemavan. You'll need a good level of fitness, and skiing experience is vital for this hugely rewarding trek across the vast wilderness and dramatic white tundra.

ALL OVER CANADA
## 34. Meet the best-dressed policemen
**When:** All year
**Latitude:** 62.4422°N
**Longitude:** 114.3975°W (for the Northwest Territories, where they were first founded)

With their wide Stetsons, scarlet jackets, and flash of yellow down the side of their pants, there's no doubt that Canada's Mounties are the best-dressed police force around. For a true pleasure, get up close to one and shake his or her hand.

SHETLAND ISLANDS, UK AND WORLDWIDE
## 35. Cycle across a continent
**When:** All year
**Latitude:** 60.5400°N
**Longitude:** 1.3843°W (Shetlands for "North Sea route")

One true pleasure of travel is to throw oneself headfirst into a new culture, and it is by bicycle that this can best be achieved. A cyclist often discovers that the real highlights are far from the beaten path. Cycling across a continent is perhaps the ultimate expression of this.

Europe is the classic home of cycling, and there are some incredible challenges out there: the 3,728 mi (6,000 km) North Sea Cycle Route (from the Shetlands around the UK, Belgium, the Netherlands, Germany, Denmark, and Sweden); the Iron Curtain Trail, which goes 4,225 mi (6,800 km) from the Norwegian-Russian border at Barents Sea down to the Black Sea in Turkey; or a route following three European rivers (Loire, Rhine, and Danube), starting in St. Nazaire, France, and ending in Constanta, Romania, next to the Black Sea. The only real limit is your imagination.

MAINLAND SHETLAND, WHITBY, AND BRIGHTON, UK
## 36. Tuck into the world's best fish and chips
**When:** All year
**Latitude:** 60.3960°N **Longitude:** 1.3510°W

Nowhere does fish and chips like the UK. Locally caught haddock, cod, and plaice wrapped in crispy batter and deep-fried, accompanied by a big greasy bag of fat hot chips—this is the stuff that Friday night dreams are made of.

But where to try them? Up and down the UK are some great "chippies" (fish and chip shops), and one of the very best is Frankie's in Brae, on Mainland Shetland. In Whitby, in Yorkshire, the Magpie Cafe is known for its fresh fish (the lemon sole is a favorite), while down on the south coast in Brighton, there's no better meal than fish and chips bought to go from Palm Court.

DENALI NATIONAL PARK AND PRESERVE, ALASKA, US
## 37. Track the Alaskan Big Five
**When:** May to September
**Latitude:** 63.3333°N **Longitude:** 150.5000°W

Denali National Park and Preserve is home to the northern hemisphere's "big five": grizzly bear, caribou, gray wolf, moose, and Dall sheep. The park takes its name from its crowning glory, Denali. This towering centerpiece is the tallest mountain in North America, measuring 20,340 ft (6,200 m). Until 2015, it was known as Mount McKinley.

Northeast of Denali lies Sable Pass, described as a "crossroads for bears," and the open tundra of the pass is the perfect place for you to spot the sandy-beige or brown fur of grizzly bears as they search for berries. You can also spot caribou at these crossroads—these wild reindeer will eat near grizzlies, but they know to choose a vantage spot above any bears, should a swift getaway be required.

For the predatory gray wolf, a little more stealth and cunning may be required. A food source, such as caribou at Sable Pass, is a good place to start. Sighting a wolf is rare, but you might hear its haunting howl.

As the brown, earthy tones of moose hide blend perfectly with its woodland habitat, the best way to find one is to find something it eats, such as bushes, tree needles, or leaves. Moose also enjoy the water, so look out for antlers poking out from the park's shimmering lakes.

To find elaborately horned Dall sheep, the best advice is simple: look up. This sure-footed native species can be found among the high-altitude ridges seeking out the lush mountain flora and vegetation.

A grizzly bear in the Denali National
Park and Preserve, Alaska, US

## 38. Canoe down the Yukon River

**When:** May to September

**Latitude:** 60.7167°N **Longitude:** 135.0465°W

Deep in the heart of Alaska, the Yukon River cuts through ancient peaks on its 2,000 mi (3,218 km) journey from the mountains of Canada, across Alaska, to the Bering Sea. This giant of a waterway offers some of the best canoeing in the world—it isn't too challenging, but its size and setting makes this a journey of a lifetime.

There are many places along its huge stretch where you can push some paddles in the water, but the 460 mi (740 km) from Whitehorse to Dawson City are particularly historic, and no specialist canoe skills are required. The route takes about three weeks to travel, broken by nightly camps up on the sandbanks.

By day, you'll pass abandoned settlements from the era of the gold rush. Keep an eye out, too, for wildlife such as bald eagles above and bears—of both the black and grizzly type. Take particular care at Lake Laberge, which can be subject to high winds, and Five Finger Rapids—going through the islands here can make the going quite choppy. Finally, you will arrive in Dawson City, where you can tread the boardwalks of this historically preserved town that was at the heart of the gold rush.

ANCHORAGE TO NOME, ALASKA, US
## 39. See "The Last Great Race on Earth"
**When:** First Saturday in March
**Latitude:** 61.2167°N **Longitude:** 149.9000°W (Anchorage)

In 1978, a British journalist taken by the scale, splendor, and sheer stamina and skill required of Alaska's Iditarod Trail Sled Dog Race called it "The Last Great Race on Earth." It is easy to see why the name has stuck: Iditarod remains the world's foremost sled race, covering more than 1,000 mi (1,600 km) of stunning snowy terrain that takes in everything from mountains to coast.

Riders (known as "mushers") fight blizzards, long hours of darkness, and temperatures that drop far below zero. Watch the action as every year, men and women with their teams of huskies battle nature and pay tribute to the country's dogsledding heritage.

ALASKA, US
## 40. Go unplugged: take a digital detox
**When:** May to August
**Latitude:** 67.7833°N
**Longitude:** 153.3000°W

In a world where technology rules so much in life, switching off is essential. Escape the city, enjoy the digital silence, and get back to the basics in the US's wildest preserve: Gates of the Arctic National Park and Preserve.

COOPER LANDING, ALASKA, US
## 41. Catch a trophy fish
**When:** June to October
**Latitude:** 60.4905°N
**Longitude:** 149.7945°W

The Kenai River is world-renowned for its supersized fish—the largest recorded salmon, weighing 97 lb (44 kg) was caught here in 1985. Feel the pull on your line and the satisfaction of reeling in your own trophy: silver salmon runs happen each September.

BARROW, ALASKA, US
## 42. Stay awake for a day that never ends
**When:** May to August
**Latitude:** 71.2956°N
**Longitude:** 156.7664°W

In early May, the sun sets for the last time each spring in Barrow, and so begins almost ninety days of continuous daylight for the US's most northerly point. Expect to see houses with windows blacked out to help people sleep. Alternatively, pack a flashlight and visit from November to January, when the sun never rises.

LOWER HERRING BAY, ALASKA, US
## 43. Watch the sea froth and bubble
**When:** Spring
**Latitude:** 60.3844°N
**Longitude:** 147.7997°W

The seas bubble and turn a milky white as thousands of herring come together each year to spawn in Lower Herring Bay. View the spectacle as it brings with it an attentive following of seabirds, eagles, bears, and wolves that come to dine on the delicious roe.

PRUDHOE BAY, ALASKA, US, TO USHUAIA, ARGENTINA

## 44. Take a road trip to beat all others

**When:** All year, weather permitting (some parts only passable during the dry season)
**Latitude:** 70.3256°N **Longitude:** 148.7113°W (Prudhoe Bay)

There are easier ways to travel from the tip of the North American continent to its end, but driving the Pan-American Highway has to be one of the most diverse. Start at Prudhoe Bay in Alaska, and follow the 19,000 mi (30,578 km) route that takes you through seventeen countries, all of which agreed to build one continuous continental highway in 1937.

Officially recorded as the "longest motorable road in the world" by Guinness World Records, the highway, from top to bottom, travels first from Alaska into Canada. From here, a series of interstates designated as part of the route takes you through the US down to the border of Mexico. Next, you'll travel through every country of Central America, before you hit the impenetrable Darién Gap at Panama.

Take up the wheel again in Colombia, where the drive south down the west of South America takes you to Ecuador, Peru, Chile, and Argentina. Finally, you pass through the stunning wilds of Patagonia to arrive at the beautiful Tierra del Fuego.

It is not a difficult drive, but it is long—give yourself at least eighteen months to complete it. A journey of this kind really isn't about getting from A to B—or in this case, north to south. Take the opportunity to savor the stops, discover new places, and meet new people.

The Dalton Highway in northern Alaska—the starting point of the world's longest road trip

A brown bear catching a leaping
salmon in Alaska (see page 101)

# CHAPTER 2
# NORTHERN HEMISPHERE

from 60° north to 45° north

▼ ST. PETERSBURG, RUSSIA

## 45. Savor stunning Soviet architecture

**When:** All year
**Latitude:** 59.9342°N **Longitude:** 30.3350°E

Built from virtually nothing into a huge monument to imperial power by Peter the Great, St. Petersburg is an architecture lover's delight, with its phenomenal palaces and cathedrals. The majestic onion domes of the Church of Our Savior on Spilled Blood feel like something from another era, while you can get lost for what seems like an eon in the Hermitage. The Russian Museum—contained across four palaces—is home to the best of Soviet art and culture anywhere, and there's also the historic marvel of the Winter Palace, and the Mariinsky Theatre, which showcases ballet and opera. Be sure to bring a big memory stick for your camera.

KRUTYNIA RIVER, POLAND

## 46. Kayak on Europe's most beautiful canoe trail

**When:** All year
**Latitude:** 53.6778°N **Longitude:** 21.4302°E

Go kayaking on one of the most elegant waterways in Europe—the Krutynia River has a cult following among paddlers, who revel in its varied 68 mi (109 km) route. It takes in twenty different lakes, six different nature reserves, a wild animal center, and a fetching monastery. It's great for beginners, too.

St. Isaac's Cathedral in stunning St. Petersburg, Russia

TALLINN, ESTONIA
## 47. Adopt another way of life for a year
**When:** All year
**Latitude:** 59.4370°N **Longitude:** 24.7536°E

The traditional gap year trip—traveling across the world—is perennially popular, but sometimes to truly see life differently, it's better to spend a year in one foreign place and get to know it well.

Living in the medieval Old Town of Tallinn, capital of the Baltic state of Estonia, is an uplifting way to change perspective. This historic district is compact enough to walk across, architecturally distinguished, quietly quirky, and delightfully laid-back.

Some sights should be on every traveler's itinerary: St. Nicolas' Church is home to Bernt Notke's spooky *Danse Macabre*; the Museum of Occupations gives a harrowing insight into the country's tragic, complex history; while the square around the Gothic town hall is lined with good restaurants and hosts a charming Christmas market.

Quiet, reserved, and polite, Estonians are an easygoing people to live among, and when they do let their hair down, the vibe can be fascinating.

HIIUMAA, ESTONIA
## 48. Sleep on the beach after a kayak odyssey
**When:** All year
**Latitude:** 58.9239°N
**Longitude:** 22.5919°E

The islets of Hiiumaa are one of Europe's best-kept secrets, and kayaking between them—through warm, sheltered waters—is undoubtedly the way to visit. You can then sleep on the southern shore beach campsite after a perfect day on the water.

SWEDEN
## 49. Enjoy the freedom of wild camping
**When:** All year (if you dare)
**Latitude:** 59.3878°N
**Longitude:** 18.7358°E

*Allemansrätten* ("the freedom to roam") is a constitutional right in Sweden, which makes wild camping here practically mandatory. There are basic sensible rules regarding safety and respecting the environment and privately owned land, but essentially, you are free to go wild. The easily accessible sandy beaches of the Stockholm archipelago are a great place to start.

STOCKHOLM, SWEDEN
## 50. Write a song for somebody
**When:** All year
**Latitude:** 59.3325°N
**Longitude:** 18.0647°E

As romantic gestures go, few can beat writing a song for somebody you love. For inspiration, head to Stockholm, the birthplace of the world's most successful songwriter, Max Martin, who has written fifty-four Top Ten hits—that's more than Madonna, Elvis, or The Beatles. Your song might not reach quite so high, but it can be filled with meaning and references to shared memories.

ROGALAND, NORWAY
## 51. Dare to stare into the abyss
**When:** All year (weather permitting)
**Latitude:** 59.0337°N
**Longitude:** 6.5930°E

Wedged in a mountain crevice on the edge of the Kjerag mountain in Rogaland, Norway, the Kjeragbolten boulder is suspended over a near-3,280 ft (1,000 m) high drop. It's accessible, after a hike, without any climbing equipment—simply jump up onto the large rock for a very memorable photo op.

STAVANGER, NORWAY
## 52. Catch a glimpse of a sleeping giant
**When:** All year
**Latitude:** 58.9633°N
**Longitude:** 5.7189°E

In 2015, French artists Ella & Pitr completed the world's largest roof mural. Painted across the tops of industrial units in Stavanger, Norway, the huge 22,6042 sq ft (21,000 sq m) artwork features a dozing woman—although you'll need an airplane to fully appreciate its full extent.

OSLO, NORWAY
## 53. Ghost hunt at a haunted castle
**When:** All year
**Latitude:** 59.9067°N
**Longitude:** 10.7361°E

Built as a medieval castle, then later used as a prison and place of execution, the history of Akershus Fortress is long and bloody—and perfect for tales of things that go bump in the night. Regularly rated in lists of the world's most haunted, come prepared to see more than just the great views from the rampart of this popular tourist spot. Do you dare to drop in?

BILLUND, DENMARK
## 54. See the world in an hour
**When:** March to October
**Latitude:** 55.7356°N
**Longitude:** 9.1261°E

The first LEGOLAND®, built near the original LEGO® factory in Denmark, is home to the first "miniland." Marvel at this miniature world built out of millions of the toy bricks that lies at the heart of each of the world's LEGOLAND® parks that followed this one.

DORNOCH, SCOTLAND, UK
## 55. Sleep in a fifteenth-century castle …
**When:** All year
**Latitude:** 57.8803°N
**Longitude:** 4.0283°W

Or a school, jail, courthouse, hunting lodge … In its time, Dornoch Castle has been all these things. Today, it is a hotel that you can check into, but one with plenty of castle features: rooms in the tower, four-poster beds, big stone hearths—there's probably even a knight in armor tucked away somewhere.

SCOTLAND, UK
## 56. Discover Scotland's Gaelic culture
**When:** All year
**Latitude:** 57.5400°N
**Longitude:** 7.3573°W

The Outer Hebrides, a chain of islands off the northeast coast of mainland Scotland, are home to the 5,000-year-old Callanish Stones, iron-age dwellings, a medieval castle, and Gaelic heritage that can be heard in the language of the islanders. Explore mountain ranges, moorland, golden sandy beaches, and 2,000 freshwater lochs.

The Kjeragbolten boulder on Kjerag mountain in Rogaland, Norway

START AT INVERNESS CASTLE, SCOTLAND, UK

## 57. Drive one of the world's best roads

**When:** All year

**Latitude:** 57.4763°N **Longitude:** 4.2256°W

The best way to see Scotland is to drive around it, and the North Coast 500—a network of roads that takes travelers on a circular route through the north of the country—is the best road on which to do it. It only officially opened in 2015 and is already earning a place among the top road trips in the world.

It is not just a drive showcasing the best Scotland has to offer in its scenery, food, drink, and culture, but also a journey through time itself. The route starts in the bustling town of Inverness, at the ancient site of Inverness Castle—there has been a castle here in one form or another for more than 900 years.

Your journey will then take you first across the west Highlands on the twisting Bealach na Bà road. When you hit Applecross, be sure to make a visit to its sandy dune beaches. Traveling almost halfway up the stunning west coast from here, you'll reach the lovely seaside town of Ullapool, and the start of the wildest corner of the North Coast 500. Windswept and isolated, there is evidence of the previous neighbors—fragments of polar bear skulls more than 20,000 years old were found in the Bone Caves here.

Continue up the west coast to Lochinver, and stop to check out the unspoiled white sands of Achmelvich Beach. The Hermit's Cave here is one of the tiniest castles in Europe. Journeying onward, you'll cross the sweeping curve of the Kylesku Bridge and pass the sixteenth-century ruins of Ardvreck Castle, jutting out into Loch Assynt. Driving east across the width of the top of the country brings you to John o'Groats—from here to Land's End in Cornwall may be the longest distance between two British mainland points (876 mi; 1,410 km), but it is not quite the UK's most northerly point. That accolade is reserved for nearby picturesque Dunnet Head.

The completion of the loop from here takes you back to Inverness via the fairy-tale castle at Dunrobin. It is a suitably romantic end to a charming drive that's full of rugged mist-covered mountains, seemingly bottomless lochs, and isolated glens inhabited only by red deer.

One of the world's best
roads, near Inverness
in Scotland, UK

A naked bungee jump off a cable car at the Guaja River in Poruka, Latvia

▲ PORUKA, LATVIA
### 58. Leap off a cable car … naked!
**When:** All year
**Latitude:** 56.9632°N
**Longitude:** 23.7485°E

Unleash your inner James Bond by leaping from a cable car. Bungee jumping is always a buzz, but doing it from the luminous yellow Sigulda cable cars that span the Gauja River in Latvia adds an extra element of spice. And real daredevils do it in the nude … .

TURAIDA, LATVIA
### 59. Pound a pagan symbol into iron
**When:** All year
**Latitude:** 57.1804°N
**Longitude:** 24.8404°E

Turaida Museum Reserve has a prepossessing redbrick castle— Turaida means "God's garden." But the highlight of a visit is the smith house, where a bona fide blacksmith can guide you through pounding Liv pagan symbols into small chunks of iron. It makes quite the souvenir.

SKYE, SCOTLAND, UK
### 60. Forage for dinner on a windswept beach
**When:** All year
**Latitude:** 57.5312°N
**Longitude:** 6.2289°W

No meal is more satisfying than one gathered yourself. Visit Skye to learn how to harvest some of Scotland's larder with Skye Ghillie (aka Mitchell Partridge), grabbing super-fresh mussels from the rocks, and cooking them over a fire made with tree resin and dried leaves.

ARBROATH, SCOTLAND, UK

## 62. Eat great foods where they taste best

**When:** All year
**Latitude:** 56.5614°N
**Longitude:** 2.5857°W

Arbroath smokie, a type of smoked haddock from the small fishing village of Arbroath in Scotland, is one of many foods named on the European Union's protected geographical indication list. This means it's only the real thing if it's produced a certain way in a certain place. Much of the UK, and indeed the world, can be traveled on a gastronomic tour of local food and drink like this: head to Bakewell, in Derbyshire, England, for their tarts, or Pastéis de Belém in Lisbon, Portugal, for theirs.

FORT WILLIAM TO MALLAIG, SCOTLAND, UK

## 61. Ride on the *Hogwarts Express*

**When:** May to October
**Latitude:** 56.8207°N **Longitude:** 5.1047°W

*The Jacobite* steam train in the West Highlands of Scotland is one of the few remaining in the world that harks back to the finer days of locomotive travel. It runs during the summer tourist season, taking visitors 41 mi (66 km) from Fort William, the largest town in the Highlands, to the small fishing harbor of Mallaig on Scotland's west coast.

It really is a step back in time, with traditionally upholstered seats, curtains, and carpet in the carriages. Yet it will feel familiar as it was popularized in the hugely successful Harry Potter movies. If you have seen them, you will no doubt recognize Glenfinnan Viaduct—overlooking Loch Shiel, the twenty-one arches of this magnificent feat of engineering have carried trains on a curved track across the valley since the turn of the twentieth century.

The West Highlands Line is regularly voted among the top railway journeys in the world, and it is easy to see why. The Scottish scenery passing by your window is up there with the best in the world. Large, fathomless lochs edged with mist-covered mountains contrast with rolling banks featuring every shade of green. Traveling in the countryside really doesn't get more charming than this.

SCHIEHALLION, SCOTLAND, UK
## 63. Bag a munro
**When:** All year (but you'll need winter equipment, skills, and experience if there's snow)
**Latitude:** 56.6664°N **Longitude:** 4.1016°W

Nowhere feels quite like the top of the world as the Scottish Highlands, and any mountain that's higher than 3,000 ft (910 m) is a *munro*. According to the Scottish Mountaineering Club, there are 282 of them, and some 4,000 people have "bagged" them all.

Want to bag the biggest? That would, of course, be Ben Nevis. It is a tough climb, up to 4,409 ft (1,344 m), and it takes some nine hours to cover the return trip. For something a little easier, Schiehallion in Perthshire is a peak so beautifully conical it was used in a groundbreaking 1774 experiment to estimate the mass of Earth—and resulted in mathematician Charles Hutton devising contour lines. Its peak is 3,553 ft (1,083 m) high and it is one of Scotland's most accessible.

▶ LOCHABER, SCOTLAND, UK
## 64. Watch a unique mating ritual
**When:** Late September to November
**Latitude:** 56.8198°N
**Longitude:** 5.1052°W

Witness one of Europe's most impressive wildlife spectacles: the frenzied, noisy, and primal testosterone-fueled tussle of 420 lb (190 kg) red deer as they lock horns to impress the ladies and win themselves a mate (or preferably several).

ST. ANDREW'S, FIFE, SCOTLAND, UK
## 65. Tee off at one of the world's oldest golf courses
**When:** April to October (although it is open all year)
**Latitude:** 56.3430°N **Longitude:** 2.8030°W

As a hobby, golf only has a short window before it becomes an obsession, and playing "the home of golf" a lifetime ambition. Play the 6,721 yd, par 72 Old Course at St. Andrews and you'll be taking on one of the most challenging courses in the world, with its double greens and 112 bunkers. According to Open champion Jack Nicklaus, "There's just no other golf course that is even remotely close."

WALES, UK
## 66. Hike the incredible Wales Coast Path
**When:** May to September
**Latitude:** 53.2110°N **Longitude:** 3.0160°W

The Welsh coastline is made up of gorgeous little coves, dramatic cliffs, and pristine beaches, and has more than 870 mi (1,400 km) of footpaths to explore. From Chepstow in the south to Queensferry in the north, it would take weeks to conquer this stunning route in its entirety. But the Wales Coast Path should be tackled slowly; there are eight sections, each as beautiful and varied as the last, and there's something for everyone on this beguiling coastal trail.

Red deer in
Scotland, UK

EDINBURGH, SCOTLAND, UK
## 67. Climb to the top of Arthur's Seat
**When:** All year
**Latitude:** 55.9442°N
**Longitude:** 3.1619°W

Arthur's Seat is a feature of so many views of Edinburgh and also the place to experience a true panoramic of the city. Take the easy climb to the top, which is an essential part of any trip to Scotland's capital.

EDINBURGH, SCOTLAND, UK
## 68. Stroll the historic Royal Mile
**When:** All year
**Latitude:** 55.9532°N
**Longitude:** 3.1882°W

Take a civilized stroll along the street that connects two wonderful attractions: Edinburgh Castle and Holyroodhouse. The Mile is dripping with history, as well as restaurants, pubs, and a fair few shops punting tartan-themed tourist bait.

NORTHERN IRELAND, UK
## 69. Follow in the footsteps of a giant
**When:** All year
**Latitude:** 55.2408°N
**Longitude:** 6.5117°W

More than 50 million years ago, a volcanic eruption left part of the coast of what is now Northern Ireland covered in hexagonal columns of hardened lava. Today, you can walk over these "stepping stones" into the past, which legend says were built by a giant.

◀ ISLE OF MULL, SCOTLAND, UK
## 70. Island-hop to a real-life TV set
**When:** All year
**Latitude:** 56.6200°N **Longitude:** 6.0700°W

Tobermory, on the Isle of Mull, is more than picture-perfect: it's TV-perfect. With its colorful quaint waterfront cottages, this small fishing port is a charming place to visit for its scenery alone, but it has also been used in many TV shows and movies, including, most famously, as the setting for the popular BBC children's TV program, *Balamory*. Filming has long since finished—it was made from 2002 to 2005, although is still shown on TV in the UK today.

ARGYLL, SCOTLAND, UK
## 71. Knit an Argyle sweater in Argyll
**When:** All year
**Latitude:** 56.2500°N **Longitude:** 5.2500°W

The tartan of clan Campbell became famous throughout the world when its diamond pattern was popularized by Pringle. But if you want to make (or even just buy) a clan Campbell tartan sweater in the beautiful location it comes from, head to the west coast of Scotland. The Duke of Windsor was a fan of this tartan for his golf sweaters and socks, and there are plenty of fantastic golf courses in Argyll where you can tee off in your new togs.

Tobermory on the Isle of
Mull in Scotland, UK

MILNGAVIE TO FORT WILLIAM, SCOTLAND, UK
## 72. Trek the West Highland Way
**When:** All year
**Latitude:** 55.9421°N **Longitude:** 4.3137°W

There is no better introduction to the Scottish Highlands than the West Highland Way walking route, from Milngavie near Glasgow in the south, to Fort William in the north.

Expect to see bucolic pastoral landscapes in the south, beneath the undulating fells of the Campsies, serene views over the bonnie banks and placid waters of Loch Lomond, awe-inspiring vistas across the boggy moorland of desolate Rannoch Moor, and a truly epic, neck-bending first sight of Ben Nevis from the glen at its foot. You will also get a peek down Glencoe and will cross the hills to the beautiful, glassy Loch Leven.

The best way to experience the Scottish landscape is to camp, and wild camping is permitted along the route (the only exception is much of the east side of Loch Lomond in the summer). Otherwise, there are hotels and bed and breakfasts at manageable intervals, many of which will pick you up at the day's end and drop you back on the route the following morning.

The West Highland
Way in Scotland, UK

▼ MOSCOW TO VLADIVOSTOK, RUSSIA

73. Take the world's longest train journey

**When:** All year (but May to September is the best for longer daylight and good weather)
**Latitude:** 55.7733°N
**Longitude:** 37.6564°E

The Trans-Siberian Railway connects Moscow in Russia's west to Vladivostok in the east. At more than 5,700 mi (9,173 km) long, it is the longest railway journey in the world that you can make on a single train line, and arguably one of its most fascinating. Whether you choose to undertake the journey nonstop in a week, or stop off en route, make sure you pack a watch that is easy to adjust: you will travel through seven time zones on the ride.

MOSCOW, RUSSIA

74. Tread inside the Kremlin

**When:** All year
**Latitude:** 55.7528°N
**Longitude:** 37.6177°E

Once the citadel of the csars and today the home of the Russian parliament, the Duma, the Kremlin is to many the symbol of Russia. Don't miss the Armoury Chamber, which houses ancient state regalia, including an impressive collection of Fabergé eggs.

The world's longest train journey: the Trans-Siberian Railway in Russia

► MOSCOW, RUSSIA
## 75. Gaze upon Moscow's postcard-perfect church

**When:** All year

**Latitude:** 55.7525°N

**Longitude:** 37.6231°E

Looking like something conjured up in a Disney studio, Ivan the Terrible's riotous sixteenth-century St. Basil's Cathedral is the very image of Russia in popular imagination. You'll find it standing at the southern end of Moscow's Red Square—it is impossible to miss.

Moscow's postcard-perfect St. Basil's Cathedral, Russia

MOSCOW, RUSSIA
## 76. See some of the best ballet at the Bolshoi

**When:** All year

**Latitude:** 55.7558°N **Longitude:** 37.6173°E

Nobody can call themselves a true fan of the pirouette and pointe until they've seen the Bolshoi. Perhaps the most famous ballet corps of them all, the company was founded in the 1770s, but it was not until the early 1900s that it emerged as one of the world's foremost companies.

Its reputation for putting on huge, bold, and extravagant performances is second to none. This is the epicenter of Moscow culture, where oligarchs come in their downtime, and the overseas visitor can't help but feel like they've stepped back in time. The Bolshoi really comes into its own when staging blockbusters from *Don Quixote* to *Swan Lake*, producing huge, spellbinding shows. It's a dizzying, overwhelming experience, and in many ways a microcosm of the newly wealthy Russia.

MOSCOW, RUSSIA
## 77. Surf the world's most beautiful subway

**When:** All year

**Latitude:** 55.7750°N

**Longitude:** 37.6542°E (The gateway at Komsomolskaya station)

Twelve lines, 196 stations, and 204 mi (328 km) of track make up the Russian capital's majestic metro system. Start at charismatic Komsomolskaya—at 38 ft (12 m) high, it's designed to show off the majesty of the Soviet empire—and marvel at each station's extraordinary, elaborate construction.

## MOSCOW, RUSSIA
### 78. Visit the house of your favorite novelists
**When:** All year
**Latitude:** 55.7500°N
**Longitude:** 37.6167°E

With its cobweb of streets and narrow lanes, the Russian capital has been the setting of many a novel. Today, you can visit the house museums dedicated to some of Russia's most renowned novelists; it was in this city that Leo Tolstoy penned *War and Peace*.

## NIZHNY NOVGOROD, RUSSIA
### 79. Go supersonic in a fighter jet
**When:** All year (weather permitting)
**Latitude:** 56.3269°N
**Longitude:** 44.0075°E

Perform thrilling rolls, loops, and vertical climbs and dives, break the sound barrier, and experience a G-force of 9 in an MiG-29 Fulcrum, a frontline fighter of the Russian Air Force, at Dolinsk-Sokol Air Base in Nizhny Novgorod. Seated behind one of the country's top gun pilots, you'll experience stunning speed and aerobatics, and have the opportunity to take over the controls.

## MOSCOW, RUSSIA
### 80. Visit the State Tretyakov Gallery
**When:** All year
**Latitude:** 55.7423°N
**Longitude:** 37.6208°E

Nowhere else in the world houses such a rich collection of Russian art—this is the world's largest, displaying masterpieces that span a thousand years. Feast your eyes upon the 170,000 works by Russian artists that incorporate religious icons and Impressionist pieces by Valentin Serov, including *The Girl with Peaches*, one of the gallery's masterpieces.

## KAZAN KREMLIN, KAZAN, RUSSIA
### 81. Marvel at Russia's other Kremlin
**When:** All year
**Latitude:** 55.8000°N
**Longitude:** 49.1000°E

Wait. There's more than one Kremlin? There is, and you can visit this sumptuous UNESCO World Heritage site, some of which dates from the sixteenth century. You'll find a feast of galleries, museums, parkland, and religious buildings.

## COPENHAGEN, DENMARK
### 82. Trip the light fantastic in the Tivoli Gardens
**When:** Open for summer (April to September), Halloween (October), and Christmas (mid-November to December 31) each year
**Latitude:** 55.6747°N
**Longitude:** 12.5656°E

Get festive at the second-oldest amusement park in the world (open since 1843)—and Walt Disney's inspiration for Disneyland. The park dons thousands of fairy lights, lamps, and illuminations over Christmas to create a truly magical winter wonderland.

## ROSKILDE, DENMARK
### 83. Be a Viking for a day
**When:** All year
**Latitude:** 55.6500°N
**Longitude:** 12.0833°E

Experience what it was like to be a seafaring warrior a thousand years ago at Roskilde's Vikingeskibsmuseet ("Viking Museum"). There are five original longships on display and a working boatyard, plus there's the chance to set sail onboard a Viking warship.

BETWEEN SWEDEN AND DENMARK
## 84. Take the world's most elegant link between two countries

**When:** All year
**Latitude:** 55.5832°N **Longitude:** 12.7943°E

Bridges are a great punctuation mark in any journey, and the world's longest road and rail bridge, the Øresund Bridge—which connects Malmö in Sweden and Copenhagen in Denmark—is like a delicate hyphen. You'll catch your breath as you pass.

Magnificent aerobatics by European starlings in Tønder, Jutland, Denmark

▲ TØNDER, JUTLAND, DENMARK

## 85. Witness magnificent aerobatics in the sky

**When:** Spring and fall
**Latitude:** 54.9516°N
**Longitude:** 8.8818°E

Witness one of nature's most riveting displays as hundreds of thousands of perfectly choreographed European starlings turn the sky dark with their whirling, wheeling dance as day turns to night. Sometimes referred to as the "Black Sun," these avian acrobats create artwork in the sky. According to experts, the performance is to confuse potential predators—safety in numbers it may be, but what an incredible show they put on.

CUMBRIA, ENGLAND, UK

## 86. Amaze your friends by mastering magic

**When:** All year
**Latitude:** 54.6733°N
**Longitude:** 3.2778°W

Magic is a great way to get people talking and where better to try it out than in one of Britain's many mystical stone circles, such as the Elva Plain Stone Circle? These are found all over the country, and many are close to public footpaths, so are easily accessible. As they date back to pre-Christian times, not much can be said about them with any certainty. But whatever their origins, they're a great place for mystery and magic.

WHITBY, ENGLAND, UK

## 87. Go Gothic in Dracula country

**When:** April and November
**Latitude:** 54.4858°N
**Longitude:** 0.6206°W

In the decade since it was established, Whitby's Goth weekends have grown into lively alternative music events that attract hundreds of the weird and wonderful to this northeastern English coastal town. Join them in the place that featured in Bram Stoker's stark novel.

COAST TO COAST WALK IN ENGLAND, UK
## 88. See the best bits of Britain as you cross on foot

**When:** May to September (for better weather)
**Latitude:** 54.4038°N **Longitude:** 2.1639°W (Midpoint of Keld)

Walks are good when they have a very definite accomplishment. By taking you from the Irish Sea on Britain's west coast to the North Sea on the east, the Coast to Coast route certainly ticks that box. It was devised by Britain's great fell walker, Alfred Wainwright.

Tradition states that at the start of the walk you dip your boots in the sea at the starting point of St. Bees so you can do this again when you end at Robin Hood's Bay. The route takes you through three national parks: the magnificent Lake District has great mountains and clear lakes; the Yorkshire Dales has dry stone walls crisscrossing green fields; and the North York Moors is all windswept heather moorland. This is where you'll find Robin Hood's Bay, where you can dip those walking boots again and reflect on the many steps you've taken.

▼ ŠIAULIAI, LITHUANIA
## 89. Explore the Hill of Crosses

**When:** All year
**Latitude:** 56.0154°N
**Longitude:** 23.4142°W

The Hill of Crosses is home to an estimated 100,000 crucifixes—as well as effigies, rosaries, and statues of the Virgin Mary—that tinkle in the wind. Visit this enigmatic site and you'll be reminded of how the deeply Catholic locals here defied the Soviets throughout their recent occupation.

The Hill of Crosses in Šiauliai, Lithuania

GIANT'S CAUSEWAY, NORTHERN IRELAND, UK
## 90. Walk around an entire country
**When:** All year
**Latitude:** 55.2408°N **Longitude:** 6.5117°W

Take in all six counties that make up Northern Ireland
on the mammoth 625 mi (1,006 km) circular walk that
is the magnificent Ulster Way.

Opened in the 1970s, the project's aim was to take
long-distance hikers through some of the most beautiful
scenery the Northern Irish countryside has to offer.
The most popular place to start is the curious Giant's
Causeway, with its ancient stone "steps," which jut out
in the sea of the country's northern coastline. Clockwise
from here, take the path that follows the forests and
folklore of the green rolling Glens of Antrim and the
Glenariff Forest Park, with its steep gorges cut through
with waterfalls, before traveling along the east coast
and dropping down to Belfast, the capital.

The Mourne Mountains in the south offer a mix of
forest trails and mountain paths alongside the highest
peaks in the country, before the route heads into the
most rural part of the walk, through the many lakes
and streams of the Sliabh Beagh Way. Then it is on to
the lake lands and small islands of County Fermanagh,
and the celebrated views from the Cliffs of Magho.
Finally, the path takes you through the Sperrin Mountains
of the west before heading back north where it
all began.

Summer is the best time to undertake this walk—the
majestic landscapes can quickly turn bleak in rough
weather. But even in the better months, remember
this is Ireland, so pack your rain gear—for you and
your backpack.

The Giant's Causeway,
Northern Ireland

LISDOONVARNA, IRELAND
## 91. Find love at a matchmaking festival
**When:** September
**Latitude:** 53.0303°N
**Longitude:** 9.2894°W

Lisdoonvarna may be a tiny Irish town, but that doesn't stop it from being the love capital of the world. Join thousands of lonely hearts, who each September arrive for a month of matchmaking, music, and dancing at a festival that is more than 150 years old.

NORFOLK, ENGLAND, UK
## 92. See the world's slowest race
**When:** July or August
**Latitude:** 52.7819°N
**Longitude:** 0.5399°E

"Ready ... Steady ... Slow!" And so begins the annual World Snail Racing Championships, the least-speedy sprint in mollusk athletics, which have been held in Congham for more than twenty-five years. On a nominated day in summer, you can watch as 200 or so snails are brought to this small English village to test their slither ability against their peers.

SNOWDONIA, WALES, UK
## 93. Look down at Wales from its highest point
**When:** All year (dependent on weather)
**Latitude:** 53.0917°N
**Longitude:** 3.8026°W

The UK's highest point outside of Scotland is absolutely captivating, and climbing it is achievable for those of even just moderate fitness (in fact, you don't even need to climb it at all—there's a train right to the summit). From the top, drink in stunning views of Ireland, Scotland, England—and, of course, the rest of Wales.

CROAGH PATRICK, MAYO, IRELAND
## 94. Climb a mountain barefoot
**When:** The last Sunday in July
**Latitude:** 53.7595°N **Longitude:** 9.6584°W

The tradition of pilgrimage to Ireland's holiest mountain is thought to date back more than 5,000 years to the Stone Age—long before Christianity came to Ireland. Then, pagans were thought to gather here to celebrate the harvest season. Today, the annual summer pilgrimage in honor of St. Patrick is the big draw—it was from this mountain that St. Patrick was said to have banished snakes from Ireland forever.

Pilgrims traditionally climb the mountain barefoot as a penance, but the mountain can be climbed any time of year, weather permitting, and footwear is not only optional, but recommended. Join the hill climbers, archaeologists, and nature lovers who come from all over the world to accompany the traditional pilgrims on this energetic, yet moderate, two-hour climb to the top.

▶ CANADA
## 95. Be transfixed by a spirit bear
**When:** August to October
**Latitude:** 53.7267°N
**Longitude:** 127.6476°W

Spirit bears are a subspecies of black bears that have white or creamy fur. It gives them a magical allure and it's no surprise that British Columbia has made it its official mammal. Look for the bears in the Great Bear Rainforest in this Canadian state, where they are predominantly found.

A spirit bear in the Great Bear Rainforest, Canada

WAKEFIELD, ENGLAND, UK
## 96. See Henry Moore sculptures in Yorkshire
**When:** Open daily (except December 24 and 25)
**Latitude:** 53.6140°N **Longitude:** 1.5671°W

One of the first things that greets you when you enter Yorkshire Sculpture Park (YSP) is a sign for Arcadia by the artist Leo Fitzmaurice, alluding to an image or idea of life in the countryside that is believed to be perfect. Travel farther down the rolling fields that lead into the park and it's not long before you catch a glimpse of a sculpture by one of Yorkshire's most famous artists, a founding patron of YSP and a true champion of its landscape and cultural heritage—Henry Moore.

Several of Moore's bronze sculptures are situated in this wonderful open-air celebration of sculpture, their megalithic, curvaceous silhouettes standing strong against the undulating hills and distant views of the surrounding countryside. Indeed, the park provides the setting for one of the largest displays of his bronzes in Europe.

To witness the full power of these sculptures, take a walk around the park—and what a walk it is, with the view changing as you approach; stand alongside the smooth bronze, and then retreat, just as Moore intended his sculptures to be viewed.

Alongside the Moores you'll stumble upon other permanent or transitory sculptures from various artists, such as Barbara Hepworth, Sophie Ryder, and Tim Paul.

LIVERPOOL, ENGLAND, UK
## 97. Take a ticket to ride to John Lennon's house
**When:** All year (booked tours only)
**Latitude:** 53.3772°N **Longitude:** 2.8813°W

Behind the gray, stone exterior of 251 Menlove Avenue, in Liverpool's suburb of Woolton, lies the story of one of the greatest musical groups of all time.

From July 1946 to mid-1963, this property was home to John Lennon, who along with childhood friend Paul McCartney, was one of the powerhouse songwriting duo behind The Beatles. Now, fans of the Fab Four can take a guided tour around the place where a legend was molded. It's a fascinating journey into the past and gives a remarkable insight into the postwar environment that nurtured a band that retain their magic more than fifty years later.

You can also catch The Beatles Magical Mystery Tour, a bus trip that visits many key sites in the band's history.

DUBLIN, IRELAND
## 98. Go local with your tipple
**When:** All year
**Latitude:** 53.3498°N
**Longitude:** 6.2603°W

Buy a bottle of something special on vacation, and strangely enough, it never quite seems as good back at home as it did wherever it came from. There's science behind this: a recent study into why Guinness tastes better in Ireland identified several key factors, including the fact that the drink doesn't get spoiled by travel, and that its high demand there means it's fresher when imbibed. This theory can be applied to many other tipples, so go local for the same reasons.

Trinity College's Library in Dublin, Ireland

LIVERPOOL, ENGLAND, UK

## 99. Walk among the *Another Place* figures

**When:** All year
**Latitude:** 53.4875°N
**Longitude:** 3.0507°W

Sir Antony Gormley's *Another Place* consists of a hundred cast-iron figures, spread across 2 mi (3 km) of the shore of Crosby Beach and almost a mile (1 km) out to sea. Having been exhibited in Germany, Norway, and Belgium, they're now a permanent Scouse fixture; mingle with them to explore man's relationship with nature.

LIVERPOOL, ENGLAND, UK

## 100. Get by with a little help from your friends

**When:** All year
**Latitude:** 53.4061°N
**Longitude:** 2.9872°W (Cavern Club)

More than 300 tracks were recorded by The Beatles. Listen to every single one where it all began, in the historic city of Liverpool. Take a stroll around town, starting at the Cavern Club—the band's birthplace—and take in Penny Lane, Strawberry Fields, and the rest.

▲ DUBLIN, IRELAND

## 101. Get lost in a book at Trinity College's library

**When:** All year
**Latitude:** 53.3453°N
**Longitude:** 6.2578°W

Trinity College is simply one of the most stunning study centers on Earth. Its library is home to the ancient masterwork *The Book of Kells*, which you can pay to see, but you are unable to just wander into the iconic Long Room; non-student readers need to jump through hoops to prove they can't access the book they're after elsewhere.

## 102. Enjoy an island for every day of the year

**When:** All year

**Latitude:** 53.4333°N **Longitude:** 9.2333°W

Legend has it that Lough Corrib in Ireland has 365 islands—one for every day of the year. You'd be forgiven for thinking this an exaggeration, but you'd be wrong—this gorgeous loch actually has an astonishing 1,327 islands.

The west coast of Ireland is dotted with freshwater lakes and is known as Ireland's Lake District. Lough Corrib is the largest at 68 sq mi (176 sq km) and definitely the most atmospheric: swirling mists spread above the water as a dawn chorus fills the air. Some of the best fishing in Europe can be found here.

See how many you can pack into your summer vacation.

THE NETHERLANDS
## 103. Scale a really high urban rock face
**When:** All year

**Latitude:** 53.2408°N **Longitude:** 6.6008°E

Tackle the world's highest freestanding climbing wall that rises out of the flat Dutch countryside. Excalibur has a height of 121 ft (37 m) and 36 ft (11 m) of overhang, so you'll be taking on the ultimate climbing challenge. It is definitely not one for those who suffer from vertigo …

The Crooked Forest of Nowe Czarnowo, Poland

ACROSS THE UK
## 104. Drift away with "TM"
**When:** All year
**Latitude:** 51.5000°N
**Longitude:** 0.1167°W (UK)

Using repetition of a unique mantra, transcendental meditation is undeniably a great way to relax and mentally escape the hurly-burly of modern life. Exponents (as varied as The Beatles and Rupert Murdoch) also claim it has health benefits. Visit one of numerous learning centers across the UK.

▲ NOWE CZARNOWO, POLAND
## 105. Walk through the Crooked Forest
**When:** All year
**Latitude:** 53.1833°N
**Longitude:** 14.4833°E

What makes the trees in this forest grow with a 90-degree bend in their trunk is an unsolved mystery. Was it a snowstorm? Or the work of man, growing curved wood for furniture? A trip to the forest will inspire you to come up with your own theories.

SILESIAN HIGHLANDS, POLAND
## 106. Head into the desert … in Poland?!
**When:** All year
**Latitude:** 50.3716°N
**Longitude:** 19.4308°E

Europe isn't somewhere most people traditionally associate with deserts, but Europe's largest sandy plain, the Błędówska Desert in Poland, is a fascinating 12 sq mi (31 sq km) territory. Walk or trek on horseback in this oddly charming place that's only an hour from Kraków.

## 107. Cycle through the Canadian Rockies

**When:** May to September
**Latitude:** 52.8731°N **Longitude:** 118.0822°W (Jasper, most northerly point)

The 143 mi (230 km) long ride along Alberta's Icefields Parkway, from Jasper in the north to Lake Louise in the south, is regarded as one of the most beautiful cycle journeys in the world. Cyclists who set off on the four- to five-day ride through the untouched wilderness in the UNESCO-listed Rocky Mountains National Park are rewarded with unspoiled views of ancient ice fields, hundreds of glaciers, waterfalls cascading from rock spires, the snow-covered peaks of the Canadian Rockies, and azure-blue lakes set among sweeping valleys. The abundant wildlife is equally spectacular: grizzly and black bear, elk, golden eagle, moose, and wolf.

Traveling on the pathway, you can enjoy well-earned breaks at one of the many creekside campsites, complete with a permit for making a warming fire, and a bear-proof locker (of course!). Or there are cabin-style hostels where you can mix with fellow travelers.

SPANDAU, BERLIN, GERMANY
## 108. From Berlin to the Baltic by boat
**When:** May to September
**Latitude:** 52.5361°N **Longitude:** 13.2033°E

Sometimes, the slow way is the best way. You can get from Germany's history-laden capital Berlin to the shores of the Baltic Sea in the charming Polish city of Szczecin by train in a little more than two hours. But where is the romance and sense of adventure in that?

Much more interesting, given a few days to travel and a hankering for the relaxed pace of waterborne transport, is to take the 100 mi (161 km) journey by canal, perhaps detouring slightly to pause en route. From Spandau, waterways head off in all directions, including northeast to the Baltic. Several companies offer everything from boat hire to guided tours.

Traveling by canal boat allows plenty of time to take in the surroundings, giving an entirely different view of the land as you chug serenely by.

BERLIN, GERMANY
## 109. Hold an exhibition of your work
**When:** All year
**Latitude:** 52.5233°N
**Longitude:** 13.3839°E

Berlin is a hotbed of contemporary art galleries, so hire some exhibition space here to put your paintings, photography, or other artwork on display, and join hundreds of other artists doing the same. For inspiration, check out the Boros Collection, held in a bunker built in 1942 as a bomb shelter—its walls are 6 ft (2 m) thick. It is open on weekends only, so be sure to book by appointment.

KIEL, GERMANY
## 110. Send a message in a bottle
**When:** All year
**Latitude:** 54.3333°N
**Longitude:** 10.1333°E

Just don't forget to include your email address for a reply—something that was understandably lacking in the note found in a bottle in the Baltic Sea off Kiel in 2014. It had been adrift for more than a century and is thought to be the world's oldest such message.

GERMANY
## 111. Drive without limits on the autobahn
**When:** All year
**Latitude:** 52.5167°N
**Longitude:** 13.3833°E (Berlin)

Germany's "autobahn" motorway system (all 8,046 mi; 12,949 km of it) is famous for long stretches of road without speed restrictions for cars (although it does have a recommended limit). You can access it easily from most cities, including the capital, Berlin.

▶ FLEVOLAND, THE NETHERLANDS
## 112. Take a journey on the Tulip Route
**When:** Mid-April to May (for blooms)
**Latitude:** 52.6926°N
**Longitude:** 5.7378°E

It's almost impossible to drive along the Tulpen Route (Tulip Route) in Noordoostpolder without getting out and running through the flower-filled furrows. All around are colorful tulips, nodding in their thousands in more than 2,500 ac (1,012 ha) of fields. This candy-striped, living landscape is a fitting tribute to The Netherlands' most famous bloom, but also is an extravagant display of horticultural prowess.

On the Tulip Route in
Flevoland, The Netherlands

BERLIN, GERMANY
## 113. Walk the most infamous collection of bricks and mortar in history
**When:** All year
**Latitude:** 52.5200°N **Longitude:** 13.4049°E

The Berlin Wall divided East and West Germany from 1961 to 1989, epitomizing the global power struggle between the west and communism, and preventing huge waves of defectors from traveling out of the eastern bloc. It was an intimidating structure with guard towers, anti-vehicle trenches, and the notorious "death strip," where many trying to cross it were killed.

Now, however, the site of the former barrier has been transformed into a historic trail. The route runs for 99 mi (160 km), almost all of which you can hike or cycle along. It can leave you feeling overwhelmed by the sheer scale of the former wall's reach, better educated—and a little fitter.

The most infamous collection of bricks and mortar: the Berlin Wall, Germany

▶ THE NETHERLANDS
## 114. Experience history at Anne Frank House
**When:** All year
**Latitude:** 52.3752°N
**Longitude:** 4.8840°E

Wander through the rooms where Anne Frank and her family lived for two years during World War II. They hid in an annex behind her father's office and it is in these very rooms that the young Jewish girl wrote her famous diary. Step through the secret entrance behind a bookcase to what is now a museum that opened in 1960 to discover more about her life and her writings. Visiting can leave you feeling both awe and horror, as you reflect on all the warmth and love of Anne's writings set against the stark cruelty of the holocaust.

Anne Frank House in Amsterdam, The Netherlands

BERLIN, GERMANY
## 115. Watch—and hear—Simon Rattle in action
**When:** Check performance dates
**Latitude:** 52.5200°N
**Longitude:** 13.4049°E

Widely regarded as the best conductor in the world, Rattle led the Berlin Philharmonic from 2002 to 2017, when he took the helm of the London Symphony Orchestra. Watch the bubbly Liverpudlian musical force transform interpretations of classic works—it truly is a sight to behold.

TIERGARTEN PARK, BERLIN, GERMANY
## 116. Get naked in the middle of a busy city
**When:** Whenever it's warm enough …
**Latitude:** 52.5145°N
**Longitude:** 13.3500°E

Disrobing with zero sense of self-consciousness is a peculiarly German thing, with nudity on the beach and sunbathing starkers in public parks a common sight. Tiergarten Park in Berlin—the capital's biggest green space—is a good place to give this liberating experience a go, with a designated nudist area.

69

THE HAGUE, THE NETHERLANDS
### 117. Stare at the *Girl with a Pearl Earring*
**When:** All year
**Latitude:** 52.0803°N **Longitude:** 4.3142°E

Submit to the wide-eyed allure of the "Mona Lisa of the North" at Mauritshuis museum. Just who was the girl and why was she wearing a blue turban and that eponymous and improbably large pearl earring?

COUNTY CORK, IRELAND
### 118. Kiss the Blarney Stone
**When:** All year
**Latitude:** 51.9343°N **Longitude:** 8.5669°W

Puckering up to this bit of rock apparently bestows the kisser with the gift of the gab. The tradition dates back to the builder of Blarney Castle winning a lawsuit after giving it a peck; so climb to the top of the castle, lean backwards over a parapet, and plant your kiss for some good luck.

▶ THE NETHERLANDS
### 119. Cruise Amsterdam on two wheels
**When:** All year
**Latitude:** 52.3667°N
**Longitude:** 4.9000°E

Whether it's Rembrandt and Van Gogh, or coffee shops and the nighttime economy, the Netherlands' biggest city is best explored by pedal power. One of the great pleasures of Amsterdam is getting lost while cycling alongside scenic canals, past narrow gabled buildings and bobbing houseboats. There are more than eighty waterways in the "belt of canals" that make up the center of the city (1,500 in total)—cross them all to capture all the main sights.

Amsterdam, the Netherlands

▶ PEMBROKESHIRE COAST NATIONAL PARK, WALES, UK
## 120. Discover coasteering and make a big splash

**When:** May to September
**Latitude:** 51.8812°N **Longitude:** 5.2660°W (St. Davids)

Described as "sideways mountaineering," coasteering was invented in Pembrokeshire, on the west coast of Wales, in the mid-1980s and the area remains its spiritual home. The sport involves wetsuit-clad coasteerers traveling around the coastline with a mix of climbing, scrambling, cave exploring, swimming, bodysurfing, and from time to time, leaping off cliffs. Changing tides, waves, and wildlife make every coasteering trip unique, and it is invigorating and serious fun for all the family. So don your wetsuit and start exploring—but be sure to make use of the services of a qualified tour guide with good local knowledge.

Coasteering on the west coast of Wales, UK

DUNGENESS, ENGLAND, UK
## 121. See the wilder side of a postmodern garden

**When:** All year (from the roadside)
**Latitude:** 50.9193°N **Longitude:** 0.9652°E

On the shingle shore near Dungeness nuclear power station sits an unlikely paradise—that of the late artist, writer, theater designer, and filmmaker, Derek Jarman (1942–1994). "Paradise haunts gardens, and some gardens are paradises. Mine is one of them," he wrote in his last book, *Derek Jarman's Garden*, published posthumously. Jarman's paradise continues to evolve today, around his final home at Prospect Cottage in Dungeness. On the black timber wall of the cottage are lines from John Donne's poem, "The Sun Rising." Observe the garden from the road or walk along the neighboring beach into which it poetically creeps.

OXFORD, ENGLAND, UK
## 122. Grow your own vocabulary

**When:** All year
**Latitude:** 51.7519°N
**Longitude:** 1.2578°W (Home of the *Oxford English Dictionary*)

You're never too old to learn, and having a new word to work into a conversation can provide endless fun. Pick up a dictionary or download an app and set yourself the task of a new word every day. Start with "pogonophobia"—the fear of beards.

SKELLIG MICHAEL, KERRY, IRELAND
## 123. Climb to the end of the universe
**When:** Summer (weather permitting)
**Latitude:** 51.7711°N **Longitude:** 10.5406°W

In the remotest part of the universe, Luke Skywalker has been hiding out for years on a craggy island surrounded by sea, where he is discovered in the closing scenes of 2015's return to the Star Wars saga, *The Force Awakens*. Back in the real world, the stunning location where this movie was set is only marginally easier to reach in real life than its fictional intergalactic incarnation. But just as in the movie, your efforts to get here will be amply rewarded: the island of Skellig Michael sits in the Atlantic Ocean off the coast of County Kerry, Ireland. A UNESCO World Heritage site, the steep steps and precipitous drops are not for the fainthearted, and access to the island is very weather dependent.

▼ OSS, THE NETHERLANDS
## 124. Stay in a sand castle hotel in Oss
**When:** Summer
**Latitude:** 51.7611°N
**Longitude:** 5.5140°E

Spend the night in a life-size sand castle made by Dutch sculptors—it's a children's fantasy made real. Surprisingly luxurious, this fantastical place, complete with drawbridge and turrets, gets knocked down at the end of summer (presumably with a massive spade).

A sandcastle hotel in Oss, the Netherlands

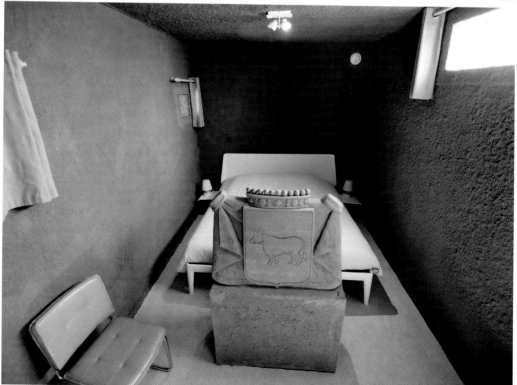

START AT THE THAMES HEAD, ENGLAND, UK
## 125. Follow a river from its source to the sea
**When:** All year
**Latitude:** 51.6943°N **Longitude:** 2.0297°W

To experience the full passage of nature, walk—or run, or cycle, or even swim—the length of a river from its source to the sea. The River Thames in England is great for this since it is easily accessible. It is the longest river in the country at more than 200 mi (322 km), but there are plenty of great places to stop off en route. Starting at Thames Head, near the village of Kemble in Gloucestershire, it ends in Essex, after passing through London, an adventure in itself.

The River Thames from its source at Thames Head in Gloucestershire (left) through London (below) to the sea

RHONDDA VALLEY, WALES, UK
## 126. Sing with a Welsh choir
**When:** All year
**Latitude:** 51.6159°N
**Longitude:** 3.4175°W

Wales has a long and distinguished history of singing, from the folk songs that survived attempts to suppress the Welsh language, to the male voice choirs of the coal industry, to hip-swiveling stalwart Tom Jones. Choirs have existed in the Rhondda Valley for more than 150 years, making it a good place to join in—so what's stopping you?

LONDON, ENGLAND, UK
## 127. Kiss someone famous
**When:** All year
**Latitude:** 51.5228°N
**Longitude:** 0.1553°W

Let's face it, it's unlikely to happen in real life, so head instead to Madame Tussauds, the waxwork museum that started in London and now has branches in cities across the world, filled with uncanny likenesses of the rich and famous. But beware if you decide to peck your favorite: Ozzy Osbourne, Arnold Schwarzenegger, and One Direction are just a few of the stars who have stood in place of their figures in the past to prank unsuspecting visitors.

LONDON, NEW YORK, TOKYO
## 128. Shop in the three meccas of fashion
**When:** All year
**Latitude:** 51.5149°N
**Longitude:** 0.1445°W (London's Oxford Street)

The holy trinity for serious shopaholics. If you can't find what you're looking for in the boutiques, markets, and mega department stores of these three shrines to the art of shopping, then it may be time to stop searching.

LONDON, ENGLAND, UK
## 129. Brew your own beer
**When:** All year
**Latitude:** 51.5333°N
**Longitude:** 0.1333°W

What better way to celebrate the revival of British brewing culture than by enjoying a hoppy ale created by your own hand? Spend the day on a brewing experience at the Brewhouse and Kitchen in Islington, London, and you'll leave with a 176 fl oz (5 l) keg of your own creation.

LONDON, ENGLAND, UK
## 130. Catch an innings at Lord's
**When:** Summer
**Latitude:** 51.5306°N
**Longitude:** 0.1695°W

The "Home of Cricket" is a wonderful collision of the old (they've batted and bowled here since 1814) and modern (due to a tasteful £200m regeneration). Every cricketer wants to play here at St. John's Wood, and its quintessentially English setting is the definitive place to hear leather smack willow.

LONDON, ENGLAND, UK
## 131. See justice being done
**When:** Monday to Friday
**Latitude:** 51.5158°N
**Longitude:** 0.1019°W

The historic Central Criminal Court, affectionately known as Old Bailey, has seen infamous characters such as Dr. Crippen and the Krays pass through its dockets. Entry to the public gallery is free, but be prepared to wait in line, especially for cases of high media interest.

LONDON, ENGLAND, UK
## 132. Play soccer at Wembley
**When:** Depends on availability
**Latitude:** 51.5560°N
**Longitude:** 0.2795°W

How do you get to play at Wembley Stadium? Practice. One of soccer's most famous homes, the 90,000 capacity, £800m facility with its defining arch is somewhere every soccer player wants to play. There are competitions to win the chance to play there, and there's a five-a-side complex next door for those who don't make it.

▼ LONDON, ENGLAND, UK
## 133. Cross Abbey Road, Fab Four style
**When:** All year
**Latitude:** 51.5367°N **Longitude:** 0.1830°W

Anywhere else in the world, a set of painted markings designed to help pedestrians across a busy street and manage traffic flow would be considered pretty mundane. The crossing on Abbey Road, St. John's Wood, however, has become a tourist trap thanks to its role on the front cover of The Beatles' eleventh album (also named *Abbey Road*). Located close to the studio where the record was cut, the crossing now has a Grade II listed status, and is a mecca for Fab fans, who inevitably have to be photographed recreating the shot. Add your photo to the website abbeyroadcrossing.com along with thousands of others who have shared a wildly differing array of images.

Crossing Abbey Road Fab Four style in London, England, UK

Julia Roberts and Hugh Grant in the movie *Notting Hill*, in London, England, UK

▲ LONDON, ENGLAND, UK
## 134. Follow Julia Roberts' and Hugh Grant's lead
**When:** All year
**Latitude:** 51.5096°N
**Longitude:** 0.2043°W

From bustling Portobello Road market, to the famous blue front door at 280 Westbourne Park Road, a walk through London's trendy Notting Hill is great fun in its own right—for fans of the 1999 movie of the same name, it's a must.

LONDON, ENGLAND, UK
## 135. Get on your soapbox
**When:** Sundays
**Latitude:** 51.5132°N
**Longitude:** 0.1589°W

A bastion of free speech and the right to protest, Speakers' Corner has been the place to go to hear, or air, opinions for more than 150 years. Start a debate here and you'll join the prestigious ranks of the suffragettes, Karl Marx, and George Orwell.

LONDON, ENGLAND, UK
## 136. Search for your very own piece of history
**When:** At low tide
**Latitude:** 51.5097°N
**Longitude:** 0.1044°W

A stroll along an exposed beach on the River Thames can be a rewarding experience for the budding historian. You might find fragments of clay pipes, pieces of pottery, old bones, and flints. Not all of it will date back to Roman times, but some might.

LONDON, ENGLAND, UK

### 137. Take in a West End musical

**When:** All year
**Latitude:** 51.5133°N
**Longitude:** 0.1286°W

From French political history to a pop group's early years or even a lion who doesn't want to be king, every story can be further enhanced with a cast of dancing extras, some amazing costumery, and, of course, unforgettable tunes. Be transported by the joy of song.

LONDON, ENGLAND, UK
## 138. Cross London's landmark bridge
**When:** All year
**Latitude:** 51.5045°N
**Longitude:** 0.0761°W

One of London's most iconic sights, this feat of nineteenth-century engineering still opens three times a day for passing boats. Wander from the eleventh-century Tower of London in the north, to the energetic south bank across the city's lifeblood river.

LONDON STUDIOS, ENGLAND, UK
## 139. Perform under pressure
**When:** All year
**Latitude:** 51.5073°N
**Longitude:** 0.1277°W

If you've ever shouted at a quiz show on TV that the questions are too easy, it's time to get off your sofa and see how you perform under pressure. Auditioning is surprisingly easy, and you could even win yourself a prize—that or a red face.

LONDON, ENGLAND, UK
## 140. Wild swim in the UK capital
**When:** All year
**Latitude:** 51.5073°N
**Longitude:** 0.1277°E

Throughout the year, those who choose to can don their bathing suits and breaststroke next to the aquatic life in London's leafy suburb of Hampstead. There are three ponds to choose from (women only, men only, and mixed) and an open-air changing room, so take your pick.

ENGLAND, UK AND WORLDWIDE
## 141. Plant a seed and nurture it to grow
**When:** Spring
**Latitude:** 51.4792°N
**Longitude:** 0.2928°W (Kew Gardens, UK)

Whether it's an acorn growing into an oak, or a pea growing into a cascade of flowers, there's something quietly magnificent about the power of nature to take something small and make it big. Be a part of it by growing your own little piece of wonder.

ENGLAND, UK AND WORLDWIDE
## 142. Tread the boards
**When:** All year
**Latitude:** 51.5073°N **Longitude:** 0.1278°W (London)

Stepping out onto the stage as part of a play isn't TV or a movie—nobody can shout "cut" and let the actor do it again if they mess up their lines, and that lack of a safety net is part of the thrill.

Where to start? It's advisable to dip a toe into the theatrical waters before taking on a big part. There are thousands of amateur dramatic associations right across the world with small roles for most people who want to give it a go, and many find that after having been on stage once, they want to do it again and again. Stage fright and nerves are an inevitable part of the process, and diminish over time. So break a leg, and remember not to mention *Macbeth* …

LONDON, ENGLAND, UK
## 143. Run in the London Marathon
**When:** Late April
**Latitude:** 51.5073°N **Longitude:** 0.1277°W

The best-supported marathon in the world sees 750,000 spectators line a 26.2 mi (42.2 km) course to cheer on 38,000 athletes. It would feel like one big party if it wasn't for the painful legs, but it is a joy to run. Take your place among the wealth of celebrities and crazy fancy-dress outfits, and hear the huge roar as runners turn onto the Mall.

BRUGES, BELGIUM
## 144. Propose or renew vows in Bruges
**When:** All year (although twilight wintry scenes are made for romantic liaisons)
**Latitude:** 51.2167°N
**Longitude:** 3.2333°E

Other towns have medieval buildings, cobbled streets, and meandering canals, but none of them have put them together in quite such a charming way as Bruges. It's the perfect place to give voice to your romantic intentions and a good way to make Bruges "your" city.

HANNUT, BELGIUM
## 145. Find a missing piece of the puzzle …
**When:** October
**Latitude:** 50.6667°N
**Longitude:** 5.0833°E

Jigsaw fans unite: the world's most prestigious jigsaw competition is held over twenty-four hours in Hannut, Belgium, every October. The best puzzlers from around the world convene here, presumably starting with those from the four corners …

BRUSSELS AND ACROSS BELGIUM
## 146. Savor Belgian beers, chocolate, and mussels
**When:** All year
**Latitude:** 50.8503°N
**Longitude:** 4.3517°E

The Belgians have cornered the market in several gastronomical areas, especially the holy trinity of beer, chocolate, and *moules* (mussels). Any visit to these European lowlands—from charming spots like Bruges, to the bureaucratic bustle of Brussels—is always hugely enhanced by enjoying at least one, but preferably all three.

**147. Cycle a piece of Olympic history**
**When:** March to October
**Latitude:** 51.4510°N
**Longitude:** 0.0915°W

Journey down to south London and get ready to race on the last remaining venue from the 1948 Olympics – the Herne Hill Velodrome. With beginner lessons and track bikes for rent by the day, there's no reason why you, too, can't be flying round the track like British cyclist Bradley Wiggins.

**148. Play tennis in Wimbledon**
**When:** All year
**Latitude:** 51.4387°N **Longitude:** 0.2052°W

So the famous Centre Court isn't open to the public for play, and you'll have to jump through a gazillion hoops to become a member and play on the other courts, but yes, you can play tennis in the hallowed SW19 postcode: the courts next door in Wimbledon Park to be precise. Better yet, go there on the middle Saturday of the tournament for a drop-in coaching session, which traditionally includes visits from some of the Wimbledon players.

**149. Dine with strangers at a supper club**
**When:** All year
**Latitude:** 51.4617°N **Longitude:** 0.1396°W

The idea of inviting complete strangers into your home for a meal took off in the Internet age, as online foodies reached out to other like-minded munchers via social media and established underground supper clubs founded on a love of fine food and good company. Londoners were the first to embrace the scene in the UK, and there are now established regular supper clubs with their dinner parties listed online. Or why not set up your own?

LONDON (ONE OF THE WORLD'S MOST VISITED CITIES), ENGLAND, UK
## 150. Be a tourist in your own city
**When:** All year and your whole lifetime
**Latitude:** 51.5055°N **Longitude:** 0.0754°W

There's nothing like knowing one place really, really well: where to get a drink after hours; the streets that have figured in famous movies and novels, the parks hidden down side streets. It's amazing to discover and know your city in such depth.

London receives almost 17 million visitors a year. Most of them will wave at the windows of Buckingham Palace, jump on the top deck of a bus, and hear the sounds of Big Ben striking the hour, but in that small section of London alone, there's so much more to discover. If they walked down the Mall from Buckingham Palace to Trafalgar Square and stopped as they passed under the left-hand side of Admiralty Arch, did they know they could look up and see what looks like Nelson's spare nose embedded in the brickwork? (It's probably shrapnel from World War II, but which makes the better story?)

It would take a lifetime to truly get to know every part of your city, but to even start scratching at the surface is to open up a whole new world of interest. How well do you know yours?

LONDON, ENGLAND, UK
## 151. Be waited on with an English afternoon tea
**When:** All year
**Latitude:** 51.5072°N
**Longitude:** 0.1417°W (Ritz Hotel, London)

Fancy being treated like royalty? The English ritual of afternoon tea at a high-end hotel is an experience not to be missed. From dainty sandwiches to exquisite cakes and pastries, plus lashings of piping-hot tea, it is tradition on a (fine china) plate.

LONDON, ENGLAND, UK
## 152. Photobomb a news story
**When:** Any time
**Latitude:** 51.4992°N
**Longitude:** 0.1247°W

If you're unlikely to become a politician making the news, you can always try stealing their limelight instead. One of the easiest places to photobomb a news broadcast has to be outside the Houses of Parliament in London, because there aren't many days when politics isn't making the news here. A smaller news story is likely to give you more chances to sneak up close, and inconspicuously wander past ... before frantically waving at your nearest and dearest on the other side of the camera lens.

KENT, ENGLAND, UK
## 153. Drive on a racetrack
**When:** All year
**Latitude:** 51.3567°N
**Longitude:** 0.2625°E

Get behind the wheel of a supercar and take on the iconic racing circuit at Brands Hatch, the home of British motorsport. One of the world's best-loved racing venues, it has hosted motoring greats such as Jackie Stewart, Stirling Moss, and Ayrton Senna. Follow in their tire tracks as you take on the infamous Paddock Hill Bend, a fast-sweeping downhill corner.

MINEHEAD TO POOLE, ENGLAND, UK

154. **Walk the South West Coast Path**

**When:** All year
**Latitude:** 51.2038°N
**Longitude:** 3.4738°W (Minehead)

Few walks are as genuinely enjoyable as England's South West Coast Path, rugged cliffs topped with heather and wildflowers, the bright, blue waters of the Atlantic at turns lapping at the soft smooth beaches and crashing into the sturdy cliffs below.

This is the country's longest trail, running 630 mi (1,014 km) from Minehead in Somerset, along the coast of Exmoor's open moorland, to North Devon and Cornwall beyond, before looping back along the south coast to Devon and Dorset, ending up in Poole. Along the way you can enjoy sunsets over the islets of the Atlantic, watch seals reclining on the rocks, and spot birds, such as peregrine falcons and cirl buntings wheeling. You can tackle the path all in one go (more than at least thirty days) or walk just one or two of the fifty-two short sections, some of which are less than 10 mi (16 km) long.

THE DUTCH COASTAL ROUTE, THE NETHERLANDS
## 155. Bicycle a hundred miles in one day

**When:** All year

**Latitude:** 51.3333°N **Longitude:** 3.4833°E (Sluis, the Netherlands)

Cycling became and remains a popular way to travel in the Netherlands most notably because the country is flat, and the Dutch have always been very bike-friendly in their urban planning.

Outside the towns, interurban cycling tracks connect towns and villages as part of the Dutch National Cycle Network. Known as LF routes, these long-distance bicycle routes crisscross the country—there is no better place in the world for cyclist enthusiasts to fulfill an ambition to clock 100 mi (161 km) in a day.

LF1—the Noordzeeroute (or "North Sea Route")—and LF10—the Waddezeeroute (or "Wadden Sea Route")—together are known as the Dutch Coastal Route. It's a 354 mi (570 km) ride along beautiful coast, the Zeeland islands, and seaside resorts from Sluis to Den Holder. You can then head to the north, from Callantsoog to Bad Nieuweschans, on the second part of the route. You'll also get to cycle over the Afsluitdijk, the 20 mi (32 km) long causeway constructed as a dam in the 1920s.

If you want to go bigger and better, the Dutch Coastal Route is part of the North Sea Cycle Route, which passes through eight countries that border the North Sea. And this in itself is one part of fourteen long-distance European cycle routes currently being completed, known as the EuroVelo network. When these are finished (estimated by 2020), they will make up a staggering 43,500 mi (70,000 km) of bicycle touring across the continent.

◀ NEAR KLEVEN, UKRAINE
## 156. Stroll through the "tunnel of love"

**When:** April to September (for best leaf coverage)

**Latitude:** 50.7503°N **Longitude:** 26.0438°E

Deep in the woods of Ukraine lies a perfect green tunnel formed by trees growing alongside and meeting above a rail track. This is nature's response when a train passes along a route just three times a day and the rest of the time the trees grow undisturbed. The result is something quite magical. Take a stroll through this enchanting passageway, which has captured the hearts of romantics everywhere, and led to the tunnel being known locally as the "tunnel of love."

LONDON, ENGLAND, UK
## 157. Live it up in a luxury hotel

**When:** All year

**Latitude:** 51.4975°N **Longitude:** 0.1456°W

There is something that feels delightfully decadent about ordering room service. At upscale hotels, there's a thrill in ringing down to the front desk and beckoning a uniformed member of staff to tap politely on the door with a tray full of food, drinks—whatever your heart desires. One UK hotel offers guests pet goldfish to keep them company overnight, while the royalty-approved Goring in London will press your daily newspaper before delivering it to the room. Now that's service.

The "tunnel of love" near
Kleven, Ukraine

▶ BRUSSELS, BELGIUM
## 158. Soak up the splendor of Brussels Grand-Place
**When:** All year
**Latitude:** 50.8467°N
**Longitude:** 4.3525°E

An immense open space surrounded by intricate detailed baroque buildings has earned Brussels' Grand-Place UNESCO World Heritage status. Dig a little deeper into the history of this iconic square and you'll discover it goes all the way back to the twelfth century.

ALDERMASTON, ENGLAND, UK
## 159. Become passionate about a campaign
**When:** Easter
**Latitude:** 51.3830°N
**Longitude:** 1.1500°W (Original destination of CND marches)

One of the world's most recognized symbols is that of anti-nuclear weapon campaigners, CND. All campaigns begin with a group of like-minded people taking action, so whatever your passion, don't bury it—get out there and shout about it!

The splendor of Brussels Grand-Place, Belgium

▼ GIVERNY, FRANCE
## 160. Visit Monet's garden in Giverny

**When:** March to November
**Latitude:** 49.0770°N
**Longitude:** 1.5257°E

Stand in the spot where the great Impressionist Claude Monet painted his famous water lily paintings. "I must have flowers, always, and always," said the artist, inspiring him to paint, and also create, one of the most beautiful gardens in the world: Jardin de Monet à Giverny.

LA FÉE VERTE, PARIS, FRANCE
## 161. Drink absinthe like a French intellectual

**When:** A night when your schedule is clear the next day
**Latitude:** 48.8578°N
**Longitude:** 2.3801°E

Few drinks have quite such an aura of mystique as absinthe. Popular with the French thinkers of La Belle Époque, it was banned in France from 1915 until the 1990s among fears that it produced hallucinations and madness. It's not banned any more, so you can sup the green stuff in dedicated bars, such as La Fée Verte.

BANKS OF THE SEINE, FRANCE
## 162. Have a bacchanalian picnic in the park

**When:** June to September
**Latitude:** 48.9333°N
**Longitude:** 2.3333°E

Monet, Manet, Cezanne—they all have their *déjeuner sur l'herbe* paintings that take the humble picnic to a more elaborate dining form. Join them by gathering together your favorite friends, creating sumptuous food, and serving it on a white tablecloth in a beautiful setting—with or without naked ladies!

Monet's garden in Giverny, France

BANFF NATIONAL PARK, CANADA

## 163. Stare in wonder at the beauty of Moraine Lake

**When:** Late June for the best colors
**Latitude:** 51.3225°N **Longitude:** 116.1855°W

The still, clear turquoise waters of Moraine Lake reflecting the towering scenery of Banff National Park make it one of those scenes you could sit and contemplate for hours. Don't miss this truly special view of Earth's natural beauty.

## Celebrate the solstice with druids at Stonehenge

**When:** Around June 21
**Latitude:** 51.1788°N **Longitude:** 1.8262°W

The gathering to witness sunrise on the longest day of the calendar year, usually on June 21, and usually at around 4:50 a.m., has long been a pagan ritual, and there's no better time or place to share a collective transcendental spiritual moment as when the sun peeks alluringly through Wiltshire's world-famous Neolithic stone sculptures.

Of course, this being the UK, sunshine levels can be somewhat temperamental and visitors need to dress for a mixture of weather.

All kinds of characters show up: the druids are always in attendance, conducting ancient rites in stern-looking circles, but so are the New Age revelers. In a gathering somewhat resembling Glastonbury Festival before its commercialization, there are plenty of travelers, and an attendant police presence too, even though the solstice tends to be a jolly, crime-free affair, attracting a good number of families with children.

It's also one of the few times of the year that visitors are allowed to actually touch the stones themselves, permitting a spiritual connection with these grounding obelisks.

Spending the short night anticipating dawn, with drummers filling the air with tribal beats and fire jugglers lighting up the skies, is enough to access anyone's inner hippie, and get them pondering about this ancient architectural mystery. Where did these vast, 20-plus ton (18,000-plus kg) stones appear from, given that the closest quarry is more than 20 mi 32 km) away and the ancient peoples had no modern-day machinery? Could this be proof of something as bizarre as alien visitation or supernatural forces?

There is no written history from this time, more than 2,500 years ago, so we'll never know, of course—but those present for the solstice will happily share their theories.

The event may be attended by those who want to forget modern life and rampant commercialization for just a moment, but that hasn't stopped a few entrepreneurs from turning this into a quick buck, either: just down the road there's a four-day camping festival, with music, food, beer, and cider—plus a shuttle bus to the site on solstice day—so if you want to turn the event into a real weekender, you can do just that.

▼ SOMERSET, ENGLAND, UK
## 165. Join the great Glastonbury party
**When:** June
**Latitude:** 51.1676°N **Longitude:** 2.5789°W

The most famous festival on Earth is an ever-changing beast: it began as a bucolic rock gathering in a farmer's field, became a vast, psychedelic free-for-all hippie haven through the 1970s and 1980s, before erecting an impenetrable superfence and commercializing itself in the mid-noughties. It is still the largest greenfield music gathering in the world—more than 100,000 people attend every year. In addition to acts on the famous Pyramid Stage, you can also stumble across a cosmopolitan smorgasbord of talks, comedians, and musical acts that simply won't gather together anywhere else.

HAMPSHIRE, ENGLAND, UK
## 166. See ponies run free in the New Forest
**When:** All year
**Latitude:** 50.8189°N
**Longitude:** 1.5757°W

Created as a royal hunting ground in 1079 for King William I, and covering a vast swathe of Hampshire, the New Forest National Park is a beautiful slice of British countryside. More than 3,000 ponies roam the unspoiled moors and woodland, so you are never far from one. Spot them grazing amid campsite tents or roaming alongside the numerous woodland cycling trails. Go in spring or summer if you want to see foals.

The great Glastonbury party in Somerset, England, UK

DOVER TO CALAIS, STARTING IN ENGLAND, UK

## 167. Grease up and swim the English Channel

**When:** All year

**Latitude:** 51.1278°N **Longitude:** 1.3134°E

Swimming the English Channel—almost always starting from Shakespeare Beach in Dover—is one of those "challenges" that really defines the word. It's tricky to even get into a position to do it: to qualify for an attempt, you must first do a verified six-hour swim in cold water (below 60°F; 15°C) and send it off to the Channel Swimming Association to seek a slot. All swims must be supported by an official pilot—which costs and needs to be booked up to three years in advance. The French have banned the pursuit, believing it to be too dangerous, meaning England to France is the only legal direction to make the swim.

Other factors that might put you off? Wetsuits are not allowed, and hypothermia accounts for a lot of abandonments. Slathering goose fat all over the body helps with insulation and to avoid chafing (but can clog up the goggles), and there's also the seasickness from the choppy swells. Dehydration, hunger, and exhaustion are constant worries. Then there's the pollution. And jellyfish. It's also deeply grueling. The record crossing took seven hours; the slowest ever took twenty-seven. Many abandon, and fewer than 2,000 people—half the amount who have climbed Everest—have ever done it.

So what is there to enjoy about such a task? Many report of a magnificent sense of isolation and connection with nature. And as with many of these things, it is the finish that makes the whole thing worthwhile.

START WITH THE SOUTH DOWNS NATIONAL PARK, ENGLAND, UK

## 168. Discover the dramatic beauty of the English countryside

**When:** All year

**Latitude:** 50.9685°N **Longitude:** 0.6953°W

You don't have to be on vacation to visit a national park; it's well worth discovering the national parks of your homeland, too. Those in Canada might want to reserve a few years for the job—there are forty-three parks there, while for those in Afghanistan, it's a simpler task: there's only one national park, the Band-e Amir National Park in the Hindu Kush.

The UK has 8 percent of its land area in designated national parks, with fifteen parks in all. The newest is the South Downs National Park, which received the status in 2011. It takes in the rolling chalk hills and gentle farmland of the Downs as well as a coastline that includes the dramatic Seven Sisters cliffs. The South Downs Way is a 100 mi (161 km) walking route within the boundaries of the park, from Winchester in the west to Eastbourne in the east.

ACROSS THE UK AND WORLDWIDE

## 169 Complete a triathlon

**When:** All year

**Latitude:** 51.5000°N

**Longitude:** 0.1167°W (UK)

There are numerous different levels of triathlon available—from a starter initiation of just 656 ft (200 m) swim/6 mi (10 km) bike/1.5 mi (2.5 km) run, to the hardcore madness of an Ironman. Experience the satisfaction that comes from completing any of these unique trebles that offer an unlikely combination of deep addiction and fitness-boosting pleasure.

A steam train in Dorset, England, UK

▲ DORSET, ENGLAND, UK
## 170. Get hot and steamy on a heritage railway
**When:** June to September
**Latitude:** 50.6100°N
**Longitude:** 1.9600°W

Drive a steam train, stoke the fire, and blow the whistle at crossings on a journey from Swanage around a delightful Dorset peninsula graced by wildflowers, castles, and rivers. It is an unforgettable experience that will, for many, fulfill a lifelong ambition.

DORSET, ENGLAND, UK
## 171. Sit behind the wheel of an armored vehicle
**When:** All year (although wet and muddy is best)
**Latitude:** 50.6952°N
**Longitude:** 2.2436°W

Take the opportunity to live out a childhood fantasy by taking the wheel of some serious military hardware as you tear around some of the UK's finest countryside. Unforgettable tank-driving experiences include obstacle courses, car crushing, tank paintball, and gun firing.

DORSET, ENGLAND, UK
## 172. Follow a map to its edges
**When:** All year
**Latitude:** 50.5500°N
**Longitude:** 2.4400°W

What better edge to head to than the beautiful Isle of Portland? This "tied" island marks the western limits of the first area mapped by the British mapping company Ordnance Survey in 1791. Follow footpaths through dunes and along sweeping sandy beaches until you run out of map.

LONDON, ENGLAND, UK
## 173. Buy a bespoke suit from Savile Row
**When:** All year
**Latitude:** 51.5119°N
**Longitude:** 0.1414°W

This central London street in the UK became synonymous with bespoke suit making (suits made and cut by hand) at the turn of the eighteenth century. You can still find the family-run establishment of Henry Poole, creator of the tuxedo, here today.

START IN PADSTOW, ENGLAND, UK
## 174. Discover the Cornish countryside on The Camel Trail
**When:** Best in summer
**Latitude:** 50.5421°N **Longitude:** 4.9390°W

You don't have to be super-fit to take in the stunning views of the Cornish Coast by bike. The Camel Trail, which stretches 18 mi (29 km) along North Cornwall between Padstow, Wadebridge, and Bodmin, follows the path of a disused railway track, ensuring the majority of it is effortlessly flat and family friendly.

The long trail takes in beautiful sea views across the Camel Estuary as well as woodland and rolling valleys. There are plenty of picturesque points along the way and you are spoiled for choice when it comes to pretty towns and villages en route to explore.

Renting a bicycle is easy, but it's best to phone ahead and book in the busy summer months as bikes get snapped up quickly.

YORKSHIRE, ENGLAND, UK
## 175. Recognize birds by their song alone
**When:** All year (but best in springtime)
**Latitude:** 53.7437°N
**Longitude:** 1.3175°W

It is always a beautiful experience to listen to birdsong, but it is even more fulfilling if you can identify what you are listening to. At the UK's Fairburn Ings Nature Reserve, listen out for the chiffchaff which, for example, says its name, while yellowhammers go "a little bit of bread and no cheese."

VANCOUVER, CANADA
## 176. Cross the Capilano Suspension Bridge
**When:** All year
**Latitude:** 49.3437°N
**Longitude:** 123.1125°W

Suspension bridges shout of man's all-conquering nature: "I will cross this gorge, as if I were born to fly." The Capilano Suspension Bridge is a true sensation, 230 ft (70 m) high, two-people wide, and 450 ft (140 m) long. Set foot on it and you'll feel like you're stepping into thin air.

DARMSTADT, GERMANY
## 177. Visit a crooked apartment block
**When:** All year
**Latitude:** 49.8856°N
**Longitude:** 8.6558°E

Translated as "forest spiral," the name Waldspirale is particularly apt for the apartment complex built by Austrian architect Friedensreich Hundertwasser. Twelve floors rise up in a colorful spiral, topped by a green "living" roof—visit the café at the top for fabulous views.

BRITISH COLUMBIA, CANADA
## 178. Build an epic sand castle
**When:** July and August
**Latitude:** 49.3150°N **Longitude:** 124.3120°W

Each year in July and August, the most stunning display of sand castles appears on the beach of Parksville in Canada. Actually, the term "sand castles" doesn't begin to do justice to these magnificent works of art that are here as part of the annual Parksville Beach Festival competition. Watch the sculptures being constructed by artists who arrive here from all over the globe, but be sure to also pop back when they are completed, to view the finished articles in all their splendor.

BRITISH COLUMBIA, CANADA
## 179. Spot a grizzly bear
**When:** September and October
**Latitude:** 49.5701°N
**Longitude:** 116.8312°W

Deep in an unspoiled valley in the Selkirk Mountains, the Grizzly Bear Ranch offers visitors a 95 percent chance of glimpsing this rare, fascinating beast without—on their record so far—getting injured. Grizzlies can run as fast as racehorses, swim rapids, and climb trees, but contrary to what *The Revenant* would have us believe, spend most of their time rooting out leaves. Visit in the fall, the best bear-spotting season, when they descend from the mountains to the rivers to seek spawning salmon.

VANCOUVER ISLAND, BRITISH COLUMBIA, CANADA
## 180. Paddle up close to breathtaking orcas
**When:** Mid-June to October
**Latitude:** 50.5458°N **Longitude:** 126.8332°W

Canadians are spoiled for whale-watching choice, with more than thirty species lurking off the country's 126,000 mi (202,777 km) coastline. But it is the waters around Vancouver Island that contain the "holy grail" of this particular pastime. Here, awe-inspiring orcas (also known as killer whales) join the humpbacks and gray whales patrolling the Pacific. The best spot to begin the search for orcas is Robson Bight/Johnstone Strait, Canada's only killer whale sanctuary. The epicenter of orca watching is remote Telegraph Cove, a six-and-a-half-hour drive from Vancouver city. More than 200 northern resident orcas return to the cove every summer to feast on salmon and exfoliate on the beaches.

The site of a barnacle-covered orca breaking the surface, water cascading from its powerful tail, before breaching and sliding gracefully back beneath the waves just feet from you is truly breathtaking and a genuine never-to-be-forgotten moment.

▶ CANADA
## 181. Try heli-skiing where it all began
**When:** Winter
**Latitude:** 50.7458°N
**Longitude:** 116.7892°W

Heli-skiing was born in the 1960s in the Bugaboos mountains, so where better to try this adrenaline-filled sport? You'll start with a thrilling helicopter ride that takes you high up in the territory of long runs through virgin powder snow. Then it's all downhill from there—but only in terms of direction, of course.

Heli-skiing in Canada

Snow falling on Charles Bridge in Prague, Czech Republic

▲ PRAGUE, CZECH REPUBLIC

## 182. Watch snow fall from a medieval bridge

**When:** November to March

**Latitude:** 50.0865°N

**Longitude:** 14.4111°E

Charles Bridge in Prague is a magical place, but never more so than when the surrounding city is white with snow. Admire the beautiful vistas of Prague's Old Town at one end and the castle at the other from this 2,000 ft (610 m) long cobbled masterpiece.

START AT THE UK'S SOUTHWESTERLY TIP AND KEEP HEADING NORTH

## 183. Cover the whole of Britain … on foot

**When:** All year (although spring and summer may be most enjoyable)

**Latitude:** 50.0686°N **Longitude:** 5.7161°W

From the most southwesterly point of England, to the northeast tip of Scotland (or, if you prefer, the other way around), this is not a stroll for the fainthearted. But it passes through some glorious scenery: the Atlantic Coast around Land's End in Cornwall is some of the most spectacular in England, while the all-but-deserted mountains and glens on sections of the Scottish leg of the trip stand without comparison with any in the world.

If you traverse the entire length of Great Britain by road, the official journey covers 874 mi (1,407 km) between Land's End in the south and John o'Groats in the north. But if you use your feet to travel, you'll walk about 1,200 mi (1,931 km) and on average take between two and three months to complete the distance.

KUTNÁ HORA, CZECH REPUBLIC
## 186. Pray at a chapel made of bones

**When:** All year
**Latitude:** 49.9620°N
**Longitude:** 15.2883°E

In an unassuming suburb in the Czech town of Kutná Hora lies the macabre Sedlec Ossuary. In this "bone church," as it is known, you'll find an interior ornately decorated with the remains of 40,000 people, who died in the fourteenth and fifteenth centuries.

SUSSEX, ENGLAND, UK
## 184. Ride in a "spaceship" in Brighton

**When:** All year
**Latitude:** 50.6083°N **Longitude:** 1.9608°W

If you have a head for heights, a trip up the British Airways i360 in Brighton is a must. Shaped a bit like a spaceship (or a gigantic lollipop, or a mushroom—take your pick), and opened in 2016, it is the world's first vertical cable car, and world's tallest moving observation tower—it takes you up to 450 ft (137 m). From the top, you'll enjoy panoramic 360-degree views of the quirky town below, and all along the Sussex coast.

KARLOVY VARY, CZECH REPUBLIC
## 185. Blow glass with the Bohemian king of glass

**When:** All year
**Latitude:** 50.2333°N **Longitude:** 12.8667°E

Bohemian crystal is renowned worldwide for its quality and craft, and Moser is a luxury manufacturer of highly collectible decorative glassware. Visitors to its factory in the company's hometown of Karlovy Vary may get a chance to turn their hand—or rather mouths—to the art of glass blowing. Glassmakers start by placing molten glass into a wooden mold and then blowing through a spinning mouth pipe until the glass coats the interior of the mold to take on its shape. You'll find it takes more puff than you might imagine.

MONTANA, US
## 187. Skim a stone in a pristine setting
**When:** All year
**Latitude:** 48.5787°N **Longitude:** 113.9225°W

Ever managed to master the art of bouncing a flat stone over water? One of the most picturesque places to do so is on Lake McDonald in Glacier National Park, Montana. If you're particularly good, you could also join the annual World Stone Skimming Championships in Easdale Island, Scotland—the winner's stone must travel the farthest distance and bounce at least three times.

ALASKA, US
## 188. See a brown bear catch a leaping salmon
**When:** July to October
**Latitude:** 58.5533°N
**Longitude:** 155.7927°E

As if it's not amazing enough to watch a fish jump up a waterfall, seeing a brown bear pluck that leaping fish from the air in its jaws is testament to just how incredible nature is. And to see forty bears in action in one waterfall is the pinnacle of that display. Get along to Brooks Falls in Alaska's Katmai National Park and Preserve for the chance to see this happen.

▼ SEATTLE, WASHINGTON, US
## 189. Unleash your inner rock star
**When:** All year
**Latitude:** 47.6097°N **Longitude:** 122.3331°W

Who has never harbored a secret desire to take to the stage, grab the mic, and release their inner rock star? (Or pop idol, or rap guru, or … well, you get the idea). And where better to unleash your hidden talents than in one of the most musically diverse cities on Earth?

Seattle boasts an illustrious musical heritage. The number of opportunities to take to the stage in this city are so vast, your best bet is to head to four of the city's eight historic districts and seek out a venue that fits your musical style: join the talented buskers of the Pike Place Market area; look to the bars, cafés, and restaurants of the Ballard Avenue area for an acoustic folksy-tinged sound; grab your five minutes of fame in the Columbia City district; or pop over to West Seattle for open-mic nights.

Also welcome on stage: poets, orators, storytellers—anyone with something to sing, say, or recite will find a venue of like-minded listeners in this city.

Rock star Kurt Cobain was a big part of the Seattle music scene in the US

## 190. Take your cycling up a gear in the Carpathian Mountains

**When:** Summer is best

**Latitude:** 49.1803°N

**Longitude:** 19.9194°E

The Carpathian Mountains are the highest range in Central Europe, crossing seven European countries from the Czech Republic to Romania. In Slovakia you'll find the Western Carpathians, which, depending on the time of year, draw skiers, hikers, and cyclists in abundance. Their appeal lies in feeling remote and virtually undisturbed by the passage of time: cycling here feels like it may have done a hundred years ago, as much of the area remains largely underdeveloped and is historically preserved.

The tallest part of the Carpathians—the High Tatras—are in what is now the largest national park in Slovakia. It is a good place to start a cycling tour of this area of the country. Sixteen well-marked and well-maintained bike trails wind their way among alpine lakes and plenty of spectacular waterfalls.

Then head south to the Low Tatras, the largest national park in Slovakia. It has fifty cycling routes through the densely forested mountains that are home to wolves, bears, and lynx. Some of the views here are wonderfully otherworldly, with mountains as far as the eye can see staggering toward the horizon.

Onward to Vel'ká Fatra for more of the same stunning landscapes and carnivorous inhabitants. There are many Heritage sites to explore in this area of Slovakia, should you have any energy left after your cycling.

▼ TSAGAANNUUR, OUTER MONGOLIA
## 191. Spend a night in Outer Mongolia
**When:** Summer is best
**Latitude:** 51.3544°W **Longitude:** 99.3533°E

The Dukha communities of reindeer herders are not the most accessible of hosts, but they are the most hospitable. They dwell in the remote northern mountains of Mongolia that border Russia, and visiting them is a day-long bumpy drive (bring motion-sickness pills!) and a trek of at least a day or two on horseback.

In return, you will be rewarded with the experience of a lifetime with one of the last remaining nomadic reindeer herders on Earth, which move camp up to ten times a year to suit the reindeers' grazing and breeding needs. Conditions are basic, but you're warmly welcomed to join every part of life in the camp.

ASTANA, KAZAKHSTAN
## 192. Feel the energy of nations at a World Expo
**When:** June to September 2017
**Latitude:** 51.1667°N **Longitude:** 71.4333°E

A World Expo is undoubtedly one of the world's most innovative and global experiences. Countries showcase themselves in pavilions that are at the forefront of modern architecture. Inside each is a mini museum about an aspect of that country, and the whole event provides a theatrical stage for high-energy parades and shows. Plus, you could be the first to see lasting attractions—after all, the Eiffel Tower was built for a World Expo in 1889. If you don't make the one in Kazakhstan in 2017, the next one will be in Dubai in 2020.

A Dukhan with his reindeer at Tsagaannuur, Outer Mongolia

ALTAI MOUNTAINS, MONGOLIA

## 193. Hunt with eagles

**When:** All year

**Latitude:** 49.0000°N

**Longitude:** 89.0000°E

One way of feeding the family on the Eurasian steppes is hunting with golden eagles, which can catch wolves and foxes, and have a lifelong bond with their trainers. This way of hunting is a dying tradition, but a visit to the Altai Mountains will give you the chance to see these nomads practice this ancient Kazakh art.

MONGOLIA

## 194. Hear a sound that defines a culture

**When:** All year  **Latitude:** 47.9167°N  **Longitude:** 106.5399°E

At first listen, it might not sound like something you'd travel thousands of miles for. But Tuvan, Khoomei, or Mongolian throat singing is actually pretty awe-inspiring. Firstly, because it's an incredible feat of musicianship—one person is simultaneously producing two pitches at the same time—and secondly, because it's all about context. This is a pastoral tradition that's all about mimicking nature. This could be anything from the gentle breezes of summer to birdsong, swirling rocks, traveling brooks, and chirruping crickets—meaning some singers will trek miles to find the right river or mountainside to go with their songs. And doesn't that sound like something that would be great to hear live?

KOSTOMAROV, RUSSIA

## 195. Visit one of the most natural churches

**When:** All year

**Latitude:** 50.6846°N

**Longitude:** 39.7554°E

There is something truly magical about the Spassky Cave Church near Kostomarov. Spot the colorful domes on top of chalky outcrops on a beautiful hillside, and inside you'll find a church that has been carved out of the rocks and can accommodate 2,000 worshippers.

▼ POISSY, PARIS, FRANCE
## 196. See Le Corbusier's elegant modernist villa
**When:** All year
**Latitude:** 48.9244°N
**Longitude:** 2.0283°E

Swiss-French architect Le Corbusier is viewed by many as the father of the modernist style. Step back in time to the 1930s with a visit to his stunning Villa Savoye, in Paris' western suburbs, one of the world's leading examples of his art. With its clean lines, huge windows, graceful internal curves, and spacious open-plan design, this style-defining villa moved from being a luxury second home to a World War II hayloft for occupying German forces before the French government safeguarded its future in 1965 by declaring the property a national monument.

PLACE DU TERTRE, PARIS, FRANCE
## 197. Become a cartoon
**When:** All year
**Latitude:** 48.8865°N
**Longitude:** 2.3408°E

Those brave enough to sit for a caricature in Paris could discover that the mole on their nose that they thought no one else noticed is actually their most dominant feature. But that's the whole point: have a portrait that makes you laugh—and was drawn in a memorable place.

Le Corbusier's elegant modernist villa: Villa Savoye in Poissy, Paris, France

► PARIS, FRANCE
## 198. Drink coffee at a real-life movie location

**When:** All year
**Latitude:** 48.8849°N
**Longitude:** 2.3336°E

In the historical Montmartre district of Paris, once famed for its artistic residents such as Picasso, van Gogh, and Toulouse-Lautrec, to name just three, lies Café des Deux Moulins, which became famous in another art—that of filmmaking, as the workplace of Amélie in the 2001 movie of that name. The area is full of movie locations—the café itself has appeared in two other films. Life imitates art here: expect to see lots of movie buffs taking photos with their small screens of these places that have appeared on the big screen.

Café des Deux Moulins is a real-life movie location in Paris, France

CHAMPS-ÉLYSÉES, PARIS, FRANCE
## 199. Win the Tour de France—in your head

**When:** Sundays
**Latitude:** 48.8705°N
**Longitude:** 2.3082°W

The Champs-Élysées on the Tour de France's final day bears very little resemblance to its everyday state when it has eight lanes of traffic. However, on Sundays, it is blessedly quiet, so why not cycle down it and create your own winning moment?

THE LOUVRE, PARIS, FRANCE
## 200. Peruse the *Mona Lisa*

**When:** All year
**Latitude:** 48.8641°N
**Longitude:** 2.3425°E

This is one of those works of art that retains its ability to astonish, even though almost everyone who sees it is already familiar with the image. You'll probably have to stand in line to view Leonardo da Vinci's masterpiece of portraiture, but it's absolutely worth it to admire and analyze the unknowable thoughts behind that enigmatic grin.

START AT THE MUSÉE D'ORSAY IN PARIS, FRANCE
## 201. Visit the world's "Big Five" art museums
**When:** All year
**Latitude:** 48.8600°N **Longitude:** 2.3266°E

An art lover's bucket list must include our pick of the "Big Five:" the Musée d'Orsay in Paris, the Hermitage in St. Petersburg, the Prado in Madrid, the Tate Modern in London, and MoMA in New York. Each offers a unique cornucopia of sensory delights, each will vie with each other for the title of the greatest collection for a long time, and you'll have a ridiculously good time trying to decide which one you like the most.

Paris' Musée d'Orsay is housed in the Gare d'Orsay, a former railway station on the Left Bank of the Seine—it's an almost magical place to set foot in.

The Hermitage in St. Petersburg occupies a series of six historic buildings, including the Winter Palace, in an absolutely massive, domineering building.

The Museo del Prado in Madrid is an understated and airy place in which to wander and ponder. The Tate Modern on London's South Bank is based in the former Bankside Power Station, and its Turbine Hall is the perfect place to profile huge, imposing pieces of art. Then to the Big Apple, and the Museum of Modern Art (or MoMA) is an alluring labyrinth to potter in. You just need to decide which is your favorite.

Musée d'Orsay, in Paris, France, is one of the world's Big Five art museums

FRANCE
## 202. Pedal power along a stage of the Tour de France
**When:** All year
**Latitude:** 48.8567°N **Longitude:** 2.3508°E

What began as a promotional exercise to increase sales of *L'Auto* magazine has since become one of the most watched, and at times, controversial sporting events in the world. The exact route of the annual event—held every year since 1903, with the exception of a brief hiatus during both World Wars—changes, however, the format remains the same, with time trials, passage through the Pyrenees and Alps mountain ranges, and a thrilling climax at the Champs-Élysées in Paris.

The thrill of a Tour route can be easily experienced at any time of year, although in July there'll already be a fair few riders, including one in a yellow shirt, on the roads. But be warned: tour routes are not for the fainthearted, with some very big mountain passes to traverse.

It is possible to ride sections of the course just hours before the pros pass through, their endeavors all the more impressive when you yourself are still wincing from the pain of saddlesore. You can also take part in the thrill of timed sections of routes, giving amateur riders an idea of the pressure of competition. The only thing missing will be the overexcited spectators heckling as they run in front of the action.

A stage of the
Tour de France

GARE DE LYON, PARIS, FRANCE
## 203. Go to bed on a train, wake in a new country
**When:** All year
**Latitude:** 48.8447°N
**Longitude:** 2.3739°E

Catch an international night train that carries you through borders and mountain tunnels as you sleep, so that you wake up in a whole new country at dawn.

VERSAILLES, FRANCE
## 204. Lap up the life of France's gilt-edged past
**When:** All year (closed Mondays)
**Latitude:** 48.8044°N
**Longitude:** 2.1232°E

As far as opulence and luxury go, it is hard to look past the vast, glittering Palace of Versailles, situated 13 mi (21 km) southwest of Paris. Built in the seventeenth century, and home to the royal family until Louis XVI and Marie-Antoinette were beheaded in 1793, the palace remains a living example of the finest things money can buy. The French revolutionaries may not have liked the affluence, but today, you can marvel at all the gold, marble, frescoes, and never-ending gardens.

▶ NOTRE DAME, PARIS, FRANCE
## 205. Listen to great cathedral bells
**When:** All year
**Latitude:** 48.8530°N
**Longitude:** 2.3499°E

The sound of great cathedral bells is full of beauty and emotion. Yet for many years, a lot of Parisians wouldn't have agreed. The original bells of Notre Dame Cathedral were victims of the French Revolution, melted down and turned into cannons. The replacements were discordant and not a pretty listen. But visit today and you can rejoice in the sound, as new bells were finally commissioned in 2013.

Great cathedral bells can be heard in Notre Dame cathedral in Paris, France

VAL THORENS, FRANCE
### 206. Fly like an eagle across an alpine valley
**When:** December to April
**Latitude:** 45.2982°N
**Longitude:** 6.5824°E

The highest zip line in the world is La Tyrolienne in Val Thorens. It takes skiers from a 10,600 ft (3,231 m) mountain peak across a valley almost a mile wide to the other side. The journey takes one minute and forty-five seconds, in which time you fly, free as an eagle (well, almost).

PÈRE-LACHAISE CEMETERY, PARIS, FRANCE
### 207. Write your own epitaph
**When:** All year
**Latitude:** 48.8600°N **Longitude:** 2.3960°E

Bit of a morbid thought, but have you ever wondered what you might want written on your gravestone when the time comes to take your final journey and become a root inspector? Maybe you need some inspiration? In which case the best place to head to has to be Père-Lachaise in Paris, the world's most visited cemetery. Wander among the 70,000 ornate tombs, including plenty of the rich and famous. Rock star Jim Morrison's spot is popular with visitors, as is Oscar Wilde's. Composer Chopin; playwright Molière; and many poets, writers, and painters can be found here in their final resting place.

NORMANDY, FRANCE
### 208. Walk to an island
**When:** All year
**Latitude:** 48.6360°N
**Longitude:** 1.5114°W

Mont Saint-Michel is a beautiful pile of buildings spiraling up narrow cobbled streets to the abbey at its peak. It is also a tidal island, so take a walk across the sands at low tide to reach it—although there's also a permanent raised causeway that was added more than a hundred years ago.

▶ FONTAINEBLEAU, FRANCE
## 209. Dine like French nobility
**When:** All year
**Latitude:** 48.3365°N
**Longitude:** 2.6982°E

Dine in a regal château surrounded by a medieval moat nestled on the edge of the mighty Fontainebleau forest—it is arguably the best way to enjoy a flavor of the glory days of the French nobility. The picturesque seventeenth-century Château de Bourron offers a gastronomic experience courtesy of the Michelin-listed local chef.

Beyond the grandeur of the château and its adjoining pavilions is a 99 ac (40 ha) estate to explore; and close by is the opulent Fontainebleau Palace.

French nobility dining near Fontainebleau, France

STRASBOURG, FRANCE
## 210. Shop at a traditional Christmas market
**When:** November to December
**Latitude:** 48.5734°N
**Longitude:** 7.7521°E

Strasbourg hosts the oldest Christmas market in Europe—it has been running since 1570. From late November every year, its streets and squares are lit up by mile upon mile of Christmas lights beneath which 300 wooden stalls sell an array of arts, crafts, food, and drink. Let Christmas sink into your soul as you wander at leisure, before topping it all off by ice-skating under the stars.

FORÊT D'ORIENT, FRANCE
## 211. Pick wild mushrooms
**When:** October to December
**Latitude:** 48.3000°N
**Longitude:** 4.41667°E

Enhance a walk in the woods by keeping your eyes on the ground looking for the alien formations of chanterelles, ceps, and hedgehog mushrooms. Know the picking laws and what to look out for, and you can forage yourself a fine meal.

VIENNA, AUSTRIA
## 212. Drink in the company of revolutionaries
**When:** All year
**Latitude:** 48.2082°N
**Longitude:** 16.3738°E

Visit Café Central in Vienna and you'll not only enjoy a fine coffee, you'll also rub shoulders with history—Russian revolutionary exiles Vladimir Lenin and Leon Trotsky were regular patrons. Amid the café's old-world charm, it's easy to picture them enjoying their fix of caffeine and news.

▼ VIENNA, AUSTRIA
## 213. Fall into a deeeep sleeeep in the home of hypnosis
**When:** All year
**Latitude:** 48.2000°N **Longitude:** 16.3667°E

Franz Mesmer was an eighteenth-century German physician widely acclaimed for popularizing hypnotism; using the power of suggestion to change people's behavior. Although it wouldn't be known as hypnotism while he was alive, he did leave the world the word "mesmerized." Mesmer's heyday was his practice in Vienna, where famous patients included Mozart and the empress Maria Theresa.

Today, you can find hypnotherapy practitioners almost anywhere. Vienna, like any large city, has plenty of hypnotherapy clinics waiting to treat anything from depression and stress disorders, to quitting smoking or losing weight.

HOTEL SACHER, VIENNA, AUSTRIA
## 214. Celebrate a chocolate cake
**When:** December 5 (National Sachertorte Day)
**Latitude:** 48.2039°N
**Longitude:** 16.3694°E

It was only after a lengthy legal battle that Vienna's Hotel Sacher was allowed to claim its delicious chocolate and apricot cake as the original Sachertorte—a famous Viennese specialty. So make sure you sample this gâteau when you visit this city—a trip here would not be complete without a tasting.

The home of hypnosis: Vienna, Austria

## 215. Reenact *The Sound of Music*

**When:** Springtime (for authenticity)
**Latitude:** 47.6958°N
**Longitude:** 13.0450°E

Whose heart is not filled with joy as Julie Andrews—or rather, Maria—twirls around in a Tyrolean meadow singing that the hills are alive with the sound of music? Recreate the moment on a Tyrolean mountain—Austrian national dress optional.

Julie Andrews as Maria in
*The Sound of Music*, in Austria

SALZBURG, AUSTRIA
## 216. Slide around in underground ice caves

**When:** All year
**Latitude:** 47.4950°N
**Longitude:** 13.2894°E

Discover the stunning ice monuments in the caves of Eiskogelhöhle, in the Austrian mountains. An enchantingly atmospheric frozen ice hall offers up every shade of blue in this underground adventure playground for grown-ups.

BREGENZ, AUSTRIA
## 217. Float on sound at Lake Constance

**When:** July to August
**Latitude:** 47.6363°N
**Longitude:** 9.3892°E

There are plenty of great venues to watch classical music and theater, but surely none that rival the floating stage in the alluring setting of Lake Constance. Don't miss the Bregenz Festival, which is rightly acclaimed and features orchestral presentations.

SWITZERLAND
## 218. Eat breakfast in the home of muesli

**When:** All year
**Latitude:** 47.3667°N
**Longitude:** 8.5500°E

Sometimes an adventure comes just from changing your normal habits. So, wake up, throw open the patio doors, and eat breakfast in the fresh air; it will change your mood for the whole day (even if you're wrapped in a fence to do it).

MOLDAVIA, ROMANIA
## 219. See Romania's painted churches
**When:** All year
**Latitude:** 47.7782°N
**Longitude:** 25.7112°E

Visiting the Sucevița Monastery is both a visual delight for the eyes and a testament to the heritage of Byzantine art and religion. Inside and out, the entirety of this sixteenth-century church is decorated with mural paintings. Walls 19 ft (6 m) high are filled from top to bottom with Biblical scenes that extend around the whole site. Sucevița Monastery is one of eight such buildings that together make up the UNESCO World Heritage Site-protected painted churches of Moldavia, all built in the fifteenth and sixteenth centuries. As you view them today, you'll see how outstanding they look in their well-preserved state.

Romania's painted churches in Sucevița Monastery, Moldavia

START AT THE SOURCE AT DONAUESCHINGEN, GERMANY
## 220. Pedal through Europe on a riverside ride along the Danube

**When:** May to September
**Latitude:** 47.9531°N **Longitude:** 8.5033°E

From the Danube's source in Germany down to the Black Sea is a journey of around 1,800 mi (2,897 km). If two-wheeled travel is the order of the day, then a trip along one of Europe's finest cycle routes could be just the thing to get the pedals spinning.

The slow, winding Danube is the longest river in the European Union and makes for a dreamy, enjoyable ride through the very heart of this fascinating, varied continent. Rising in Donaueschingen, in Germany's beautiful Black Forest region, the Danube's marathon journey offers fabulous views along the majority of its length as it touches ten countries and meanders through twenty-one national parks and ninety-seven cities before spilling out into the Black Sea.

One of the many beauties of the path is that the decisions are all in the hands of you, the rider. The rich culture, stunning scenery, and pretty medieval towns are not going anywhere.

OBERAMMERGAU, GERMANY
## 221. See the Passion play in Oberammergau

**When:** Every ten years (next one is in 2020)
**Latitude:** 47.5956°N
**Longitude:** 11.0723°E

An extraordinary tradition, this is the oldest continuously running piece of Christian drama in existence, dating back to 1634. Catch the story of Jesus' arrival in Jerusalem and crucifixion, put on by the Bavarian village en masse—it is a raw, somewhat grueling, day-long performance, lasting five hours, and staged daily for around three months.

NEUSCHWANSTEIN CASTLE, GERMANY
## 222. Visit a real-life Disney castle

**When:** All year
**Latitude:** 47.5575°N **Longitude:** 10.7500°E

Picture a Disney castle and the chances are your imagination will conjure up a near-perfect image of Neuschwanstein Castle. Which is hardly surprising, as this Bavarian palace was the inspiration for Sleeping Beauty's castle, as seen in Disneylands the world over, and as the logo on the opening credits of countless Walt Disney movies.

Set on a rugged hill amid idyllic alpine mountains, this romantic palace was built for King Ludwig II in the nineteenth century. Ironically, the castle was opened to the public just seven weeks after his death in order to recoup some of the enormous costs of its build. Be one of 1.4 million who come to admire the "Disney" castle every year.

BADEN-BADEN, GERMANY
## 223. Wash away your cares in the Black Forest

**When:** All year
**Latitude:** 48.7628°N
**Longitude:** 8.2408°E

Nestled in the foothills of the Black Forest mountains, this charming spa town is popular among sports enthusiasts, with excellent golf, tennis, horseracing, hiking, and in winter months, skiing. But it is the restorative powers of its famous waters that have attracted visitors since the days of Roman emperor Caracalla in AD 210s, so wash away your aches in one of the city's baths.

MUNICH, GERMANY
## 224. Drink a giant ale at Oktoberfest
**When:** September 17 to October 2
**Latitude:** 48.1351°N
**Longitude:** 11.5819°E

A one-stop shop to immerse any visitor in the boozy, jolly Bavarian culture: you'll find gargantuan beers (all brewed in Munich and conforming to strict quality standards), roast wurst galore (accompanied by dumplings and sauerkraut), music, amusement parks, stalls, and jigging men in lederhosen. *Prost*!

ROTHENBURG, GERMANY
## 225. Step into a storybook past in Germany's romantic heart
**When:** All year
**Latitude:** 49.3801°N **Longitude:** 10.1867°E

This medieval German town has existed in some state since AD 950 and looks like it has been taken straight out of the pages of a fairy tale, complete with Gothic spires and atmospheric timber-framed houses. It comes as little surprise that Rothenburg was the "setting" for Disney's 1940 movie *Pinocchio*, or that parts of the Harry Potter franchise were filmed here. Visit at Christmas, when the festive market is in full swing.

▶ POLAND
## 226. Paddle through Poland
**When:** May to September
**Latitude:** 49.4164°N
**Longitude:** 20.3986°E

Soak up the idyllic scenery as you are guided 15 mi (24 km) through the beautiful Dunajec Gorge in the heart of the Pieniny National Park onboard a traditional Polish flatboat. In some sections, the forested cliffs rising 1,000 ft (305 m) all around are within touching distance on both sides.

Paddling through pretty Polish scenery in Pieniny National Park

Chess moves in Budapest's Széchenyi Baths in Hungary

▲ BUDAPEST, HUNGARY
## 227. Conquer a game of chess—in a bath
**When:** All year
**Latitude:** 47.5186°N
**Longitude:** 19.0819°E (Széchenyi Baths)

There's a good reason that Budapest is known as the "City of Baths," with almost 120 spas offering thermal springs in often lavish surroundings. While relaxing in the hot waters, local Hungarians like nothing more than working their minds with a game of chess. Be one of many pondering their next move in one of the city's baths, with the vast Széchenyi Baths a favorite.

▶ BUDAPEST, HUNGARY
## 228. Learn to juggle at the home of the art's first lady
**When:** All year
**Latitude:** 47.4925°N **Longitude:** 19.0514°E

Martha "Trixie" Firschke was born into a Hungarian circus family in 1920 and grew up to become known as the first lady of juggling. Rumor had it she was able to balance a ball on a stick held in her mouth from the first time she tried it, and she could even bounce two balls on her head at the same time. Travel to her hometown of Budapest to start working on your skills—best start with small balls rather than the plates she used, though.

Juggling's first lady, Martha "Trixie" Firschke, was from Budapest, Hungary

The ultimate in luxury is Lake Como, Italy

MILAN, ITALY
## 229. Splurge on shoes in Milan
**When:** All year
**Latitude:** 45.4667°N
**Longitude:** 9.1833°E

Italy is world-famous for its high fashion, particularly when it comes to shoes. Head to fashion capital Milan to find the best shoe designers the country has to offer today.

▲ COMO, ITALY
## 230. Stay at the ultimate in luxury at Lake Como
**When:** All year
**Latitude:** 46.0160°N
**Longitude:** 9.2571°E

For many, the glacial Como is the last word in luxury: it's an incomparably dramatic setting, with the deep waters set against alpine foothills. Stay in its lavish hotels, which are the perfect base for swimming, walking, cycling—or doing nothing much bar relaxing.

ALBERTA, CANADA; MONTANA, US
## 231. Shake hands across a border of peace
**When:** All year
**Latitude:** 49.0000°N
**Longitude:** 113.9167°W

The world's first international peace park at Waterton Glacier is a beautiful wilderness of lakes and mountains that also represents the harmony of nations. It was formed when the US and Canada merged two separate national parks into one. Shake hands across the border in a sign of peace.

GROSSGLOCKNER HIGH ALPINE ROAD, AUSTRIA
## 232. Take off into the mountains
**When:** May to October
**Latitude:** 47.0833°N **Longitude:** 12.8427°E

The Grossglockner's High Alpine Road is one of the most popular tourist attractions in the country, drawing in almost a million tourists in more than a quarter of a million vehicles annually.

The road runs from Heiligenblut in Carinthia to Bruck in Salzburg, taking in the High Tauern National Park. It has thirty-six hairpin bends, and the dramatic falls away from the roadside are breathtaking. For the motoring enthusiast there are few sights that swell the heart as much as an empty mountain road curving in and out of view for miles ahead.

The green of the slopes and pines, the white and granite gray of the peaks, the blue of the sky, and the suddenly descending patches of white swirling mist among it all: this is mountain driving at its best. Get behind the wheel for the best way to experience this majestic peak and its environs.

The mountains of Grossglockner High Alpine Road, Austria

▶ QUÉBEC, CANADA

## 233. Explore the French-speaking province of Canada by bike

**When:** Spring and summer
**Latitude:** 46.8167°N **Longitude:** 71.2167°W (Québec City, Québec, Canada)

For lovers of the outdoors, it is hard to beat the enormous swathes of forest, glorious water views, plentiful wildlife, and innumerable lakes and rivers of Québec. And what better way to enjoy it than from the saddle?

Winding for more than 3,000 mi (4,828 km) through the beautiful province of Québec, Canada's La Route Verte ("the Greenway") is a network of interconnecting cycle routes through this huge and varied area. With urban trails in and around metropolitan Montréal and Québec City, and tracks following the majestic St. Lawrence River before heading out into remote areas to the north, the Greenway also borders the US at Vermont, Maine, and New York State.

Like many long-distance routes, hardcore cyclists aim to pedal every inch of its trails. But it is perfectly possible to follow an independent itinerary and tackle sections of the course at different times. Check various websites to plan your trip, which also offer accommodation suggestions, maps, and valuable advice.

Cycling to see the best of Québec, Canada

MONTRÉAL, QUÉBEC, CANADA

## 234. Laugh at the world's biggest comedy festival

**When:** July
**Latitude:** 45.5000°N **Longitude:** 73.5667°W

Laughs don't come much bigger than those at the Just for Laughs comedy festival in Montréal. What started as a two-day French language-only event more than thirty years ago quickly turned into an annual summer laughathon, which welcomes the world's top comedians for a month of japes and jests. The French aspect is still strong, with the first half of the festival devoted to this, before English speakers join for the second. Head along and laugh your head off.

SWISS ALPS, SWITZERLAND

## 235. Savor a delectable cheese fondue

**When:** November to April
**Latitude:** 46.5592°N **Longitude:** 8.5614°E

Since at least the 1700s, the Swiss have been dipping bread into a communal pot of melted cheese, but they waited until the 1930s to introduce the rest of the world to this most sociable form of comfort eating. Enjoy this treat in a wood-beamed mountain chalet next to an open fire.

WORLDWIDE, BUT START IN BURGUNDY, FRANCE
## 236. Embark on a worldwide wine odyssey
**When:** All year
**Latitude:** 49.3493°N **Longitude:** 4.0695°E

It's a simple truth that somehow wine tastes better at its home vineyard. Frankly, it doesn't get much better than supping your way around the winemaking universe.

Classic wine buffs would start in France: Burgundy, Bordeaux, and the Loire Valley are still home to arguably the best drops anywhere. Piedmont in Italy combines vineyards with Michelin-starred restaurants, while also in Europe, La Rioja in Spain, Douro Valley in Portugal, and Mosel Valley in Germany should be considered.

Napa Valley is the US's wine capital, while its neighbor, Sonoma County, is also gorgeous. The Willamette Valley in Oregon is also hot on the heels of Napa in the quest for New World wine supremacy.

South Africa's Western Cape is hard to top as a setting, with its wining and dining hub, Stellenbosch, while notable in Australia are Barossa Valley and the Hunter Valley.

Central Otago in New Zealand is the planet's southernmost wine-growing region, while the Maipo Valley in Chile is considered the bordeaux of South America. Cheers!

MONTREUX, SWITZERLAND
## 237. Listen to a song in the place it was written
**When:** Tie it in with the jazz festival in July for true authenticity
**Latitude:** 46.4333°N
**Longitude:** 6.9167°E

Deep Purple's "Smoke on the Water" describes a fire that broke out at the Casino Barrière de Montreux where the band was just about to start recording its album, *Machine Head*. Sit by the shores of Lake Geneva, with headphones on for a true rock pilgrimage.

TICINO, SWITZERLAND
## 238. Take a high dive with an unequaled vista
**When:** May to September
**Latitude:** 45.9676°N
**Longitude:** 8.6532°E (Lake Maggiore)

While few are likely to want to emulate Laso Schaller's 193 ft (59 m) world record leap from a Ticino clifftop in 2015, Switzerland's alpine lakes, each vying for the title of "world's best view," provide a multitude of breathtaking spots to dive in for a refreshing dip. Take your pick.

APPENZELL, SWITZERLAND
## 239. Sing until the cows come home
**When:** May to September
**Latitude:** 47.3349°N
**Longitude:** 9.4066°E

Sing like the alpine farmers who have used yodeling to call their cattle for more than 500 years. There is something hugely liberating about standing on a mountaintop belting out this distinctive musical chant that originated in the Swiss village of Appenzell in the sixteenth century.

▼ ADELBODEN, SWITZERLAND
## 240. Take a dip in an infinity pool with a view
**When:** All year
**Latitude:** 46.4930°N
**Longitude:** 7.5595°E

Perching on the side of an infinity pool, overlooking breathtaking surroundings, is a travel brochure cliché for a reason—it feels very pleasant indeed. Find out for yourself at what is arguably the best pool with a view, at the Cambrian Hotel, commanding a picture-postcard vista of the Swiss Alps.

ST. MORITZ, SWITZERLAND
## 241. Hone your milking skills in the Alps
**When:** May to September
**Latitude:** 46.5000°N
**Longitude:** 9.8333°E

Once the snow has melted and the skiers have gone home, it is time for Switzerland's cows to enjoy the fresh air and sweet grass that go toward making coveted Alp cheese. Many farms offer the chance to get hands-on experience milking the cows, so what are you waiting for?

The Cambrian Hotel's infinity pool with a view, Adelboden, Switzerland

EIGER, SWITZERLAND
## 242. BASE jump off the Eiger

**When:** Summer (for best weather)
**Latitude:** 46.5776°N
**Longitude:** 8.0054°E

Crazy as it seems, BASE jumping is legal in some places—and one of those is the Eiger in Switzerland. For the ultimate daredevil thrill, climb to the top of the Swiss mountain and soar down, 9,000 ft (2,743 m) to the ground. Just be sure to practice on smaller jumps first.

LE PUY-EN-VELAY, FRANCE
## 243. Eat Puy lentils in Puy
**When:** All year
**Latitude:** 45.0442°N
**Longitude:** 3.8858°E

Only green lentils grown in this area of southern France are allowed to be labeled as Puy lentils, which are world-renowned for their flavor. Wash them down here with a glass of the famous local Verveine, a lemon verbena liqueur.

TERME 3000, SLOVENIA
## 244. Go up and over in a loop-the-loop waterslide
**When:** All year
**Latitude:** 46.6857°N
**Longitude:** 16.2225°E

Terme 3000 in Slovenia was the world's first waterpark to have a slide featuring a 360-degree loop. As if hurtling toward a pool at 50 mph (80 kph) wasn't enough, here you can be turned almost upside down on the way!

▶ LES HOUCHES, NEAR CHAMONIX, FRANCE
## 245. Enjoy the Blanc canvas with this incredible trek
**When:** Mid-June to early September
**Latitude:** 45.8908°N **Longitude:** 6.7992°E

Take in stunning scenery in the mountains of three of Europe's most beautiful countries, covering 106 mi (171 km) and around 33,000 ft (10,058 m) of ascents on the Tour du Mont Blanc, one of the world's most memorable walking experiences.

Traditionally starting and finishing in Les Houches, the full walk takes around ten days, although it is possible to dip in and out. As well as France, you'll take in mind-expanding views in Switzerland and Italy as you circle the Mont Blanc massif. At 15,781 ft (4,810 m), it towers relentlessly over proceedings, providing a spellbinding backdrop. Fitness and preparation are important, but fear not: creature comforts are never too far away. Welcoming villages, hamlets, and mountain huts (referred to as refuges) en route provide beds, food, and drink.

As well as the anticipated mountain peaks and glaciers, you'll puff your way through glorious pine-scented woodland and brightly colored meadows, as well as pass over thrashing, boiling mountain rivers and encounter plentiful wildlife, including deer and eagles. It sounds astonishing, and it is.

An incredible trek on the Tour du Mont Blanc at Les Houches near Chamonix, France

THE FRENCH ALPS, JAPANESE ALPS, AUSTRALIAN ALPS, WHISTLER, CHILE, AND ALGERIA
## 246. Ski on every continent before climate change stops play
**When:** November to March (northern hemisphere), June to October (southern)
**Latitude:** 45.8326°N **Longitude:** 6.8527°E (French Alps)

A scorched planet totally devoid of snow is still an apocalyptic scenario that seems some way off, but for lovers of the piste, whether on skis or snowboard, the chance to glide down the slopes on every continent may become limited, or very expensive. It's an apt time then, to take to a slope on every populated continent.

Each has its own selling points: the French Alps have a broader range of pistes than anywhere else in Europe. Chamonix, Tignes, Val d'Isere, and Les Trois Vallées are classic venues.

The four key areas in North America are California, Colorado, Utah, and New England; while in Canada, there's magnificent snow to be found in British Columbia and the Rockies. South America's finest options are in Chile's Andes, with popular resorts like Portillo, Valle

Nevado, and La Parva, and volcanic terrain like Llama and Pucón.

Japan's skiing thrives at its many micro resorts, where the slopes aren't always too steep or challenging, but there is fresh powder and a lack of crowds. Snow and Australia aren't two things that many people would put together, but there are decent pistes in New South Wales and Victoria; Perisher and Thredbo are probably the pick of the bunch.

Finally, skiing in Africa? It can be done. Algeria's Chréa resort, in the Djurdjura Mountains, contains alpine forests few would associate with the country. It's somewhere every adventurous skier should tick off their list.

So where will you start your skiing grand slam?

---

TRENTINO, ITALY
## 247. Follow a trail in the Dolomites
**When:** All year
**Latitude:** 46.2366°N
**Longitude:** 11.8830°E

You'll have to prepare for snow, wind, and rain no matter what time of the year, but the spectacular views in Paneveggio National Park more than compensate. With its razor-sharp peaks, the awe-inspiring Pale di San Martino plateau is crisscrossed with a series of thrilling trails for you to hike.

MILAN, ITALY
## 248. Learn to bake a signature cake
**When:** All year
**Latitude:** 45.4654°N
**Longitude:** 9.1859°E

Baking is back in a big way thanks to the popularity of many TV shows, and learning to make a signature cake is easy—and a great way to impress family and friends. Get deeply into sugar craft and choose from numerous competitions to enter—including the Cake Designers World Championship in Milan.

MILAN, ITALY
## 249. Sit by the catwalk in the home of fashion
**When:** February to March (for fall/winter event); September to October (for spring/summer event)
**Latitude:** 45.4654°N
**Longitude:** 9.1859°E

Adore Armani? Giddy about Gucci? Milan is a mecca for fashion lovers, and in recent years charities have offered a way for the public to take a coveted front-row place at the leading shows. If the $50,000-plus per show price tag is a bit high, you can watch them online, as most are also streamed.

TURIN, ITALY
## 250. Soak up historic Turin and its plethora of royal palaces

**When:** All year
**Latitude:** 45.0727°N **Longitude:** 7.6893°E

Most would be hard pushed to name the first capital of unified Italy. Beautiful Turin was also the seat of the House of Savoy, one of the oldest ruling families in the world. Between the seventeenth and eighteenth centuries, the Savoy constructed magnificent royal palaces, once venues for court life, hunting lodges, and vacation resorts. The heart of the city was Piazza Castello, home to opulent palaces that, together with villas outside the city center, were nicknamed *corona dell delizie*, or "crown of delights." In 1997 fourteen palaces were designated a UNESCO World Heritage site.

Stroll the lavish interiors of the city's royal palaces: elegantly sitting on the main square is the Palazzo Reale, or "Royal Palace." In the middle of the square is Madama Palace, with Roman, medieval, and baroque features; a short walk away is Carignano Palace. Equally as lavish are the city's opulent cafés, the Museo Egizio, plus, cinema is celebrated at the Museo Nazionale del Cinema in the towering Mole Antonelliana.

Historic Turin's royal palaces, Italy

TURDA, CLUJ, ROMANIA
## 251. Go with the grain in this underground wonderland
**When:** All year
**Latitude:** 46.5877°N **Longitude:** 23.7874°E

Think salt is just for your fries? Think again. Take a trip to the extraordinary Turda Salt Mine in the heart of Romania and you'll discover a fascinating—and surprisingly picturesque—insight into a glittering, crystalline underworld that was once voted the most beautiful underground attraction in the world.

LA PLAGNE, FRANCE
## 252. Toboggan like an Olympian
**When:** December to April
**Latitude:** 45.5217°N **Longitude:** 6.6778°E

Toboggan wrapped up in woolies down a hill in fresh snow and feel all the joy of fast, free abandon: lungs filled with fresh air, an element of danger, and a lot of laughing. For many, that joy is enough, but for others who crave longer hills and bigger thrills, there is the Olympic bobsled run at La Plagne, France. In the time it takes to read this paragraph, you could slide a mile down the mountain, round nineteen bends, and reach speeds of 50 mph (80 kph).

BRAN CASTLE, BRAN, ROMANIA
## 253. Connect with your inner vampire
**When:** All year
**Latitude:** 45.5150°N
**Longitude:** 25.3672°E

Pack your garlic and crucifix and take a trembling tour of the spectacular edifice that many believe was the inspiration for the creaking hilltop home of Bram Stoker's Dracula. This fairy-tale fortress is, naturally, to be found in the heart of Transylvania.

MURANO, ITALY
## 254. Drink wine from a crystal glass
**When:** All year
**Latitude:** 45.4590°N
**Longitude:** 12.3523°E

Luxuries aren't just for the rich. Everybody should have the chance to drink wine from a true Venetian crystal glass made on the "glass" island of Murano. Tap the glass on the side to hear the music of crystal ring out, and you'll know it's authentic.

NAQUANE, LOMBARDY, ITALY
## 255. Decipher prehistoric rock carvings
**When:** All year
**Latitude:** 46.0275°N
**Longitude:** 10.3508°E

Surprisingly, Italy's first inscribed UNESCO World Heritage site of Val Camonica remains off the tourist trail. Discover one of the world's most extensive collections of prehistoric rock carvings at the Parco Nazionale delle Incisioni Rupestri, which is dotted with thousands of engravings.

VENICE, ITALY

## 256. Get serenaded in a Venetian gondola

**When:** All year
**Latitude:** 45.4408°N **Longitude:** 12.3155°E

A romantic cliché for a good reason: it's simply a wonderful experience to glide through serene Venetian waters while being serenaded by a gondolier. Drink in the baroque buildings—and perhaps a glass of prosecco with a loved one, or even solo.

VENICE, ITALY
## 257. Get lost in a labyrinthine floating city
**When:** All year; high summer is always crowded, so late spring is ideal
**Latitude:** 45.4408°N **Longitude:** 12.3155°E

Little can prepare visitors for the delights that overwhelm the senses in this most romantic of world cities. Wandering aimlessly and getting gently lost is a vital part of the experience and is quite easy to do too.

There's a maze of charming alleyways to poke about in: walk without a real goal and pick up a coffee, gelato, or aperitif; rummage around tiny shops selling Venetian masks, colorful glass, and intricate lace and linens; witness tiny neighborhood churches covered with priceless marble; savor some of the freshest seafood available anywhere; stare in awe at the Grand Canal, overseen by the Palazzo Ducale; and hop into a gondola and be serenaded by the gondolier, with the lovely buildings reflected back.

It's not as if getting lost is going to be a problem—all roads eventually lead back to somewhere central.

PADUA, ITALY
## 258. Swim in the world's deepest swimming pool
**When:** All year
**Latitude:** 45.3190°N
**Longitude:** 11.7844°E

Take a dip with a difference in Hotel Terme Millepini's Y-40 Deep Joy, the futuristic name of the world's deepest swimming pool. An incredible fourteen stories deep, it features underwater caves, ledges, and even a glass walkway. Its balmy 90°F (32°C) water temperature means anyone with just a regular bathing suit can enjoy a swim.

▶ VENICE, ITALY
## 259. Be incognito for a day at the Venice Carnival
**When:** Approximately two weeks before Shrove Tuesday
**Latitude:** 45.4408°N
**Longitude:** 12.3155°E

For the sense of illicit excitement that comes from anonymity, the Venice Carnival is the place to be. Around 3 million people descend annually for the event, which dates back 900 years. The celebrations are built around parties, dinners, and events like the Grand Carnival Masquerade Ball (or the less traditional Fifty Shades of Casanova Grand Ball) at the city's palazzo. If you don't have an invite you can just wander the streets in a mask looking mysterious, and it's a perfect preeners' forum to pose and philander.

The Venice Carnival, Italy

Juliet's balcony at "Juliet's House" in Verona, Italy

### VENICE, ITALY
### 260. Soak up art at the Venice Biennale

**When:** May to November, every other year
**Latitude:** 45.4408°N
**Longitude:** 12.3155°E

There is nowhere quite like the Venice Biennale International Art Exhibition for immersing yourself in the world of contemporary art. Eighty-nine countries participated in 2015 at venues throughout the city. What better excuse do you need to visit?

### VENICE, ITALY
### 261. Live like a star for one night in Venice

**When:** All year
**Latitude:** 45.4408°N
**Longitude:** 12.3155°E

Created by Giuseppe Cipriani, who invented the Bellini cocktail, the Belmond Hotel Cipriani is a sumptuous hotel with superb views of Venice. Splurge on a room that typically costs $1,000-$4,000 per night to share a hotel with such famous patrons as Henry Kissinger, Gwyneth Paltrow, and José Carreras.

### ▲ CASA DI GIULIETTA, VERONA, ITALY
### 262. Call for your Romeo on Juliet's balcony

**When:** All year
**Latitude:** 45.4333°N
**Longitude:** 10.9833°E

"Juliet's House" is a fourteenth-century house in Verona where every young girl—or boy—can imagine themselves as Shakespeare's Juliet, stepping out onto her purported balcony. Sound too good to be true? That may be because it is: historians say the balcony was actually added to the house well after Shakespeare's time.

Perfect lines in powder snow in Washington, US

▲ WASHINGTON, US
## 263. Cut a perfect line in powder snow
**When:** December to March
**Latitude:** 48.7773°N
**Longitude:** 121.8132°W

The resort with the most snow in the world is surely the destination to head to when you're planning to leave a perfect track down the mountain. So head to Mount Baker, where in nature's huge expanse, you can create a simple wavy line drawn in the snow. Perfect.

BEAVERCREEK, OREGON, US
## 264. Find hidden treasure while geocaching
**When:** All year
**Latitude:** 45.2879°N **Longitude:** 122.5353°W

First done on May 2, 2000 in Beavercreek, Oregon, geocaching is a truly twenty-first century activity. It involves using a GPS to track and find small waterproof containers—the "cache"—as part of a high-tech treasure hunt. Most caches, now located all over the world, contain a logbook where discoverers can add the date they found it, sign with their codename, and return it. Some contain fun items for trading and swapping—the original Oregon cache contained software, videos, books, food, a small amount of money, and a slingshot. Become a geocacher and think about setting up a cache yourself—you can also share your findings on various websites.

265. Gaze upon awesomely cool (get it?) ice sculptures

**When:** January
**Latitude:** 45.8037°N **Longitude:** 126.5349°E

China's eighth-biggest metropolis, and northernmost major settlement, is nicknamed "Ice City" due to its very low winter temperatures, but they've turned all that frozen water into a major asset. The International Ice and Snow Sculpture Festival sees teams of up to 15,000 workers beavering away for up to three weeks, and actual full-size buildings are made as part of the show.

View the two major display areas: Sun Island features exhibits like temples and reproductions of famous landmarks such as the Sphinx, and the Ice and Snow World area displays illuminated works, often best viewed at night. The thought that these structures will soon melt away can blow the mind.

The Guggenheim Museum Bilbao in Spain (see page 180)

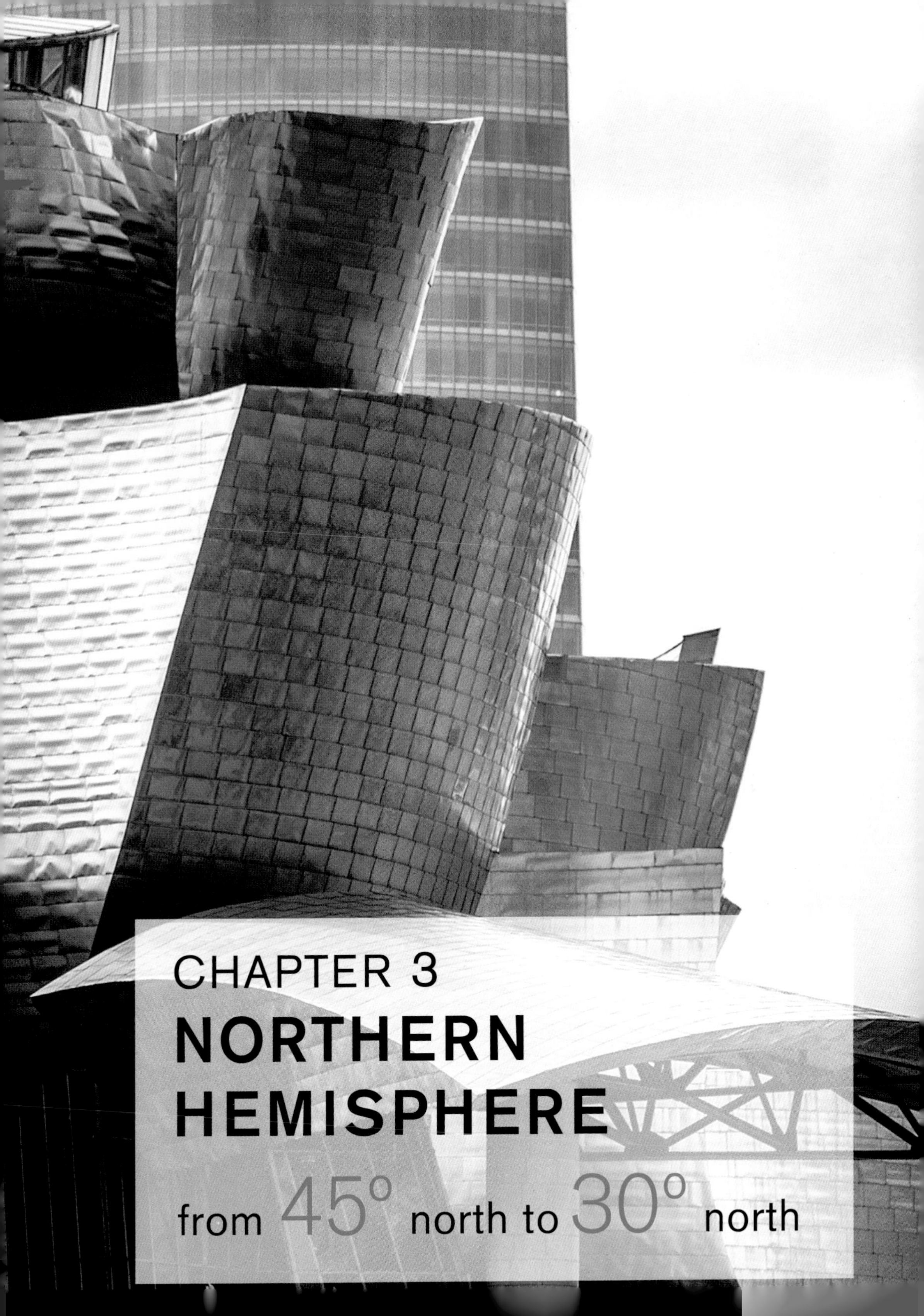

# CHAPTER 3
# NORTHERN HEMISPHERE

from 45° north to 30° north

Wondrous waterfalls at Plitvice Lakes in Croatia

ZADAR, CROATIA
### 266. Hear the sea transformed into music
**When:** All year
**Latitude:** 44.1194°N
**Longitude:** 15.2314°E

On the rebuilt seafront in Zadar, marble steps lead down to the sea; hidden within the steps is a thirty-five-note musical organ. Hear the hypnotic sound created as each wave pushes air through the organ's pipes.

▲ PLITVICKA JEZERA, CROATIA
### 267. Stroll among a hundred waterfalls
**When:** All year
**Latitude:** 44.8588°N
**Longitude:** 15.5904°E

One of Europe's most beautiful natural features is this series of sixteen lakes connected by hundreds of streams and waterfalls. Watch the water glow in every blue of the spectrum as the limestone lakes reflect the Croatian sky.

DALMATIAN COAST, CROATIA
### 268. Sip a cocktail in a gin palace
**When:** All year
**Latitude:** 43.1729°N
**Longitude:** 16.4411°E

Forget the Côte d'Azur or Ibiza: all the cool rock-star types are now hanging out in Croatia, where Hvar Island has become one of Europe's party capitals. Sipping a fine cocktail in a floating gin palace is a must and isn't as expensive as the south of France—yet.

▶ MAJORCA, SPAIN

### 269. Wind up and down Hollywood's favorite road

**When:** All year
**Latitude:** 39.8500°N
**Longitude:** 2.7998°E

A road most will have already seen in a hundred movies and car ads, the snaking hairpins of the Carretera must surely be the most scenic drive in the world. Take a spin on this road that has a 7 percent gradient and 800 turns, and you can be forgiven for rolling down the windows and pretending to be Bond.

MALI STON, CROATIA

### 270. Eat a dozen fresh oysters on a waterfront

**When:** All year
**Latitude:** 42.8469°N
**Longitude:** 17.7030°E

The Dalmatian coast is full of wondrous little seaside towns like Mali Ston, and the seafood is ocean-fresh and utterly delicious. Grab a seat on the waterfront and knock back some of the best seafood anywhere on Earth.

Hollywood's favorite road: Carretera de Sa Calobra in Majorca, Spain

FLORENCE, TUSCANY, ITALY

## 271. Marvel at Michelangelo's *David*

**When:** All year (less busy off-season)
**Latitude:** 43.8001°N **Longitude:** 11.2258°E

The inevitable line at the Galleria dell'Accademia is worth it: This sculpture is the jewel in the crown of Europe's most beautiful city. See Michelangelo's huge marble masterpiece, glaring threateningly toward rival Rome. It really is a miracle of sculpture and a still-stunning symbol of strength and youthful perfection.

▼ PORTOFINO, LIGURIA, ITALY
## 272. Get snap happy in picturesque Portofino

**When:** All year (but May to September is best)
**Latitude:** 44.3032°N
**Longitude:** 9.2098°E

You're unable to take a car to jet setters' favorite Portofino (vehicles are banned), but you can take a camera to capture memories of this exquisite Italian village. Nestled around a yacht-filled harbor fringed by pretty pastel houses, see how the other half lives.

LIGURIA, ITALY
## 273. Trek the cinematic Cinque Terre in Italy

**When:** May, June, or September (to avoid the crowds)
**Latitude:** 44.1349°N **Longitude:** 9.6849°E

No hike can really rival the Italian Riviera's Cinque Terre for rugged beauty and romance. Found in Liguria, the "Five Lands" consists of five near-perfect villages: Vernazza, Monterosso al Mare, Corniglia, Manarola, and Riomaggiore. It's a UNESCO World Heritage site, thanks to its unspoiled charm—indeed, it's so difficult to build on, it's almost impossible to spoil. Stunning terraces overlook the Mediterranean, connected only by paths and boats.

The connecting walks are fairly short—the towns are spread across just 10 mi (16 km)—but despite none taking much more than a couple of hours, they all contain glute-bothering steep stretches. These lead to views that will stun even the most seasoned of travelers.

Picturesque Portofino in Italy

▶ LANGUEDOC REGION, FRANCE
### 274. Canoe under the Pont du Gard aqueduct

**When:** May to September

**Latitude:** 43.9473°N

**Longitude:** 4.5355°E

Three tiers of perfectly proportioned Roman arches rise 161 ft (49 m) out of the Gardon River. Their ocher hues contrast with the almost guaranteed blue skies this area enjoys in the summer. Canoe along the river and underneath this piece of history—it beats any other way to view it.

Canoeing under the stunning Pont du Gard aqueduct in the south of France

CANNES, FRANCE
### 275. Mix with movie royalty

**When:** May (usually)

**Latitude:** 43.5504°N

**Longitude:** 7.0174°E (Palais des Festivals et des Congrès, Cannes)

The height of sophistication, Cannes Film Festival is a who's who of the movie world's power brokers. You'll need an invitation—and formal wear—for official screenings, but there are lots of chances to join in and attend movies at the parallel festivals.

PARMA, ITALY
### 276. Pig out in Parma

**When:** All year

**Latitude:** 44.8100°N

**Longitude:** 10.3333°E

It's no secret that a trip to Parma, Italy, is a gastronomical delight. The area is famed for its delicious prosciutto and tasty Parmesan, although you should also take time to savor the mouthwatering architectural and cultural delights of this Renaissance city, too.

FLORENCE, TUSCANY, ITALY
### 277. Ride around like a European, on a scooter

**When:** All year

**Latitude:** 43.7833°N

**Longitude:** 11.2500°E

When it comes to scooters, there is only one name that counts—Vespa—and one place to ride it: Italy. Rent one for an afternoon in Florence and head out to the scenic hills of Tuscany.

## BOLOGNA, ITALY

### 278. Take an Italian cooking class

**When:** All year
**Latitude:** 44.4949°N
**Longitude:** 11.3426°E

From pizza to pasta, pretty much everybody has a soft spot for Italian food. What better way to enjoy it than by learning to cook it where it was created—in Bologna (Bolognese sauce), Genoa (pesto), Naples (pizza), or Turin (grissini).

## PISA, TUSCANY, ITALY

### 279. Put yourself in the most touristy of photos

**When:** Best in summer (for clear blue skies as a backdrop)
**Latitude:** 43.7230°N
**Longitude:** 10.3966°E

It's an old one but a good one: that photo where you use the perspective to make it look like you're holding up the Leaning Tower of Pisa with your hands. And you get to see a feat of twelfth-century engineering.

## START IN FLORENCE, ITALY

### 280. Eat ice cream in every region of Italy

**When:** Summer
**Latitude:** 43.7695°N
**Longitude:** 11.2558°E

Florence is gelato's epicenter—it was invented here—so eat it at La Carraia and Vivoli. Elsewhere, Il Massimo of Milan, I Caruso in Rome, La Sorbetteria in Bologna, Alberto Marchetti in Turin, Alaska in Venice, and Emilia Cremeria in Parma all come highly recommended.

## FLORENCE, TUSCANY, ITALY

### 281. Compare the two best views of Florence

**When:** All year
**Latitude:** 43.7695°N **Longitude:** 11.2558°E

Soak up the fantastic sights of Tuscany's most stunning city by climbing to the top of the cathedral. It's a long clamber and very narrow in parts—definitely not one for the claustrophobic—but the 463 steps are well worth the climb. For the less energetic, the Boboli Gardens, just south of the River Arno, also has beautiful views across the terracotta rooftops of the city.

AMALFI, ITALY

## 282. Holiday at the Amalfi Coast

**When:** All year
**Latitude:** 40.6340°N
**Longitude:** 14.6026°E

The Amalfi Coast is a region so beautiful that it has been listed as a UNESCO World Heritage site. Visit the haven for unspoiled little villages, fresh seafood, limoncello liqueur, boat trips, and a dip in the Mediterranean.

▼ THE CAMARGUE, FRANCE
## 283. Ride a white horse in the wilds of Camargue
**When:** All year
**Latitude:** 43.5939°N **Longitude:** 4.4689°E

The Camargue is one of Western Europe's last truly wild-feeling places, an exotic cocktail of marshy, windswept lagoons. It's also home to the famous white (technically gray) Camargue horse—one of the oldest breeds in the world. Built to survive in this sometimes-harsh environment, these sturdy, calm, and intelligent beasts are the absolute best way to explore this exquisite environment, and—luckily for beginners—are easy to learn to ride. A number of riding schools will put you through your paces in the morning before leading expeditions out in the afternoon through the waterlines and down to the beach.

CANNES, FRANCE
## 284. Make your own movie
**When:** All year (film festival in May)
**Latitude:** 43.5528°N
**Longitude:** 7.0173°E

Making a movie is now easier than ever: it's possible to produce a cinema-ready reel using an SLR and a laptop. Do it really well, and the results might even lead a budding cinematographer to that megastar magnet, Cannes Film Festival, for the Palme d'Or … .

The white horses in the wilds of Camargue, France

A tree-lined avenue in France

▲ ALL OVER RURAL FRANCE
## 285. Drive down a tree-lined avenue
**When:** All year
**Latitude:** 43.6667°N
**Longitude:** 3.1667°E (for Languedoc, where these avenues are still easily found)

The tree-lined avenues of rural France are iconic, and there's only one true way to experience them: riding pillion on a vintage French motorcycle. See the dappled shade, feel the wind in your hair, and hear the distinctive swoosh of the passing trees.

PROVENCE, FRANCE
## 286. Soak up the scents of Provence lavender
**When:** June to August
**Latitude:** 44.0144°N
**Longitude:** 6.2116°E

It gladdens the heart that a plant this beautiful can be grown en masse as a crop that turns views of fields into surreal paintings and tinges the air with the scent of bath oil. Don't miss the experience or the Provençal cuisine and many local lavender festivals held every year.

CÔTE D'AZUR, FRANCE
## 287. Create a memory from the glittering Med
**When:** All year
**Latitude:** 43.1204°N
**Longitude:** 6.9209°E

The beaches of the Côte d'Azur, on France's sunshine-soaked Mediterranean coast, are made largely of flat gray stones called *galets*, which help give the sea its incredible blue color. Take some home and paint them—they make for a beautiful souvenir of a memorable trip.

SAN GIMIGNANO, TUSCANY, ITALY
## 288. Climb a tower for scenic views
**When:** All year
**Latitude:** 43.4654°N **Longitude:** 11.0485°E

From a distance, the thirteen towers of San Gimignano can fool the visitor into thinking they are heading to a town of skyscrapers. But these towers date back to the fourteenth century, when families built towers to show their wealth, and act as fortified homes. Climb Torre Grossa for fabulous views of the Tuscan countryside.

SAINT-TROPEZ, FRANCE
### 289. Get a tan with the international jet set
**When:** June to September
**Latitude:** 43.2676°N
**Longitude:** 6.6407°E

Saint-Tropez beaches are not about finding a hidden-away cove and a secret beachfront seafood shack. They are busy, and that's why you're here—to see and be seen. Spot the celebrities on the yachts, delight in paying a small mortgage for a sun lounger—and don't forget the sunscreen.

GAIOLE IN CHIANTI, ITALY
## 290. Bicycle the Strade Bianche
**When:** October
**Latitude:** 43.4667°N
**Longitude:** 11.4333°E

The L'Eroica race in Italy is a noncompetitive, vintage bike-race that is 124 mi (200 km) long (predominantly on white graveled roads that give the route its name). You'll ride on a machine probably older than you are, from Gaiole in Chianti, through beautiful Tuscan countryside, and back again.

SIENA, TUSCANY, ITALY
## 291. Experience the thrills and spills of the Palio di Siena
**When:** July 2 and August 16
**Latitude:** 43.3188°N **Longitude:** 11.3307°E

The most spectacular of horse races anywhere—and one of the best displays of pride, passion, and pageantry—is the Palio di Siena. Held twice a year, the race's history dates back to medieval times.

The race is a minute-plus of madness contested by ten horses and their bareback rider from a selection of seventeen wards, or *contrade*. With brightly colored outfits, each rider carries the hopes of a different area of the city, and support is fierce.

Join the frenzied crowds to witness the Palio di Siena: an explosion starts the race, three times around, and the place goes bananas; on the treacherous track, many jockeys tumble into the dirt. A horse can win without a rider and locally, coming in second is considered worse than last. The victor gets a banner and bragging rights for the year.

LOURDES, FRANCE
## 292. Take the healing waters of Lourdes
**When:** All year
**Latitude:** 43.0915°N
**Longitude:** 0.0457°W

The waters at Lourdes became holy in 1858 when the Virgin Mary appeared here to a girl, Bernadette, and described the location of the spring. The spring is now protected by a glass screen, but you can get the freely available water from taps at the site to heal your ailments.

MONACO
## 293. Spray a bottle of champagne over friends
**When:** All year
**Latitude:** 43.7384°N
**Longitude:** 7.4246°E

When in Monaco, do as the Monégasque do and celebrate like a Formula 1 Grand Prix winner by spraying champagne over your friends. At $550 for the jeroboam that race winners routinely receive, you'd be well-advised to stick to prosecco.

FRENCH RIVIERA, MONACO
## 294. See the Grand Prix from the French Riviera
**When:** May
**Latitude:** 43.7384°N
**Longitude:** 7.4246°E

Perfect for people watching, as well as high-octane action, the Formula 1 Grand Prix in the rich man's playground of Monaco is glamour personified. See the action from the best place in which to sample the atmosphere of the street circuit: at the marina—ideally, on board a yacht.

VARIOUS ROUTES TO SANTIAGO DE COMPOSTELA, SPAIN
## 295. Follow the pilgrim's path
**When:** All year
**Latitude:** 42.8782°N **Longitude:** 8.5448°W

The Camino de Santiago, also known as the Way of St. James, is possibly the most-walked route in history. It became a Catholic tradition as early as the ninth century to embark on a trip from home to the Cathedral of Santiago de Compostela in Galicia, where legend has it that St. James, the first of Jesus' apostles to be martyred, is laid to rest.

Join the 200,000 people per year that still complete the journey. There are many routes, but the most popular starting point is the Galician city of Sarriá. The reason is simple: Those who wish to officially recognize their journey receive a *compostela* ("certificate of accomplishment") upon completion. To earn this, you need to walk a minimum of 62 mi (100 km) or bicycle more than 124 mi (200 km). It's a serene and stunning walk, given gravitas by the fact that popes have done it, but the highlight will always be entering Santiago de Compostela.

◀ VIS, CROATIA
## 296. Swim into the Blue Cave in Vis
**When:** All year
**Latitude:** 43.0602°N
**Longitude:** 16.1828°E

This incredibly cinematic and appropriately named waterlogged sea cave on the island of Vis positively glows azure. It's only the size of a large swimming pool, but swim or row in it at around noon, and it's a phenomenal, romantic experience, regardless of crowds.

MOUNT VESUVIUS, NAPLES, ITALY
## 297. Climb a dangerous, active volcano
**When:** All year
**Latitude:** 40.8167°N
**Longitude:** 14.4333°E

Mount Vesuvius in Italy is the volcano that erupted above Pompeii almost 2,000 years ago, suspending the ancient Roman city in a lava time capsule, which has been excavated and restored as a unique tourist destination today. The volcano is still active, but it is open to the public—take a walk up the spiral path to the top and peer into the depths of its eerie crater.

Croatia's Blue Cave
on the island of Vis

BAGNÈRES-DE-BIGORRE, PYRENEES, FRANCE
## 298. Feel on top of the world
**When:** All year
**Latitude:** 42.9103°N **Longitude:** 0.1828°E

Enjoy the glorious vistas of the Pyrenees without climbing a single step. A cable car from the ski resort of La Mongie glides effortlessly to the 9,000 ft (2,743 m) summit of Pic du Midi, where a huge terrace affords unparalleled views of 185 mi (298 km) of snowcapped mountains.

▶ KORTEZUBI, URDAIBAI BIOSPHERE RESERVE, SPAIN
## 299. Feel the connection between nature and art
**When:** All year

**Latitude:** 43.3400°N **Longitude:** 2.6549°W

A stroll through the peaceful Oma Painted Forest amid colorful Monterey pine trees is a feast for the senses. In the 1980s sculptor and artist Agustín Ibarrola painted unique patterns on the tree trunks here, some of which change shape and perspective as you move through the forest. This open-air museum is a form of "land art"—where nature is used as the artist's frame—and features artworks that are representative of nearby Paleolithic cave art. Contemplate the relationship between man and nature as you walk among the trees and ferns in this magical place.

BALKAN MOUNTAINS, BULGARIA
## 300. Bicycle through the Balkan Mountains
**When:** All year

**Latitude:** 42.7468°N

**Longitude:** 25.0788°E

Most cycling tourists think of heading to the Alps or Pyrenees to emulate their Tour de France idols, but Bulgaria's Balkan Mountains offer challenging climbs and panoramic views with far less traffic and tourism. Saddle up and explore before the rest of Europe catches on.

START AT MLJET, CROATIA
## 301. Go island-hopping in the Adriatic Sea
**When:** Summer months

**Latitude:** 42.7478°N **Longitude:** 17.5150°E

Croatia's Adriatic coastline is speckled with more than 1,000 islands, all beautiful, inviting, and very different. In the summer months, ferries make it simple to hop between many of the bigger islands. Start in Dubrovnik in the south and work up the coastline exploring the islands along the way.

The first is Mljet, most of which is a national park, covered in verdant forest, and surrounded with pretty coves and bays. North of here you'll find Korčula, packed with history and culture. Then you get to Vis, a smaller island, but full of beautiful coves and a couple of sandy beaches. It is far less developed than many of its neighbors.

At the opposite end of the spectrum to Vis is Hvar, whose port is lined with bars and the harbor filled with luxury cruise boats. A party island for the well-heeled, it is also a charming town. Farther north from here, the island of Brac is famous for its triangular spit of sand—the Zlatni Rat beach that sticks out into the ocean from two sides of a promontory—offering views over the Dalmatian coast.

At the north end of the trip, you can return to the mainland at Split—Croatia's second-largest town, but wonderfully picturesque with a Roman palace at its heart.

Nature and art combine in the
Oma Painted Forest, Spain

DUBROVNIK, CROATIA
## 302. Walk the ancient city walls of Dubrovnik's Old Town
**When:** All year
**Latitude:** 42.6403°N **Longitude:** 18.1083°E

Encircled by honey-hued battlements; crisscrossed with sinuous cobbled streets; and packed with green-shuttered, terracotta-roofed buildings, Dubrovnik at the far southern end of Croatia has few contenders for Europe's most beautiful city.

The best way to take in the beauty of the so-called "pearl of the Adriatic" is to walk the city walls, a complete circuit of crenellated battlements and sturdy forts that date back as far as the twelfth century. The narrow pathway offers fabulous views out over the Adriatic along the 1.2 mi (2 km) walk.

Most start and finish the walk at the Pile Gate. Head out in the early morning to avoid the crowds. Walk clockwise, and you'll visit Minceta Fortress first, for views up Mount Srd. The northern section of the walls continues on past the North Gate to St. Luke's Bastion and around to the city's ancient harbor.

The walls then run along the Adriatic, passing along the top of St. John's Fortress before turning west above Pustijerna, one of Dubrovnik's oldest quarters. As the walls wind their way back along toward Pile Gate, you'll see people sunbathing on the rocks below and cooling off in the Adriatic. You can get there by ducking through almost hidden doorways in the walls below.

TREVI FOUNTAIN, ROME, ITALY
## 303. Throw a coin into Italy's famous fountain
**When:** All year
**Latitude:** 41.9009°N
**Longitude:** 12.4833°E

There are few movie scenes quite as memorable as the one in *La Dolce Vita*, where Anita Ekberg jumps into the Trevi Fountain with her clothes on. Rome's carabinieri take a dim view of anyone trying to replicate that scene, but throw in a coin over your shoulder, and legend has it you'll return to Rome.

ALBA, PIEDMONT, ITALY
## 304. Go truffle hunting with pigs
**When:** End of October to early January
**Latitude:** 44.6899°N
**Longitude:** 8.0513°E

October marks the start of one of Italy's most exciting and unusual activities that you can participate in: foraging for white truffles with the aid of pigs and dogs that sniff out the fungi under the roots of trees. More valuable than gold, the prized fungus is the ultimate decadence of any fall menu.

▶ SATURNIA, TUSCANY, ITALY
## 305. Bathe like the locals in tempting Tuscany
**When:** May to September
**Latitude:** 42.6480°N
**Longitude:** 11.5123°E

Enjoy an unforgettable spa experience at one of southern Tuscany's best-kept secrets: the Cascate del Mulino in Saturnia. Take in the views while basking in the silky 99.5°F (37.5°C) water that cascades down a series of natural terraces that form outdoor pools. Best of all? It's completely free.

Bathing in the Cascate del Mulino
in Saturnia, Tuscany, Italy

ISTANBUL, TURKEY
## 306. Unwind completely at a Turkish bath
**When:** All year
**Latitude:** 41.0082°N
**Longitude:** 28.9783°E

A hammam (Turkish bath) is the perfect way to steam away the aches and pains of travel. You'll find them countrywide, but Istanbul's spectacular marble baths take some beating: a steam, wash, and an oil massage sets up a trip to Turkey pretty wonderfully.

ISTANBUL, TURKEY
## 307. Arrive in style on a yacht
**When:** All year
**Latitude:** 41.0082°N
**Longitude:** 28.9784°E

There are some places that just have an ideal way to arrive, and for Istanbul, it's on a yacht. Sail toward the towering minarets with the Bosphorus Bridge in the background suspended between Europe and Asia for a truly memorable entrance.

MADRID, SPAIN
## 308. Learn a new language
**When:** All year
**Latitude:** 40.4153°N
**Longitude:** 3.7089°W

If you want to truly immerse yourself in your surroundings when traveling, learning another language is a must. Spanish is the ideal choice: it's spoken by around 560 million people around the world.

The Caribbean in Europe … Praia das Rodas on Las Islas Cíes, Spain

### BARCELONA, SPAIN
## 309. Get weird with Gaudí at Park Güell
**When:** All year
**Latitude:** 41.4142°N
**Longitude:** 2.1521°E

Barcelona can feel like one big Gaudí exhibition sometimes: his buildings and artwork are everywhere. They are best profiled at the brilliant, beautiful Park Güell, where you can wander agog amid the Catalan modernist genius's unusual buildings and benches.

### LOGROÑO, SPAIN
## 310. Stomp grapes underfoot
**When:** September
**Latitude:** 42.4653°N
**Longitude:** 2.4802°W

Wineries these days don't call for feet to crush their grapes, but fortunately, festivals such as San Mateo still celebrate this age-old production method. Barrels are filled with grapes, and, shoeless, you can join men and women in treading all over them, feeling the soft crush of grape flesh between your toes.

### ▲ PRAIA DAS RODAS, SPAIN
## 311. Discover the Caribbean … in Europe
**When:** Summer
**Latitude:** 42.2238°N
**Longitude:** 8.9028°W

Las Islas Cíes, just north of Portugal, has inexplicably uncrowded beaches that look and feel just like St. Lucia's finest. Head to what locals call Praia das Rodas, the "Caribbean beach," with its light, soft sand; calm lagoon; and turquoise sea—although the water is cold!

VATICAN CITY, ROME, ITALY
## 312. Wonder at Michelangelo's artwork

**When:** Open Monday to Saturday, and last Sunday of every month

**Latitude:** 41.9029°N

**Longitude:** 12.4544°E

*The Creation of Adam* tells the story of Genesis with God's and Adam's fingers almost but not quite touching. As you gaze upon this wondrous image, ask yourself: is it this artful tension that draws gasps from the crowds or the unbelievable notion of painting the whole thing upside down?

VATICAN CITY, ROME, ITALY
## 313. See the light at one of the largest churches

**When:** Open Monday to Saturday, and last Sunday of every month

**Latitude:** 41.9022°N

**Longitude:** 12.4533°E

Visit the sublime St. Peter's Basilica in the afternoon to see the bright glow reflecting off the bronze and gold of the high altar.

ARBOUSSOLS, FRANCE
## 314. Experience the "Chamber of Certainties"

**When:** All year

**Latitude:** 42.6644°N

**Longitude:** 2.4861°E

Collect a key from the town mayor, then follow a mountain trail to Wolfgang Laib's "La Chambre de Certitudes," a locked room hewn from granite, whose walls are covered in beeswax and lit from a single hanging lightbulb. The color and smell is intense, yet the effect oddly tranquil.

◄ CORSICA, FRANCE
## 315. Tackle one of Europe's longest footpaths

**When:** All year

**Latitude:** 42.0396°N **Longitude:** 9.0128°E

The 112 mi (180 km) trail through the fabulous island of Corsica is on every self-respecting trekker's bucket list. Crossing diagonally via high mountain ridges, GR20 is both one of the longest and most difficult continuous footpaths in Europe.

Beyond being a physical challenge, however, its rewards are manifold. You'll pass through special scenery in a vivid range of colors, towering pinnacles, lush pine forests; past glorious glacial lakes and over snow-tipped passes. The views are enhanced by being on an island: turn a corner along the way, and you will suddenly glimpse craggy coastline and shimmering sea.

The wildlife is also unique: there's the mouflon, a hardy wild sheep, commonly found in the reserves of Asco and Bavella, and in the skies, if you're lucky, you might catch a glimpse of the super rare lammergeier, or bearded vulture, which has a wingspan of up to 10 ft (3 m). On the ground you'll find cyclamen, crocuses, anemones, red peonies, and the native Corsican hellebores.

Most walkers take somewhere between ten and fifteen days to finish the route, and you can rest your heads in *gîtes* and refuges along the way—often simple, quaint huts, staffed from June until fall, that offer a comfy bunk bed and a welcome cooked meal.

The GR20 footpath in Corsica, France, is one of Europe's longest footpaths

## 316. Spend a night in the Gobi Desert

**When:** All year
**Latitude:** 42.5898°N
**Longitude:** 103.4299°E

Do a Gobi tour and you'll travel a full day (out of Ulan Bator, Mongolia) in a rattly van to get deep into this vast expanse. But once there, you'll find it's an evocative place to spend a night in a *ger*, enjoying some Gobi grub under a twinkling blanket of stars.

ISTANBUL, TURKEY
## 317. Visit all seven continents; start with two in a day
**When:** All year
**Latitude:** 41.1194°N **Longitude:** 29.0753°E (the Bosphorus)

Setting foot on each of the planet's continents is a travel goal for many, and while it might take most people years to tick off all seven—Africa, Antarctica, Asia, Australia, Europe, North America, and South America—in cosmopolitan Turkey, you can visit two in a matter of minutes.

The endlessly fascinating city of Istanbul straddles Europe and Asia across the teeming Bosphorus Strait. Its commercial and historical heart can be found on the European side of the water, while almost a third of its 14 million inhabitants live in Asia.

Other countries at the threshold of Europe and Asia include Azerbaijan, Georgia, Kazakhstan, and Russia. Moving southwest, Egypt is considered to be a country that also straddles two continents, namely Africa and Asia, courtesy of the Sinai Peninsula.

A glance at the map suggests an equally straightforward crossing between North (via Panama) and South (via Colombia) America. But the Darién Gap presents a formidable barrier, made all the less enticing by political and armed upheaval in the area. A short flight might be easiest.

ISTANBUL, TURKEY
## 318. Step into the calm of the Hagia Sophia
**When:** All year
**Latitude:** 41.0082°N
**Longitude:** 28.9783°E

Once a Christian basilica, then an imperial mosque, now a museum, a wander around the Hagia Sofia still feels like an enlightening religious experience. Its huge dome is of great architectural significance, and it feels like a perfect microcosm of Turkey's heady cultural and religious blend.

ISTANBUL, TURKEY
## 319. Heed the call to prayer in Istanbul
**When:** All year
**Latitude:** 41.0082°N
**Longitude:** 28.9783°E

With its six slender minarets and eight cascading domes, the Blue Mosque is one of Istanbul's favorite tourist attractions, but it's also a working place of worship. Hear the call to prayer at dawn for an atmospheric and hypnotic part of the Turkish capital's soundscape.

IBIZA, BALEARIC ISLANDS
## 320. Party all night to Balearic beats
**When:** May to October
**Latitude:** 38.9067°N
**Longitude:** 1.4206°E (Ibiza Town)

If you want to party, then head to Europe's premier party island: a 355 sq mi (920 sq km) rock in the Mediterranean's Balearic Islands. Ibiza offers stunning beaches, great walking, pine-scented villages—and a riotous nightclub scene. Hardcore partygoers flock to Ibiza Town and San Antonio each summer to dance all night and take in Ibiza's legendary "disco sunrises."

IBIZA, BALEARIC ISLANDS
## 321. Create waves on a speedboat
**When:** All year
**Latitude:** 38.9089°N
**Longitude:** 1.4328°E

The Mediterranean Sea is almost completely enclosed by land, making it relatively warm and calm all year round—and perfect for a jaunt on a speedboat. Rent one from the traditional party island of Ibiza for full celebrity lifestyle points.

## 322. Join the Human Tower Competition

**When:** October (biannually)
**Latitude:** 41.1188°N **Longitude:** 1.2444°E

Competitors in this biannual Spanish contest need a hundred to 500 friends, a proper amount of time to plan their entry, as well as strength, balance, and a good amount of daring. A Tarragona tradition dating back more than 200 years, the "Concurs de Castells" sees competitors, known as *castellers*, attempt to build the highest and most complex human structures possible. If you're not participating, be sure to watch this colorful competition.

▶ BARCELONA, SPAIN
## 323. Tower above the city of Barcelona
**When:** All year
**Latitude:** 41.4044°N **Longitude:** 2.1757°E

To experience the independent nature of the Catalan region of Spain, simply ascend one of the 213 ft (65 m) towers of the Sagrada Família. This emblematic basilica sits in the heart of the Catalan capital.

Climb one of its towers to enjoy panoramic views that include the distinctive patchwork of architecture Antoni Gaudí created throughout the city, such as Park Güell. Gaudí's death meant the Sagrada Família was left unfinished. However, construction has been overseen by a number of architects, the influence of which has added to the dreamlike quality of this unique building.

ROME, ITALY
## 324. Explore the unrivaled history of Rome
**When:** All year
**Latitude:** 41.9027°N **Longitude:** 12.4963°E

Rome is a word that resonates for a reason. For three millennia, it has influenced art, politics, business, culture ... everything, really, across the rest of the planet. No travel bucket list can leave it off.

A visit must include a tantalizing trek back in time to the epicenter of the Roman Empire: the great gladiatorial stadium of the Coliseum; the Roman Forum; and the Pantheon. Then there's the Catholic Church—Rome has numerous churches and cathedrals, while the Vatican City, still HQ of a religion followed by 1.25 billion people and the seat of the pope, contains the stunning St. Peter's Basilica and Vatican Museums. In addition, step inside the legendary museums and galleries, scale the Spanish Steps, point a camera at the Piazza Navona, and toss a coin into the Trevi Fountain.

Sagrada Família in the city of Barcelona, Spain

▼ BARCELONA, SPAIN
## 325. Savor a soccer duel between two Spanish rivals
**When:** September to May
**Latitude:** 41.3809°N **Longitude:** 2.1228°E

The best way to convey the intensity of this derby between two of the world's most storied soccer clubs is to note that when Portuguese star Luís Figo returned to Barcelona after leaving them for Real Madrid C.F., the home fans threw a pig—traditional symbol of a traitor thereabouts—at him. The rivalry pits FC Barcelona, the pride of Catalonia, against Real Madrid, a team that regards itself as the symbol of Spain. Get along to one of the matches, when the clubs face off at least twice a season in an iconic encounter that has starred such greats as Zinedine Zidane and Lionel Messi and attracts a global TV audience of 150 million.

KYRGYZSTAN
## 326. Visit a popular Soviet Union resort
**When:** All year
**Latitude:** 42.5214°N
**Longitude:** 77.2713°E

Lake Issyk-Kul in Kyrgyzstan may not immediately conjure up images of a vacation destination, but this was one of the Soviet Union's most popular summer resorts. In summer you can go horseback riding and trekking, while in winter you can ski at the Karakol Ski Base.

A soccer duel between Barcelona and Madrid at Barcelona's stadium, Spain

CASPIAN SEA
## 327. Indulge in caviar and champagne
**When:** All year
**Latitude:** 41.6667°N
**Longitude:** 50.6667°E

Champagne and caviar are both the epitome of fine food and wine, yet also a perfect pairing. Eat the caviar (at its home, the Caspian Sea) directly from the pot with a nonmetallic spoon for a truly decadent experience and be sure you choose a dry champagne.

HARTFORD, CONNECTICUT, US

### 328. Recreate a Mark Twain adventure

**When:** All year
**Latitude:** 41.7637°N
**Longitude:** 72.6850°W

Which big kid wouldn't want to tread where Tom 'n' Huck have? Mark Twain's timeless novels of a Mississippi childhood have inspired a million youngsters worldwide to explore and observe the countryside around them. The best place to start off an adventure is the characterful Mark Twain House in Hartford, Connecticut, where author Samuel Langhorne Clemens (aka Twain) spent his own formative years and which featured heavily in his writing.

▶ SAVANNAH, GEORGIA, US

### 329. Creep among the Savannah cemeteries

**When:** All year
**Latitude:** 32.0835°N **Longitude:** 81.0998°W

Captured eerily in John Berendt's book, *Midnight in the Garden of Good and Evil*, Savannah is a city with a unique and sometimes dark atmosphere, full of Southern charm and ghostly mystery. Probably the most-photographed cemetery in the world is Bonaventure, where bizarre and creative headstones abound—the cover of Berendt's book featured the Bird Girl headstone, which once lay here but is now in the Telfair Museum of art.

Colonial Park Cemetery is home to many of Savannah's oldest citizens, including many killed in duels, and is a very popular stop on the city's popular ghost tours, for those with a strong nerve. The Laurel Grove Cemetery, meanwhile, is where 1,500 Confederate soldiers were laid to rest, and is one of the oldest African-American cemeteries still in use—fascinating tours run six days a week thanks to the Ralph Mark Gilbert Civil Rights Museum.

GREAT SALT LAKE, UTAH, US

### 330. Unwind by walking on the *Spiral Jetty*

**When:** All year
**Latitude:** 41.4377°N
**Longitude:** 112.6689°W

*Spiral Jetty* is the name of a 1,500 ft (4,572 m) long sculpture created by Robert Smithson from natural materials. Take a stroll on the coil that juts out of the northeastern shore of the Great Salt Lake in Utah, although be warned: it is sometimes submerged, depending on water levels.

MASSACHUSETTS, US

### 331. Spin a basketball on your fingertip like a pro

**When:** All year
**Latitude:** 42.1124°N
**Longitude:** 72.5475°W

Head to the home of basketball to perform one of its coolest moves; basketball was invented in 1891 by a sports coach from Springfield, Massachusetts. Want to know the key to spinning a basketball on your fingertip? Try using a slightly deflated ball.

NEW WINDSOR, NEW YORK, US

### 332. Wander through a vast sculpture park

**When:** All year (hours vary seasonally)
**Latitude:** 41.4249°N
**Longitude:** 74.0592°W

Lose yourself in the Storm King Art Center, which is home to more than a hundred unique sculptures set within 500 ac (202 ha) of dramatic, natural landscape. You could find yourself face to face with exhibits such as Zhang Huan's *Three Legged Buddha* or Alyson Shotz's picket *Mirror Fence*, and works by world-renowned artists Andy Goldsworthy, and Roy Lichtenstein.

A Savannah cemetery in Georgia, US

DOWN THE ROAD ..., US
## 333. Get your kicks on Route 66
**When:** All year
**Latitude:** 41.8781°N **Longitude:** 87.6297°W (Chicago)

The most romanticized, written, and sung about thoroughfare on Earth, Route 66 runs from Chicago to Santa Monica, passing through Missouri, Oklahoma, New Mexico, and Arizona—oh, so much Arizona—before finally reaching the Pacific Ocean. It is one of the most popular road trips around.

Most travel it from east to west, and although the 2,448 mi (3,940 km) drive can be done quicker, many recommend at least twelve days, with two nondriving rest days. From Chicago, pleasant farmland eventually leads to St. Louis and the famous Chain of Rocks Bridge, where the road crosses the mighty Mississippi.

The rolling hills of the Ozark Mountains come next, as the road winds down to Springfield and then on to Oklahoma, where the scenery turns dry and dusty.

Down toward Tucumcari, New Mexico, the feel of the journey turns exotic, heavy with Native American and Spanish influences. There're lots of the original road and charming adobe buildings—real Americana. Next comes Albuquerque, then Holbrook, the Navajo Nation, and the dramatic scenery of Arizona. Here, you can explore the wonders of the nearby Grand Canyon on a quick detour. Next, Las Vegas and its attendant pleasures looms into view. From there, it's just a hop to the coast, and the end of the road.

BOSTON, MASSACHUSETTS, US
## 334. Feel the pleasure of giving a gift you have sewn by hand
**When:** All year
**Latitude:** 42.3500°N **Longitude:** 71.0667°W

These days we tend to buy gifts, but there's nothing like taking the trouble to make something yourself and give it as a gift to someone you love. If dusting down an old Singer sewing machine (patented by Isaac Singer in Boston, Massachusetts, in 1851) puts you off, then invest in some hand-sewing needles—it will be worth the smile you'll receive.

FOXBOROUGH, MASSACHUSETTS, US
## 335. Watch an ice hockey match outside
**When:** January
**Latitude:** 42.0944°N **Longitude:** 71.2651°W

Ice hockey is one of the fastest and most frantic winter sports to watch, but it's generally been held inside in the modern era. America's top-level National Hockey League, however, has started to arrange the Winter Classic, held in huge-capacity baseball and American football stadiums. In 2016, fierce rivals the Montréal Canadiens and Boston Bruins battled it out at the huge Gillette Stadium on New Year's Day. It's a real return to the sport's outdoor roots, which looks set to be expanded on every year. For an unforgettable spectator experience, get yourself to one of these matches.

## 336. Enter the world of the Burning Man

**When:** Last Sunday in August through to the first Monday in September

**Latitude:** 40.9107°N **Longitude:** 119.0560°W

A crazy, sometimes bewildering, but never boring, experience: tens of thousands of people descend on the Nevada desert, set up a temporary city dedicated to art and self-expression, then head off a week later without leaving any trace. The central theme is to selflessly give over one's talents for the enjoyment of all: sculpture, building, performance, and elaborately decorated cars are all central to the experience.

Be one of the 70,000 who currently attend and witness the centerpiece of the event: the ritual burning of a huge wooden man, occurring on the Saturday.

## 337. Capture the world's best city skylines at night

**When:** All year
**Latitude:** 40.8260°N
**Longitude:** 73.9303°W

A terrific challenge for any budding photographer—or indeed, artist—is to record the iconic skylines of the world's greatest cities for posterity; spending time among the skyscrapers, shadows, and stars makes you feel at one with a city—and see it in a different way.

Start in New York and view incredible vistas of Manhattan from Jersey City, Brooklyn Bridge Park, the Staten Island Ferry, the Statue of Liberty, or the Empire State Building. Then head to Tokyo, where the appeal lies in its incredible light show, with skylines in Shibuya, Shinjuku, and from the top of the Roppongi Hill Mori Tower all being spectacular. Move on to London to see its superb silhouette from Mudchute Park and Farm, Primrose Hill, and the London Eye, while from the top of The Monument to the Great Fire of London you can enjoy a vantage of the city. Then visit Hong Kong—which dazzles from the Star Ferry, Victoria Peak, or the Avenue of Stars—and then Shanghai, whose seemingly endless skyline is bewitching from the Bund or the Park Hyatt.

Manhattan city skyline at night in New York, US

LEADVILLE, COLORADO, US
## 338. Cycle across the sky
**When:** Second Saturday in August
**Latitude:** 39.2500°N **Longitude:** 106.2917°W

Tough mountain-bike races covering more than 100 mi (160 km) of terrain have really taken off in the past few years. In Colorado the Leadville Trail 100 MTB is one of the oldest and best-known races of this type. It is a spinoff of the Leadville 100—an ultramarathon run along a similar route, which is known as the "Race Across the Sky." The route takes bikers 100 mi (160 km) through the heart of the Rocky Mountains.

High altitudes and extreme terrain are the order of the day here. The views really are breathtaking up where the air is already thin (beware altitude sickness, especially under such grueling conditions).

The current record is six hours, sixteen minutes, but twelve hours is fine—heck, finishing at all is. That you have to be fit to take this race on is a massive understatement: even those lucky enough to complete it can barely stand by the end. It is truly, utterly, life-defyingly exhausting.

LOUISVILLE, KENTUCKY, US
## 339. Cheer on your nag at the Kentucky Derby
**When:** First Saturday in May
**Latitude:** 38.2526°N
**Longitude:** 85.7584°W

Known as the "most exciting two minutes in sport" and the "run for the roses" (the winner is blanketed in the flowers), the Churchill Downs Racetrack goes utterly wild for the Derby. Follow tradition and drink a mint julep, wolf down a bowl of burgoo stew, and of course, have a small bet.

NEW YORK, US, AND WORLDWIDE
## 340. Join a flash mob
**When:** All year
**Latitude:** 40.8260°N
**Longitude:** 73.9303°W (Manhattan)

A daft, daring, and fun-filled way to fill up a few minutes—and attract some amazed looks—flash mobs are a modern phenomenon. The first successful one was organized at Macy's, in Manhattan, where 130 people gathered around a rug, as a social experiment. There have since been various wacky examples: huge "silent discos" at British railway stations and mass pillow fights in Canada. Anyone can organize them, and there are no rules. So what are you waiting for?

CONEY ISLAND, NEW YORK, US
## 341. Live the American dream at Coney Island
**When:** Summer
**Latitude:** 40.5744°N
**Longitude:** 73.9786°W

Fancy an adrenaline rush? Go to "America's playground," "Sodom by the Sea," and reputedly the only thing about the US that interested Sigmund Freud. Coney Island's amusement park has been immortalized in books and movies, most set in its heyday at the beginning of the twentieth century.

NEW YORK, US, AND WORLDWIDE
## 342. Write your own life history
**When:** All year
**Latitude:** 43.0481°N (Syracuse)
**Longitude:** 76.1474°W

Documenting a life story can take you on a trip down memory lane. You don't need to be Dickens to do it, and it doesn't have to go any farther than your own typewriter or laptop once done. A trip to the enigmatically named Memory Lane, Syracuse, New York, in the United States, is a good place to start. And if a prospective scribe thinks they've got nothing to write about, try doing some of the other 999 things in this book first … .

## CENTRAL PARK, NEW YORK, US
### 343. Row through Central Park
**When:** April to November (weather permitting)
**Latitude:** 40.7830°N
**Longitude:** 73.9712°W

There's something splendid about finding an oasis of peace in the noisy old city that never sleeps. Rent a lovely vessel at Central Park's Loeb Boathouse and gently explore the 22 ac (9 ha) lake where egrets and herons roam.

## NEW YORK, US
### 344. Hit the baseball bleachers in the Bronx
**When:** April to October
**Latitude:** 40.8295°N
**Longitude:** 73.9265°W

The home of Babe Ruth and arguably America's most iconic sports franchise, the New York Yankees moved to a new Yankee Stadium (costing $2.3 billion) in 2009. Catch a game at the sparkly facility or at the more earthy, passionate atmosphere at Citi Field, where fierce rivals, the New York Mets, pitch and bat.

## BROADWAY, NEW YORK, US
### 345. See a play on Broadway
**When:** All year
**Latitude:** 40.7590°N
**Longitude:** 73.9844°W

There's always glamour in the air along theater land's most famous street, which remains the iconic place to catch a show. Whether you're a fan of drama, comedy, or showstopping musicals, with more than forty venues and 500-plus seats apiece, you'll find something catering to every theatrical taste imaginable.

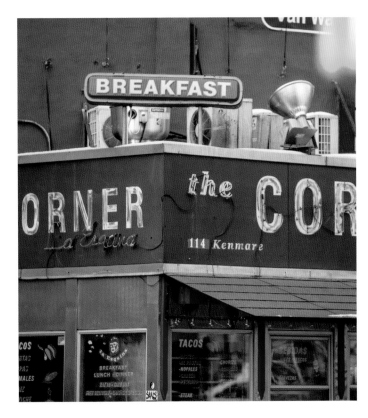

## ◀ MANHATTAN, NEW YORK, US
### 346. Start the day at a New York diner
**When:** Before noon
**Latitude:** 40.7830°N
**Longitude:** 73.9712°W

The only way to set you up for a day tramping the streets of the Big Apple is by sitting in a vinyl booth of a traditional Manhattan diner and ordering a greasy platter of fried food bigger than a human head. Pile up the pancakes, have eggs one of a million different ways, and get multiple coffee refills to fuel the fun.

Starting the day at a New York diner, US

Gliding around the Rockefeller rink in New York, US

▲ MANHATTAN, NEW YORK, US
### 347. Glide around the Rockefeller rink
**When:** October to April
**Latitude:** 40.7830°N
**Longitude:** 73.9712°W

The most recognizable rink in the world is wildly popular, and allows 150 skaters on the ice at once. Get your skates on for an early session at 7 a.m. or the Starlight Skate session from 10:30 p.m. to midnight.

MANHATTAN, NEW YORK, US
### 348. Get in an Empire State of mind
**When:** All year
**Latitude:** 40.8260°N
**Longitude:** 73.9303°W

Despite the much taller rivals that have sprung up around the globe, the enchanting art deco Empire State Building remains the definitive skyscraper. Take a trip to its observation deck, which affords the best possible views of the Big Apple.

NEW YORK, US
### 349. Attend a Greenwich Village poetry reading
**When:** All year
**Latitude:** 40.7335°N
**Longitude:** 74.0002°W

In its 1960s heyday, visitors apparently couldn't wait for a Jack Kerouac or a Bob Dylan to fill a smoky basement with revolutionary words. Open mic nights at venues like the White Horse Tavern and Café Wha? in the Village keep the tradition alive.

NEW YORK, US; BILBAO, SPAIN; AND VENICE, ITALY
## 350. Visit all the world's Guggenheim museums
**When:** All year
**Latitude:** 40.7747°N (New York) **Longitude:** 73.9653°W

Ticking off all the Guggenheim museums is a goal of any serious art buff—and considering the splendor of the buildings that house them, of any architectural fan, too. Start at the Solomon R. Guggenheim Museum, in the center of Manhattan. Opened in 1959 it is housed on Fifth Avenue in a landmark piece of architecture by Frank Lloyd Wright. Next, head to the Bilbao museum, which has put the Basque city on the map. The Frank Gehry–designed building is one of the most heralded works of contemporary architecture in Europe.

Lastly, visit the less well known, but no less worthy, Peggy Guggenheim Collection in Venice. It is situated in the Palazzo Venier dei Leoni on the Grand Canal, and approaching by boat is a particular highlight.

What does the future hold for Guggenheim fans? Plans are afoot for a Helsinki building on the South Harbour, and a Guggenheim Abu Dhabi has also been mooted.

▶ US AND WORLDWIDE
## 351. Take part in the Color Run
**When:** All year
**Latitude:** 40.7607°N
**Longitude:** 111.8910°W

Join in the fun run different from the standard trot around the park. Inspired by the Hindu festival of Holi, this race has competitors showered with colored powder along the route. It's billed as the "Happiest 5k on the Planet" and is the brightest way around to get fit.

MAROON BELLS, COLORADO, US
## 352. Document a view as it changes through the seasons
**When:** All year
**Latitude:** 39.0708°N **Longitude:** 106.9889°W

The changing of the seasons are a great meditation on nature and the circle of life, and by revisiting the same spot every day, week, or month to document its changes through words, painting, or photography, the observer can learn a huge amount. An iconic spot always helps, and Maroon Bells—with its much documented mountains reflected into Maroon Creek, making it the most photographed spot in Colorado—is an ideal place to do it. But you can also do this in a back garden pretty much anywhere.

ELLIS ISLAND, NEW YORK, US
## 353. Research your family tree
**When:** All year
**Latitude:** 40.6994°N **Longitude:** 74.0438°W

Ellis Island—home to the Statue of Liberty and the first thing the 12 million immigrants who arrived in America between 1892 and 1954 saw—is a great place to begin researching any American family tree. Head straight to the American Family Immigration History Center and scour its database of millions of Port of New York and New Jersey arrival records, and then visit the American Immigrant Wall of Honor, inscribed with the names of more than 700,000 immigrants. You can also apply to have new names added to the next phase of the memorial.

The Salt Lake City
Color Run in Utah, US

ONLINE, BUT STARTED IN US
## 354. Support something on Kickstarter
**When:** All year
**Latitude:** 40.6781°N
**Longitude:** 73.9441°W (Brooklyn)

A thoroughly modern and entrepreneurial to-do: why not lend support to a business idea or project that might just change the world? The Brooklyn-based, globally targeted crowdfunding project has already gotten more than 250,000 creative projects off the ground, such as the hugely successful Pebble smart watch from California.

LAS VEGAS, NEVADA, US
## 355. Book a penthouse suite for the night
**When:** All year
**Latitude:** 36.1699°N
**Longitude:** 115.1398°W

Nothing screams decadence quite like booking a hotel penthouse for the night. And if you're going to do decadence, you want to do it in Las Vegas, where nothing ever feels over the top. At the Mandarin Oriental you can even get change for $1,000.

MANHATTAN, NEW YORK, US
## 356. Walk the High Line
**When:** All year
**Latitude:** 40.7590°N
**Longitude:** 73.9844°W

Amble along this elevated section of disused New York Central Railroad for a leisurely and traffic-free way to get another perspective on the Big Apple. Opened in 2009, it's packed with pleasant foliage and provides unusual views of some of the city's favorite landmarks.

WALNUTPORT, PENNSYLVANIA, US
## 357. Snuggle up at a drive-in movie
**When:** Summer evenings (for full effect)
**Latitude:** 40.7671°N **Longitude:** 75.5666°W

Weirdly, going to a drive-in movie for the first time feels most like actually being in a movie—probably because so many old movies feature scenes where these settings were a byword for teen romance. Be sure to include the essentials: a convertible, a mindless blockbuster, a loved one, and popcorn.

▶ MANHATTAN, NEW YORK, US
## 358. Bid at an auction
**When:** All year
**Latitude:** 40.7403°N
**Longitude:** 73.9001°W

Sotheby's auctions are free and open to the public, although you can also watch them online. Either way, there is no obligation to bid, which may be just as well—distinguished items under the hammer here have included a complete dinosaur skeleton going for a pretty sum. What will you bid for?

Bidding at a Sotheby's auction in New York, US

FROM NEW YORK CITY TO LOS ANGELES, US
## 359. Enjoy a classic coast-to-coast American road trip
**When:** All year
**Latitude:** 40.7549°N **Longitude:** 73.9840°W

Immortalized in the 1981 Hollywood comedy starring Burt Reynolds, the Cannonball Run was a legendary car race from sea to shining sea. The classic route—named in honor of driver Edwin "Cannonball" Baker—runs from the Red Ball Garage in Manhattan to the Portofino Hotel in Redondo Beach, California. A glorious journey of more than 2,800 mi (4,506 km) across the middle of the US, the record stands at an astonishing twenty-eight hours and fifty minutes (with some highly illegal speeds). We'd recommend more fun, and less speed.

MANHATTAN, NEW YORK, US
## 360. Watch a fight at Madison Square Garden
**When:** All year, dependent on events
**Latitude:** 40.7507°N **Longitude:** 73.9944°W

Head along to Madison Square Garden, which remains a mecca for boxers and boxing fans alike. In 1971 the venue played host to the "Fight of the Century" between Joe Frazier and Muhammad Ali. Whether you're an avid fan or merely a curious spectator, you'll appreciate the significance of the arena, which is steeped in history.

## 361. Learn about nature's evolution at the world's first national park

**When:** All year

**Latitude:** 44.4280°N **Longitude:** 110.5885°W

Yellowstone, the first national park to be created in the world, is a landscape of dramatic canyons, river valleys, hot springs with steaming geysers, and home to wildlife, including bears, wolves, bison, elk, and antelope.

Most remarkable, however, is the successful reintroduction of predators to the ecosystem and the re-creation of a "natural system." Predators, such as gray wolves and cougars, were wiped out by early settlers, meaning large numbers of elk, but not so much of other species.

In 1995 the gray wolf was reintroduced; it hunted the elk, which made the elk move around more. As areas were less continuously grazed, there was more plant growth, which led to more birdlife and beavers. This in turn led to more otters, more fish, and more amphibians. The wolves also hunted the coyote, so there were more mice and rabbits, which brought in more hawks, weasels, foxes, and badgers.

So now Yellowstone offers a glimpse into the wonders of nature at its most diverse—how it looked before man tried to manage it.

Grazing buffalo at Custer State Park in South Dakota, US

▲ SOUTH DAKOTA, US
## 362. Graze with buffalo at Custer State Park
**When:** All year
**Latitude:** 43.7266°N
**Longitude:** 103.4168°W

A herd of more than 1,000 free-roaming bison enjoy roaming the 71,000 ac (28,733 ha) park, set amid the bucolic Black Hills of South Dakota. You can gaze at these mighty beasts year-round, although in September there is a dramatic roundup and auction of hundreds of animals.

NORTHERN NEW YORK STATE, US
## 363. Visit the national park that has everything
**When:** May to August or November to April (for winter sports)
**Latitude:** 44.2717°N
**Longitude:** 74.6712°W

Covering more than 6 m ac (2.4 m ha), the Adirondacks is the largest national park in the US. Offering everything from outdoor pursuits to beer and wine tasting, you can stay in a campsite accessible only by canoe, or pop into a gallery to see a Picasso.

BADLANDS NATIONAL PARK, US
## 364. Go up, up, and up in a helicopter
**When:** All year
**Latitude:** 43.8554°N
**Longitude:** 102.3397°W

The eerily named Badlands rises up out of South Dakota's prairie and the sharp pinnacles and deep canyons of striated rock can't fail to capture the imagination as you approach. They're spectacular from ground level, but go up above them on a tourist's helicopter ride and you get all the scale and majesty of the rocks.

▶ ALTON, ILLINOIS, US
## 365. Play a tune on the trumpet

**When:** All year
**Latitude:** 38.8906°N
**Longitude:** 90.1842°W

Miles Davis was introduced to the trumpet at thirteen and quickly developed a talent for it—little did he know then that he would go on to take the jazz world by storm. Take inspiration from the phenomenonally talented musician by picking up the instrument and learning a tune on it in Davis's birthplace of Alton, Illinois— you'll find it's more about vibrating your lips than just blowing into the mouthpiece.

Miles Davis playing a tune on the trumpet

START IN BROOKLYN, US, AS ALBERT PODELL DID
## 366. Visit every country in the world

**When:** All year
**Latitude:** 40.6280°N **Longitude:** 73.9445°W

Visiting every single country in the world—the United Nations reckons there are 206 at the last count, a figure that is ever changing—is perhaps the ultimate mission for the seriously committed bucket lister.

It has actually been done by one man: Albert Podell, who went to a then-complete list of 196 different countries over a fifty-year period. There are no rules, but Podell's criteria required a minimum twenty-four-hour stay in a country and a passport stamp.

Logistically, there are challenges: some places aren't safe to visit; others require a lot of money, planning, and visas. But start with *A* and see how many you've already done, then start making plans for the next few years.

NEW YORK, PARIS, OR LONDON
## 367. See the best cities in the world, from above

**When:** All year
**Latitude:** 40.7127°N **Longitude:** 74.0059°W

It is one thing seeing the skylines of a metropolis from the ground, but quite another to get up there among the buildings themselves, which is why no visit to New York, Paris, or London could be complete without a helicopter tour. It is an incredible experience to be above the landmarks, although be warned: helicopters swoop and move quite differently from even small planes, and your stomach may notice the difference. Not that you will be paying much attention to what is going on inside, when the views outside are so magnificent.

COLORADO AND WYOMING, US
## 368. Take a trip through the Rockies

**When:** All year (but not in winter)

**Latitude:** 40.3771°N **Longitude:** 105.5255°W (Estes Park, Colorado)

There's no right route to drive through the Rockies—every way you go gives a new stunning view, another geological curiosity, some more incredible wildlife. The Rocky Mountains stretch for more than 3,000 mi (4,828 km) from western Canada to New Mexico, and the area in Wyoming and Colorado must be at the heart of any great American road trip here.

Highway 34 is a good place to start, right where it enters Estes Park. Known as the Trail Ridge Road, it climbs above the tree line for 11 mi (18 km), through an eerie lunar-esque landscape of alpine tundra. The views are unparalleled from up here—the Rockies sweep before you in all directions.

It's easy to see why Rocky Mountain National Park is among the most visited national parks in the United States. Don't miss the 300 mi (483 km) of trails, mountain views, and lakes that wait to be explored.

Grand Teton is only 10 mi (16 km) south of the majestic Yellowstone. Here, you'll find (or hopefully not) wolves, grizzly bears, and moose, although the park's hot springs and geysers are the major draw, of course.

WEST COAST, US
## 369. Walk from Mexico to Canada

**When:** All year

**Latitude:** 32.6076°N

**Longitude:** 116.4697°W (Campo, California)

The spellbinding Pacific Crest Trail winds through California, Oregon, and Washington State on a 2,650 mi (km) trek that covers the length of the United States. Start at Campo on the Mexican border, and you'll cross deserts, forests, mountain ranges, canyons, glacial lakes, and volcanoes on this magnificent journey.

▶ NIAGARA FALLS, CANADA
## 370. Look up at some of the world's biggest falls

**When:** May to September

**Latitude:** 43.0845°N

**Longitude:** 79.0894°W

There are many viewpoints for Niagara Falls—and many views on which is the best. So why not experience them the way that most impressed Charles Dickens in 1842: from below, with all their thunderous noise and great power? He wrote afterward: "Great Heaven … what a fall of bright green water."

Some of the world's biggest falls: Niagara Falls, Canada

CN TOWER, TORONTO, CANADA
## 371. Take a great glass elevator up into the sky

**When:** All year (aim for sunset)
**Latitude:** 43.6426°N
**Longitude:** 79.3871°W

It's not just the sides of the CN Tower's elevators that are made of glass—parts of the floor are too. This means you can watch Earth accelerate away from you at a speed of 15 mph (24 kph) as you race to the top of the 1,815 ft (553 m) tall iconic tower.

▶ JACKSON, NEW JERSEY, US
## 372. Ride the world's tallest roller coaster

**When:** Late March to early January
**Latitude:** 40.1392°N
**Longitude:** 74.4365°W

Do you have a head for heights? Not only is Kingda Ka at Six Flags Great Adventure amusement park the tallest roller coaster in the world (measuring more than 456 ft; 139 m high), it is also one of the longest and second-fastest, accelerating up to 128 mph (206 kph) in 3.5 seconds. Only Formula Rossa, at Ferrari World in Abu Dhabi, is faster. So buckle up for the ride of your life!

New Jersey's Kingda Ka is the world's tallest roller coaster, US

LEBANON, KANSAS, THE GEOGRAPHIC CENTER OF THE CONTIGUOUS US
## 373. Visit every state in the States
**When:** All year
**Latitude:** 39.8097°N **Longitude:** 98.5556°W

Want to see the real United States? Traveling to all four corners and taking in all fifty states—from Alaska in the north all the way to Hawaii in the central Pacific—is a great way to really get under the skin of this huge and varied nation.

The list of highlights is almost endless, and there is something to satisfy all tastes. Whether it's bathing and beaches, hiking and climbing, history, adventure sport, great architecture, fine dining, or the simple pleasures of watching the horizon constantly change on an epic road trip, this expedition has it all.

How to get around is a matter of personal preference, but culture and romance make road travel the obvious choice. Whether cruising the Pacific coastline on California Highway 1, or getting your kicks on Route 66, there is no better embodiment of living the American travel dream than firing up the motor and heading off into the sunset. Flying is more of a necessity for Alaska and Hawaii, of course, but for everywhere else, the journey is as much a part of the fun as the arriving.

DENVER, COLORADO, US
## 374. Feel the thrill of chasing a tornado
**When:** March to June
**Latitude:** 39.7392°N **Longitude:** 104.9902°W

The inclination of the normal citizen when a storm is coming in is to head inside, but if you're of a more daring disposition, you can head in the other direction and experience one of nature's most powerful sensations firsthand. Storm chasing—going after tornadoes and hurricanes—can be absolutely thrilling as well as very dangerous. It's not recommended without an experienced and savvy guide, almost always in a bespoke vehicle like a TIV-2—an eight-ton monster that even a tornado can't get off the ground. Tours run from places such as Denver, into the US's "Tornado Alley." Each storm is different and poses a unique set of thrills and risks—but emerge unscathed, and you'll have a new understanding of nature's power (and hopefully, some great photos).

SKOPELOS, GREECE
## 375. Climb 110 steps to a chapel on a high rock
**When:** All year
**Latitude:** 39.1251°N
**Longitude:** 23.6800°E

The tiny chapel of Agios Ioannis Kastri perches at the top of a 328 ft (100 m) high rock. Reach it via a path of steps cut into the stone, which links it with the island down below. It's a beautiful setting and gives lovely views over the island—and you might recognize it from the *Mamma Mia!* movie.

## 376. Bike through the fabulous fall of Vermont

**When:** Late September to early October (for peak color changes)

**Latitude:** 44.5588°N **Longitude:** 72.5778°W

Vermont is rightly famous for its falls, as its foliage dramatically explodes into a million different hues of orange and red. The best way to bask in these palettes is by bike, and you'll find well-signposted trails for every skill level through this leafy wonderland. Maine and Upstate New York are also spectacular in fall.

▶ CUENCA, SPAIN
## 377. Get vertigo at the hanging houses of Cuenca
**When:** All year
**Latitude:** 40.0703°N **Longitude:** 2.1374°W

Located along the border of the ancient city near the ravine of the river Huécar, these most precarious looking of houses teeter over the mountainous edges, where only hardy residents would lean over their wooden balconies. Only a few of the original examples remain; most are private homes, but if you dare, you can step inside one at the Museo de Arte Abstracto Español ("the Spanish Abstract Art Museum"), which houses an appropriately curious collection of paintings and sculptures.

The hanging houses of Cuenca, Spain

BUKHARA, UZBEKISTAN
## 378. Stroll the medieval streets of a Silk Road stopover
**When:** All year
**Latitude:** 40.0430°N **Longitude:** 64.4448°E

The ancient town of Bukhara was once a crucial stopover on the Silk Road and a major center for Islamic theology and culture during medieval times, second only to Baghdad. Strolling around the citadel's twisting alleyways, with towering mosques topped by emerald-colored onion domes, is a highlight of any trip to Central Asia. This is the region's most complete example of a medieval city.

Visiting isn't only about history and architecture; market stalls overflow with emerald-green ceramics and beautiful crimson carpets, along with handmade robes, silk scarves, and jewelry on this once stopping-off point on the Silk Road.

SAMARKAND, UZBEKISTAN
## 379. Take in amazing Islamic architecture
**When:** All year
**Latitude:** 39.6270°N
**Longitude:** 66.9749°E

One of the oldest inhabited cities in Asia, wealthy from its prime spot on the Silk Road between China and the Mediterranean, this center of Islamic scholarship boasts some of the most incredible buildings anywhere in the world. Be sure to explore the Registan square and Bibi-Khanym Mosque.

▲ SEDONA, ARIZONA, US

## 380. Witness the magnificent Milky Way

**When:** All year
**Latitude:** 34.8697°N **Longitude:** 111.7609°W

The magnificent milky way is best enjoyed in a place like Sedona. It's a stunning part of Arizona, anyway—drawing bikers, hikers, and climbers from all over the globe—but this area is really special after sundown, when all eyes turn upward. They're proud of their lack of light pollution here—it's one of just eight areas worldwide that has been honored by the International Dark-Sky Association, and from 4,600 ft (1,402 km), it is extremely romantic to gaze upon a shimmering sheet of stars here. You could also catch the celestial magic of a "blue moon"—the additional full moon that occasionally appears in an annual cycle. It is always a time of lunar celebration, but at any time of the cycle, a nighttime moon hike into places like Boynton Canyon will provide skies that astonish, often soundtracked by the eerie cry of a pack of coyotes.

The magnificent milky way in Sedona, Arizona, US

COLORADO RIVER, US
## 381. Go whitewater rafting on the Colorado

**When:** May to September
**Latitude:** 34.3388°N **Longitude:** 114.1720°W

The sheer variety of whitewater rafting that Colorado is blessed with means that you can pick your thrill level, like skiers who choose between gentle Danish trails or death-defying black slopes. On the Colorado, you can bubble along on relatively placid waters or thunder down a spill-a-minute stretch of rampaging rapids—and most likely end up in the water at least once. With views like the Grand Canyon often part of the trip, it's a great environment to chill out in once the water cannoning has come to an end.

VALENCIA, SPAIN
## 382. Savor paella in the town of its birth
**When:** All year
**Latitude:** 39.4699°N
**Longitude:** 0.3763°W

Valencia is the undisputed home of paella—but there's no one undisputed recipe for this flavor-packed combination of rice, chicken, beans, vegetables, saffron, and seafood. Find some friends to eat this dish with communally from the pan.

PORTO, PORTUGAL
## 383. Make a triple soccer field–sized quilt
**When:** All year
**Latitude:** 41.1579°N
**Longitude:** 8.6291°W

Quilting is a very relaxing, therapeutic escape, but some people can get a bit carried away with it. In Porto, the gigantic Manta da Cultura ("Patchwork for Culture") measures a massive 270,174 sq ft (25,100 sq m). Maybe just start with a bedspread for now … .

LISBON, PORTUGAL
## 384. Chomp churros in Lisbon
**When:** All year
**Latitude:** 38.7222°N
**Longitude:** 9.1393°W

It's thought that the Portuguese brought churros to Europe from China, and the capital city is still arguably the best place to eat them. Wander through Lisbon's handsome streets with a light, hot, sugarcoated, doughy treat preferably dipped in hot chocolate—to enjoy a decadent start to any day.

▶ VALENCIA, SPAIN
## 385. Join in the madness of Las Fallas
**When:** March 15–19
**Latitude:** 39.4699°N **Longitude:** 0.3763°W

It all started back in the Middle Ages when the carpenters of Valencia celebrated the end of winter by ceremoniously burning the wood that had supported the candles they needed to work in the dark afternoons. The wood—known as "*parots*"—got more and more adorned before they were burned, leading to today's larger-than-life constructions known as "*ninots*," gathered together into "*fallas*" and burned.

Each neighborhood in Valencia constructs its own *falla*, and five days of street parties begin. Firework displays get bigger and better the closer it gets to March 19—"*la nit del foc*," or "the night of fire." This is when the *fallas* are burned. The fires rage in each neighborhood, culminating with the lighting of the final, grandest *falla* at the Plaza Ayuntamiento well after midnight.

It is a noisy, exciting, life-affirming festival that will make you smile for years to come.

The madness of Las Fallas in Valencia, Spain

▶ PUGLIA, ITALY
### 386. Sleep in a trullo
**When:** All year
**Latitude:** 40.7928°N
**Longitude:** 17.1012°E

The traditional buildings in the Puglia region of southern Italy are round with conical stone roofs. They were mainly rural dwellings or storehouses, but many have now been transformed into guesthouses. Spend a night in one of these charming buildings when you visit the area.

Traditional trulli in Puglia, Italy

BUÑOL, SPAIN
### 387. Have a food fight with thousands
**When:** Last Wednesday in August
**Latitude:** 39.4203°N **Longitude:** 0.7901°W

Wouldn't life be simpler if people could just sometimes work out frustrations by chucking fruit in other people's faces? There's a time and a place, obviously, and that is at the brilliantly childish one-day food fight called La Tomatina in the Valencian city of Buñol.

Join thousands of people who come from all over the globe for this gastronomical battle, where it's every man for himself. It's a very messy affair, so be sure to come prepared, preferably not dressed in your newest white outfit!

MATERA, BASILICATA, ITALY
### 388. Visit the troglodyte settlement of Matera
**When:** All year
**Latitude:** 40.6667°N **Longitude:** 16.6000°E

No other city in Italy evokes such wonder and awe as Matera, a troglodyte settlement whose inhabitants to this day live in cave dwellings. Wandering around the town's twisting stone alleyways will make you feel like you've stepped into a *Flintstones* movie. Pickaxes were once used to dig into stone, resulting in a unique jumble of winding steps, uneven roofs and wonky sidewalks. For the full experience, splurge on a cave hotel for a night or two.

ARIZONA, US
## 389. Hike to the bottom of the Grand Canyon and back up again
**When:** Spring and fall are ideal
**Latitude:** 36.0544°N **Longitude:** 112.1401°W

It is one of Earth's most impressive geological formations, hewn into shape over millennia by the Colorado River, and it's easy to see why the Grand Canyon is considered a holy site by the Native American people. It's also the ultimate place to hike. The spectacular views go without saying—this is a true wonder of the world—but there's so much more to learn about the canyon during a stroll through it; it may look arid, for example, but there are 1,737 known different species of vascular plants to look out for.

The classic hike is the rim-to-the-river-and-back trip, which must always involve an overnight stay. A full descent involves setting off from an elevation of around 10,000 ft (3,048 m) and carefully winding down the trails. It can be bone jarring, but the sense of solitude, wilderness, and silence you experience makes any aches or pains worthwhile.

The ever-changing environment as you descend into the canyon is a truly great pleasure. And there are many types of animals to spot, including bald eagles, beavers, coyotes, bobcats, tarantulas, six kinds of rattlesnakes, and even mountain lions (that, thankfully, tend to stay well away from humans).

After staying overnight in the canyon (many head to Phantom Ranch), the return trip—uphill—is far more demanding than the descent. Any hike in the Grand Canyon should be very carefully planned, and most people report that they found it more difficult than they had first expected. More than 250 people are rescued annually!

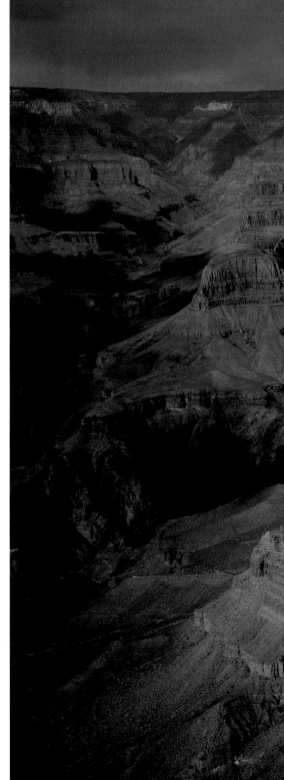

The top of the Grand Canyon in Arizona, US

CALIFORNIA, US
### 390. Rove through giant redwood trees
**When:** All year
**Latitude:** 36.1304°N
**Longitude:** 118.8179°W

Giant redwood trees are quite simply the largest living things on Earth—they can age up to 3,500 years old and reach up to 328 ft (100 m) high. Gawp at their majestic stature on a drive through the Big Basin Redwoods State Park or the Giant Sequoia National Monument.

ST. CHARLES TO PACIFIC COAST, US
### 391. Follow in the footsteps of Lewis and Clark
**When:** All year
**Latitude:** 38.7887°N **Longitude:** 90.5118°W

Captain Meriwether Lewis and Second Lieutenant William Clark set off on an expedition in 1804 from St. Charles to the Pacific Coast and back, covering 8,000 mi (12,875 km) in two years, four months, and ten days. Their exploits inspired explorers, traders, prospectors, and homesteaders to move to the West themselves, opening the country up for development and subsequent prosperity.

To enjoy the true spirit of Lewis and Clark, and in the name of adventure and discovery, dust off the hiking shoes, oil that bike, and find a life jacket for a spot of hiking, biking, canoeing, and rafting. Whether a high-spirited adventurer, keen botanist, zoologist, or historian, following in the footsteps of such intrepid explorers is an awe-inspiring experience.

▶ WASHINGTON, D.C., US
### 392. Write that novel that you know is in you
**When:** All year
**Latitude:** 38.9072°N
**Longitude:** 77.0369°E

Everyone has a novel in them. To provide the inspiration to complete the arduous journey from blank page to bookshop, arrange a visit to the Library of Congress in the US capital. The 38 million volumes in the world's largest library include 6,487 books belonging to President Thomas Jefferson.

Inside the Library of Congress, Washington, D.C., US

▶ LONG ISLAND, NEW YORK, US
## 393. Head to the Hamptons

**When:** All year
**Latitude:** 40.7891°N
**Longitude:** 73.1349°W

Want to experience summer like a wealthy New Yorker? Then head to the east end of Long Island. Here, a group of perfectly manicured villages and hamlets around Southampton and East Hampton collectively constitute the Hamptons. This contains the most expensive zip code in the US, and many of New York City's richest residents have summer homes here. Walk around the shore at Sag Harbor and admire the yachts bobbing in the sea while you fantasize about how Manhattan's genuine bigwigs live.

East Hampton Beach, Long Island, New York, US

WASHINGTON, D.C., US
## 394. Tour the Washington memorials

**When:** All year
**Latitude:** 38.9071°N  **Longitude:** 77.0368°E

If you want to really understand the United States, head to the capital, where an unrivaled collection of monuments, museums, and working government buildings reveal the country's fascinating past and present.

It'd take nearly a week to visit even just the headline attractions here, but the must-see sights to marvel at include the Capitol building and White House; the imposing, Henry Bacon–designed Lincoln Memorial; the moving Vietnam Veterans Memorial; the giant obelisk of the Washington Monument; and the National World War II Memorial.

There are a dozen more monuments of great significance, too: add in the Smithsonian American Art Museum, and National Air and Space Museum.

NEW MEXICO, US
## 395. Watch bats swarm out of a cave

**When:** April to November
**Latitude:** 32.1517°N
**Longitude:** 104.5558°W

Nestled deep in the Guadalupe Mountains, Carlsbad's dramatic caves include the dramatic retreat that is home to nearly 800,000 Mexican free-tailed bats. See them emerge and corkscrew thrillingly out of their home on summer evenings for around three hours. Not one for chiroptophobes.

► UTAH, US, AND WORLDWIDE
## 396. Learn to ride a unicycle

**When:** All year
**Latitude:** 38.5733°N
**Longitude:** 109.5438°W (Moab, Utah)

Learning to ride a cycle with one wheel rather than two is a huge amount of fun and can usually be achieved in a week. There's the childlike joy of learning to ride (and fall off) effectively that most people won't have experienced since they were kids themselves, and it's also very good for the posture. While not a great commuting option (it's not legal to ride one on a road), unicycles are light, small, easy to maintain, and can be taken on public transport.

Riding a unicycle in Moab, Utah, US

UTAH, US
## 397. Inspect God's stonemasonry at Arches National Park

**When:** All year
**Latitude:** 38.7330°N **Longitude:** 109.5925°W

"God is a stonemason," they like to say locally, and walking beneath the majestic natural arches, spires, and pinnacles that have been hewn from the rock in this national park in Utah, it's hard not to believe they're right. You can hike or ride a mountain bike around the 73,000 ac (29,542 ha) of arches, with sunrise and sunset especially magical times as radiance fills the sandstone crags and illuminates incredible horizons. There are 2,000 arches, the most famous of which is Landscape Arch—a 306 ft (93 m) whopper that has to be seen to be believed.

NEAR CORTEZ, COLORADO, US
## 398. Stand in four US states at the same time

**When:** All year
**Latitude:** 36.9990°N
**Longitude:** 109.0452°W

Four Corners Monument—where Utah, Colorado, New Mexico, and Arizona meet—is the only place in the United States where you can stand in all four states at the same time. Photographs of straddling, on-all-fours poses on the monument are practically compulsory, so get snapping.

▼ MONUMENT VALLEY, UTAH, US
## 399. Put yourself in the heart of the Wild West
**When:** All year
**Latitude:** 37.0042°N
**Longitude:** 110.1735°W

Discover the heartland of American and Navajo folklore with a 17 mi (27 km) road trip through the Wild West of John Wayne and John Ford, complete with striking sandstone spires, mesas, and buttes soaring 1,000 ft (305 m) from the desert floor. Don't forget to pack your spurs.

US AND WORLDWIDE
## 400. Lose all sense of time in a solar eclipse
**When:** Look out for the next eclipse where you live
**Latitude:** 36.8656°N
**Longitude:** 87.4886°W (Hopkinsville, Kentucky, for 2017 eclipse)

As the moon starts to move across the sun, arm yourself with a pinhole camera, welding glass, or a special astronomer's filter. There's a spiritual element to witnessing something as natural yet phenomenal as a solar eclipse.

AREA 51, NEVADA, US
## 401. Go alien hunting
**When:** All year
**Latitude:** 37.2350°N
**Longitude:** 115.8111°W

There is no guarantee a trip to the heartland of Earth's extraterrestrial activity will result in alien sightings, but a visit here is a unique experience. You can enjoy Area 51 on a kitsch level—travel along Extraterrestrial Highway before stopping off for an alien burger and a peek at the Black Mailbox of rancher Steve Medlin, which has become the unofficial meeting point for UFO enthusiasts.

Rock formation in the heart of the Wild West in Utah, US

COYOTE BUTTES, ARIZONA, US

## 402. Ride "the Wave" in a red, rocky canyon

**When:** All year
**Latitude:** 37.0016°N **Longitude:** 111.8657°W

It's hard to believe that the sweeping, red-rock formation of Paria Canyon ("the Wave") is naturally formed, such is the designed appearance of its undulating, surreal stripes. It has been carved out by a kind of wave-making machine, however, as first water, and then wind, steadily altered the ancient Jurassic-era sandstone into the mind-blowing formations seen today. If you're lucky enough to get a permit, it's worth every second of the three-hour hike to get there. Go midday when few shadows fall for the ultimate bucket list photography shoot.

THE GREAT PLAINS, US
## 403. See tumbleweed roll on the Great Plains
**When:** All year
**Latitude:** 38.0168°N
**Longitude:** 81.1218°W (Appalachian plateau)

A huge expanse of prairie, the Great Plains span an immense swathe of the central US (including Colorado, Kansas, Montana, Nebraska, New Mexico, the Dakotas, Oklahoma, Texas, and Wyoming). Think of the pioneers as you gaze at the horizon, with tumbleweed rolling through, punctuating a quiet moment.

START AT YOSEMITE, US
## 404. Trek the John Muir trail
**When:** July to September
**Latitude:** 37.8651°N
**Longitude:** 119.5383°W

Trek the US's most famous trail, named after the Scottish naturalist. It's a wonder-inspiring jaunt into the wilderness: 210 mi (338 km) of solitude that passes from the Yosemite, through Kings Canyon and Sequoia National Parks, to Mount Whitney, capturing many of the highlights of the spectacular Sierra Nevada mountain range.

CALIFORNIA, US
## 405. Float like an astronaut
**When:** All year
**Latitude:** 37.7833°N
**Longitude:** 122.4167°W (San Francisco)

The Zero Gravity Corporation offers public flights that, through a serious of acrobatic maneuvers, allow passengers to experience weightlessness. Float and flip like an astronaut aboard one of the planes that takes off from various locations, including San Francisco.

▶ CALIFORNIA, US
## 406. Hang out in a hammock tent
**When:** All year
**Latitude:** 37.8651°N
**Longitude:** 119.5383°W

It's hard to come back down to Earth once you've made like a bird and tried hammock camping between the branches of a tree or on a rock face. For the ultimate thrill, hang out in a suspended portaledge on Yosemite National Park's El Capitan.

A hammock tent suspended in midair

► SAN FRANCISCO, CALIFORNIA, US
### 407. Get slammed up in Alcatraz
**When:** Summer
**Latitude:** 37.8269°N
**Longitude:** 122.4229°W

The threat of spending the night in Alcatraz used to be enough to send a shiver down the spine of the most hardened criminal. Now a popular tourist attraction, it's possible to sleep in a cell—although only 600 people get the chance per year, thanks to the charity Friends of the Golden Gate. Spots are given out by lottery. If you're lucky enough to get picked, you'll bunk up on a small bed in spooky, atmospheric conditions.

Alcatraz in San Francisco, California, US

SAN FRANCISCO, CALIFORNIA, US
### 408. Wind up (or down) Lombard Street
**When:** All year
**Latitude:** 37.8010°N
**Longitude:** 122.4262°W

Beautiful to look at, fiendish to drive with its tight, snaking bends, Lombard Street is one of the most cinematic streets in the United States. You'll have time to see and smell its fabulous flower beds when in season, as the street's eight hairpins require a 5 mph (8 kph) speed limit.

MONTEREY, CALIFORNIA, US
### 409. Go deep at the Monterey Bay Aquarium
**When:** All year
**Latitude:** 36.6002°N
**Longitude:** 121.8946°W

Experience the combination of an unrivaled Pacific Coast location and incredible exhibits—including great whites, sea otters, bluefin and yellow tuna, stingrays, and penguins—which make this one of the most visited and fun attractions in the United States. Its exhibits about its former Cannery Row location are fascinating too.

JAMESTOWN, CALIFORNIA, US
### 410. Have a go at panning for gold
**When:** All year
**Latitude:** 37.9532°N
**Longitude:** 120.4226°W

Try your hand at a simple process that's been used since Roman days and that prompted the famous Gold Rush of the mid-nineteenth century. At places like Jamestown, gold-panning prospectors can still use a basic pan and experience the thrill of potentially striking it rich.

GOLDFIELD, NEVADA, US
### 411. See the International Car Forest of the Last Church
**When:** All year
**Latitude:** 37.7086°N **Longitude:** 117.2356°W

Formerly resident to infamous lawmen Wyatt and Virgil Earp, Goldfield, Nevada, is now home to a postapocalyptic skyline of forty or so upended cars, trucks, buses, and even an ice-cream truck. The unusual artwork is meant to represent individuality and the renouncement of organized religion; however, equally, it's just a vibrant, thought-provoking place to stop amid a sea of brown desert along Highway 95.

SAN JOSE, CALIFORNIA, US
### 412. Learn to write code in Silicon Valley
**When:** All year
**Latitude:** 37.3382°N
**Longitude:** 121.8863°W

The geeks have inherited Earth, with those early coders now running massive tech giants like Facebook, Google, and Amazon. Learn code in San Jose, the epicenter of the new-media economy, which can be done at the public library or a "coding boot camp," in preparation for becoming a tech billionaire.

COLORADO, US
### 413. Steam through Colorado in style
**When:** May to October
**Latitude:** 37.2753°N
**Longitude:** 107.8801°W (Durango)

Built to move silver and gold ore out of the San Juan Mountains, the Durango to Silverton steam railway has been running since 1882. Take a trip on its vintage steam locomotives 45 mi (72 km) through glacier-carved valleys, narrow canyon ledges, and dense forest in the San Juan Mountains.

## 414. Bicycle over the Golden Gate Bridge

**When:** Spring to fall
**Latitude:** 37.8197°N **Longitude:** 122.4785°W

A perfect day: rent a bike at Fisherman's Wharf, pedal leisurely along the handsome shore and across the iconic bridge, savoring the views of the bay along the way. On the other side, Sausalito is a picturesque, arty enclave to eat lunch at—and the boat ride back is a real pleasure, too.

CALIFORNIA, US
### 415. Hike through a rainbow of wildflowers

**When:** Blooming time March to April
(check wildflower updates)
**Latitude:** 35.3252°N
**Longitude:** 119.8000°W

In spring, near California's Temblor
Range, it can look as if someone
spilled paint over the hills and
valleys, such is the abundance of
yellow, pink, purple, orange, and
blue wildflowers on display,
providing a feast of kaleidoscopic
color and delicious layers of scent
to those lucky enough to witness it.
"Somewhere over the Rainbow"
comes to mind … .

It is often said that the Carrizo
Plain National Monument, of which
the Temblor Range forms the eastern
boundary, is reminiscent of what
California's Great Central Valley
used to be before agriculture moved
in. Hopefully, Temblor's wildflower
display will remain a wildlife haven
for many more years to come.

A rainbow of wildflowers in the
Temblor mountains, California, US

**209**

▶ GRANADA, SPAIN
### 416. Ride the Sierra Nevada by mountain bike
**When:** Summer
**Latitude:** 37.0931°N
**Longitude:** 3.3952°W

A popular ski resort in winter, during the warmer months this descent becomes one of the ultimate destinations for mountain bikers. Choose from up to 19 mi (30 km) of different marked trails—catering to novices or daredevils—and whiz down for an exhilarating, blood-pumping experience.

Riding the Sierra Nevada by mountain bike in Granada, Spain

GENALGUACIL, ANDALUSIA, SPAIN
### 417. Sleep in a yurt
**When:** May to October
**Latitude:** 36.5500°N
**Longitude:** 5.2333°W

Yurts—round, single-room tents—have been at the forefront of the glamping movement for a while, bringing glamour to camping. Experience a night in one at the Rio Genal Valley: the stunning comforts inside the canvas perfectly match the equally impressive location outside.

LANJARÓN, SPAIN
### 418. Get soaked at a water fight
**When:** June 23
**Latitude:** 36.9187°N
**Longitude:** 3.4795°W

Get drenched in the annual "water festival" at Lanjarón, where a gigantic midnight battle involves water pistols, buckets, and balloons!

GRANADA, SPAIN
### 419. Storm the fortresses at the Alhambra
**When:** All year
**Latitude:** 37.1760°N
**Longitude:** 3.5882°W

Literally meaning "the Red One," this enigmatic and otherworldly palace and fortress complex, established by Romans but rebuilt by the Moors, is one of the best examples of Islamic architecture anywhere. Explore this wonder and you'll soon understand why it's known as a "pearl set in emeralds."

CAPPADOCIA, TURKEY
## 420. Hot-air balloon over unique rock formations
**When:** All year
**Latitude:** 38.6459°N **Longitude:** 34.8424°E

There are numerous ways to describe the extraordinary geology of Cappadocia, with its ridged, layered valleys, fairy chimneys, honeycomb hills, and towering volcanic boulders. Hot-air ballooning over its landscape is a mind-blowing experience. Touching the clouds, you can gaze upon the multicolored strata and imagine you're in your own private Narnia. Most balloon flights leave very early (around 5 a.m. or 6 a.m.) to capitalize on the gorgeous sunrises, last around an hour, and drift over the soft stone with amazing churches and museums cut into the rock.

**421.** Wander back in time at the Acropolis

**When:** All year
**Latitude:** 37.9713°N
**Longitude:** 23.7260°E

The jewel of ancient Greece, nestled on a high outcrop overlooking Athens, is a site of both great beauty and massive historical significance. You can fantasize about the glorious classical era as you're engulfed by the Parthenon, Propylaia, Erqchtheion, and Temple of Athena Nike.

ARKADIKO BRIDGE, GREECE
## 422. Cross the world's oldest bridge
**When:** All year
**Latitude:** 37.5908°N
**Longitude:** 22.8267°E

Walk over the Arkadiko Bridge in Argolis, Greece, which was built in a time even before the ancient Greeks—it has been walked over for around 3,300 years. Its one arch is constructed from large rocks with no mortar binding them.

ITHACA, IONIAN ISLANDS, GREECE
## 423. Be a mentor to someone
**When:** All year (but best during the summer months of May to September)
**Latitude:** 38.4285°N
**Longitude:** 20.6765°E

Fancy following an ancient Greek tradition and becoming a mentor? Then head to the relaxing Greek holiday island of Ithaca for inspiration. According to Homer's *Odyssey*, Mentor served as teacher, counselor, and protector to Telemachus, son of the island's king. Mentor's name has become synonymous with offering guidance ever since.

PALERMO, SICILY, ITALY
## 424. Walk among the real-life dead
**When:** All year
**Latitude:** 38.1120°N
**Longitude:** 13.3410°E

The Capuchin Catacombs of Palermo, Italy, is home to the largest collection of mummies in the world. Walk through this eerie vault, which is both bizarre and creepy, and where rows of tailored and terrifyingly expressive mummies lean in toward you.

GÖREME, TURKEY
## 425. Wake up in a rock cave
**When:** All year
**Latitude:** 38.6431°N
**Longitude:** 34.8289°E

The Cappadocia region of Turkey is famed for its hoodoos—houses created in the otherworldly "fairy chimney" rock formations. At Göreme you can stay in a cave hotel, experiencing all the beauty of this ancient architecture, brought up to date with wifi and en suites.

DENIZLI PROVINCE, TURKEY
## 426. Feel like royalty in Pamukkale's hot baths
**When:** All year (spectacular in winter)
**Latitude:** 37.9186°N
**Longitude:** 29.1103°E

For an ethereal experience, bathe in these pools full of restorative minerals, with temperatures of up to 96°F (36°C). It's an awe-inspiring limestone wonder, hewn over millennia—"pamukkale" means "cotton castle," and does indeed have a soothing, fluffy feel to it.

KONYA, TURKEY
## 427. Witness the Whirling Dervishes
**When:** Saturday evenings
**Latitude:** 37.8667°N
**Longitude:** 32.4833°E

Whirling Dervishes is the name given to Sufi practitioners who use the ancient art of spinning to reach a meditative state of religious ecstasy. Witness their spellbinding dances in Konya, Turkey, where the practice began in the thirteenth century.

The world's highest motorway: Khunjerab Pass at the China–Pakistan border

KHUNJERAB PASS, CHINA–PAKISTAN BORDER

## 428. Drive the world's highest motorway

**When:** Spring or early fall

**Latitude:** 36.8500°N **Longitude:** 75.4278°E

The Karakoram Highway connects China and Pakistan at Khunjerab Pass in the Karakoram mountain range—it is the highest point on the route. Running from Kashgar in China to Abbottabad in Pakistan, the 800 mi (1,288 km) highway comes highly ranked on any list of the world's most dangerous roads. The road was never able to be perfected due to the incredibly dangerous conditions in which it was made: flash floods and landslides meant that more than 1,000 workers lost their lives in the twenty-five years it took to construct it.

Spring or early fall is the best time to travel, and a 4x4 would be recommended. Twists and turns abound on this road edged by an unforgiving rock face on one side, and crumbling into oblivion below on the other. It all makes for some serious driving challenges.

So why travel it? Well, only eight mountains in the world reach heights of more than 26,000 ft (7,925 m)—and five of them are accessible from this highway.

KESERWAN, LEBANON
## 429. Explore a captivating underground world

**When:** All year (closed on Fridays and Saturdays)
**Latitude:** 33.9438°N
**Longitude:** 35.6399°E

A short drive from Beirut, the 5.6 mi (9 km) interconnected limestone caves of Jeita Grotto are the longest in the Middle East and are jam-packed with eye-popping rock formations. Wonder at the 27 ft (8 m) long stalactite; the lower cave is accessible only by an otherworldly boat cruise.

ISPARTA, TURKEY
## 430. Eat an apple straight from the tree

**When:** September to October
**Latitude:** 37.7647°N
**Longitude:** 30.5567°E

All fruit tastes better the fresher it is when eaten, but none more so than the apple, with its satisfying crunch, deliciously fragrant juices, and gentle aroma. Pick, polish, and bite for one of life's true, simple pleasures that everyone should savor. As Turkey is the world's third most prolific producer of apples, it's a good place to eat one, straight from the tree.

FETHIYE TO ANTALYA, TURKEY
## 431. Trek through Turkey on the Lycian Way

**When:** Spring (February to May) or fall (September to November)
**Latitude:** 36.6592°N
**Longitude:** 29.1263°E

If you're up for a challenge, the 316 mi (509 km) Lycian Way is one of Asia's most breathtaking footpaths. It's a hard, stony limestone trail that takes in numerous, splendid sites, from the paragliders at Babadağ to the 11 mi (18 km) Patara Beach, the castle of Üçağiz to the lighthouse at Cape Gelidonya (where you can stay), and Mounts Olympos and Felen, which you can ascend. Be warned, the path gets more difficult as it progresses.

YANARTAŞ, NEAR ÇIRALI, TURKEY
## 432. Watch fire emerge from a mountain

**When:** All year (best at night)
**Latitude:** 36.4030°N
**Longitude:** 30.4710°E

Head along to this mountainside in the Olympos valley, where small fires constantly spring up and burn. It is the result of gases escaping through vents and has been happening for thousands of years. It could even have been the origin for the Chimera, the creature from Greek mythology.

ANATOLIA, TURKEY
## 433. Dig into history at Göbekli Tepe

**When:** All year
**Latitude:** 37.2170°N
**Longitude:** 38.8542°E

An archeologist's dream, Göbekli Tepe is mind-bogglingly ancient: it is thought to be the oldest site of a temple on Earth, possibly dating back to the tenth century BC. Visit this thought-provoking site to ponder mankind's development while it is still being unearthed and learned about.

SANTORINI, GREECE
## 434. Smash a plate at a Greek wedding

**When:** All year
**Latitude:** 36.3931°N
**Longitude:** 25.4615°E

The tradition of plate smashing may have come about from weddings of the well-off—rich hosts invited guests to break plates to show them friendship was more important than wealth. Head to the small volcanic island of Santorini, the self-styled island of romance, to give it a go.

NEAR FETHIYE, TURKEY
## 435. Jump off Babadağ Mountain and fly onto the beach
**When:** Spring and summer
**Latitude:** 36.5282°N **Longitude:** 29.1849°E

It's hard to know which is the more terrifying: the trip to the top of the mountain—which is undertaken in a swiftly driven, open-sided vehicle with sheer drops down the side of the roads—or the paragliding jump itself, which involves running at full speed off the edge of a 6,460 ft (1,969 m) peak. Either way, this is one for the more adventurous bucket lister, but the rewards are manifold.

Babadağ is a stunning mountain overlooking the glinting blue bay of Ölüdeniz. The summit's 3 mi (5 km) distance from the sea makes the landing and flying conditions perfect for the sport. Amateurs can enjoy the thrill of descending with a fully trained pilot—although the real thrill comes in the views. You'll see the nearby city of Fethiye, the aquamarine Blue Lagoon, and gradually, the golden sands of Ölüdeniz. The activity will leave you feeling utterly invigorated by the closest thing to flight a human can experience.

Jumping off Babadağ Mountain near Fethiye, Turkey

OIA, SANTORINI, GREECE

## 436. Sit back and enjoy a stunning sunset view

**When:** May to September
**Latitude:** 36.4618°N **Longitude:** 25.3753°E

Drink in the immense sight of the horizon turning a deep pink and orange as lights twinkle in the jumble of whitewashed buildings clinging prettily to the hillside. There may be more dramatic sunsets than the ones in this postcard-perfect village, but they've yet to be found.

ICHEON, SOUTH KOREA
### 437. Drink a tipple that you've never heard of
**When:** All year
**Latitude:** 37.2719°N
**Longitude:** 127.4348°E

Global sales of Jinro Soju, a Korean rice wine, are three times that of its nearest rival, Smirnoff vodka. Tour the factory in Icheon, where the factory produces 5 million bottles of soju ("fire water") every day.

SEOUL, SOUTH KOREA
### 438. Shop at a virtual supermarket
**When:** All year
**Latitude:** 37.5045°N
**Longitude:** 127.0490°E

A subway station may seem like an unlikely location for the world's first virtual supermarket, but busy commuters in Seoul have been using their phones to scan and order goods from the virtual display of products shown on Seolleung Station's walls since 2011. What will you order off the wall?

ANDALUSIA, SPAIN
### 439. Delve into the world of flamenco dancing
**When:** All year
**Latitude:** 37.5442°N
**Longitude:** 4.7277°W

Finger clicking, foot stomping, hand clapping, dress swirling, and wild guitars—there's so much to love about a flamenco dance! Experience all the passion and drama, color and vibrancy, of a true night of theater.

POHANG, SOUTH KOREA
### 440. Light up the night sky
**When:** End of July to the beginning of August
**Latitude:** 36.0322°N **Longitude:** 129.3650°E

Every summer, Bukbu Beach in Pohang is the location of South Korea's Seoul International Fireworks Festival. Every night for more than a week, the dark sky over Yeongildae Beach is lit up with the very best firework displays from across the world. No wonder it is known as the "City of Light and Fire." Head to the beach at 9 p.m. to see the action. Then head to various other locations around the city the next day to join in all the other activities on offer at the festival.

▶ START AT MYKONOS, GREECE
### 441. Sail around the Greek islands
**When:** Spring to fall
**Latitude:** 37.4467°N **Longitude:** 25.3288°E

See the Greek islands by boat for an experience you'll never forget: a warm breeze on the face, a sip of retsina, leaping into crystal-clear waters from the deck, the soul-enriching sense of isolation—despite this being one of the most popular tourist regions anywhere. The sheer volume and proximity of the country's 6,000 different landmasses means no two visits will be the same, and it's quite easy to stop off somewhere completely isolated and have a private beach for the afternoon.

Sailing around the Greek islands

DEATH VALLEY NATIONAL PARK, CALIFORNIA, US
## 442. Spend a night in the hottest place on Earth
**When:** October to April (open all year, but too hot for most visitors in summer months)
**Latitude:** 36.2469°N **Longitude:** 116.8169°W

Spending the night somewhere comparable to the imagined temperature of hell may not at first seem like a must-do experience, but Death Valley in eastern California offers some of the most stunning, varied, and occasionally dangerous areas of natural beauty in the world. An amateur photographer's dream come true, the 200 sq mi (518 sq km) of corrosive saltwater flats at Badwater Basin offer a less traditional sunrise experience, while the sand dunes outside Stovepipe Wells are romantic in their rolling allure. Experience the most colorful sunset at Zabriskie Point, dusk at Artist's Drive, and lie under the stars at Dante's Point.

MONUMENT VALLEY, UTAH–ARIZONA, US
## 443. Gallop a horse like a "real" cowboy
**When:** All year
**Latitude:** 37.0042°N **Longitude:** 110.1734°W

If it's good enough for John Wayne, it's good enough to go on the cowboy fantasist's bucket list. Monument Valley is a Western come to life; characterized by those vast sandstone buttes, its 2 sq mi (5 sq km) are as familiar to most moviegoers as Manhattan. Get on horseback with a tour guide—and optional ten-gallon hat—and it's frankly impossible not to have a private, little cinematic moment.

SEWARD, NEBRASKA, US
## 444. Bury a time capsule
**When:** All year
**Latitude:** 40.9111°N
**Longitude:** 97.0969°W

Take inspiration from Nebraskan grandpa Harold Keith Davisson and fill your time capsule with something a little more unusual than photos and a diary. In 1975 he buried a giant capsule filled with 5,000 items, including a brand-new Chevy Vega car. The capsule in Seward is due to be opened on July 4, 2025, a poignant date, as the city is known for its large and lavish annual Fourth of July celebrations, which attracts tens of thousands of visitors.

NASHVILLE, TENNESSEE, US
## 445. Take in Nashville's eclectic music scene
**When:** All year
**Latitude:** 36.1667°N **Longitude:** 86.7833°W

Nashville is home to rhinestone cowboys Dolly, Kenny, Patsy, and Shania, to name a few. But the so-called "Music City, USA" isn't just about wailing women bemoaning the loss of their man, and men lamenting the loss of a good woman. Nashville is first and foremost about music. Since the 1960s, the city is second only to New York in terms of music production. All the "Big Four" record labels have offices in Nashville, and Gibson guitars have called it home since 1984. This is where Jimi Hendrix cut his teeth, where Bob Dylan recorded *Blonde on Blonde*, and where everyone from Robert Plant to The Black Eyed Peas have come to write. Bluegrass for breakfast, Americana for lunch, honky-tonk blues for dinner, followed by an aperitif of country twangs, music engulfs the city. The avenues are littered with buskers of the kind that beggars belief they don't have a recording contract they're so good.

The dancing Bellagio fountains in Las Vegas, Nevada, US

AUGUSTA, GEORGIA, US
### 446. Master your swing on a national course
**When:** All year (most beautiful in spring)
**Latitude:** 33.4734°N
**Longitude:** 82.0105°W

To take a swing around the impeccably groomed, but fiendishly difficult, Augusta National Golf Club is the golfing dream. Home to the US Masters every year—the only major tournament held at the same location—each hole is named after a tree or shrub, and the flora and fauna found around the course are a botanist's delight, so players can keep a smile on their faces, even if they're hitting a lot of balls into the water.

▲ LAS VEGAS, NEVADA, US
### 447. See the dancing Bellagio fountains
**When:** All year
**Latitude:** 36.1699°N
**Longitude:** 115.1398°W

When in Vegas, you must witness this spectacular son et lumière show, which is one of Sin City's most enduring attractions. The magnificently choreographed water feature outside one of Vegas' most glam casinos leaps 1,000 ft (305 m) into life, perfectly choreographed to classical, operatic, and Sinatra-style musical favorites.

LAS VEGAS, NEVADA, US
### 448. Bet it all on black
**When:** All year
**Latitude:** 36.1214°N
**Longitude:** 115.1689°W

Step onto the Las Vegas Strip, where 4 mi (6 km) of casinos wait to part you from your money, and there are hotels to take your breath away. They are like nowhere else on Earth, in every style from Gothic to Venetian (with canals and gondolas) to an Egyptian pyramid. Immense!

APACHE COUNTRY, ARIZONA, US

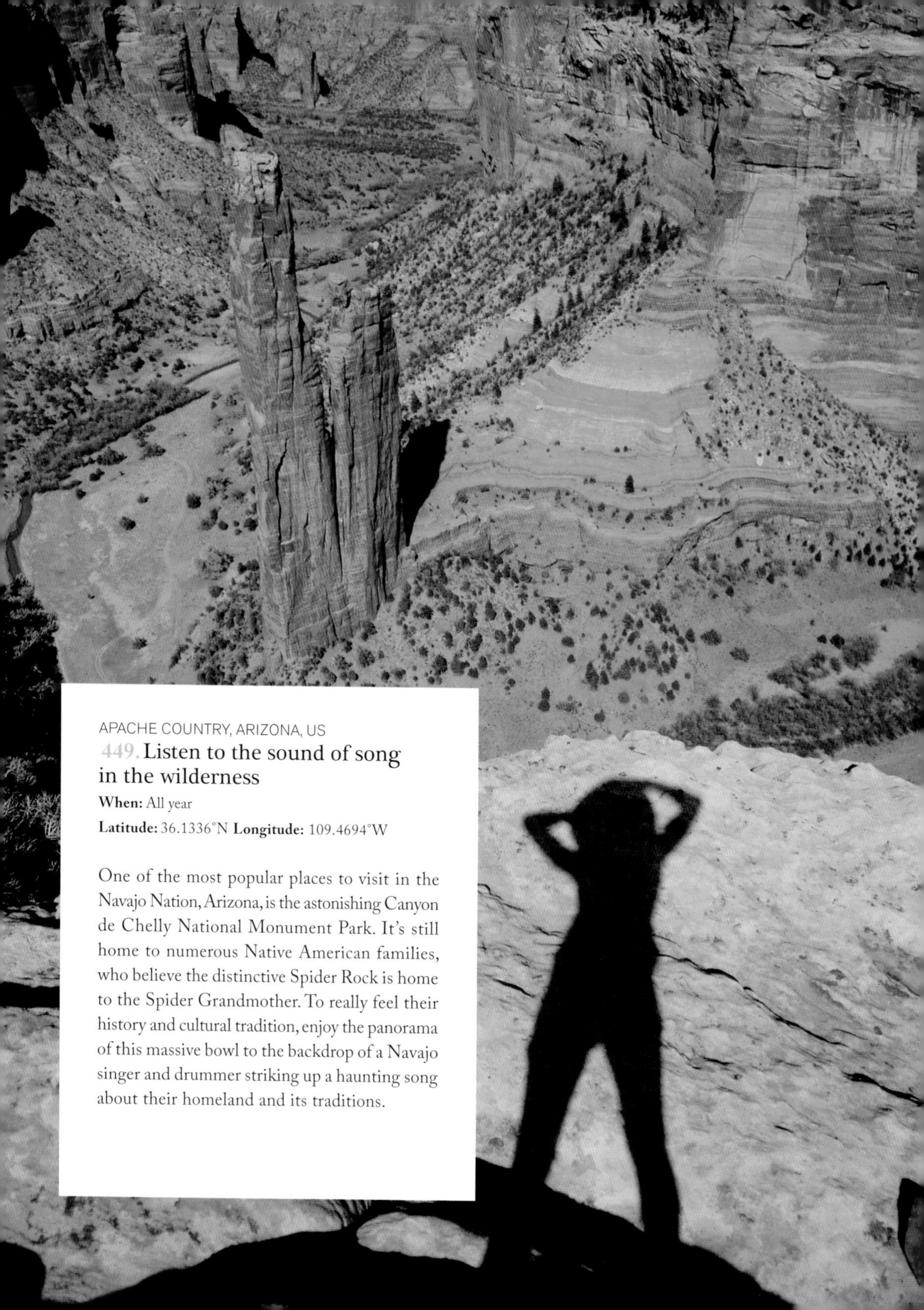

## 449. Listen to the sound of song in the wilderness

**When:** All year

**Latitude:** 36.1336°N **Longitude:** 109.4694°W

One of the most popular places to visit in the Navajo Nation, Arizona, is the astonishing Canyon de Chelly National Monument Park. It's still home to numerous Native American families, who believe the distinctive Spider Rock is home to the Spider Grandmother. To really feel their history and cultural tradition, enjoy the panorama of this massive bowl to the backdrop of a Navajo singer and drummer striking up a haunting song about their homeland and its traditions.

▶ LAS VEGAS, NEVADA, US

## 450. Experience steel between your legs

**When:** All year

**Latitude:** 36.1699°N **Longitude:** 115.1398°W

Las Vegas may be synonymous with roulette wheels, blackjack tables, and glitzy shows by singers worthy of single-name recognition—Celine, Britney, Elton—but it's also home to swinging upside down from a metal pole. Pole dancing has experienced a surge in popularity thanks to being a liberating and sexy way to get fit. To bust a few myths, men can do pole dancing; skin is exposed, but for reasons of grip and not titillation; and advancing years is not a reason to shy away—just watch Greta Pontarelli, a champion at age sixty-three. So why not give it a go?

Pole dancing in Las Vegas, Nevada, US

ALL OVER SANTA FE, US

## 451. Soak up the culture in a US capital

**When:** All year

**Latitude:** 35.6870°N

**Longitude:** 105.9378°W

Arguably the most "artsy" city in the United States, the New Mexico capital wears its creativity with pride. It was the home of Georgia O'Keeffe, the "mother of American modernism," and many of her works are on show around the city. When you visit, be sure to go down gallery-laden Canyon Road, the city's beating heart.

NORTH CAROLINA–TENNESSEE, US

## 452. See fireflies in a national park

**When:** Late May to mid-June

**Latitude:** 35.3964°N

**Longitude:** 83.2041°W

Catch one of the highlights of the most visited national parks in the United States: the Great Smoky Mountains National Park at the North Carolina–Tennessee border. Among its mesmerizing fauna, famous synchronous fireflies flash simultaneously en masse for two weeks every year in an attempt to attract a mate.

NASHVILLE, TENNESSEE, US

## 453. Learn to play a song on the harmonica

**When:** All year

**Latitude:** 36.1626°N

**Longitude:** 86.7816°W

The Deep South and its music are inseparable, with gospel, blues, and country traditions that run deep. "Amazing Grace" is a hymn and gospel standard beloved of the area, so why not pick up a harmonica in one of the numerous music shops and learn how to play a tune?

▶ GANSU, CHINA
### 454. Walk in the colorful Zhangye Danxia

**When:** All year
**Latitude:** 38.9252°N
**Longitude:** 100.1331°E

Depicted in numerous paintings for their extraordinary pastel colors, it's impossible to believe that the artistic interpretations are true until you actually lay your eyes on the Zhangye Danxia mountains. They inherit their striking colors from the different rock formations and sandstone deposits going back around 24 million years. Take a daylong hike through this photogenic place, and you'll find that no two towers, pillars, or ravines are the same shape or shade.

BEIJING, CHINA
### 455. Step inside the Forbidden City

**When:** All year
**Latitude:** 39.9159°N
**Longitude:** 116.3979°E

For 500 years after its construction in 1420, no one could enter or leave the Chinese imperial palace in Beijing without the express permission of the emperor, earning it the nickname "the Forbidden City." In stark contrast, today it is the most visited museum in the world, so be sure to pop inside when you're in China's capital.

The colorful Zhangye Danxia in Gansu, China

Madrid's legendary Mercado de San Miguel, Spain

▲ MADRID, SPAIN

### 456. Have breakfast at Madrid's mercado

**When:** All year
**Latitude:** 40.4153°N
**Longitude:** 3.7089°W

Perhaps the best market on Earth to turn up to with an empty stomach, the centrally located Mercado de San Miguel is a Madrid favorite and a huge gourmet tapas experience. Take your pick from thirty-three stalls, which vend world-class meats, olives, oysters, *gambas* ("prawns"), caviar, and Rioja in atmospheric iron-and-glass surroundings.

MADRID, SPAIN

### 457. Peruse antiques in a flea market

**When:** Sunday mornings
**Latitude:** 40.4089°N
**Longitude:** 3.7075°W

Join thousands of visitors every Sunday as they head to El Rastro de Madrid, a hugely popular open-air flea market in an area south of La Latina Metro station in Spain's capital. Soak up the atmosphere and pick up a treat from the many collectibles, knickknacks, and other rarities and curiosities on sale here.

SEVILLE, ANDALUSIA, SPAIN

### 458. Go on a tapas trail in the city that invented it

**When:** All year
**Latitude:** 37.3890°N
**Longitude:** 5.9869°W

Tapas was invented in Andalusia, and sultry Seville is the best place to hit the tapas trail (or to *tapear*, in Spanish). A late lunch is needed— no Sevillano would dream of heading out pre-10 p.m. Swing by Calle Mateos Gago on the edge of Barrio Santa Cruz or Plaza del Salvador and dive into the bars drawing the largest crowds. Order just one dish in each (salty sardines, perhaps, or juicy tomato atop bread), grazing, and cruising on to other bars as the mood strikes.

MADRID, SPAIN
### 459. Contemplate the futility of war in front of *Guernica*

**When:** All year (closed Tuesdays; check for Sunday and public holiday opening times)
**Latitude:** 40.4076°N **Longitude:** 3.6948°W

*Guernica* was Picasso's immediate reaction to the Nazis' devastating and casual bombing practice on the Basque town of Guernica during the Spanish Civil War. The painting, an epic 11 ft (3.5 m) tall and 25.6 ft (7.8 m) wide, is one of the most moving, antiwar paintings in history. Let *Guernica* be your guide to help prevent war in Museo Nacional Centro de Arte Reina Sofía.

COSTA DE LA LUZ, SPAIN
### 460. Explore southern Spain by motor home

**When:** May to September
**Latitude:** 36.0143°N **Longitude:** 5.6044°W

Rather than travel the well-worn route of Costa del Sol, with its crowded beaches and high-rise buildings, head west. The Costa de la Luz is the antithesis of its neighbor, boasting vast sweeping beaches and open unspoiled countryside.

The bohemian town of Tarifa on the most southerly tip of Europe is a good starting point, before making your way west, taking in Jerez de la Frontera and Huelva as you motor toward Portugal. Campsites are easy to find, but be warned that you can also expect strong coastal winds blowing in from the Atlantic, which is why this region is a kitesurfing paradise.

SHIBUYA, TOKYO, JAPAN
### 461. Reenact a famous karaoke scene

**When:** All year
**Latitude:** 35.6640°N
**Longitude:** 139.6982°E

In the mood for singing? Bill Murray and Scarlett Johansson famously embrace the Japanese love of karaoke in room 601 at Karaoke-kan in the lively district of Shibuya in the movie *Lost in Translation*. Other notable landmarks in the movie include Tokyo Tower, the Rainbow Bridge, and the top-floor bar of the Park Hyatt.

MOUNT FUJI, HONSHU ISLAND, JAPAN
### 462. Make a pilgrimage to the snowcapped peak of Mount Fuji

**When:** Climbing permitted early July to mid-September (trails open subject to weather conditions)
**Latitude:** 35.3605°N **Longitude:** 138.7277°E

On a clear day the exceptional symmetry and pristine beauty of Mount Fuji's cone is visible high above Tokyo, some 100 mi (60 km) to the northeast. It is Japan's highest peak at 12,389 ft (3,776 m) and World Heritage–listed as a site that has "inspired artists and poets and been the object of pilgrimage for centuries."

Although Japanese Buddhist and Shintoists consider the active stratovolcano one of their most sacred mountains, it is not sacrilegious to climb it, and pilgrims have been making their way to the summit for centuries. Most are agreed that the best and most spiritual time to arrive is at sunrise, when the valley below is bathed in sunlight.

Snow monkey near Shibu Onsen in Japan

▲ YAMANOUCHI, JAPAN

463. Have a shared bath in Shibu Onsen

**When:** All year
**Latitude:** 36.7446°N **Longitude:** 138.4125°E

Wandering the lovely alleyways of Shibu—nestled in the Yokoyugawa valley—is reason enough to visit this town, but its main attraction has always been its nine public bathhouses, which have for centuries attracted religious pilgrims, artistic types, and even samurai. Locals are free to use all nine facilities, but apart from one completely open bath, visitors will need to book an inn for a night in order to enjoy the *onsen*. Each bathhouse has a different feel and is said to cure different ailments, and you can collect stamps (and souvenirs) at all nine, as well as walk the streets in bathhouse kimonos; refresh in the 400-year-old Japanese inns, or *ryokan*; and marvel at the snow monkeys that sometimes swing through the buildings from the local forests (there's even a snow monkey park nearby).

TOGAKUSHI, NAGANO, JAPAN

464. Learn to think like a ninja

**When:** All year
**Latitude:** 36.7413°N **Longitude:** 138.0845°E

From the outside, the large white house at the Togakure Ninpo Museum seems to be a traditional Japanese dwelling, but once you have gone through the front door, you'll find it's anything but. This is a ninja house, and every room is full of tricks and obstacles that ninja warriors used to evade their enemies. Doors are hidden behind bookcases, and secret passageways connect different rooms in the house. The element of surprise is key to ninja techniques, and elsewhere in the museum there are displays of tools, weapons, and photographs that give a fantastic insight to the practices and techniques employed in this ancient warrior tradition.

NIIGATA PREFECTURE, JAPAN
## 465. Go to the world's most considerate rock festival
**When:** July
**Latitude:** 36.7928°N **Longitude:** 138.7782°E

There are certain credentials that people look for in a music festival: good music, a good setting, and a good vibe. Fuji Rock Festival, which takes place in the beautiful Japanese Alps, delivers on all fronts.

High up in the Alps, away from towns and villages, the festival creates its own little bubble in meadows. Musically, it pulls in all the big names, and with crowds of 100,000 people, you're guaranteed a good atmosphere.

What makes the festival stand out, however, is that even with a crowd the size of many small towns, it remains unfalteringly friendly and polite, and amazingly clean. It is perfectly normal to set up a mat with a picnic to act as your "base camp" for the day. And it is perfectly normal for that base camp to remain entirely undisturbed by others.

All litter is recycled, and smokers carry their own ashtrays with them. And when campers pack away their tents at the end of the weekend, nothing—not even a peg—is left behind. The former campsite looks like pristine fields again. It's just perfect.

NAGANO, JAPAN
## 466. Write a haiku
**When:** All year
**Latitude:** 36.6513°N
**Longitude:** 138.1810°E

The ancient art of haiku poetry isn't just about condensing thoughts into just three lines and seventeen moras, or syllables (although a challenge in itself). It's more about examining the physical world and questioning the nature of existence. Take a shot at haiku in the home of haiku master Kobayashi Issa—this is probably one of the more challenging entries here.

SAPPORO, JAPAN
## 467. Play culinary Russian roulette
**When:** November to February (when the fish fatten up to survive the cold)
**Latitude:** 43.0621°N
**Longitude:** 141.3544°E

Fugu (blowfish) is more toxic than cyanide, leading some unfortunate diners to follow their main course with rapid paralysis and violent death. Those who survive the culinary delicacy, however, savor the delicate and fresh-tasting translucent fish, which some have compared to chicken. Bon appétit?

KANAZAWA, ISHIKAWA PREFECTURE, JAPAN
## 468. Marvel at the precision of a Japanese garden
**When:** All year
**Latitude:** 36.5613°N **Longitude:** 136.6562°E

Japanese design and precision stands alone in many fields, but nowhere more so than in the country's legendary ornamental gardens. Spending time in one is guaranteed to increase your Zen levels, and according to many experts, Kenroku-en, situated next to Kanazawa Castle, is the jewel in Japan's gardening crowd. This place is like a living art gallery, with breathtaking work at every turn. Its sheer scale (27 ac; 11 ha) is only matched by its microlevel majesty.

Kenroku-en's centerpiece is a huge artificial pond, the Kasumigaike, with houses dotted along the surrounding hills. It has a mythical feel despite being manmade. *Kenroku-en* literally means having "six factors," referring to the different elements that its gardeners believe were required for perfection. These are spaciousness, tranquility, artifice, antiquity, water features, and great panoramas. It's fair to say—any visitor will attest—that all six are palpable.

ASHIKAGA, JAPAN

469. **Inhale the scent of a wisteria canopy**

**When:** Best blooming season: April to June (check for public holiday closures)

**Latitude:** 36.3140°N

**Longitude:** 139.5202°E

Imagine walking through a tunnel of the most deliciously scented flowers, with millions of purple, yellow, white, or pink cascading petals glowing in the sun or the moonlight overhead. This is Ashikaga Flower Park in April. Prepare to be mesmerized.

OMIYA, TOKYO, JAPAN
## 470. Grow a bonsai tree for posterity
**When:** All year
**Latitude:** 35.9064°N
**Longitude:** 139.6287°E

Bonsai is part and parcel of Japanese culture. A peaceful exercise of calm ingenuity for the grower, and a form of contemplation for the admirer, take inspiration from the gardens at Omiya before heading to one of the nurseries in the village to start your own horticultural meditation.

TOKYO, JAPAN
## 471. Transform yourself in the world's karate capital
**When:** All year
**Latitude:** 35.7076°N
**Longitude:** 139.7441°E

Karate—"the way of the empty hand" in Japanese—is good for your body and soul. Take lessons in the ancient martial art—where progress is really measured by personal enrichment and not black belts—at the Japan Karate Association's headquarters in downtown Tokyo.

TOKYO, JAPAN
## 472. Book into a love hotel for naughtiness
**When:** All year
**Latitude:** 35.6894°N
**Longitude:** 139.6917°E

Feeling in the mood? Most guests looking to check into a hotel for a little afternoon delight risk running the gauntlet of raised eyebrows on reception, but not in Tokyo's kitsch love hotels. With garish designs and eccentric flourishes like mirrored walls, they're a Tokyo tradition that anyone amorous passing through the city would be mad not to try.

HONSHU, JAPAN
## 473. Learn to make an origami animal
**When:** All year
**Latitude:** 36.0786°N
**Longitude:** 138.0804°E

Origami, the Japanese skill of folding paper, dates back to the sixth century and has evolved and developed with time. Originally restricted to religious ceremonies, it is now something of an art form. Have a go in Honshu, the home of origami innovator Akira Yoshizawa. It might be worth considering a children's class to begin with.

JAPAN
## 474. Eat at all the world's three-Michelin-star restaurants
**When:** All year
**Latitude:** 35.6833°N **Longitude:** 139.7667°E

Michelin's coveted three-star award is defined as those restaurants offering "exceptional cuisine, worth a special journey." Admittedly, visiting all three-star establishments is an ambitious feat in anyone's book, not least the organization needed to secure a table. For example, calling a few months in advance for a reservation at Tokyo's Sukiyabashi Jiro just won't cut it—a local Japanese friend with a spare ¥20,000 to vouch for diners is also required. But it's not impossible: food critic Andy Hayler managed to eat at all 110 three-Michelin-star restaurants in 2014.

Japan's edition of the acclaimed Michelin guide is a hotly anticipated event thanks to the country ranking number one in the world since 2009 for most three-star restaurants. Eating in any three-star restaurant should represent an assault on the senses. It's not just about the food consumed, but it's also about impeccable yet unintrusive service, tenable ambience, and surroundings befitting the experience.

TOKYO, JAPAN
## 475. Get caught up in an Olympic atmosphere
**When:** July 24 to August 9, 2020
**Latitude:** 35.6894°N **Longitude:** 139.6917°E

There's nothing quite like the Olympic spirit, and Tokyo is next in line after Rio 2016, hosting the twenty-ninth modern-era Olympic Games in 2020.

Tickets can be in high demand, but remember that events like the marathon and cycling road race can be viewed for free. Soaking up the atmosphere at designated points around the host city is also a thrill, and Tokyo promises to be particularly strong on this front. Seven venues will be contained within a designated "heritage zone," including the Yoyogi National Gymnasium, the pretty Imperial Palace East Garden, and the legendary Nippon Budokan. Tokyo's enchanting bay will also host events.

Don't forget the Paralympics, either, the sister event running from August 25 to September 5. It includes fascinating events, such as goalball (contested by the blind), boccie (a type of bowling for those with cerebral palsy), and wheelchair rugby—aka "murderball"—which produce moments just as inspiring as the Olympics. At either event it's hard not to leave with the feeling that the world is a better place for them.

JAPAN
## 476. Watch Kabuki theater
**When:** All year
**Latitude:** 35.6833°N
**Longitude:** 139.6833°E

Kabuki is about surrendering to your imagination. To enjoy this highly stylized form of Japanese theater, it's essential to embrace the assault on the senses, with its elaborate costumes, striking make-up, exaggerated movements, and all-male cast, many of whom specialize in female roles (*onnagata*). Catch one in Tokyo, Osaka, or Fukuoka.

HITACHINAKA, JAPAN
## 477. Bathe in a sea of flowers
**When:** All year (but baby blue eyes are in bloom late April to early May)
**Latitude:** 36.4006°N
**Longitude:** 140.5914°E

See for yourself how the vibrancy of the colors here can make it appear a little unreal, like a retouched photograph. The 190 ac (77 ha) Hitachi Seaside Park is famed for its 4.5 million baby blue eyes flowers, but there are also 170 varieties of tulip, a million daffodils, and swathes of blazing red Kochia.

▶ TOKYO, JAPAN
## 478. Wrestle with sumo in Tokyo
**When:** All year
**Latitude:** 35.6894°N
**Longitude:** 139.6917°E

To the unrefined eye, it may seem like two big lads shoving, but this ancient and subtle art is wildly popular in Japan, with six grand tournaments attracting particular fervor. Take in one of these, three of which are held at Tokyo's Ryōgoku Sumo Hall, the spiritual home of sumo; the last day is always earsplittingly exciting.

Japanese sumo
wrestling in Tokyo

NAGARAGAWA RIVER, GIFU, JAPAN

## 479. Witness the art of *Ukai*—fishing with cormorants

**When:** May to October

**Latitude:** 35.4167°N **Longitude:** 136.7667°E

Charlie Chaplin was said to have been a fan of this 1,300-year-old tradition and it's easy to see why. Performed at night, with sake flowing, the fishermen manipulate both the water, trapping the sweetfish in the shallows, and ten to twelve cormorants at a time.

◀ LINTONG DISTRICT, XI'AN, CHINA
## 480. Join the Terra-cotta Army
**When:** All year
**Latitude:** 34.3841°N
**Longitude:** 109.2783°E

It's a mind-boggling vision: more than 8,000 terra-cotta figures, dating back to the third century BC, were found buried in pits close to the Mausoleum of the First Qin Emperor. Each of the thousands of warriors is unique, thought to have been carved in the likenesses of the workers who created them around 250 BC. Spot also chariots, horses, musicians, and even acrobats among the lineup.

▶ CHANG'AN-TIANSHAN CORRIDOR, CHINA
## 481. Travel the ancient Silk Road
**When:** All year (best in May to October)
**Latitude:** 34.5594°N **Longitude:** 12.9678°E

Traveling along the ancient Silk Road of the East harks back to the earliest days of travel, when the wild and exotic landscape was traversed by caravans of camels and horses. China had a monopoly on silk, hence the name for the network of roads.

The ancient Silk Road was created in the second century BC and used well into the sixteenth century. The route is mammoth, but a few years ago one section was designated a UNESCO World Heritage site, so this is a good place to experience what it is like to travel along it today. It is more than 3,000 mi (4,828 km) of often remote roads, which connect many protected sites of historical interest on its way from central China into Kazakhstan and Kyrgyzstan. This route passes cities, palaces, religious buildings, ancient paths, and sections of the Great Wall. It is history on a grand scale.

Chang'an-Tianshan Corridor on the ancient Silk Road, China

The road itself is as immense as the history it depicts, traveling as it does through geographical extremes—from below sea level to 24,000 ft (7,315 m) above. The best time to visit is from early May to late October, when the warm, long days offer lots of time for exploring, and many festivals also take place.

The Terra-cotta Army in Lintong District, Xian, China

BEIJING, CHINA
## 482. Whizz around a frozen lake … on a chair
**When:** All year
**Latitude:** 39.9442°N
**Longitude:** 116.3818°E

Beijingers love to take to the frozen lakes during their brutal winters—it's no coincidence that the city produces so many world-class ice dancers. But rent a chair on skis at the city's Houhai Lake, and you can speed around, full of childlike glee.

BEIJING, CHINA
## 483. Take up a new sport—table tennis
**When:** All year
**Latitude:** 39.9042°N
**Longitude:** 116.4073°E

Stimulate different parts of the brain, make friends, or find a hidden talent. There are plenty of reasons to try a new sport. Table tennis is a good option—it's simple to start, and cheap—and as the seventh most popular game in the world, there's always an opponent available.

BEIJING, CHINA
## 484. Explore Beijing's backstreet culture
**When:** All year
**Latitude:** 39.9042°N
**Longitude:** 116.4073°E

Take a wander down Beijing's old backstreets—where you can watch someone skin a live snake for lunch—to explore a fascinating part of old Chinese culture that needs to be seen before it's gentrified out of existence.

BEIJING, CHINA
## 485. Eat Peking duck … in Peking
**When:** All year
**Latitude:** 39.9042°N
**Longitude:** 116.4073°E

This dish has been prepared in Peking—now known as Beijing, of course—since the imperial era, and is mouthwatering for its thin, crispy skin and succulent meat. The duck is seasoned and served with cucumber, hoisin sauce, and mandarin pancakes. So feast on this best starter in the world.

PANJIN, CHINA
## 486. See the rivers run through red
**When:** September to October
**Latitude:** 40.6764°N
**Longitude:** 122.1420°E

Visit the Liaohe River Delta in the fall to witness a spectacular scene that looks as though it's been Photoshopped, as river tributaries snake their way through a bright-red landscape. There's no trickery involved, though—the seaweed that grows on this alkaline soil turns bright red in fall, for as far as the eye can see, turning a pretty landscape into a beautiful one.

ALL OVER CHINA
## 487. Recuperate with a hot-stone massage
**When:** All year
**Latitude:** 39.9042°N
**Longitude:** 116.4074°E (Beijing)

Head to the home of the hot-stone massage—designed to ease tension, improve circulation, and relax aching muscles—which originated in China some 2,000 years ago. Although it is now popular throughout the world, China remains the original and best place to seek out this wonderfully relaxing therapy.

## 488. Stroll along the Great Wall of China

**When:** All year
**Latitude:** 40.4405°N **Longitude:** 116.5595°E

In *The Bucket List* movie, starring Morgan Freeman and Jack Nicholson, the daring duo break out of hospital and end up motorbiking along the Great Wall of China. Alas, this isn't actually legal in real life, but it's far better is to do it on foot, anyway. The whole 13,171 mi (21,196 km) stretch isn't feasible—or is it?—but you can join in some great walking tours, which take in highlights, including Beijing, the Old Dragon's Head (where wall meets sea), and the imperial tombs at Qing.

▶ ECHIGO-TSUMARI, NIIGATA PREFECTURE, JAPAN
## 489. Attend the world's largest outdoor arts festival

**When:** All year (triennial held every three years; next one is in 2018)

**Latitude:** 33.8403°N **Longitude:** 134.3973°E (Echigo)

If you're interested in the idea of living in harmony with nature—a *satoyama* existence—then it's well worth making a trip to the Echigo-Tsumari Art Field in Japan, home to the Echigo-Tsumari Art Triennial. The overarching theme is "humans are part of nature," to help present a model for how humans can relate to nature and avoid further environmental destruction.

Artworks are dotted across approximately 200 villages and 293 sq mi (760 sq km) in the Echigo-Tsumari region, deliberately at odds with the rationalization and efficiency of modern society that would potentially choose a single center or site instead; around 160 artworks are displayed by artists from all over the world.

Those viewing the artworks pass through the region, encountering festivals and local customs along the way. The idea is to emphasize the beauty and richness of *satoyama*, open the senses to the wonder of existence, and connect people to one another and the land.

Indeed, this is the best way to see the world's largest outdoor arts festival and the mist-swirled, haiku-inspired landscape in which it is set—stay for a week, reside among the artworks, and get back a little bit of *satoyama* for yourself.

YAMANASHI, JAPAN
## 490. Ride the fastest-accelerating roller coaster in the world

**When:** All year

**Latitude:** 35.4870°N **Longitude:** 138.7800°E

Dodonpa in Fuji-Q Highland amusement park is no longer the world's fastest roller coaster—it is now ranked a more humble fourth—but it retains pole position for fastest acceleration. Ride this and experience a force of up to 2.7Gs, which is just slightly less than that exerted on an astronaut at takeoff.

HAKONE, JAPAN
## 491. Feel the calm of staying in a *ryokan*

**When:** All year

**Latitude:** 35.2324°N **Longitude:** 139.1069°E

Spend the night in a *ryokan*—a traditional Japanese inn. The best are a study in tasteful simplicity—paper walls, low-level furniture, and amazing food and hospitality, and where better to find these than in Hakone, on the historic road between Tokyo and Japan.

The Echigo-Tsumari Art Trienniale in Niigata Prefecture is the world's largest oudoor arts festival, Japan

SPRINGER MOUNTAIN, GEORGIA, TO MOUNT KATAHDIN, MAINE (OR VICE VERSA), US

## 492. Hike a celebrated US trail

**When:** Late March to mid-May start date (if you're heading northbound)

**Latitude:** 34.6267°N **Longitude:** 84.1936°W

The Appalachian Trail is a wilderness trail that stretches from Springer Mountain in Georgia to Mount Katahdin in Maine. Along with the Pacific Crest and Continental Divide, the Appalachian Trail is one of the Triple Crowns of long-distance US hikes.

Since its inauguration in 1937, the trail has inspired millions of people. Some will just do a day or two, while others (known as Thru Hikers) will attempt to walk the entire trail in one season. Join them, and you'll be looking at something of a six-month hike.

The trail has a well-marked route, plus more than 250 campsites and shelters that make great meeting places. These hubs are often where you find Thru Hikers sharing stories of the incredible scenery they've seen that day, tips for picking up food in the next town along the route, and tales of close encounters with the local wildlife, which does include the odd bear or two.

At the end of September, when most Thru Hikers aim to finish, you're likely to have trekked around 2,180 mi (3,508 km) and climbed an elevation gain roughly equivalent to climbing Mount Everest sixteen times. No doubt, it's an arduous journey but one that, for many, becomes a truly life-changing experience.

LOS ANGELES, CALIFORNIA, US

## 493. Be a movie extra

**When:** All year

**Latitude:** 34.0928°N

**Longitude:** 118.3286°W

The TV and movie industries wouldn't be able to function without its army of extras, and playing a bit part in a movie or show is easier than you might think. The work is generally low pay for a long day, but what could be better than being a zombie in *The Walking Dead* or lurking in the background of a blockbuster?

YOSEMITE, CALIFORNIA, US

## 494. Watch the sun slowly set in Yosemite

**When:** All year (but best in summer)

**Latitude:** 37.8651°N

**Longitude:** 119.5383°W

As a setting for a setting, this one is hard to top: the World Heritage site's waterfalls, valleys, glorious meadows, and huge trees provide a preposterously pulchritudinous place to watch evening turn to night, especially after a day exploring this vast wilderness. Go during summer for the best sunsets.

BEVERLY HILLS, CALIFORNIA, US

## 495. Try speed dating in the place where it began

**When:** All year

**Latitude:** 34.0731°N

**Longitude:** 118.3994°W

Speed dating was invented, believe it or not, by a rabbi. The first event—where singles sit down for just a couple of minutes with a potential partner, before moving on to the next, in the hope of finding a match—was held at Peet's Café in Beverly Hills in 1998. So what better place to give it a go?

MOUNT HUA, WEINAN SHI, CHINA
## 496. Make a dangerous religious pilgrimage
**When:** Avoid winter—ice and snow make it even more dangerous
**Latitude:** 34.4779°N **Longitude:** 110.0848°E

Mount Hua in China has long-held religious significance for Daoist and Buddhists alike. It has five peaks, and each has a temple on top of it. One of these temples is also a teahouse—presumably to supply something to calm the nerves of the (mainly Chinese) visitors who reach it.

Get training before going: at the base of Mount Hua are the "Heavenly Stairs," a daunting (and exhausting to scale) set of steps. The view here is truly one to savor, but an eye is best kept on the trail, as fatalities still occur here, and certain sections of the steps are very narrow. Once up the first section, many take a gondola to the southern peak of the mountain. Beyond this, the most notorious section, the plank path, awaits; there's literally nothing but planks of wood and a rail of chains to hold on to here. In areas, the drop is thousands of feet down, and certain parts must be "climbed," too, with just chains and footholds. Safety harnesses can be deployed, and are strongly recommended, but it's still a nervy mission too far for many. For those who do take part, the adrenaline rush of edging along, clinging to a sheer cliff face, is unbeatable.

For others, there are easier ways to get a cup of tea.

A dangerous religious pilgrimage takes you over wooden planks on the side of Mount Hua in Weinan Shi, China

SAN DIEGO, CALIFORNIA, US
## 497. Be a zookeeper for a day
**When:** All year
**Latitude:** 32.7357°N **Longitude:** 117.1516°W

California's San Diego Zoo is an ideal place for adventurers to embark on a mini worldwide safari. For a close-up experience with some of the zoo's 650 species, would-be naturalists can join a keeper on a behind-the-scenes adventure across this 100 ac (41 ha) park. Explorers will travel through the world's climatic zones and get up close with elephants, koalas, polar bears, and rare giant pandas.

Keeping wild animals captive can be a cause for concern for many, but San Diego Zoo has a leading reputation for conservation and the reintroduction of wild species into native habitat. Its pioneering approach to animal welfare can also be seen in the park itself. Many of the exhibits use open-air pools and moats instead of cages. There is also the Skyfari—a gondola lift that takes visitors on a ride high above the enclosures, causing minimal disturbance to the animals below.

PIGEON FORGE, TENNESSEE, US
## 498. Go ditzy at Dollywood
**When:** All year
**Latitude:** 35.7884°N
**Longitude:** 83.5543°W

Tennessee's most popular attraction is owned by probably the most famous Tennessean of them all, and Dolly Parton's Dollywood, an adventure playground, is a fun, frivolous way to spend a day. So ride the thunderous roller coasters and revel in the famous Southern charm—and music.

▶ DETROIT, MICHIGAN, US
## 499. Rev up a Shelby Mustang
**When:** All year
**Latitude:** 42.4015°N
**Longitude:** 82.9239°W

Justifiably included in the Morgan Freeman and Jack Nicholson *The Bucket List* movie romp was to drive a Shelby Mustang, the high-performance, all-American car of many a teenager's Motor City fantasy. Classic or modern, it's a muscular and mesmerizing drive—perhaps it's one for you to consider if attempting Route 66.

Morgan Freeman in a Shelby Mustang in the movie *The Bucket List,* US

▶ ALBUQUERQUE, NEW MEXICO, US
## 500. Go up, up, and away in a hot-air balloon
**When:** October
**Latitude:** 35.1961°N
**Longitude:** 106.5975°W

Every year in the first week of October, hundreds of hot-air balloons gather in Albuquerque for the International Balloon Fiesta. It is the largest balloon festival in the world, so expect lots of spectacular sights in the sky and plenty of enthusiasts talking hot air.

International Balloon Fiesta in Albuquerque, New Mexico, US

COLUMBUS, NEW MEXICO, US
## 501. Trek the Continental Divide trail
**When:** All year
**Latitude:** 31.8276°N
**Longitude:** 107.6400°W

Reckon that things like dehydration, lightning, falls, avalanches, hypothermia, bears, mountain lions, and blisters are all merely obstacles to be overcome? Then the Continental trail might just be the hike to top your bucket list. An ambitious 3,100 mi (4,989 km) mission running from Canada to Mexico, this walk takes around six months to complete.

MEMPHIS, TENNESSEE, US
## 502. Discover how it feels to live like the King
**When:** All year
**Latitude:** 35.0480°N **Longitude:** 90.0260°W

As soon as Graceland's gates open, you enter Elvis Presley's gaudy, compelling world. He bought the house for his mother in 1957—she died a year later—and the dining room and living room have, at the behest of ex-wife, Priscilla Presley, been conservatively restored to their early 1960s look.

The kitchen, where the notorious fried peanut butter and banana sandwiches were made, is merely a prelude to the house's pièce de résistance: the TV room. A riotous blue-and-yellow masterpiece with a mirrored ceiling and three TV sets (so he could watch three American football games at once), it feels like an adolescent fantasy of bachelorhood. The tragic denouement to Elvis's unprecedented career is reflected in the Meditation Garden, where many a tear has been shed by the King's graveside.

The Leh-Manali Highway in the Himalayas, India

LEH-MANALI HIGHWAY, INDIA
## 503. Ride high in the Himalayas
**When:** May or June till September (but August and and September are best)
**Latitude:** 34.1454°N **Longitude:** 77.5676°E (Leh)

The Leh-Manali Highway in North India travels almost 300 mi (483 km) through remote Himalayan mountain passes, villages, monasteries, and fantastic scenery. But be warned: driving this route takes some seriously skilled driving. Fast-flowing icy streams, formed from the melting of snowcapped mountains and glaciers, cross the road frequently, and the only way forward is straight through them.

The road is also fairly basic and subject to landslides, which make it even more damaged and dangerous to drive. It is only open for around four and a half months of the year in summer; August and September are the best months to travel it.

This beautiful journey is one of the highest in the world—its average elevation is 13,000 ft (3,962 m), and at its peak it reaches an incredible 17,500 ft (5,334 m). Starting in Leh gives your body the best chance to acclimatize to the lack of oxygen, because along with the tough driving conditions, altitude sickness should be your main concern here.

The journey includes dramatic hairpin bends; river valleys; and brown, arid desert conditions that give a stunning, endless moonscape appearance. There isn't another drive quite like it anywhere else.

LOS ANGELES, CALIFORNIA, US
## 504. Stay in Hollywood's glitziest hotel
**When:** All year
**Latitude:** 34.0981°N **Longitude:** 118.3686°W

A set of keys to a room at the luxurious Chateau Marmont hotel, a castle on the edge of the Hollywood Hills, gives you the chance to mix with Tinseltown royalty. To fit in, you need to arrive at this A-lister's hangout on Los Angeles' Sunset Boulevard wearing your biggest sunglasses and with a suitcase filled with your most glamorous outfits.

The turrets and colonnades of this Gothic-style hotel exude the vintage glamour of 1930s Tinseltown. Inside, the guest list reads as a who's who in the world of movies, music, and entertainment.

Celebrities have long been drawn to the palm-fringed grounds of the Chateau Marmont, craving its paparazzi-free atmosphere and a reputation for discretion, ever since the hotel was built in 1929. Of course, it's impossible not to indulge in some celeb spotting ….

Situated away from the hustle and bustle of the city, the hotel offers a perfect base from which to indulge in glamour and luxury while remaining close to the hot spots, such as the Viper Room, with the luxury boutiques of Rodeo Drive just a short drive away.

US AND WORLDWIDE
## 505. Meet someone through Tinder
**When:** All year
**Latitude:** 34.0221°N
**Longitude:** 118.2852°W (University of Southern California, Los Angeles)

Mobile-dating app Tinder has revolutionized the way people meet one another. California-founded Tinder links Facebook profiles so that users can sit and compile a virtual list of people they like the look of nearby. It should certainly be on the bucket list of anyone single who wants to get out there, whether it's for a casual meet-up or a long-term relationship. It's a fun and sometimes frivolous ego boost.

▶ LOS ANGELES, CALIFORNIA, US
## 506. Tread the Hollywood Walk of Fame
**When:** All year
**Latitude:** 34.0928°N **Longitude:** 118.3286°W

You're nobody in Hollywood until you've got a star. Los Angeles is the city built on dreams, and any wannabe actor, actress, director, producer, singer, or musician who moves to the city must walk among these 2,500 five-pointed stars along the sidewalk and fantasize. The attraction, located along fifteen blocks of Hollywood Boulevard and Vine Street, is a great place to promenade, spotting favorite names from movies, TV, the music business, radio, and theater. Beginning as a collection of eight stars in 1956, twenty new ones are added every year, making it an ever-expanding attraction that effectively serves its purpose of celebrating Los Angeles as a world-famous culture hub.

The Hollywood Walk of Fame in California, US

The down and dirty sport of drag racing at Pomona Raceway in California, US

▲ POMONA RACEWAY, CALIFORNIA (FINALS), US
## 507. Watch the down and dirty sport of drag racing
**When:** February to November
**Latitude:** 34.0950°N **Longitude:** 117.7698°W

Loud, dirty, brash, downright dangerous, and a whole ton of fun, drag racing has brought a modern, exciting take on the illegal pastime of street racing from a standing start. It pits two incredibly fast vehicles against each other over a short, straight course. The NHRA Mello Yello Drag Racing Series, held across twenty-four cities, is its zenith. Join the huge, yee-hawing crowd of gearheads, who drool over the cars—and often tune up their own, too.

LOS ANGELES, CALIFORNIA, US
## 508. Celeb spot at a red-carpet event
**When:** All year
**Latitude:** 34.1000°N **Longitude:** 118.3333°W

The best place in the world to go celeb hunting has to be LA. Attend a movie premiere to get as close as you can—unless you are on first-name terms, you are unlikely to secure a ticket, but anyone can turn up and hang over the barriers, hoping to grab a selfie with a star.

Another way to catch a star is at on-location filming, where you may be lucky enough to stumble upon some celeb action. Or you can join the studio audience of your favorite shows. Alternatively, there are plenty of organized tours into the Hollywood Hills to see the homes of the stars.

LOS ANGELES, CALIFORNIA, US
## 509. Spar at a gym with pedigree
**When:** All year
**Latitude:** 34.0591°N **Longitude:** 118.3271°W

Boxing gyms, once temples of intimidating testosterone, have flung open their doors to noncombatants of any age and gender. And there's nowhere better to hit the pads than in the spiritual home of prizefighting, the United States. Just off LA's Santa Monica Boulevard is the Wild Card gym made famous by world champ Manny Pacquiao and his trainer Freddie Roach. You are free to train or simply sit ringside when fight night is approaching and watch the pros go through their paces. Alternatively, for a gym steeped in pugilistic history, head to Gleason's Gym in New York.

LONG BEACH, CALIFORNIA, US
## 510. Fly in a biplane
**When:** All year
**Latitude:** 33.7700°N **Longitude:** 118.1937°W

As much as modern aircraft have evolved, there's no aviation experience to match the utter thrill and exhilaration of flying in a biplane. Long Beach is where pioneer Amelia Earhart, the first female aviator to venture solo across the Atlantic, learned her art, and gorgeous 1930s-inspired biplanes still launch from here. In the hands of an experienced pilot, you can enjoy astonishing vistas across the port of Los Angeles, including the *Queen Mary* ocean liner and Long Beach harbor.

LINCOLN, NEW MEXICO, US
## 511. See where Billy shot the sheriff
**When:** All year
**Latitude:** 33.4920°N
**Longitude:** 105.3839°W

It's become a cliché to say you can walk in history's footsteps, but in this perfectly preserved Wild West town, it is possible. In the courthouse you can stand on the spot where, on April 28, 1881, legendary outlaw Billy the Kid shot the sheriff. The whole town is a state monument, which recaptures the feel of a nineteenth-century Western town.

OUTSIDE PHOENIX, ARIZONA, US
## 512. Soak up a meteor shower in Arizona
**When:** Mid-December
**Latitude:** 33.4483°N
**Longitude:** 112.0740°W (Phoenix)

Arizona's wide-open skies and lack of light pollution make it the salient spot to see meteors disintegrate as they enter the atmosphere—a mind-bending celestial event. Head there to see the annual Geminids shower—caused by the Apollo asteroid's 3200 Phaethon—which occurs in December.

LONG BEACH, CALIFORNIA, US
## 513. Get on the waiting list for space
**When:** You can apply now (but you'll have to wait till the scheme starts, which is TBC)
**Latitude:** 33.7683°N
**Longitude:** 118.1956°W

Spaceflights are coming, and Virgin has been busy developing a spacecraft that it says will be the world's first commercial space line any year now. Pay $200,000 for a ticket and join tens of thousands of others on the waiting list.

KII MOUNTAINS, JAPAN
## 514. Go trekking in the Kumano Kodo
**When:** All year
**Latitude:** 34.0000°N **Longitude:** 135.7500°E (center Kii Hanto trail)

The ancient, sacred feel of the routes weaving through the Kumano Kodo—their historical significance and their tradition in connecting sites of great religious importance—means that stepping along these paths still feels like a pilgrimage, just as it did as early as the ninth century.

Zigzagging across the Kii Hanto, the largest peninsula in Japan, the Kumano Kodo pass through the Kii Mountains overlooking the Pacific Ocean, and are cinematically beautiful. Huge waterfalls cascade through valleys and whip up a mist over centuries-old temples. Sunlight cuts through thousands of rigidly straight tree trunks that line the paths. In the fall it is a rhapsody of reds and oranges; and for a few tantalizing days in spring, the cherry blossoms make the paths a carnival of color. This is living Japanese culture: on the right day, you will see modern-day pilgrims in large straw hats and veils, an outfit unchanged for millennia.

The pathways connect three sacred sites of UNESCO World Heritage importance: the Kumano Hongu Taisha, the Kumano Nachi Taisha, and the Kumano Hayatama Taisha. Linking the ancient capitals of Nara and Kyoto, the pilgrims who would have roamed these paths followed multiple different traditions, reflecting a combination of Shinto, which is Japan's ancient system of worship, and a Buddhism that was imported from Korea and China. Little has changed over the 1,200 years that the paths have been walked, with perfect preservation of the environment and fascinating shrines along the way.

The real joy is in walking the lush, verdant trails; the sunrises and sunsets; the rolling hills; and the luminous flora. Far more than just a walk.

A Kumano Kodo route in the Kii Mountains, Japan

KOBE, OSAKA BAY, JAPAN
## 515. Tuck into Kobe, the world's best steak
**When:** All year
**Latitude:** 34.6900°N
**Longitude:** 135.1956°E

The "caviar of meat," Kobe cattle are fed beer, are massaged, and their coats brushed with sake to enhance the tender, juicy flavor and marbled appearance of their meat. Since it's rarely exported, try it in Kobe, where prices are reasonable, and chefs meticulously cut bite-size chunks before cooking to match your pace of eating.

TOKYO, JAPAN
## 516. Join the cherry blossom parties in Japan
**When:** Spring
**Latitude:** 35.7331°N **Longitude:** 139.7467°E

Although there are many places where you can enjoy Japan's cherry blossom season, Tokyo remains one of the highlights, due not only to its huge number of the trees, but also the popularity of *hanami* ("flower viewing") here. *Hanami* is the Japanese tradition of welcoming the arrival of spring and honoring the country's national flower, the cherry blossom, while it is in full spectacular bloom. Stroll among the trees and picnic under them, but don't limit your festivities to the day—at night the parks' thousands of cherry trees are beautifully lit up, looking incredibly romantic and making them popular places for friends and lovers to gather.

ABASHIRI, JAPAN
## 517. Travel on an ice-breaking ship
**When:** Winter
**Latitude:** 44.0206°N
**Longitude:** 144.2733°E

Experience the majesty of our ocean in an invigorating way that's a million miles away from your standard cruise. Travel on a mighty breaker out of Abashiri, an isolated corner of Japan, as it cuts through drift ice.

KYOTO, JAPAN
## 518. Sip tea in Kyoto
**When:** All year
**Latitude:** 35.0117°N
**Longitude:** 135.7683°E

Making a brew is a means of rejuvenation, but in the heart of the tea-growing world, it is considered the highest truth of Zen Buddhism. The cleansing of utensils, the three clockwise stirs before that first sip of the purest, delicate-tasting tea offers time for contemplation and relaxation. Find your inner peace with a soothing cup of tea.

OSAKA, JAPAN
## 519. Experience a capsule hotel
**When:** All year
**Latitude:** 34.6939°N
**Longitude:** 135.5022°E

A very Japanese experience, capsules have failed to catch on in the West, possibly because you won't necessarily sleep, especially if you're claustrophobic. But staying in a fiberglass pod marginally larger than a coffin, complete with TV, is worth doing once. Just not twice.

TSUKIJI, TOKYO, JAPAN

520. Sample sushi at a Tokyo fish market

**When:** All year

**Latitude:** 33.6273°N **Longitude:** 135.9426°E

The frantic pace, pungent aromas, and visual spectacle of 5 a.m. tuna auctions at the world's largest and busiest fish market is not complete without a sushi breakfast. You'll have to line up for three hours, but this is an indication of the caliber of the *omakase* (dishes selected by the chef), which is not to be missed by connoisseurs.

MATMATA, TUNISIA

### 521. Spend a night with Luke Skywalker—sort of

**When:** All year
**Latitude:** 33.4552°N
**Longitude:** 9.7679°E

Movie fans can get very excited about visiting exotic locations that were featured in their favorite flicks. *Star Wars* fans can get even more excited as they get the chance to sleep in the house where Luke Skywalker grew up in *Star Wars Episode IV: A New Hope*—it's the Hotel Sidi Driss in the Tunisian Desert.

DERWEZE, TURKMENISTAN
## 522. Feel the heat at the Door to Hell
**When:** All year
**Latitude:** 40.2526°N
**Longitude:** 58.4394°E

Peak into the Door to Hell—the "affectionate" name given to a natural gas crater in Derweze, Turkmenistan. It was set on fire in 1971 to prevent the spread of methane gas and has been burning solidly ever since—for more than forty years.

DAMAVAND, IRAN
## 523. Find glaciers in an unlikely location
**When:** All year
**Latitude:** 35.9556°N
**Longitude:** 52.1100°E

Iran may not be the first place you think of when it comes to finding glaciers, but they can be found in the mountains above the arid landscape in the north of the country. See them while they're still around: the impact of climate change means they are rapidly disappearing.

▼ ISFAHAN, IRAN
## 524. Step into a picturesque Persian city
**When:** All year
**Latitude:** 32.6333°N
**Longitude:** 51.6500°E

"Isfahan is half of the ancient world" goes the Persian proverb, and this pearl of a city, once the capital of Persia, remains as glorious today. Tree-lined boulevards, picturesque enclosed bridges, and wonderful gardens—this is a place to simply wander and wonder.

The picturesque Persian city of Isfahan, Iran

IBUSUKI, KYUSHU, JAPAN
## 525. Bury yourself in a bath of hot sand
**When:** All year
**Latitude:** 31.2528°N
**Longitude:** 130.6331°E

Japan is well known for its healing hot springs, but aquaphobes may prefer a drier way to benefit from the heat. "Burial ladies" on the beach will bury you up to your neck in sand warmed by the springs below, in the name of aiding circulation.

▶ KYUSHU, JAPAN
## 526. Feel the peace of old trees in Kirishima
**When:** All year
**Latitude:** 31.8872°N
**Longitude:** 130.8559°E

Some Japanese believe that Kirishima-Yaku National Park is where the Gods first descended, and it's certainly pretty and peaceful enough to believe it. Situated across the northern Kagoshima-ken and western Miyazaki, the island's incredible old trees also have a near-religious aura. These ancient cedars, known as Yakusugi trees, are enormous: some are more than 1,000 years old and have a circumference of 53 ft (16 m); elsewhere, you can spot wild azaleas and the huge Senrigataki waterfall.

One of the old trees in Kirishima-Yaku National Park, Kyushu, Japan

▶ TAJIKISTAN
## 527. Trek in Asia's highest mountain ranges
**When:** July to September
**Latitude:** 38.5618°N **Longitude:** 73.2312°E

Tajikistan offers some of the world's most dramatic landscapes of turquoise lakes, jagged mountains, and steaming geysers. Dubbed the "Roof of the World," the country's soaring Pamir Mountains are more than 9,843 ft (3,000 m) high, with the most towering peaks located in the Gorno-Badakhshan Autonomous Region. Some of the world's highest mountains are found here.

At such an altitude, summers are short and winters are long. Local transport is limited, maps scarcely available, and a lack of Russian or Tajik may mean you'll soon be out of your depth. Yet, brush these difficulties aside and you'll find the rewards by far outstrip the drawbacks. Due to the high altitudes and waterless expanses, trekking with a guide is essential.

Your efforts will be rewarded with glacial otherworldly landscapes with emerald-green lakes punctuated by arid desertlike expanses of land. One of the major highlights is the Pamiris' warm sense of hospitality. You will likely be invited in for tea or for a meal.

Exploring Asia's highest mountain ranges, Tajikistan

ALL OVER JAPAN
## 528. Feed the fish … with human flesh
**When:** All year
**Latitude:** 35.2324°N
**Longitude:** 139.1069°E (Hakone, first-known fish pedicure venue in Japan)

The rumors are true. Fish pedicures have stepped out of sci-fi and into Japan's famous *onsen* (hot springs). Freshwater "doctor fish" suck the dead skin off feet dangled in the soothing waters, leaving lovely, smooth flesh after fifteen minutes. Not for the squeamish.

MCLEOD GANJ (AKA UPPER DHARAMSALA), INDIA
## 529. Enjoy a joke with a god-king in his home
**When:** All year
**Latitude:** 32.2433°N **Longitude:** 76.3210°E

About 6,500 ft (1,981 m) above the gentle chaos of the town of McLeod Ganj is the home of the Dalai Lama, who is, depending on one's point of view, a god-king, a Buddhist master, an inspirational example, or—if you're a Chinese official—an imperialist puppet. In person, the man at the center of such controversy, adulation, and tragedy exudes intellect, humor, and a kind of peace that is an extraordinary tribute to his faith—and/or resilience—given the turmoil his homeland Tibet (from which he has been exiled since 1959) has experienced under Chinese rule. Thousands flock here every year to hear the Dalai Lama lecture in his compound. Audiences with His Holiness usually feature a few good jokes and the blessing gift of a white scarf.

257

MARRAKECH, MOROCCO
## 530. Soak up the intense cobalt blue of the Jardin Majorelle
**When:** Open all year (times vary according to season)
**Latitude:** 31.6414°N **Longitude:** 8.0023°W

The artist Jacques Majorelle constructed the Jardin Majorelle in Marrakech more than forty years ago. It's made up of several buildings of different styles (Moorish, Berber—complete with high adobe tower—and Cubist), with an Arab-inspired pergola. These are set in an oasis he created around it, filled with exotic plants and rare species that he gathered from across five continents during his extensive travels.

Visit the enchanting property (now a museum) and wander through the vibrant-colored buildings and exquisitely atmospheric gardens.

AMRITSAR, PUNJAB, INDIA
## 531. Pray at the Golden Temple
**When:** All year
**Latitude:** 31.6200°N **Longitude:** 74.8769°E

The Golden Temple, Harmandir Sahib, in Amritsar, Punjab, is the most important shrine in Sikhism. The water that surrounds the gleaming central shrine is said to have healing powers, and pilgrims come here from across the world to bathe in its sacred waters. The temple itself is an exquisite blend of a carved-marble lower level, followed by a beautifully engraved-gold second level, topped with domes. Inside, the building rings with the continuous chanting of the Sikh holy book. All in all, it's an intensely spiritual experience.

MASADA, ISRAEL
## 532. Follow in the footsteps of rebels
**When:** All year
**Latitude:** 31.3109°N
**Longitude:** 35.3640°E

Take a predawn trek 1,300 ft (396 m) up Masada, the site of a legendary Jewish rebel stronghold against the Romans in AD 73, and you'll see just why this ancient, isolated outcrop was chosen as a fortress. The glorious views of the sunrise from the top make the effort worthwhile.

HAIFA, ISRAEL
## 533. See modern-day hanging gardens
**When:** All year
**Latitude:** 32.7940°N
**Longitude:** 34.9896°E

In front of the Baha'i Shrine of the Báb in Haifa, Israel, are eighteen terraces, also known as the Hanging Gardens of Haifa, formed on concentric circles and representing the first eighteen disciples of the Báb. Could this be what the ancient wonder, the hanging gardens of Babylon, once looked like? Take a trip there to see what you think.

JERUSALEM OLD CITY, ISRAEL
## 534. Bask in a golden glow over Jerusalem
**When:** All year (closed on Muslim holy days)
**Latitude:** 31.7780°N
**Longitude:** 35.2354°E

A breathtaking confection of marble, mosaic tiles, and shimmering gold, the mesmerizing Dome of the Rock on the Temple Mount bestrides an iconic site for three religions—Judaism, Islam, and Christianity. See how remarkable it is inside and out—there is no denying the affecting beauty of this extraordinary building.

BETHLEHEM, PALESTINE
## 535. Celebrate Christmas in Bethlehem
**When:** Christmas, but visitable all year
**Latitude:** 31.7054°N **Longitude:** 35.2024°E

There are few places more resonant to those with even a tenuous grip on the Christian faith than the little town of Bethlehem, accepted birthplace of Jesus Christ, and an attraction for pilgrims, historians, and interested travelers alike. For anyone who grew up in a Christian environment, a Christmas visit to this holy site can feel like stepping into the pages of history, so alive is it with familiar stories and imagery.

While the dusty outskirts of town are jammed with souvenir shops and streets named to reflect the Bible story, central Manger Square and its pièce de résistance, the Church of the Nativity, is a suitably imposing and thought-provoking place. The oldest continuously operating church in the world—a religious site has operated here since AD 339—visitors enter by crouching through the tiny Door of Humility before descending to the Grotto of the Nativity, said to be the place of Christ's birth. The precise spot is marked by an inlaid fourteen-point silver star.

A fascinating visit at any time of year, around Christmastime—not surprisingly—is when everything ramps up.

TIBERIAS, ISRAEL
## 536. Take a cleansing dip in historical waters
**When:** All year (although winter can be chilly)
**Latitude:** 32.8244°N
**Longitude:** 35.5880°E

Its name may be misleading, but the world's lowest freshwater lake has an important place in Christian tradition. Now popular with beachgoers, you can refresh yourself with a dip in the Sea of Galilee, which features heavily in the Holy Bible.

▶ WESTERN WALL, JERUSALEM, ISRAEL
## 537. Leave a prayer note in the Western Wall
**When:** All year
**Latitude:** 31.7767°N **Longitude:** 35.2345°E

The Western Wall of the Temple Mount in Jerusalem is the only surviving part of this once-massive ancient holy structure. According to Jewish tradition, behind the wall lies the mount where Abraham was said to have prepared to sacrifice his son Isaac to God. For centuries, thousands have visited here annually, to pray at the wall or leave prayer notes tucked into its cracks. More than a million notes are said to be placed here each year (today, online organizations offer the ability to e-mail notes to the wall).

Jerusalem's Western Wall, Israel

The heart of Jemaa el Fna in Marrakech, Morocco

▲ MARRAKECH, MOROCCO

## 538. Feel the pulsing heart of Jemaa el Fna

**When:** All year

**Latitude:** 31.6260°N **Longitude:** 7.9890°W

Jemaa el Fna in Marrakech is a town square that is a bustling marketplace, an outdoor food court, an open-air theater, and a museum of the exotic. By day, it is relatively quiet. By night, however, Jemaa el Fna positively explodes with life. Food stalls set up shop with outdoor grills, and plumes of smoke drift in the evening breeze as the smell of roasted meat fills the air. Locals come out in their hundreds for an evening stroll and to enjoy the many entertainments: storytellers, magicians, acrobats, musicians—every few paces there is another crowd gathered around another spectacle.

Retreat to a rooftop café and enjoy the spectacle from above: watch the different scenarios as they unfold and then return to the melee for a mint tea imbued with all the energy of the square.

ESSAOUIRA, MOROCCO

## 539. Play soccer with sand between your toes

**When:** All year

**Latitude:** 31.5085°N

**Longitude:** 9.7595°W

The beach at Essaouira isn't just impressively long; at low tide, it's also wonderfully wide. A fact that hasn't gone unnoticed by the local soccer fans. As the sand appears, so do the makeshift goalposts and the teams of players—who are more than happy for you to join in.

JORDAN
## 540. Get no sinking feeling in the Dead Sea

**When:** All year (although winter can be chilly)

**Latitude:** 31.5590°N

**Longitude:** 35.4732°E

The extraordinary Dead Sea is a not-to-be-missed destination. Lying at the lowest point on Earth, its mineral-rich high salinity—ten times saltier than the ocean—means the only living things you'll likely see in it are superbuoyant tourists.

MOROCCO
## 541. Trek in the High Atlas
**When:** All year
**Latitude:** 31.4300°N **Longitude:** 6.9400°W

They're not called the High Atlas without good cause: Morocco's premier trekking destination—and arguably the most fascinating trekking in all Africa—contains twelve summits, more than 13,600 ft (4,145 m) high. Winding through them, you'll encounter fascinating people, spectacular scenery, splendid isolation, aeons-old villages, pastoral valleys, and cinematic hidden tunnels that lead to sheer ledges and crags with panoramic views.

There are a number of ways to do a trek: some are simply day trips out of Marrakech, but the more ambitious can attempt a three-day or five-day ascent, taking in at least a couple of peaks. A guided tour with an English-speaking local expert is always recommended. A sturdy mule will usually be deployed to carry supplies, and guides tend to cook up all the food, too. Choosing a route will depend on fitness and budget, but the options are limitless.

Whether wandering through derelict casbahs, riding a camel, or enjoying the local villagers' well-tended gardens, it's a time to forget the bustle of the modern world, breathe the fresh air, and connect with a simpler life.

The High Atlas mountain range in Morocco

SHANGHAI, CHINA
## 542. Experience the world's fastest commute
**When:** All year
**Latitude:** 31.1433°N
**Longitude:** 121.8053°E

The Shanghai Maglev Train operates at speeds of a whopping 268 mph (431 kph)—almost twice as fast as the world's fastest roller coaster—making it the world's fastest commercial train. Jump onboard with the commuters, who have no excuse for being late for work.

▶ SHANGHAI, CHINA
## 543. Cruise on the Yangtze River
**When:** All year
**Latitude:** 31.2304°N **Longitude:** 121.4737°E

Stretching nearly 4,000 mi (6,437 km) from Shanghai into China's heartland, the Yangtze River is a mythical-feeling place. The lifeline of China for thousands of years, it has been a cradle to its commerce and culture. Cruising this mighty body of water—the third longest in the world—allows you to see China from a fresh perspective. There's a steady flow of historically significant sites where you can stop off and explore, as well as impressive views for those perched on deck.

Numerous commercial vessels run cruises here, with the iconic stretch of river being the Three Gorges. This is actually a stretch of the Golden River. Beyond, it winds through incredible canyons. Photographers will have a field day with the twists and turns of the Wu Gorge, including the magical Twelve Peaks of Wushan, and their famed "Goddess." Qutang Gorge is a sheer, narrow limestone beauty, while Xiling Gorge—the longest of the three—links Jiangxi and Yichang City via some bewitching scenery.

A weeklong cruise is enough for many, who often tie it in with visits to the Great Wall, Shanghai, and Xian—but the more committed can undertake an eleven-day, 1,400 mi (2,253 km) trip that allows you to really relax and drift into another mindset during your time aboard.

MARRAKECH, MOROCCO
## 544. Sleep in a traditional riad
**When:** All year
**Latitude:** 31.6295°N
**Longitude:** 7.9811°W

Step off a Moroccan street and into a riad and you're stepping from the hubbub and into the calm. Rooms are arranged around a central courtyard, often with a fountain or small pond at its center, creating an enclosed world of its own—and all steeped in centuries-old history.

MARRAKECH, MOROCCO
## 545. Haggle in a Moroccan market
**When:** All year
**Latitude:** 31.6294°N **Longitude:** 7.9811°W (Marrakech)

From Fez to Rabat, Essaouira to Taroudant, Morocco's market tradition is an essential part of the country's lifeblood and a must-do for anyone passing through. Wherever hagglers go, the rules remain the same: try to get there early, before the heat and crowds arrive, drift, and debate for hours before making a decision on what to buy; and always, always haggle—it's rude not to.

Moroccan markets sell pretty much everything these days, although the country's renowned crafts remain the favorite purchase. To haggle well, try to seem indifferent, always be polite, and offer about a third of what the seller originally wants.

Cruising on the Yangtze River in China

▶ IRAQI KURDISTAN, IRAQ
## 546. Visit the oldest town on Earth

**When:** All year
**Latitude:** 36.1910°N
**Longitude:** 44.0090°E

Visit the Citadel of Erbil in Iraq, which is said to have been continuously inhabited since at least 2,300 BC, making it the oldest town on Earth. Pottery found here even suggests its history may extend further back, to the Neolithic period—the last era of the Stone Age.

Jalil Khayat Mosque in the oldest town on Earth: the Citadel of Erbil, Iraq

MESOPOTAMIAN MARSHES, IRAQ
## 547. Take a trip to a floating village

**When:** All year
**Latitude:** 31.0000°N **Longitude:** 47.0000°E

It is quite an otherworldly sight to see the floating basket homes of the Ma'dan, or Marsh Arabs, where the Tigris meets the Euphrates in Iraq. These are the ultimate sustainable dwellings, made from reeds and a giant bamboo-like grass—no nails, no wood, no glass. It has been a simple way of life for these seminomadic people for hundreds of years, but that hasn't stopped the age-old problem of boundary issues: houses are built on boggy islands, and villagers have to anchor them to stop them drifting into a neighbor.

Unfortunately, the traditional dwellings and their people suffered greatly under Saddam Hussein, almost completely disappearing. The wetlands were drained and residents forced to flee, many abandoning their traditional way of life for good. Since 2003 the wetlands have begun to be restored, and efforts are in place to begin reviving the small Ma'dan community that survived.

DHI QAR GOVERNORATE, IRAQ
## 548. Get creative where pottery began

**When:** All year (although summer can be uncomfortably hot)
**Latitude:** 30.9626°N
**Longitude:** 46.1018°E

Forge links with the "cradle of civilization" in modern-day Iraq by attempting to throw a pot. As part of Mesopotamia, the ancient city of Ur (called Tell el-Muqayyar today) was a hub of ceramics production—the world's oldest potter's wheel was discovered there around 3,000 BC.

ALEXANDRIA, EGYPT
## 549. Dive into an underwater palace
**When:** All year
**Latitude:** 31.2000°N
**Longitude:** 29.9187°E

One era's misfortune is another's wonder: when an earthquake sank Queen Cleopatra's palace and Alexandria's old lighthouse, little did the Egyptians know that centuries later, it would create an astonishing, artifact-packed underwater playground for divers. Get your wetsuit on to explore this amazing underwater museum.

ALEXANDRIA, EGYPT
## 550. Live like a pharaoh and bathe in milk
**When:** All year
**Latitude:** 31.2001°N
**Longitude:** 29.9187°E

The silky caress of warm milk on skin was part of the beauty regime of renowned stunner Cleopatra, who favored donkey's milk for the purpose. Science has since found truth in her claims—the lactic acid gets rid of dead skin cells. And where better to treat yourself than in Cleopatra's hometown?

SAHARA DESERT
## 551. Conquer the Marathon des Sables
**When:** Annually in April
**Latitude:** 31.1458°N
**Longitude:** 3.9677°W

Billed as the toughest footrace on Earth, the MdS is a grueling 156 mi (251 km) slog, taking around six days and battling 122°F (50°C) temperatures. Do not attempt it without a modicum of training and professional advice first … .

UTTARAKHAND, HIMALAYAS, INDIA
## 552. Lose yourself in myriad colors
**When:** Main blooming season between July and October
**Latitude:** 30.7280°N **Longitude:** 79.6053°E

It was a fortunate moment in 1931, when three British mountaineers—Frank Smythe, Eric Shipton, and R. L. Holdsworth—lost their way in the West Himalayas, in what is now the Nanda Devi Biosphere Reserve, and stumbled upon one of the most beautiful wildflower displays in the world. They named it "the Valley of Flowers," with Smythe later authoring a book of the same name.

What they saw were the most alluring emerald-green slopes of birch forest, gently cascading waterfalls, mysterious swirls of cloud, and meadows carpeted with dainty, sherbet-colored alpine flowers. It must have been somewhere between July and October when those three mountaineers made their first foray into the "playground of the fairies," as this is when the valley is at its most blooming.

EASTERN LADAKH, INDIA
## 553. Sneak a peak at an evasive snow leopard
**When:** August to October
**Latitude:** 33.7563°N
**Longitude:** 77.2833°E

It's not easy to catch a glimpse of a snow leopard, but in winter this endangered animal comes down from the high mountaintops of the Himalayas in search of food. A trek into its habitat in Rumbak Valley is your best chance of seeing one.

AÏT-BENHADDOU, MOROCCO

## 554. See the sunrise over a fortified Moroccan city

**When:** All year
**Latitude:** 31.0500°N **Longitude:** 7.1333°W

Watch the sunrise over the Moroccan fortified city of Aït-Benhaddou and see the whole hillside bathed in an orange glow reflected from the mud-brick buildings. Found at the foot of the High Atlas Mountains, Aït-Benhaddou has been used as a location for *Gladiator* and *Game of Thrones*, among others, and is often used to stand in for Jerusalem.

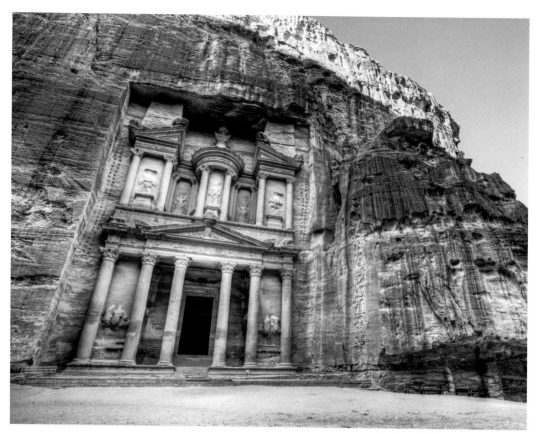

PETRA, JORDAN
## 555. Take in the spectacle that is Petra at sunrise
**When:** March to May
**Latitude:** 30.3286°N **Longitude:** 35.4419°E

Forged by the Nabateans in the fourth century, Petra is a unique city half built, half carved into the enclosing rock. A crossroads between Arabia, Egypt, and Syria, the "Rose City" boasts a mystical aura—partly due to the surrounding mountains, well-known to be riddled with caves and secret passageways, and partly because it is literally like stepping back in time 2,000 years.

There is no bad time to visit, but sunrise captures the city in all its glory. You enter via the narrow Al Siq canyon, whose twists and turns can feel quite claustrophobic, as do the constant requests from Bedouin children to buy their wares, but it's all part of the majesty and magic of the city. The gorge immediately opens out onto the most famous landmark, Al-Khazneh or "the Treasury," its notoriety thanks largely to a starring role in director Steven Spielberg's archeological adventure, *Indiana Jones and the Last Crusade*. The Greek-style facade is simply breathtaking both in terms of its sheer scale, but also the ornate detailing on the building and the colors of the sunrise, which change in the blink of an eye.

Even those who arrive early to take in the spectacle of the morning sun crashing against the rose-pink backdrop still find themselves soaking up the ambience and hustle and bustle atmosphere as the sun sets.

JORDAN
## 556. Bicycle from the Dead Sea to the Red Sea
**When:** All year
**Latitude:** 31.1806°N **Longitude:** 35.7014°E (Al-Karak Castle)

Take the cycling trip of a lifetime, between two of the most atmospherically named bodies of water: from the east side of Jordan, the Dead Sea, to the south of the country, the Red Sea.

The Dead Sea is technically a lake and is the deepest, saltiest lake in the world. Due to its high salt content, life struggles to survive here—hence its eerie moniker. By contrast, the Red Sea, an inlet of the Indian Ocean, may have gotten its name from a type of algae found in its water. Unlike its Dead Sea counterpart, there is a fantastic array of life in the sea here. So your biking days through Jordan can be top and tailed with a much-needed spot of water refreshment at either end.

And you'll need those refreshing dips. It takes between six and nine days on a mountain bike to cycle between the seas. The route is mainly dirt tracks or quiet roads, but there is desert sand to tackle and long climbs, all under a hot sun. The reward is a simply stunning ride through incredible sights and sites.

This trip is as much about the culture, heritage, and tradition of Jordan as it is about the fantastic ride through it.

ALL OVER EGYPT (OR ANYWHERE)
## 557. Bake like an Egyptian
**When:** All year
**Latitude:** 30.0444°N
**Longitude:** 31.2357°E (Cairo)

A fresh loaf of warm bread is one of life's simple pleasures, and even more so when you've made it yourself. Discovered in ancient Egypt, the first evidence of sourdough dates back to around 1500 BC. Tasty, easy to digest, and natural, it is still baked all over the country.

OLD CITY, BAKU, AZERBAIJAN
## 558. Step back in time in Azerbaijan's capital
**When:** All year
**Latitude:** 40.3667°N
**Longitude:** 49.8352°E

Who doesn't want to utter the sentence "I'm just back from Azerbaijan"? Head to this wonderfully named country to see the UNESCO-listed medieval Old City, complete with city walls and a labyrinth of beguiling narrow streets.

CAIRO, EGYPT
## 559. Predict the future in the past
**When:** All year (although summer can be uncomfortably hot)
**Latitude:** 30.0444°N
**Longitude:** 31.2357°E (center of Cairo)

Where better than mysterious Egypt to explore your mystical side with a fun tarot card reading? Playing cards were invented in the ancient city of Cairo, entering Europe in the late fourteenth century, and some believe that the way the tarot cards fall can predict your future.

EGYPT
## 560. Learn to strum a guitar
**When:** All year
**Latitude:** 30.0444°N
**Longitude:** 31.2357°E

It's never too late to learn an instrument, and the guitar, which has its earliest origins in Babylon (known as Egypt these days) is a fine choice. Whether it's a classical example or an amplified heavy-metal Flying V ax, there's a six-stringed style for every taste.

Scuba diving with turtles in the subaqua world of Honduras (see page 338)

CHAPTER 4
# NORTHERN HEMISPHERE
from 30º north to 15º north

▼ EVERGLADES, FLORIDA, US
### 561. See crocodiles and alligators together
**When:** All year
**Latitude:** 26.0000°N
**Longitude:** 80.7000°W

Alligators love freshwater marshes. Crocodiles prefer salt water. So while they may look similar to us, their paths rarely cross, with the exception of in the Florida Everglades, where the wetlands offer the perfect habitats for both. Alligators are usually darker and have blunter snouts; crocs have more teeth protruding—although you might not want to get close enough to find this out!

NEW ORLEANS, LOUISIANA, US
### 562. Play poker where it all began
**When:** All year
**Latitude:** 29.9500°N
**Longitude:** 90.0667°W

Poker is said to have started in New Orleans, spreading to the rest of the country via the Mississippi riverboats upon which gambling was a common pastime. Play a hand or two in any of the bars here, or on the riverboats that still cruise the Mississippi today.

NEW ORLEANS, LOUISIANA, US
### 563. Party with the locals in a second line parade
**When:** All year (notably as part of festivals in April and August)
**Latitude:** 29.9511°N
**Longitude:** 90.0715°W

Descendants of New Orleans' legendary jazz funerals, second line parades are a boisterous, jubilant celebration of life that surges through neighborhood streets throughout the year. Take part in one of these colorful, musical, mobile, brass band-led parties.

The search for crocodiles and alligators in the Florida Everglades, US

Mardi Gras in New Orleans, US

NEW ORLEANS, LOUISIANA, US
## 564. Let your hair down at Mardi Gras
**When:** January to February
**Latitude:** 29.9500°N **Longitude:** 90.0667°W

Despite the devastation inflicted by Hurricane Katrina in 2005, New Orleans has proven to have an indomitable spirit, characterized by its annual carnival celebration, Mardi Gras. A time for overindulging on food, wine, and song before the fasting period of Lent begins, it is just one of many carnival celebrations in a city that you'd forgive if it just wanted to lick its wounds and mourn its dead. But that's not its style.

A visit to New Orleans should be a staple of any bucket list, any time of year. The architecture is bold and brassy; the food innovative, bordering on eccentric;

the music loud and never ending. Barely a week goes by when there isn't some kind of parade or party, but the city pulls out all the stops during the two weeks of Mardi Gras, also called "Fat Tuesday."

There are two ways to enjoy Mardi Gras: take in the drama and performance from the balcony of one of the many lodging houses lining the parade routes of the French Quarter, or down in the streets, where jazz vibrations reverberate and senses are teased with the potent smell of gumbo and jambalaya. This is where to truly experience the hedonism of Mardi Gras.

Miami's funky South Beach in Florida, US

▲ MIAMI, FLORIDA, US
### 565. Visit Miami's art deco playground
**When:** All year
**Latitude:** 25.7616°N
**Longitude:** 80.1917°W

They don't call it the American Riviera for nothing: Ocean Drive on Miami's South Beach is unsurpassed for US art deco architecture. See palm trees set against grand, pastel buildings—nowhere else looks quite like it; and it's a true nightlife hot spot too.

NEW ORLEANS, US
### 566. Have a road food-feast
**When:** All year
**Latitude:** 29.9510°N
**Longitude:** 90.0715°W

Americans love both driving and eating, so the rise of "road food-culture"—appreciation of the very best fare from homegrown eateries dotted along the highways and back roads of the country—was inevitable. Grab everything from the finest crab cakes in Maryland to Texan bulls' testicles; how deep you want to experiment into it is up to you, but from brawny burgers to rocking ribs, there's something ready in the diner for every taste.

ORLANDO, FLORIDA, US
### 567. Feed your inner child at Walt Disney World
**When:** All year
**Latitude:** 28.4186°N
**Longitude:** 81.5811°W

It's billed as the "Happiest Place on Earth," and the smiles plastered across every face—children and adults alike—make it hard to argue. Join the throngs at the world's consistently top-ranked amusement park—the Cinderella Castle and ride-packed Adventureland are among the myriad highlights.

KENNEDY SPACE CENTER, FLORIDA, US

## 568. Watch a rocket launch into space

**When:** All year

**Latitude:** 28.5241°N **Longitude:** 80.6509°W

Watching a space rocket fire up its boosters and blast off into the atmosphere isn't an everyday occurrence, but at the Kennedy Space Center in Florida, it may happen more often than you might imagine.

Of all the space centers, Kennedy has the closest viewing platform for the public, so you won't see better anywhere else. Or hear better—the thundering roar of the rocket's engines will reach you shortly after the flames ignite, so you may want to bring earplugs. Expect your skin to prickle with the thrill of it all.

Tickets are available to buy online, although be aware that launch dates can change due to weather or technical issues. If you don't manage to see a launch, you can still visit to soak up the atmosphere of a ride into space. Check out, too, the 525 ft (160 m) tall "rocket garage," and 3 mi (5 km) long shuttle-landing facility. Parking these things takes some serious room.

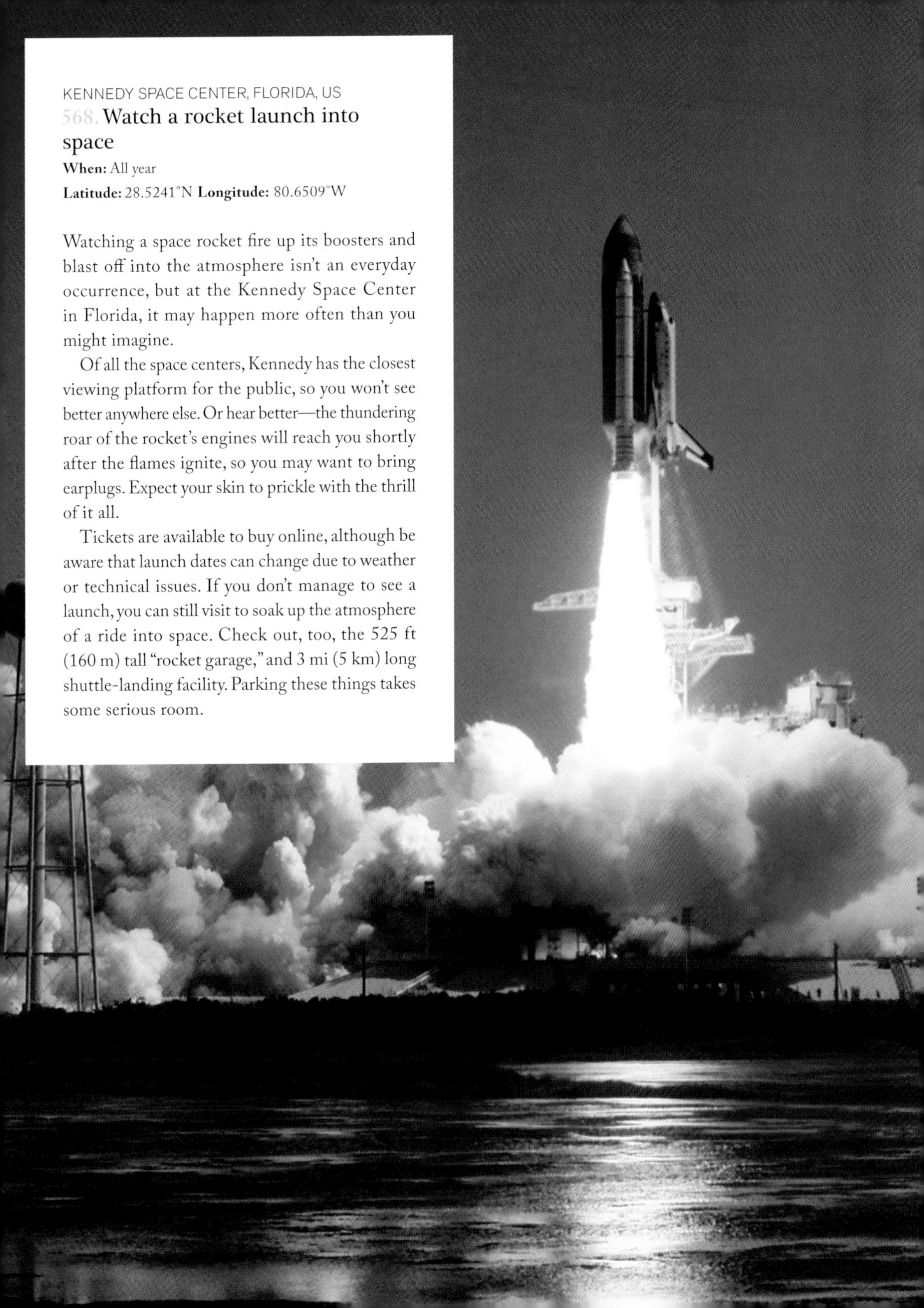

SAN ANTONIO, TEXAS, US
## 569. Enter a tree-climbing championship
**When:** Annually in August
**Latitude:** 29.4241°N
**Longitude:** 98.4936°W

Most people haven't climbed a tree since they were in short pants, but there's no reason not to—the nimble athleticism required, the thrill of getting a little bit too high, and the view from the top all make it worthwhile. If you think you've got what it takes, you can get competitive with it, too. The International Tree Climbing Championship in Texas, now in its fortieth year, sees competitors scored for speed, accuracy, poise, and strength, all while safely attached to a rope—and wearing a helmet, it should be added.

▶ CRYSTAL RIVER, FLORIDA, US
## 570. Swim with manatees
**When:** April to October
**Latitude:** 28.9024°N
**Longitude:** 82.5926°W

These prehistoric-looking animals roam the coast of Florida during the warmer sea months. Head to Crystal River, the only place where it's legal to swim alongside the gentle, slow-moving mammals, although there are numerous other options available to observe them in summer.

A manatee in Crystal River, Florida, US

KATHMANDU VALLEY, NEPAL
## 571. Explore the heritage of the Kathmandu Valley
**When:** All year (although avoid the mid-June to September monsoon season)
**Longitude:** 27.6722°N (at Bhaktapur) **Latitude:** 85.4278°E

Despite the ongoing expansion of Nepal's hectic capital, the Kathmandu Valley remains a cultural treasure trove. Well-preserved medieval towns—most notably Bhaktapur—are tightly packed with houses, temples, palaces, and squares that appear little changed in hundreds of years. The area is also home to some of Nepal's holiest Hindu sites. Pashupatinath, on the banks of the Bagmati River, is home to an important Shiva temple and a series of cremation ghats (riverside steps), while Dakshinkali is a center of animal sacrifice—a bloody but compelling place. The town of Boudha, meanwhile, is the center of Nepal's Tibetan Buddhist community, its focal point the glorious white dome of the Great Stupa.

Don't let Nepal's 2015 earthquakes put you off: although the Kathmandu Valley was badly affected, many of the key sites escaped serious damage, and most of those that were hit have been restored.

SAURAHA, NEPAL
## 572. Stroke a baby elephant
**When:** All year (although avoid the mid-June to September monsoon season)
**Latitude:** 27.5747°N
**Longitude:** 84.4936°E

Just outside the town of Sauraha, close to the main gate of Chitwan National Park, the Elephant Breeding Centre enables pachyderms to mate in peace and safety. It is open to visitors, so you can see—and even stroke—the playful, impossibly cute calves.

LHASA, TIBET, CHINA
## 573. Touch heaven in the Place of the Gods
**When:** All year
**Latitude:** 29.6578°N
**Longitude:** 91.1169°E

"Lhasa" means "place of the gods," and is aptly named, not least because it reaches up into the heavens as one of the highest cities in the world. Look up to see, rising above it all, the splendor of the Dalai Lama's Potala Palace.

SICHUAN, CHINA
## 574. Feel the force at the Jinping-I Dam
**When:** All year
**Latitude:** 28.1822°N
**Longitude:** 101.6314°E

Wonder at the 1,000 ft (305 m) tall Jinping-I Dam, the world's tallest, which has created a massive reservoir to produce hydroelectricity. The dam has four gates to control flooding, and when water is let out of these at a huge 800,000 gallons a second, you can feel the force.

TIBET, CHINA
## 575. Cleanse your karma with a prayer wheel
**When:** All year
**Latitude:** 29.6475°N
**Longitude:** 91.1175°E

An essential when in Tibet: prayer wheels—generally wood, metal, or stone—have Buddhist mantras written on them, and spinning the wheel is similar to reciting a prayer. It's acceptable when done respectfully by non-Buddhists, so help yourself to some good karma.

## 576. Take a sail on the holy Ganges

**When:** November to March

**Latitude:** 25.3176°N **Longitude:** 82.9739°E

One of the most spiritual and important Hindu sites in India, and one of the oldest living cities in the world, Varanasi is as frenetic as it is serene. Thousands of travelers—Indians and foreigners—come each year to bathe in the holy Ganges on the ghats (stone steps) or to die and be cremated on the riverbanks.

There is no better way to soak up the serenity of this city than on a sunrise cruise in a rowboat on the Ganges, during which you'll witness hundreds of pilgrims performing their ritual ablutions on the riverside. At sunset you'll discover a similar feeling of tranquility; as the sky turns pink, you can take to the waters to perform an *aarti*—a devotional ceremony involving fire. Believers float candles in cups made from leaves and flowers on the venerated river, as an offering to the gods.

When darkness falls, the city reaches its spiritual climax: from your wooden boat, feel the electric atmosphere as crowds gather to see priests perform the daily Agni Pooja ritual on the Dashashwamedh Ghat.

## 577. Hike to one of Buddhism's most holy sites

**When:** May to October

**Latitude:** 28.8187°N **Longitude:** 99.7022°E

Choose from a rewarding day hike to a demanding two-week *kora* trail—or anything in between—over the 112 mi (180 km) spiritual Meili Xue Shan. There are twenty breathtaking peaks, and the towering 22,000 ft (6,706 m) Kawa Karpo is one of Buddhism's most holy sites.

## 578. Hike to Everest Base Camp
**When:** October to April
**Latitude:** 28.0072°N (at Everest Base Camp) **Longitude:** 86.8594°E

The trek to Everest's Southern Face Base Camp gets you as close to the world's highest mountain as you can get without actually climbing it. Nepal's most famous trek, which takes you through fabulous Himalayan scenery, lasts fourteen to eighteen days. This allows you enough time to properly rest and acclimatize to the altitude—you reach more than 18,045 ft (5,500 m) above sea level at one stage of the trail. It is strenuous—you walk for three to six hours a day at altitude—but achievable for anyone who is reasonably fit. En route you'll stay in teahouses with Nepali, Tibetan, and Western food, as well as beer and local spirit *rakshi* on offer.

The trek starts at Lukla, home to a perilous-looking airstrip into which most travelers fly. Following the path of the Dudh Kosi River, the trail leads up to Namche Bazaar, a town known as the "Sherpa capital of the world." After Namche Bazaar, the trail heads northwest through small settlements, across the Dudh Kosi, and bisects the juniper forests of Tengboche, from

where there are breathtaking views. After a brief descent through fir and birch woods, the route takes you to Pangboche, home of the region's oldest Buddhist *gompa* ("monastery"). From here, the altitude steadily rises, passing remote villages, tiny teahouses, and monasteries strung with colorful prayer flags, passing poignant monuments to those who have died attempting the ascent of Everest.

The trek's final stages take you across the Khumbu Glacier, following in the tracks of mountaineering parties, their yaks, and porters, to Everest Base Camp itself. Set at 17,598 ft (5,364 m) on the southern side of Everest, the vistas here are breathtaking but for an even better view of the mountain, scale the nearby 18,192 ft (5,545 m) peak of Kala Pattar.

Choosing when to attempt the hike can be tricky. During the peak season (early October to early December), the route—and the lodges strung along it—can be uncomfortably busy. The mid-December to January period is much quieter, but the colder and snowier weather (in places the temperature can plunge to -4°F; -20°C) means that it is not really suitable for amateur hikers. In springtime (February to April), the weather is warmer and the trail is not overly busy, though haze, rain, and snowstorms mean views may be obscured. Regardless of when you decide to do it, however, the trek to Everest Base Camp is an unforgettable experience.

Hiking to Everest Base Camp in northern Nepal

THE RED SEA, EGYPT
## 579. Discover a wonder of the underwater world
**When:** All year
**Latitude:** 27.9158°N **Longitude:** 34.3300°E (Sharm el-Sheikh)

In addition to its extraordinary ancient civilization, Egypt is also the location for what has been described as one of the seven wonders of the underwater world: the Red Sea. From Taba—on the border with Israel and the northern tip of the Gulf of Aqaba—through renowned diving spots at Dahab and tourist-friendly Sharm el-Sheikh, and on to Hurghada in the south, the warm waters of this 220 mi (354 km) wide belt are teeming with marine life and spectacular coral reefs.

Snorkel or dive at any of these sites to discover the delights of this remarkable underwater playground.

VRINDAVAN, UTTAR PRADESH, INDIA
## 580. Experience an uplifting Hindu ceremony
**When:** August to September
**Latitude:** 27.5650°N **Longitude:** 77.6593°E

Situated roughly halfway between New Delhi and Agra—home of the awe-inspiring Taj Mahal—lies the temple-filled town of Vrindavan. This holy town arguably holds a greater place in the country's psyche than either of those internationally famous places.

According to tradition, the religious deity Lord Krishna (worshipped as supreme being by the country's 1 billion Hindus) first took human form in nearby Mathura and spent a large part of his early life in Vrindavan. Each year, to celebrate this momentous occasion, spectacular ceremonies are held in the city, and their bright colors, pageantry, and religious fervor make for an absorbing spectacle.

Experience one of India's joyful, uplifting religious ceremonies and take home a memory to be treasured.

▶ LUNANA, BHUTAN
## 581. Escape reality on the Snowman Trek
**When:** All year
**Latitude:** 27.5141°N **Longitude:** 90.4336°E

Don't be misled by its fabulous name—the Snowman Trek is a high-altitude mission that involves six- to eight-hour walks every day; but for those who are willing to rise to the challenge, it's also one of the most rewarding.

With a month-long adventure around blissfully beautiful, remote Bhutan, it is truly possible to lose yourself among the otherworldly landscape, friendly people, and absorbing Buddhist culture. Based in Lunana, it involves walking around—and sometimes up—six mountains more than 22,966 ft (7,000 m) high. Nine passes above 14,764 ft (4,500 m) must be overcome during the month, and it is this element that makes it so challenging. A degree of fitness is naturally required before participating, although you don't need to be young or an international athlete: it's often completed by those over sixty.

On the Snowman Trek
in Lunana, Bhutan

LA GOMERA IN SPAIN TO ANTIGUA
## 582. Cross the Atlantic—in a rowboat …
**When:** All year
**Latitude:** 28.1033°N **Longitude:** 17.2193°W (La Gomera)

More people have climbed Everest than have rowed the Atlantic; roughly the same number have gone into space. It is a notoriously difficult task. Generally done in crews of four or two, it requires money and hours and hours of training.

While crossing, crews tend to row in pairs—two hours on, two hours off, for twenty-four hours a day, for up to fifty days, sleeping only sporadically—so it is enormously draining. There are also often treacherous storm conditions, plus the slight madness of sensory deprivation; with nothing but sea for miles around, the feeling that the boat isn't traveling anywhere can mess with the strongest minds.

So why do it? Those who have conquered this challenge talk in awed tones about the greatest sunsets and sunrises they've ever seen; the clearest night skies; glorious encounters with whales, dolphins, and seals; and a sense of teamwork that cannot be rivaled.

CHITWAN NATIONAL PARK, NEPAL
## 583. Explore Nepal's thriving jungle
**When:** December to April
**Latitude:** 27.5000°N
**Longitude:** 84.3333°E

It's not exactly a walk in the park, but if you're willing to brave creepy-crawlies, a stroll through Chitwan can be the best way to experience this lush Nepalese wilderness. Chitwan National Park is home to a plethora of wildlife within its 360 sq mi (932 sq km) of dense forest. If you're extremely lucky, you could see sloth bears, leopards, and even a majestic Bengal tiger.

BHAKTAPUR, NEPAL
## 584. Commission a painting
**When:** All year
**Latitude:** 27.7165°N
**Longitude:** 85.4298°E

The search for nirvana is easier when you have a few timely tools to help keep you on the right spiritual path—a *thanka*, for example. You don't need to be a Buddhist to appreciate them, however. The highly geometric profusion of eyes, noses, mouths, animals, and spiritual symbolism is both meditative and beautiful. Commission your own from Sunapati Thanka Painting School, one of Nepal's only academies of this ancient art, and keep it rolled up in your travel bag for moments of personal contemplation.

TRONGSA, BHUTAN
## 585. Explore a little-known corner of the Himalayas
**When:** Spring, summer, and fall
**Latitude:** 27.4997°N **Longitude:** 90.5050°E

A mysterious landlocked kingdom perched high in the foothills of the Himalayas, Bhutan is a joy to explore, with hiking a particular treat. Despite its inhabitants being known as the "Dragon People," Buddhist Bhutan is a gentle, welcoming place packed with fascinating history and glorious views. Head to the center of the country to see the imposing Trongsa Dzong, an intriguing multi-leveled latticework of courtyards, alleyways, and temples, as well as home to 200 monks. The end-of-year Tshechu festival is a particularly good time to visit.

MOUNT TEIDE, TENERIFE, SPAIN
## 586. Stand atop a smoldering volcano
**When:** All year (though the summit is sometimes closed in midwinter)
**Latitude:** 28.2725°N **Longitude:** 16.6421°W

Mount Teide towers over the Canary Island of Tenerife, beckoning beachgoers upward, to the highest point of Spain. The summit is 12,198 ft (3,718 m) above sea level (making it the third-highest volcano in the world).

You can catch a cable car from the main road up to 11,663 ft (3,555 m), but for those who want to stand on the crater itself, a permit is needed for access to Route No. 10, which must be applied for several weeks in advance. The cable car may be easy, but far more satisfying is the walk up from Montaña Blanca. Stay overnight in the basic refuge, then leave it two hours before sunrise, and you'll reach the top in time to see the sun pop out of the Atlantic.

LA GOMERA, CANARY ISLANDS, SPAIN
## 587. Hear the whistling people of La Gomera
**When:** All year
**Latitude:** 28.1033°N **Longitude:** 17.2193°W

In a world of Snapchat, WhatsApp, and wifi, there's something deeply heartwarming about hearing the silbo gomero—an ancient language used on the mountainous Canary Island of La Gomera, where people still whistle from hilltop to hilltop to communicate. Using two whistled vowels and four consonants, the method is perfect for getting messages across deep valleys and ravines, with sound traveling more than 2 mi (3 km)—much farther than shouting. It is still taught in the schools here in order to preserve the tradition. It sounds like pleasant birdsong and adds a unique air to this hikers' paradise that you can reach by ferry from Tenerife.

▶ SARANGKOT, POKHARA, NEPAL
## 588. Soar like a hawk over mountain vistas
**When:** October to April
**Latitude:** 28.2439°N
**Longitude:** 83.9486°E

Fly like a bird in an exhilarating parahawking adventure. It is paragliding with a difference: a trained Egyptian hawk is your aerial guide. This tandem experience—a trained pilot is in control of the actual flying—allows you to feed the hawk in flight while tracking its swooping and soaring progress across the thermals. Amazing.

Parahawking over mountain vistas in Nepal

▶ LUMBINI, NEPAL
## 589. Pay your respects at the birthplace of Buddha

**When:** All year (although avoid the mid-June to September monsoon season)
**Latitude:** 27.4840°N **Longitude:** 83.2760°E

In the Terai lowlands of southern Nepal, just beyond the dusty town of Bhairahawa, is Lumbini, the source of one of the world's great religions. Set in a garden strung with colorful prayer flags, and populated with meditating devotees, is the Maya Devi Temple, which marks the spot where the Buddha is reputed to have been born in 623 BC. Whatever your religious beliefs, it is a wonderfully tranquil, contemplative spot.

Surrounding the Maya Devi Temple is a vast, peaceful park studded with monasteries founded by Buddhist groups from around the world and built in an eclectic range of national styles. At the far end, beyond a sanctuary for the endangered sarus crane, is the gleaming white, Japanese-style Shanti Stupa ("Peace Pagoda"). If you can put up with the blistering heat, the best time to visit is in May, to celebrate Buddha Jayanti, Buddha's birthday (the exact date varies according to the Nepali lunar calendar).

The birthplace of Buddha—Lumbini in Nepal

BHANGARH, INDIA
## 590. Dare to visit a haunted village

**When:** All year (daytime only!)
**Latitude:** 27.0947°N
**Longitude:** 76.2906°E

Visit the Indian fortified village of Bhangarh—famed for its ancient ruin—during the day, as it is prohibited during the hours of sunset and sunrise. This is because, legend has it, this place is one of the most haunted in the world!

DELHI, INDIA
## 591. Ride in an Indian rickshaw

**When:** All year
**Latitude:** 28.6139°N
**Longitude:** 77.2090°E

You haven't traveled properly in India until you have traveled in an auto-rickshaw: India's omnipresent three-wheeled taxi. They command the roads like nothing else, squeeze into spaces that seem smaller than they are, and round corners without indicators—just a lot of tooting horns. It's the perfect way to turn a standard A to B journey into a mini-adventure every time.

DARJEELING, INDIA
## 592. Pick tea in Darjeeling

**When:** March to November (although avoid the mid-June to September monsoon season)
**Latitude:** 27.0500°N
**Longitude:** 88.2667°E

Indians love tea, and around a quarter of what it makes is the popular blend grown on the hillsides of Darjeeling. Visit between March and November for tea plucking, but avoid the monsoon season from June to September.

AGRA, INDIA

## 593. Be stunned by the Taj Mahal

**When:** November to March
**Latitude:** 27.1750°N **Longitude:** 78.0419°E

No matter how many pictures you see before you visit Agra's
Taj Mahal, nothing can quite prepare you for the captivating
grandeur and beauty of this towering, white-marble mass.
Built by Mughal Emperor Shah Jahan to house the body
of his favorite wife—Mumtaz Mahal ("Jewel of the
Palace")—who died after the birth of their fourteenth
child, the Taj is a majestic centerpiece in a
flourishing walled garden.

Visit at sunrise, when the grounds are
a little quieter, and watch the growing
light change the colors of the marble
pillars and curved domes from
blue to pink to orange,
and finally, to a pristine,
glittering white.

▼ JAIPUR, RAJASTHAN, INDIA

### 594. Feast your senses in an Indian bazaar

**When:** All year
**Latitude:** 26.9000°N
**Longitude:** 75.8000°E

Rajasthan is an Indian state famed for its market bazaars—and nowhere do they come more iconic than those in Jaipur, the largest city in, and capital of, the state. Crowded, noisy, narrow-alley markets provide the perfect place to get lost in, where everything you could imagine is on sale and every sense is assaulted. Remember to haggle—the price you are quoted is never the price you should pay!

JAIPUR, RAJASTHAN, INDIA

### 595. Take a peek at the Pink City's palace

**When:** All year
**Latitude:** 26.9239°N
**Longitude:** 75.8267°E

Built over five stories, the elaborate Hawa Mahal ("Palace of the Winds") in the opulent "Pink City" was built to allow the ladies of the court to watch outside life without being observed. Nowadays, you can go to observe the palace.

ASSAM, INDIA

### 596. Lock eyes with a rhino

**When:** November to April
**Latitude:** 26.5775°N
**Longitude:** 93.1711°E

Few animals epitomize strength like a rhinoceros. Yet look one in the eye (from a safe distance), and they seem to have a certain vulnerability about them. Try it with a greater one-horned rhino in Kaziranga National Park.

A bustling Indian bazaar in Jaipur, Rajasthan

## 597. Work through the UNESCO World Heritage list
**When:** All year
**Latitude:** 26.8578°N
**Longitude:** 40.3293°E (Ha'il, Saudi Arabia)

If you visited one UNESCO World Heritage site a week, you would have more than twenty years of nonstop travel ahead of you. You'd need a limitless budget and probably some good contacts to transport you to some of the harder-to-reach places.

All 1,031 UNESCO World Heritage sites (as of April 2016) have something unique and outstanding about them, whether it is to do with a natural world or a cultural contribution. The sites are spread over more than 163 different nations, and Italy tops the list of entries with fifty-one. There are no records of anyone having visited all of the World Heritage sites—but with twenty or so sites being added each year, it's not easy to keep up.

## 598. Marvel at the miraculous "Tree of Life"
**When:** All year (but best outside summer, which is April to October)
**Latitude:** 26.0386°N
**Longitude:** 50.5459°E (Jabal Al Dukhan)

Somehow eking enough water to survive in the desert, Bahrain's Shajarat-al-Hayat ("Tree of Life"), near Jabal Al Dukhan, has, not surprisingly, earned mythical status. Join other visitors who have been coming to see the only natural growth for miles around for 400 years.

## 599. Take time to tour Timbuktu
**When:** November to February
**Latitude:** 16.7666°N
**Longitude:** 3.0026°W

The Malian city of Timbuktu has long held an air of remoteness and mystery. Perched on the southern edge of the vast Sahara Desert, a twenty-hour 600 mi (966 km) off-road drive from the capital Bamako, it is often used as shorthand to describe the "middle of nowhere." You'll find, though, plenty more to this beautiful and haunting adobe city, which has been a UNESCO World Heritage listed site since 1988. Seek out its fascinating history, extraordinary architecture, and three magnificent mosques.

## 600. Be a Berber for the night
**When:** April to May
**Latitude:** 23.4162°N **Longitude:** 25.6628°W

Just 150 mi (250 km) from the chaotic city of Marrakech lies the vast Sahara. It stretches out through western and southern Morocco and spans right across the African continent from Egypt to Mauritania.

Join a tour from Marrakech and spend a night in the desert with the nomadic Berber men, who have lived here for hundreds of years. They were Morocco's original inhabitants, before the Arabs arrived at the end of the seventh century. Take the long and bumpy ride on a camel into the wilderness, until every horizon is far, wide, and punctuated by sand dunes.

Temperatures drop to well below 32°F (0°C) in the Sahara, but a night by the bonfire, with traditional music and dancing, will keep you warm. Once the party has ended, you'll find the night sky is at its most spectacular in the depths of the desert.

PUSHKAR, RAJASTHAN, INDIA

## 601. Help judge the camel beauty pageant

**When:** November

**Latitude:** 26.4897°N

**Longitude:** 74.5511°E

Join hundreds of thousands of hump-loving visitors as they flock to Pushkar's crazy camel fair each year. As well as camel trading, there is a lively carnival, with prizes for longest mustache, turban tying, snake charming, markets, and even a beauty contest. For the camels, naturally.

GUWAHATI, ASSAM, INDIA
### 602. Dare to dine on the world's hottest chili
**When:** All year
**Latitude:** 26.1445°N
**Longitude:** 91.7362°E

Enjoy hot food? Like testing your taste buds? Then get your teeth into the eye-watering *bhut jolokia* ("ghost chili"). Burning to the top of the official hotness-ometer (the Scoville heat unit), this fiery spice is a staple in Assam cooking.

RAJASTHAN, INDIA
### 603. Explore the regal palaces of Rajasthan
**When:** October to February
**Latitude:** 26.5727°N
**Longitude:** 73.8390°E

Rajasthan's forts and palaces are some of India's most majestic structures. Explore these opulent monuments from the country's princely past—some standing since the sixteenth century, and some perfectly preserved and just as impressive as when they were built.

WADI AL-HITAN, EGYPT
### 604. Discover whale fossils in a desert
**When:** November to April
(to avoid the heat)
**Latitude:** 29.2725°N
**Longitude:** 30.0405°E

Be impressed by the massive collection of whale fossils at Wadi Al-Hitan, which is almost the missing link in the evolution of these great beasts. It is also 115 mi (185 km) from the sea, which shows how the land has changed in the past 50 million years.

GIZA, EGYPT
### 605. Discover the secrets of the pyramids
**When:** All year
**Latitude:** 29.9791°N **Longitude:** 31.1343°E

The pyramids at Giza are far more accessible than you might imagine. Visible in the skyline of Cairo, these magnificent tombs were built around 2,500 BC. Hop in a taxi for a ride to the ancient site—preferably at sunrise to see the amazing hues of the warming stones. You can explore the fascinating, humid tunnels within, although more claustrophobic visitors may prefer an airier camel ride around the massive monuments and iconic sphinx instead.

LUXOR, EGYPT
### 606. Walk in the footsteps of pharaohs
**When:** All year
**Latitude:** 25.6872°N
**Longitude:** 32.6396°E

Walking in the footsteps of the pharaohs is a dizzying feeling. Karnak is the place to do it; it dates back to the rule of Senusret I, who reigned nearly 4,000 years ago. Part of the huge city of Thebes, it was a key center of worship and is now one of the largest ancient centers of worship in the world. The precinct of Amun-Ra is the only one of its four sections open to the public and is majestic. With vast statues, colossal halls and gateways, and a 95 ft (29 m) obelisk, you'll be awed by the scale of the ancients' architectural acumen.

FARS PROVINCE, NORTH OF SHIRAZ, IRAN
## 607. Take the time to discover Persepolis
**When:** All year
**Latitude:** 29.9355°N
**Longitude:** 52.8915°E

The ceremonial center of the Persian Empire (it was the capital between the years 550 and 330 BC), the sheer scale of the place also known as the Throne of Jamshid is mind-boggling. Explore the ruins, which are in good shape. There are eighteen pillars of a huge building on the terrace, richly decorated sepulchers in the hillsides, and the Naqsh-e Rostam—7 mi (12 km) from the main site—is an exceptional example of an Achaemenid necropolis. All of this is enough to give you an overwhelming sense of history.

HUNAN PROVINCE, CHINA
## 608. Get your head in the clouds in China
**When:** All year (although summer can be very humid)
**Latitude:** 29.2057°N
**Longitude:** 110.3238°E

The ethereal splendor of mist-shrouded Tianzi Mountain—with its gullies, forests, and needlelike peaks peeping through the clouds—makes for an otherworldly experience. Catch a cable car that runs 6,500 ft (1,981 m) to the summit from the Wulingyuan entrance of Zhangjiajie National Forest Park—or you can walk up the 3,878 steps.

◀ SICHUAN PROVINCE, CHINA
## 609. Peek into the pandas' private world
**When:** All year
**Latitude:** 29.5347°N
**Longitude:** 102.0845°E

Is there a cuter animal in the world than the giant panda? Judge for yourself at Sichuan's network of seven nature reserves that houses 30 percent of the world's panda population. With prior arrangement, you can help care for these bamboo lovers.

Pandas in their private world in Sichuan Province, China

WADI RUM, JORDAN

## 610. Make a *Lawrence of Arabia* journey

**When:** All year

**Latitude:** 29.5846°N

**Longitude:** 35.4263°E

Wadi Rum provided the locations for most of the *Lawrence of Arabia* movie. T. E. Lawrence did pass through the area on his travels, but he was far from being the first. See for yourself: the rocks here are home to many prehistoric drawings and signs.

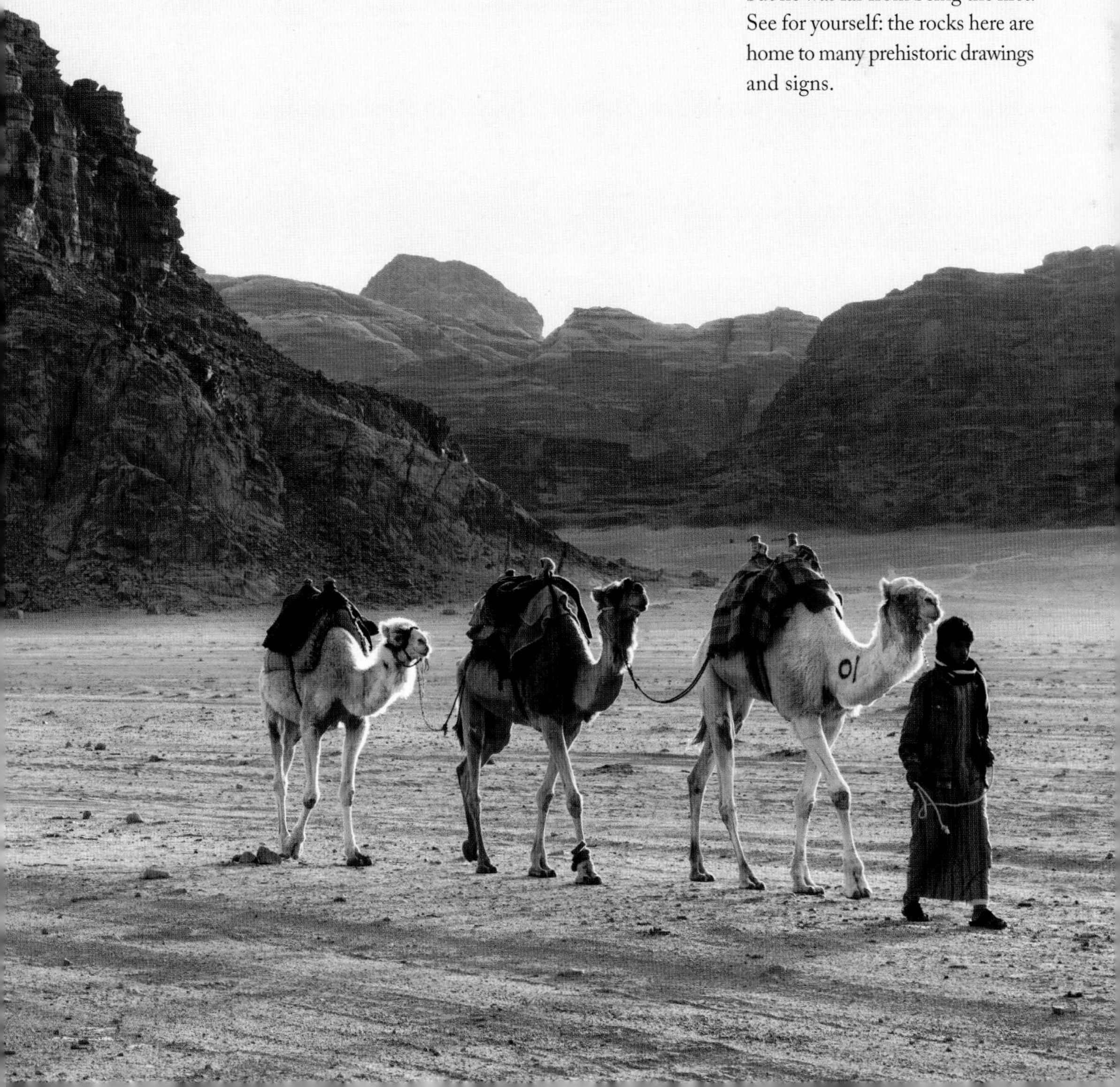

▼ MEGHALAYA, INDIA

### 611. Discover the best root across the river

**When:** January to May and September to December

**Latitude:** 25.2717°N

**Longitude:** 91.7308°E

They might just be the weirdest bridges in the world. Created from rubber tree roots guided across rivers by the Khasi tribe of northern India, the living-root walkways can support up to fifty people. Marvel at the double-decker bridge in Nongriat village, in the Cherrapunji rain forest.

ST. LOUIS, SENEGAL

### 612. Attend the Saint-Louis Jazz festival

**When:** May

**Latitude:** 16.0333°N

**Longitude:** 16.5000°W

The vibrant Senegalese city of Saint-Louis comes into its own in May, when jazz heads from all over the globe convene to sing, scat, and dance. Join the crowds in venues big and small to hear some of the world's best acts.

SAHARAN ALGERIA REGION

### 613. Get on the trail of the Saharan sand cat

**When:** All year

**Latitude:** 25.5000°N

**Longitude:** 9.0000°E (Tassili n'Ajjer National Park, Algeria)

The arid Sahara Desert may not be the obvious place to go looking for cute kittens, but with its large eyes and outsized ears, the nocturnal sand cat certainly provides the *aaw* factor. Visit Algeria's awe-inspiring national parks to see one of these adorable creatures for yourself.

Tree root bridge in the Cherrapunji rain forest, India

Al Mahara restaurant at Dubai's Burj Al Arab Jumeirah Hotel, UAE

MADHYA PRADESH, INDIA
## 614. Encounter the erotic carvings at Khajuraho Group of Monuments
**When:** All year (although avoid the mid-June to September monsoon season)
**Latitude:** 24.8500°N **Longitude:** 79.9300°E

Tucked away in a remote corner of the hot, dusty central Indian state of Madhya Pradesh are some of the most exquisitely preserved—and erotically charged—ancient carvings in the subcontinent. The walls of Khajuraho's temples are covered with eye-catching carvings depicting amorous couples, trios, and groups in a beguiling variety of combinations and positions. They have been dubbed the "Kamasutra temples."

Built between the tenth and twelfth centuries AD by the Chandela dynasty, the temples were abandoned soon after completion, following the arrival of waves of Afghan invaders. They were later swallowed up by the jungle and remained hidden for centuries before being "rediscovered" by the British in the 1830s. The carvings captivate visitors like few others in India.

▲ DUBAI, UAE
## 615. Drink at the top and bottom of one building
**When:** All year
**Latitude:** 25.1409°N
**Longitude:** 55.1857°E

Enjoy the impressive view along Dubai's coastline from the cocktail bar on the twenty-seventh floor of the Burj Al Arab Jumeirah Hotel. Then take a quick elevator journey below, to the underwater restaurant with floor-to-ceiling glass walls, for a very different view of the sea.

▶ AL JAYLAH, OMAN

616. Find water in the desert the Omani way

**When:** All year

**Latitude:** 24.5328°N

**Longitude:** 56.4923°E

Not all deserts are without water. For more than 2,000 years in Oman they have had an irrigation system known as *aflaj*—small channels that cling to cliff faces and cross arid deserts taking water from springs to settlements and fields. So you need never go thirsty in the Oman desert.

Finding water in the desert the Omani way: Al Jaylah irrigation system

◀ BODHGAYA, BIHAR, INDIA

617. Sit in the shade of the tree of enlightenment

**When:** All year

**Latitude:** 24.6961°N **Longitude:** 84.9870°E

As you approach the Mahabodhi Temple Complex in Bodhgaya, you can see its spire from 6 mi (10 km) away, as it rises above the tree line to a height of 180 ft (55 m). This is the place where Buddha attained enlightenment meditating under a Bodhi tree without moving for seven days.

There is still a sacred tree here, the Mahabodhi Tree, said to be a direct descendant of the original. This is the most important place for Buddhist pilgrimages, and people come to meditate and contemplate Buddha's teachings under the shade of the tree's heart-shaped leaves. Sit in its shade and experience the peace and reverence of that which exudes from this magical place.

CHERRAPUNJI, INDIA

618. Sing in the rain at Cherrapunji

**When:** June to August (for most chance of rainfall)

**Latitude:** 25.2717°N

**Longitude:** 91.7308°E

Sometimes, instead of pulling up your hood and putting up your umbrella lest any stray raindrop should touch your body, don't you just want to throw your arms wide, toss your head back, and sing in the rain? Do it. And do it loudly at Cherrapunji.

The tree of enlightenment: the Mahabodhi Tree in Bodhgaya, Bihar, India

START IN GUANGZHOU, CHINA
## 619. Create the sensation of travel in your own kitchen
**When:** All year
**Latitude:** 23.1333°N **Longitude:** 113.2667°E

Breakfast like a king, so the saying goes, and what better way to do it than to choose a different nationality to feast from every morning? Start with filled steamed buns from China; arepa, a corn cake from Colombia topped with eggs or jam; or a full English breakfast that includes sausages, bacon, eggs, mushroom, and tomatoes. Then there are French croissants; Russian griddle cakes, often made with cheese; and Jamaicans like ackee, a fruit that looks like scrambled eggs when cooked. You'll be around the world in a week.

NEAR HUIZHOU, GUANGDONG, CHINA
## 620. Visit an Austrian town, in China
**When:** All year
**Latitude:** 23.0667°N **Longitude:** 114.4000°E

If you've ever wondered what billionaires spend their money on, look no further than Hallstatt in Guangdong province, China. Actually, look a bit farther and also check out Hallstatt in Austria—the former is a replica of the latter, built at a price tag of almost $1 billion.

The original picturesque alpine town of Hallstatt is a UNESCO Heritage site. Narrow cobblestone streets, brightly painted homes, and a scenic lake make it traditionally Austrian in feel. The two towns are twinned, with the Austrian Hallstatt reportedly receiving many more Chinese visitors today. The Chinese have previously built miniversions of Barcelona and Venice near Shanghai.

◄ HAVANA, CUBA
## 621. Travel in style in a classic car in Havana
**When:** All year
**Latitude:** 23.1136°N
**Longitude:** 82.3666°W

The classic 1950s cars in Cuba have stayed on the road out of necessity. Much loved, and much used, they are as much a part of Cuba as posters of Che Guevara, and a testament to the survival spirit of the island. A ride in one might not feel smooth, but it will certainly look it.

Traveling in style in a classic car in Havana, Cuba

Big game fishing off Cuba in the Caribbean

HAVANA, CUBA
### 622. Smoke a cigar in the country it was made
**When:** All year
**Latitude:** 23.1136°N
**Longitude:** 82.3666°W

You don't need to be a smoker to want to roll the smoke of a Cuban cigar around your mouth on a visit to the tobacco-rich country of Cuba. The production technique of a true Cuban cigar is the same now as it was a hundred years ago, giving it its strong, but authentic, flavor.

▲ OFF CUBA
### 623. Feel the thrill of hooking a big game fish
**When:** Choose your month based on the month for your species
**Latitude:** 23.1799°N
**Longitude:** 81.1885°W

Hemingway captured the drama of big game fishing perfectly in his book *The Old Man and the Sea*. The book came from his love of the sport: the waiting game, the luring of the majestic blue marlin or a sailfish, then the skill and the battle of reeling it in. Hook your big game fish in the Caribbean.

LA CECILIA, HAVANA, CUBA
### 624. Dance under the stars to Cuban salsa
**When:** All year (avoid the rainy season from May to October)
**Latitude:** 23.1012°N
**Longitude:** 82.4493°W

Cuba has an energy all of its own, and when that energy is put into partying and salsa dancing, Cubans really get going. Throw back the rum, loosen up your hips, and join in—under a starry night sky in Cuba, it's seriously fun.

BIMMAH SINKHOLE, OMAN
## 625. Take a dip in a hole in the earth

**When:** All year
**Latitude:** 23.0361°N
**Longitude:** 59.0717°E

The Bimmah sinkhole in Oman formed when waters dissolved the rock below and the roof fell in. It is simply a hole in the earth, but a very beautiful one. Take a dip in its clear turquoise waters, with striated rock faces rising up 66 ft (20 m) all around.

The International Kite Festival in Ahmedabad, India

▲ AHMEDABAD, GUJARAT, INDIA

### 626. Go fly a kite

**When:** January 14
**Latitude:** 23.0225°N
**Longitude:** 72.5714°E

The sight of thousands of colorful kites bobbing and dancing in the sky fills the heart with a childish wonder as the end of winter is celebrated in this annual festival. The city is open for business twenty-four hours a day, and you can either watch the spectacle or take part.

HOWRAH, INDIA

### 627. Be posh where it all began

**When:** All year
**Latitude:** 22.5818°N
**Longitude:** 88.3423°E

The word posh is rumored to come from "port out, starboard home." This refers to the sides of the cabins on the steamship to India that well-to-do English passengers opted for, to stay out of the sun. Go posh in India today by first-class rail, leaving from one of the busiest and oldest stations, Howrah Junction.

MAHARASHTRA, INDIA

### 628. Marvel at the art of the Ajanta Caves

**When:** All year (although avoid the mid-June to September monsoon season)
**Latitude:** 20.5524°N
**Longitude:** 75.7004°E

Set your eyes upon some of the finest and best-preserved examples of ancient art in the world at the Ajanta Caves. The caves have been cut into the sides of a precipitous, horseshoe-shaped ravine—high above the narrow Waghora River—by Buddhist monks who carved them out of the basalt rock and painted an array of evocative images depicting the life of the Buddha.

MUMBAI, INDIA

### 629. Sample street food in Mumbai

**When:** All year
**Latitude:** 18.9664°N
**Longitude:** 72.8136°E

There is no better introduction to south Indian food than a trip to Swati Snacks in Mumbai. Feast on everything from *pav bhaji* to *pani puri*, all washed down with a traditional lassi.

MUMBAI, INDIA

### 630. Brave rush hour at a Mumbai train station

**When:** All year
**Latitude:** 18.9690°N
**Longitude:** 72.8188°E

Mumbai's main railway terminal, Chhatrapati Shivaji, is a splendid Gothic building, complete with domed arches and carved pillars. Its crowded rush-hour trains, however, are a little less serene, but if you're traveling for fun, the jostle and crush, with its lack of tension and malice, is really quite enjoyable, too.

▼ KOLKATA, INDIA

### 631. Buy a posy at India's largest flower market

**When:** All year
**Latitude:** 22.5667°N
**Longitude:** 88.3667°E

Next to the Hooghly River in Kolkata, you'll find the bustling Malik Ghat Flower Market, India's largest flower market, where a couple of thousand sellers provide the bouquets and garlands so important to Indian culture in festivals, temples, and celebrations.

India's largest flower market: Malik Ghat in Kolkata, India

NIZWA, OMAN
## 632. Travel back in time in Nizwa Fort
**When:** All year
**Latitude:** 22.9171°N
**Longitude:** 57.5363°E

One of the oldest forts in Oman, Nizwa Fort is both a fascinating insight into civil defense in the seventeenth century and a beautiful and impressive piece of architecture. Admire its round central tower that's 141 ft (43 m) across, topped with gentle crenellations all built in the soft pinky hues of Oman's desert sand.

HONG KONG, CHINA
## 633. Feel the scale of the world's super ships
**When:** All year (you can track the CSCL Globe online)
**Latitude:** 22.3964°N
**Longitude:** 114.1095°E

Usually when you see a container ship, you're on shore and it's at sea, but get up close to one to feel the huge scale of these beasts that plow across our oceans. They make the containers look like little bricks of LEGO®. *CSCL Globe*, the world's largest ship, is registered in Hong Kong.

HONG KONG, CHINA
## 634. Sail a junk into Victoria Harbour
**When:** All year
**Latitude:** 22.3964°N
**Longitude:** 114.1094°E

Hong Kong may be one of the most forward-looking places on Earth, but a traditional, old red-sailed Chinese junk is still the best way to see the electric Victoria Harbour—especially when it is lit up at night. Take a trip on one to see why this city is such a vibrant clash of old and modern.

▶ RAS AL-JINZ TURTLE RESERVE, OMAN
## 635. Watch baby turtles hatch from their nest
**When:** July to October
**Latitude:** 22.4242°N **Longitude:** 59.8303°E

There is not much that can beat staring at the sand and seeing the grains start to move as a tiny flipper battles its way out of the darkness, and soon, a tiny turtle emerges. Its mother will have pulled herself out of the sea around seven to nine weeks earlier, dug a hole in the sand at the back of the beach, and laid around a hundred eggs. She's now long gone.

The babies now have to find their way to the sea. Scrabbling over driftwood and running the gauntlet of gulls overhead and crabs on the sand, they strive toward that first cooling splash of surf. As you watch, it's impossible not to wonder at the miracle—and harshness—of nature.

Newly hatched baby turtles at Ras al-Jinz Turtle Reserve, Oman

▶ MADHYA PRADESH, INDIA
### 636. Spot a wild tiger in the jungle
**When:** National parks are open November to June
**Latitude:** 22.3333°N **Longitude:** 80.6333°E (Kanha Tiger Reserve)

Nothing can prepare you for your first sight of a tiger in the wild. It feels like an incredible privilege.

The best place to see these big cats in the wild is eastern Madhya Pradesh, whose tiger reserves cover lands that, ironically, were once vice regal hunting grounds. The jewel of the parks is Kanha Tiger Reserve, home to around forty Bengal tigers.

Although you have a better chance of spotting a tiger in one of Madhya Pradesh's parks than anywhere else in the world, sightings are not guaranteed. The best time to see one is between March and June, when the stifling pre-monsoon heat forces them out into the open to drink from rivers and waterholes. Plan on spending three days at the parks and going on five to six "game drives" with guides to find them.

If you want to spot a tiger in the wild, however, you should visit as soon as you can. Around the world, the big cats remain severely endangered: there are as few as 3,200 tigers left in the wild.

A wild tiger in a Madhya Pradesh tiger reserve, India

UDAIPUR PROVINCE, INDIA
### 637. Live the high life in a floating hotel
**When:** All year
**Latitude:** 24.5720°N
**Longitude:** 73.6790°E

The floating palaces of Udaipur are a byword for romance and splendor. Soaring majestically out of the water of Lake Pichola, the Taj Lake Palace and the Lake Garden Palace have, for hundreds of years, housed royalty and movie stars. Book a stay here yourself, as they now serve as glamorous hotels.

WEST BENGAL, INDIA
### 638. Hike with a view of Mount Everest
**When:** April to May
**Latitude:** 27.0600°N
**Longitude:** 88.0000°E

Hike up Sandakphu in the freshest of air, with wildflowers at your feet and rhododendron in bloom all around. The views are amazing. You can see Mount Everest and its neighbors Lhotse and Makalu as well as the locals' favorite, Kangchenjunga, whose form resembles a man lying on his back.

ABU DHABI, UAE
### 639. Ride the world's fastest roller coaster
**When:** All year
**Latitude:** 24.4832°N
**Longitude:** 54.6074°E

Don your pair of compulsory protective goggles to take a seat on the world's fastest roller coaster. Formula Rossa, in Abu Dhabi's Ferrari World, takes just five seconds to reach its top speed of 150 mph (240 kph).

HOANG LIEN SON MOUNTAINS, LÀO CAI PROVINCE, VIETNAM
## 640. Explore spectacular Vietnamese mountains
**When:** All year (late September for the harvest)
**Latitude:** 22.3033°N
**Longitude:** 103.7750°E (Phan Xi Pang mountain)

Savor glorious views as you trek through the lush Hoang Lien Son range, with its foothills marked by spectacular rice terraces. There are countless trails to enjoy, all overlooked by the towering Phan Xi Pang mountain, which at 10,300 ft (3,139 m) is the highest in the region. The views are worth the trip at any time, but are particularly enticing just before the annual rice harvest—around late September—when the rice fields turn a luminous shade of yellow to warm the senses.

▼ MANDALAY, MYANMAR
## 641. Take the road to Mandalay
**When:** All year
**Latitude:** 21.9750°N
**Longitude:** 96.0833°E

Immortalized in Rudyard Kipling's poem, and later in songs by Frank Sinatra and Robbie Williams, the road to Mandalay takes you to Myanmar's second-largest city. Explore the country's cultural and religious center for Buddhism; it is home to more than 700 pagodas.

A horse and cart on the road to Mandalay, Myanmar

THE SUNDARBANS, BANGLADESH
## 642. Stalk the Bengal tiger in the Sundarbans mangrove forest
**When:** All year (between November and February for the best chance of spotting a tiger)
**Latitude:** 21.9497°N **Longitude:** 89.1833°E

When it comes to Asian wildlife, the Sundarbans mangrove forest of Bangladesh is the absolute apex. Situated on the delta of three of the region's great rivers: the Ganges, Brahmaputra, and Meghna, on the Bay of Bengal, its series of islands, mudflats, and groves support an astonishing kaleidoscope of wildlife, including Bengal tigers.

Covering 25,900 sq mi (10,000 sq km), the Sundarbans contains three wildlife sanctuaries of renown, teeming with biodiversity. Prone to severe storms, cyclones, and tidal waves, it's a hazardous place, and tourist numbers remain fairly low. It is difficult to reach, there isn't much in the way of organized transport, and there's a lack of accommodation. Overcome these humps—and it can be done—and any visitor is richly rewarded.

Tiger spotting is the key draw for many. Bengals here are unique for their habit of swimming in salty waters—but also have an unfortunate reputation for eating human beings (they kill around ten people a year). Accompanied by a guide, however, they can be relatively safely spotted on riverbanks between November and February.

PHÔNGSALI, LAOS
## 643. Solve the mystery— how does rice grow?
**When:** June to December (rice-growing season)
**Latitude:** 21.6819°N
**Longitude:** 102.1090°E

You don't have to visit the Phôngsali rice paddies to answer the question, but it's a beautiful and dramatic location to do so. It's cool and peaceful, with many traditional farmers growing rice—a grain that grows on stalks in fields that are flooded to keep down weeds.

PALEIK, MYANMAR
## 644. Visit a snake pagoda
**When:** All year
**Latitude:** 21.8333°N
**Longitude:** 96.0667°E

When three pythons set up home in this pagoda near Mandalay, coiling themselves around the statue of Buddha, local monks decided the pythons must be holy, and now, they treat them as such. Watch them being bathed daily in a tub topped with flower petals.

ARAKAN, MYANMAR
## 645. Watch the sunrise from Shwe Taung Hill
**When:** All year
**Latitude:** 19.8100°N
**Longitude:** 93.9878°E

Shwe Taung is a small town on the Yangon to Pyay Road and is well-known for its Buddha of the Golden Spectacles and its Arakan mountain range, which rises out of the Bay of Bengal. Head to Shwe Taung Hill for the ideal spot to sit and soak up some spectacular sunrises and sunsets.

HONOLULU, HAWAII, US
## 646. Throw yourself out of a plane
**When:** March to August
**Latitude:** 21.5799°N **Longitude:** 158.1839°W

The question "why?" is probably on most people's lips when told someone is going to jump out of a plane for fun. That falling feeling is something many are afraid of—but it's something that plenty of other people crave.

Skydiving is undoubtedly one of the most exhilarating adrenaline rushes you can get. It's an exposing, invigorating, and breathtaking experience—but perhaps only for the most adventurous of thrillseekers.

The toughest part of any skydive is at the start: when you have to put your faith in your parachute cord, then jump from the door of a plane and submit yourself to gravity. It is probably one of the most difficult things you'll do. But once you're past that hurdle, skydiving presents the chance to feel complete freedom: for up to a minute you are in free fall, plummeting toward the Earth from up to 14,000 ft (4,267 m), before the cord is pulled and your parachute yanks you to the safety of a gentle glide. The next ten minutes are spent peacefully soaring beneath your canopy, allowing time to admire the landscapes below until you touch down, feeling more alive than you've ever felt before.

For the most awe-inspiring skydive, head to Hawaii. Honolulu is an astounding place to find yourself hurtling through the sky. You'll ascend high above the clouds, and strapped to an experienced professional, exit the plane to reach up to 120 mph (193 kph) in free fall. As the parachute opens, you're afforded some of the most incredible views in the Hawaiian archipelago, as the azure ocean stretches out toward the horizon, and the verdant, mountain landscape of Honolulu invites you back down to Earth.

MONTEGO BAY, JAMAICA
## 647. Dance the night away in the Caribbean
**When:** July
**Latitude:** 18.4762°N **Longitude:** 77.8939°W

Where better to take in the thick and heavy bass sounds of reggae than in the place where it all began: Jamaica? The Caribbean island's annual weeklong Reggae Sumfest festival, held each July in Montego Bay, is one of the world's great musical gatherings, bringing together a relaxed vibe, plenty of sunshine, and a passion for partying.

After dancing all night, you can revive yourself at the beautiful palm-fringed Doctor's Cave Beach. The crystal clear water is perfect for a refreshing dip or a bit of snorkeling, while there are plenty of shady spots to catch up on some much-needed rest before doing it all again the following evening.

COPPER CANYON, MEXICO
## 648. Take a dramatic train ride through a canyon
**When:** All year
**Latitude:** 26.6858°N **Longitude:** 97.7961°W

Regularly voted the most dramatic train ride of them all, the Ferrocarril Chihuahua al Pacifico ("Copper Canyon Railway") is a 404 mi (650 km) delight, crossing thirty-six bridges as it chugs through the mountainous interior of northern Mexico's Pacific Coast. Highlights include dramatic, sheer canyon walls that'll give vertigo sufferers pause for thought; huge waterfalls; and views across vast desert plains. The journey is set up to savor the vistas of the Sierra Tarahumara. Be sure to stop off along the way, because the indigenous tribes in the canyon are just as interesting as the views.

OAHU, HAWAII, US
### 649. Get lost in a massive planted maze
**When:** All year
**Latitude:** 21.5258°N
**Longitude:** 158.0379°W

Left, left, right … or was it right, right, left? Try to find your way through more than 3 ac (1 ha) and 2.5 mi (4 km) of paths in Dole Plantation's giant Pineapple Garden Maze in Hawaii. Prepare for a mixture of both fun and frustration in the world's largest planted maze.

▼ HAIKU STAIRS, HAWAII, US
### 650. Climb the stairway to heaven
**When:** All year (or never—it's illegal!)
**Latitude:** 21.4046°N
**Longitude:** 157.8250°W

Almost 4,000 steps take you up Hawaii's luscious Ko'olau mountain range—and despite the no trespassing sign and a guard routinely stationed at the bottom, many people risk a potential fine to climb the phenomenal Haiku Stairs, installed in the 1940s to reach a radio station at the summit. Will you risk it?

HAWAII, US
### 651. Chase rainbows in the Rainbow State
**When:** All year
**Latitude:** 19.8967°N
**Longitude:** 155.5827°W

There's a long-standing joke in Hawaii—you have to try to avoid a rainbow. That's hard to do when they appear every day, often in more than one place at the same time, and sometimes for as long as thirty minutes—an extra bonus for an already idyllic destination.

The stairway to heaven: Haiku Stairs in Hawaii, US

HONOLULU, HAWAII, US
## 652. From "aloha" to "*zdravstvuyte*"
**When:** All year
**Latitude:** 21.3069°N
**Longitude:** 157.8583°W

The sign of a good traveler is the ability to communicate, wherever on Earth they find themselves. Learning to say hello in as many languages as possible is a decent place to start. Begin with the Hawaiian "aloha" and work all the way through to the Russian greeting of "*zdravstvuyte.*"

◀ HAWAII, US
## 653. Ride the big waves in Hawaii
**When:** All year
**Latitude:** 21.2893°N **Longitude:** 157.9174°W

Nothing is cooler than surfing in the spiritual home of the sport, the Hawaiian Islands. Set amid the vastness of the Pacific Ocean, this archipelago offers the greatest concentration of surfable shoreline in the world. The famous North Shore of Oahu alone has fifty-five beaches in the space of a mere 11 mi (18 km).

Although beginners may want to avoid the winter months, when surf spots such as Jaws and Banzai Pipeline earn their fearsome reputations, from Honolulu to Maui, there are surfing beaches to suit all levels. Sign up for surf school, and within a few days, you will be sitting in the lineup, waiting for a wave before paddling hard, head down, as a wave lifts you up and propels you toward the beach. Then the adrenaline takes over … .

MAUI, HAWAII, US
## 654. Hawaii drive-o!
**When:** All year (wet season is November to March)
**Latitude:** 20.8810°N
**Longitude:** 156.4438°W

Life, a philosopher once said, is about the journey and not the destination. Nowhere is that sentiment more true than on the woozy, winding roads of Hawaii's spine-tingling Hana Highway. With the glittering blue ocean to one side, and lush rain forest and waterfalls to the other, it is a drive through paradise. Take in more than 600 curves and fifty-five bridges on the road that is carved into Maui's precipitous coastline.

MAUI, HAWAII, US
## 655. Cliff jump like a king
**When:** All year
**Latitude:** 20.9178°N **Longitude:** 156.6966°W

Follow in the footsteps of a legendary king by taking a leap of faith off Maui's famous Pu'u Keka'a ("Black Rock") into crystal clear waters. Splitting sundrenched Ka'anapali Beach, the imposing volcanic outcrop of Black Rock looms over the deep, blue Pacific.

The great King Kahekili, who ruled Maui from 1766 to 1793, was a big fan of cliff jumping at Black Rock and was celebrated by locals, who believed only a blessed person could jump off the rock unharmed. Partly as a result, the activity has become something of a national sport in Hawaii, and every evening a lone diver recreates the king's feats in a sunset ceremony.

Watch others launch themselves off the rock, or better still, take the leap yourself and plunge into the ocean below. Choose a spot where locals line up to leap for a less risky place to jump.

Riding the big waves in Hawaii, US

**656.** Go kayaking in paradise

**When:** March to May (when the mist is less prominent)
**Latitude:** 20.9101°N
**Longitude:** 107.1839°E

There's an element of danger involved in kayaking here, as caves along the coastline are prone to sinkholes. Yet, there is no better way to take in the crystal clear waters surrounding the 3,000-plus limestone and dolomite islets, and unspoiled beaches.

HAMPI, KARNATAKA, INDIA
### 657. Discover musical pillars at Hampi
**When:** All year (but popular between October and February; check opening times of temples)
**Latitude:** 15.3350°N
**Longitude:** 76.4600°E

The bewitching fourteenth- to sixteenth-century ruins of Hampi sit among heaps of giant boulders that look as if they are part of a *Flintstones* movie set. See for yourself that they are real, as are the extraordinarily intricate carvings that adorn the temples and bazaar, and those brilliantly engineered "musical pillars."

MUMBAI, INDIA
### 658. Mix with Bollywood stars at afternoon tea
**When:** All year
**Latitude:** 18.9220°N
**Longitude:** 72.8334°E

Join the hoi polloi of Mumbai's Bollywood for a lavish spread of expertly prepared, fresh Indian street snacks and famously sugary, delectable sweets in one of the world's most luxurious hotels: the elegant and grand Taj Mahal Palace.

AL WUSTA, OMAN
### 659. Help bring back the Arabian oryx
**When:** All year (although summer can be uncomfortably hot)
**Latitude:** 20.1739°N
**Longitude:** 56.5616°E

Revered throughout the Middle East, the distinctive Arabian oryx was hunted almost to extinction in the early 1970s. Based in Oman's atmospheric central desert, the Al Wusta Wildlife Reserve is one of several organizations working to stabilize the population—stop in for the chance to see this beautiful creature.

MECCA, SAUDI ARABIA
### 660. Take the pilgrimage to Mecca
**When:** All year
**Latitude:** 20.3941°N **Longitude:** 40.8531°E

Every Muslim on Earth is required to perform the Hajj pilgrimage to the Grand Mosque in Mecca. Once there, they must complete the Tawaf, walking around its Khana Kaaba, the most sacred site in Islam, seven times in a counterclockwise direction. This demonstrates unity and harmony among the worshipers.

But you don't have to follow Allah to follow the trail: this is a stunningly beautiful and educational place to visit for people of any faith—preferably away from the incredible crowds of Hajj, although it is busy year-round. The Kaaba, a cube-shaped building in its center, is the center point to which all Muslims point when they do daily prayers. The Black Stone was set by the Holy Prophet Muhammad in AD 605, while the Maqam Ibrahim has an imprint of Abraham's foot. Take a drink from the Zamzam Well, where pilgrims traditionally refresh themselves.

JEDDAH, SAUDI ARABIA
### 661. Marvel at a towering fountain
**When:** All year
**Latitude:** 21.2854°N
**Longitude:** 39.2376°E

Feast your eyes upon King Fahd's Fountain (it was his gift to the city), which is set in the sea off Jeddah and shoots water 1,000 ft (305 m)—that's higher than the Eiffel Tower—into the air. It was modeled on the freshwater fountain in Lake Geneva, although with a measly 460 ft (140 m) reach, that wasn't felt to be quite impressive enough.

MUMBAI, INDIA
## 662. Discover the benefits of laughter

**When:** All year
**Latitude:** 18.9750°N **Longitude:** 72.8258°E

Laughter Yoga was born in Mumbai in the 1990s and is as insane, and fun, as it sounds. Based on his research into the beneficial health properties of a good giggle, Indian hospital registrar Dr. Madan Kataria started a quest to discover how he could use laughter to alleviate the physical and mental stresses of modern living for the people who need it most.

Laughter Yoga is best done with others, so get over your self-conscious inhibitions and join in. There are thousands of Laughter Clubs worldwide, with many more local Laughter Yoga groups joining in the fun every day.

EMPTY QUARTER, SAUDI ARABIA
## 663. Fill your boots in the Empty Quarter

**When:** All year
**Latitude:** 20.0952°N **Longitude:** 48.7191°E

Few names are quite as evocative as Rub' al Khali ("Empty Quarter"): a vast empty expanse of the Arabian Desert crossing Saudi Arabia, Yemen, Oman, and the UAE. It is that very emptiness that has drawn in adventurers across the years.

It is possible to visit (advisably with a guide) for a couple of nights or weeklong trips. And it's well worth it: expect to see wonderful star-filled nights, impressive 656 ft (200 m) high sand dunes, and occasional salt flats. This is not a place you visit for the wildlife; you come because nowhere else on Earth offers such a huge array of nothingness—and such an epic name.

▶ GUJARAT, INDIA
## 664. Spot Asia's last wild lions

**When:** Mid-October to mid-June
**Latitude:** 21.1356°N
**Longitude:** 70.7967°E

The little-visited Gir National Park, a 444 sq mi (1,150 sq km) swathe of forest, is home to the last 523 wild Asiatic lions. View the smaller and shaggier—but no less impressive than their African cousins—big cats on a jeep safari.

Asia's last wild lions in Gir
National Park, India

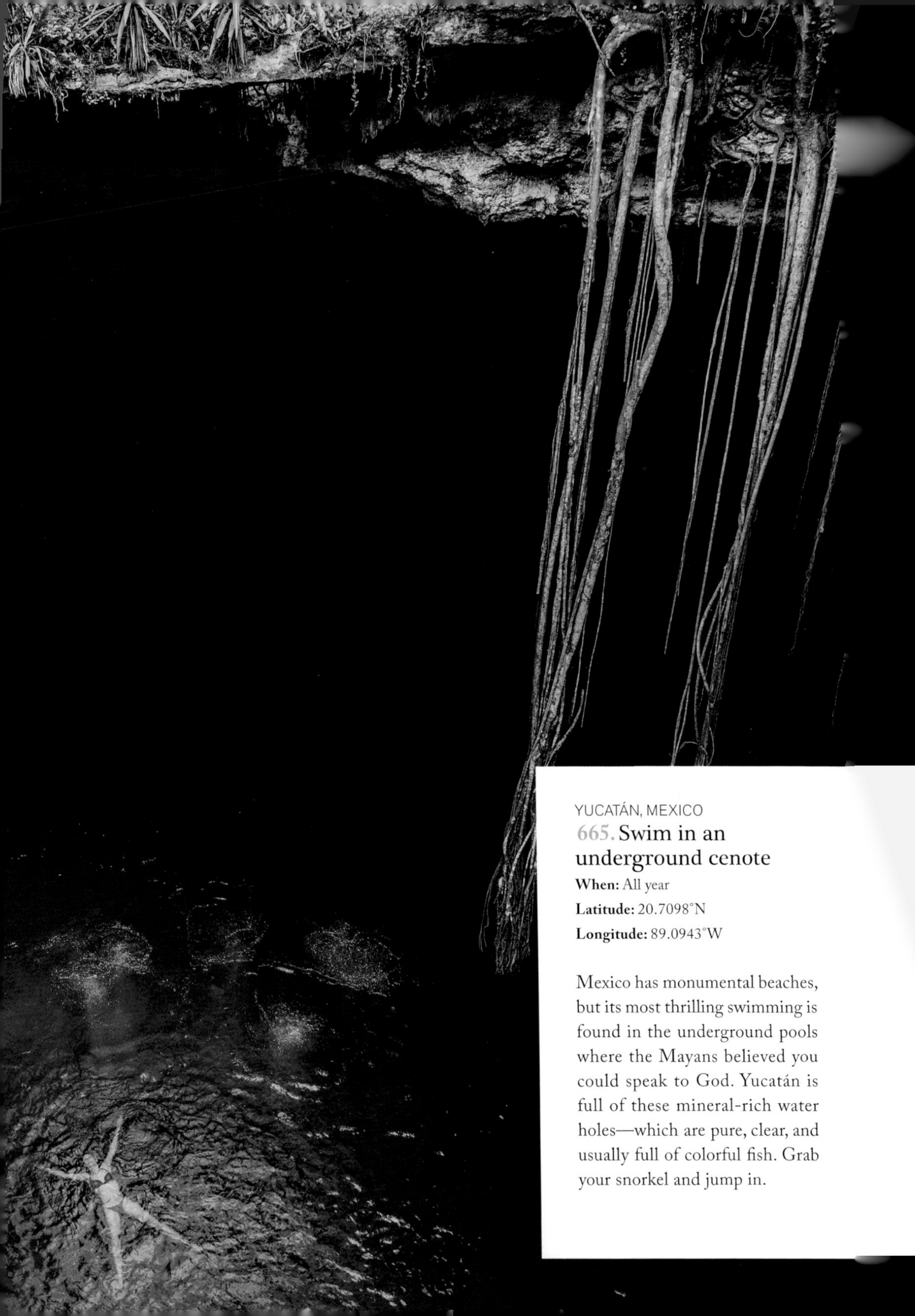

YUCATÁN, MEXICO
## 665. Swim in an underground cenote
**When:** All year
**Latitude:** 20.7098°N
**Longitude:** 89.0943°W

Mexico has monumental beaches, but its most thrilling swimming is found in the underground pools where the Mayans believed you could speak to God. Yucatán is full of these mineral-rich water holes—which are pure, clear, and usually full of colorful fish. Grab your snorkel and jump in.

▼ MICHOACÁN, MEXICO
### 666. See massed Monarch butterflies
**When:** Winter (from October)
**Latitude:** 19.5665°N
**Longitude:** 101.7068°W

A barely believable congregation of millions of monarch butterflies arrives in the pine-oak forests of Michoacán every winter. Visit two of eight colonies that are open to the public: Sierra Chinch and El Rosario.

ZÓCALO, MEXICO CITY, MEXICO
### 667. Visit the center of the universe
**When:** All year
**Latitude:** 19.4328°N
**Longitude:** 99.1333°W

Visit the Zócalo, the huge main square in Mexico City, which is one of the largest city squares in the world. It has been a gathering place for locals since Aztec times—a block away is the Templo Mayor historical temple site, which the Aztecs considered the center of the universe.

TAXCO, MEXICO
### 668. Treat yourself in the world's silver capital
**When:** All year
**Latitude:** 18.5564°N
**Longitude:** 99.6050°W

Nestled on a hillside in southern Mexico, the charming colonial town of Taxco has a long history of silver mining and silversmithing. Today, you'll find workshops and stores selling locally produced jewelry and other silver creations on almost every picturesque corner, so start shopping.

Massed monarch butterflies in Michoacán, Mexico

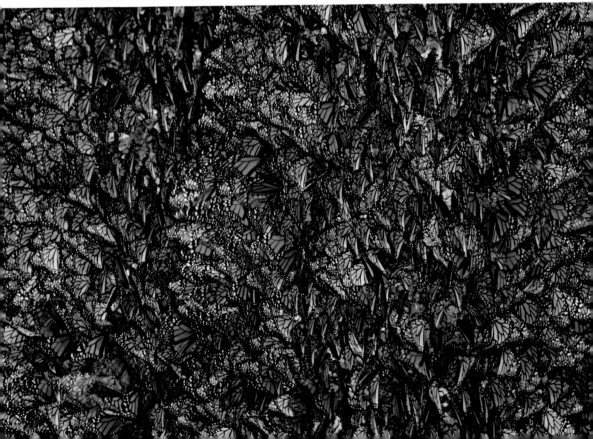

▶ HAWAII, US
## 669. See volcanoes erupting in front of you
**When:** All year
**Latitude:** 19.4100°N
**Longitude:** 155.2864°W

There is something primal about the natural power of a volcano spilling lava. On the "Big Island" of Hawaii, you can see the lava flowing at Hawaii Volcanoes National Park or the Kalapana viewing area, with the Halema'uma'u crater particularly striking at sunset.

Erupting volcano in Hawaii, US

MEXICO CITY, MEXICO
## 670. Explore Mexico City via its bohemians
**When:** Between March and May
**Latitude:** 19.3496°N
**Longitude:** 99.19743°W

Take a trip to the Blue House, now the Museo Frida Kahlo, home to the great, but tortured, Mexican artist from 1907–1954. This is Mexico's most famous monument to Kahlo, and where the largest collection of her work can be found, but her ghost is everywhere: in her home district of Coyoacán and in the homes and museums dedicated to artist and revolutionary Diego Rivera—the man she married twice.

HO'OKENA BEACH, HAWAII
## 671. Sleep on a beach and wake up to dawn
**When:** All year
**Latitude:** 19.3827°N
**Longitude:** 155.9005°W

In truth, the romance of this is slightly jaded when you wake up with a sleeping bag full of sand and crabs trying to climb through your hair, but to fall asleep utterly under the stars, with waves lapping at the shore, is a wondrous feeling.

ALL ACROSS HAWAII, US
## 672. Say hello to hula
**When:** All year
**Latitude:** 21.3069°N
**Longitude:** 157.8583°W

Learn to swing and sway the Polynesian way by taking lessons in the traditional Hawaiian dance. The hula originated in religious ceremonies, and is often performed as a blessing or celebration. Lessons are both great fun and free across most of the islands.

The colorful *trajineras* in the canals of Xochimilco, Mexico

▲ XOCHIMILCO, MEXICO

## 673. Discover the floating side of Mexico City

**When:** All year
**Latitude:** 19.2572°N
**Longitude:** 99.1030°W

In a country that is bursting with color, the canals of Xochimilco, just south of Mexico City, take it one step further. The canals are full of *trajineras*—boats painted in bright reds, blues, greens, and yellows—some of which take visitors on tours of the canals. At the same time other boats take the entertainment in the form of mariachi bands or marimba players, while others sell sweet corn or tacos. Cruise on the canals amid this wonderful jumble of color and life.

GUADALAJARA, MEXICO

## 674. Cheer on a *charreada*

**When:** All year (Sundays)
**Latitude:** 20.6667°N **Longitude:** 103.3500°W

A *charreada* is a Mexican rodeo and celebrated as a national sport in some areas of the country. Charros wearing traditional, colorful cowboy costumes take part in events that include roping a horse by its hind legs, riding a wild mare, and traditional bull riding—hanging on to a bull for dear life. The final event—affectionately known as "the Pass of Death"—involves jumping bareback from one horse to a wild mare. Attend one of these rodeos, which are held every Sunday in Guadalajara, or catch the national championship here in September.

NEW PROVIDENCE, THE BAHAMAS
## 675. Wonder at the underwater *Ocean Atlas*
**When:** All year (hurricane season June to November)
**Latitude:** 25.0519°N
**Longitude:** 77.4013°W

The clear waters off the Bahamas are perfect for diving and snorkeling. While exploring, take time to discover *Ocean Atlas*, a 17 ft (5 m) tall statue of a hunched woman, symbolizing the weight of the environmental burden on the young generation.

CAYMAN ISLANDS
## 676. Perform tricks at the world's best skate park
**When:** All year
**Latitude:** 19.3221°N
**Longitude:** 81.2408°W

Acknowledged by those in the know as the finest place on Earth to ollie, rail-slide, and 720°, the Black Pearl Skate and  Surf Park in Grand Cayman's George Town is gigantic (64,584 sq ft; 6,000 sq m, with 62,000 ft; 18,898 m of vertical and street elements), iconic, and in a beautiful setting. Are you up for the challenge?

SANTIAGO DE CUBA, CUBA
## 677. Catch a baseball game in Cuba
**When:** All year
**Latitude:** 20.0344°N
**Longitude:** 75.8122°W

Watching a baseball match in Cuba, particularly at the home of the country's most successful team, Santiago de Cuba, is more like going to a festival than a game. Join the party atmosphere—plus theatrical booing/going crazy for badly/well-played balls.

CUBA
## 678. Play dominoes in the street
**When:** All year
**Latitude:** 22.1456°N
**Longitude:** 80.4364°W

People playing dominoes in the parks and public areas of Cuban towns and cities such as Cienfuegos is commonplace. Follow the distinctive *click-clack* sound of the tiles to join in—but brush up on the slightly variant Cuban rules first.

CUBA
## 679. See ballet Cuban style
**When:** All year
**Latitude:** 23.1368°N
**Longitude:** 82.3596°W

The state-funded Ballet Nacional de Cuba is frequently heralded as one of the best ballet schools in the world. Catch its highly praised choreography and dancers in the crumbling Gran Teatro de la Habana for a feast for the senses.

VIÑALES, CUBA
## 680. Scoot past *guajiros* along *mogotes*
**When:** All year
**Latitude:** 22.6188°N
**Longitude:** 83.7066°W

Viñales is real rural Cuba, where you'll see *guajiros* ("peasant farmers") plowing their fields, and simple one-story village homes. It's also home to steep-sided *mogotes* (tall, rounded hills)—and the ideal way to explore its appealing web of roads is on a cheap, easy-to-rent (and drive) scooter.

MEXICO CITY, MEXICO
## 681. Be serenaded by a mariachi band

**When:** All year
**Latitude:** 19.4326°N
**Longitude:** 99.1332°W

Dating back to nineteenth-century Western Mexico, mariachi is a noble tradition, and being serenaded by a charro-wearing ensemble is one of the most thrilling musical experiences available in Latin America. Make sure to get on up—and dance the hacienda down.

ZACATECAS, MEXICO
## 682. Cross a city by cable car

**When:** All year (as long as it is not too windy)
**Latitude:** 22.7667°N
**Longitude:** 102.5500°W

The best way to see Zacatecas, a historic silver-mining city in the middle of Mexico, is to travel on its cable car that runs for more than 700 yd (640 m) above the famous pink city, built from stones of the distinctive hue. Hop aboard and enjoy magnificent vistas.

BAJA CALIFORNIA, MEXICO
## 683. Watch the whales in the Sea of Cortez

**When:** February to May
**Latitude:** 28.0331°N
**Longitude:** 111.7749°W

The Sea of Cortez, once described as the "world's aquarium," is the best place to get up close to humpback and blue whales. The blue whale is the largest creature on the planet, and you'll find these gentle giants and their humpback cousins around the waters of Baja California.

◀ FAJARDO, PUERTO RICO
## 684. Kayak in a sea lit up from within

**When:** All year (at night)
**Latitude:** 18.3258°N
**Longitude:** 65.6524°W

Each dip of the paddle leaves a glow in the water when you kayak through the magically beautiful bioluminescent waters in Fajardo, Puerto Rico. The ecosystem here is perfectly balanced for this amazing natural phenomenon.

The sea lit up from within by beautiful bioluminescence in Fajardo, Puerto Rico

▶ TULUM, MEXICO
## 685. Explore the only Mayan ruin on a beach

**When:** All year
**Latitude:** 20.1373°N
**Longitude:** 87.4633°W

The ancient Mayans knew what they were doing when they sited Tulum overlooking one of the most beautiful beaches on Mexico's Caribbean coast. Who wouldn't want to live here? Explore the dramatic ruin in a striking setting that was built as a seaport for trading jade and turquoise.

The only Mayan ruin built on a beach in Tulum, Mexico

START IN TEQUILA, MEXICO
## 686. Create a Big Five of drinks to-do list

**When:** All year
**Latitude:** 20.7883°N **Longitude:** 103.8414°W

Follow wildlife's method of Big Five animal spotting by creating your own "Big Five drinks" to try in the place they come from. Your list should be compiled to suit individual tastes—both of the palette and for where you want to travel.

Tequila should earn its place on the list because a visit to the town is so eye-opening. The surrounding countryside is full of fields of spiky blue agave plants, which are used in making tequila.

Champagne would grace most people's lists. To be a true champagne—and not a sparkling wine—it has to be produced in the Champagne region of France and has to go through a double-fermentation process—the second one happening in the bottle.

Port needs to be drunk in the city of Porto, which sits across the river Douro. On one side is Ribeira, on the other, in Vila Nova de Gaia, are the port wine lodges that produce the city's famous tipple.

Pisco is the unofficial national drink of Chile, produced primarily in the Elqui Valley, north of Santiago. There is a small town deep in the valley called Pisco Elqui, which has two pisco distilleries. Order a pisco sour—pisco with lemon and egg white—at a bar in town.

Some drinks are more created than made, and the Manhattan is one of those. As with many of the best cocktails, the precise origins of the drink are now a little fuzzy—although many claim it links back to the Manhattan Club in New York.

## MORELOS, MEXICO
### 687. Experience a hip festival in Mexico
**When:** February
**Latitude:** 18.7056°N
**Longitude:** 99.0972°W

Forget sticking to the dance floor; at Bahidorá, half the crowd cools down in the river that the DJ's stage is set over. This is a hip festival in a beautiful location, and when the music stops playing, you can always go kayaking.

## CHIHUAHUA, MEXICO
### 688. Climb through gigantic crystals
**When:** Whenever you're lucky enough to get access
**Latitude:** 27.8508°N
**Longitude:** 105.4964°W

This incredible cave of giant crystals was discovered by miners at the Naica silver mine. If you're lucky enough to gain access to the cave, you'll find spectacular crystals, some of which are up to 36 ft (11 m) long, dwarfing you. Professional equipment and exceedingly good contacts are needed.

## XOCHIMILCO, MEXICO CITY
### 689. Pay your respects on the Island of the Dolls
**When:** All year
**Latitude:** 19.2901°N
**Longitude:** 99.0965°W

Overcome your fear of Chucky and step upon the island with a sad background—and possessed dolls. Named Isla de las Muñecas ("Island of the Dolls"), this small island is dedicated to the soul of a girl who mysteriously drowned many years ago. Some believe the dolls are possesed by her spirit. Visit it and decide for yourself whether the rumors are true.

## ▶ TIKAL, GUATEMALA
### 690. Watch the jungle wake up at ancient Mayan ruins
**When:** All year
**Latitude:** 17.2171°N **Longitude:** 89.6233°W

Tikal is the largest of the ancient Mayan cities that have been discovered. The former city covered more than 20 sq mi (52 sq km); had around 3,000 buildings; and was home to an estimated 50,000 people. All this has left plenty for archaeologists—and tourists—to discover.

Because of its setting in the heart of the jungle, the best time to set off on a discovery of Tikal is before dawn. That way you can be sitting at the top of a pyramid, up above the tree canopy, listening to the sounds of the jungle as the sun starts to peep over the horizon. The sound is best described as a cacophony. Howler monkeys howl. Loudly. Waking birds join them with an almighty dawn chorus. The noise carries on as the sun rises.

The dawn's light gradually starts to pick out the silhouettes of the temples that poke above the trees, and you can start to spot the wildlife you've been hearing. With daylight you can also start to explore the huge expanse of Tikal.

The center of the site is the Grand Plaza, which has two temples at its north and south ends, while along each side, acropolises rise from the grassy lawn in a series of terraces. Paths lead from one excavated site to another. As well as numerous temples, buildings also include palaces, tombs, altars, causeways, and even a ball court. There is such a wealth of ruins here that archaeologists have been able to discover incredible details about Mayan life.

Some visitors to Tikal will want to piece together the past and learn about the lost Mayan civilization, while others will come to enjoy the atmosphere of ruins in the heart of a jungle taken over by wildlife. Both will leave this place full of awe and wonder.

Ancient Mayan ruins at Tikal, Guatemala

◀ LUANG PRABANG, LAOS

## 691. Meet the monks of Luang Prabang

**When:** All year
**Latitude:** 19.8833°N
**Longitude:** 102.1333°W

Serenity flows through Luang Prabang's dusty lanes and pretty streets all day, but you'll feel it most at sunrise, when hundreds of orange-robed Buddhist monks come out to receive alms from the locals lining the streets.

The monks of Luang Prabang in Laos

SAGADA, PHILIPPINES

## 692. See the hanging coffins of Sagada

**When:** All year
**Latitude:** 17.0996°N
**Longitude:** 120.9102°E

The awe-inspiring hanging coffins of Sagada are nailed or tied to the sides of steep cliffs in the Echo Valley in Mountain Province. The tradition of burying the dead in coffins has existed for more than two millennia and continues to be practiced today—albeit on a much smaller scale. Corpses are buried in the fetal position, so coffins tend to measure no more than 3 ft (1 m) long. The wooden coffins, hanging precariously off jagged rock, are truly a sight to behold.

KABAYAN, BENGUET, PHILIPPINES

## 693. Enter the Philippines' "fire mummy caves"

**When:** All year
**Latitude:** 16.5500°N
**Longitude:** 120.7500°E

Trek the mountain slopes near Kabayan in the Philippines and you'll find the Kabayan Mummy Burial Caves, containing the remains of "fire mummies." These human remains were preserved after death by being smoked—tobacco smoke was blown into the bodies to mummify the insides.

OAXACA, MEXICO
## 694. Celebrate Day of the Dead in Mexico
**When:** November 1–2
**Latitude:** 17.0833°N **Longitude:** 96.7500°W

Think there's nothing cheery about death? Think again. Día de los Muertos, or Day of the Dead, is a national holiday in Mexico. It is, in fact, two days—the first and second of November—dedicated to honoring the dead through the living. This is not a time for mourning, but a celebration of those who have passed away.

In many places in Mexico it is the most celebrated day of the year, and it derives from the ancient Aztec belief in Mictlan—a kind of limbo between life and death, from which spirits can make a special trip home once a year. To help them find their way and welcome them, tombs and altars are created and decorated with food and drink offerings for the dead when they come back—it is a long journey, after all.

Oaxaca City is known for its ornately rich Day of the Dead celebrations, and the fun actually starts a week before November 1, with the opening of the festive markets. Mercado de Abastos is the biggest one, where you will find everything you need to prepare for the upcoming festivities.

Strolling through the city is the best way to soak up the atmosphere. To see decorated graves and tombs, head to Oaxaca's Panteón General Cemetery—one of the main city cemeteries—or try Xoxocotlan Cemetery, just outside the city.

Public places also come alive with people dressed as skeletons, adorned with jewels, hats, and feather boas. Comparsas—theatrical displays by musicians and costumed performers with painted faces—go from house to house playing music, dancing, and eating the offerings on the altars.

Day of the Dead celebrations in Oaxaca, Mexico

SANTA MARÍA DEL TULE, OAXACA, MEXICO

**695.** Pay your respects to the world's oldest tree

**When:** All year

**Latitude:** 17.0447°N **Longitude:** 96.6330°W

It's billed as the "world's wildest tree." That doesn't mean it gets drunk and smashes up hotel rooms; rather this whopping *Taxodium mucronatum* has the stoutest trunk anywhere, with a 138 ft (42 m) circumference. Some claim it could be 6,000 years old. Able to shade 500 people, it's well worth napping under.

BANAUE, PHILIPPINES
## 696. Trek through expansive rice terraces
**When:** All year
**Latitude:** 16.9241°N **Longitude:** 121.0573°E

It is said that if you laid the Philippines Cordilleras rice terraces flat, they'd stretch halfway around the world. Dating back more than two millennia, the UNESCO rice terraces of the Cordilleras gently follow the contours of the mountainside. They were hewn from land with primitive tools, and serve as a telling example of sustainability, reflecting the harmony between humankind and the environment. The stone and mud rice terraces are the products of the Ifugao people, who have occupied the area for centuries, handing down age-old traditions to each generation. Elaborate farming techniques and irrigation systems that harvest water from the mountaintops reflect the Ifugao's mastery of engineering that ranks alongside the construction of the pyramids.

Trekking through the rice terraces and overnighting in traditional Ifugao huts is a major highlight of any trip to the Philippines. You'll snake your way through impressive mountain scenery, where the rice terraces stretch out for miles on end, stopping off in local villages where life has remained largely unchanged for centuries.

Depending on the time of year you visit, the terraces will be of different hues. They are at their greenest in April, while in June and July they morph into shades of yellow. In August they are golden, while later in the year they turn a light shade of brown. No matter when you visit, you are sure to be awestruck by this impressive sight.

Trekking the expansive Banaue
Rice Terraces, Philippines

KYAUK KA LAT, HPA-AN, MYANMAR
## 697. Find peace in the mountains
**When:** All year
**Latitude:** 16.8182°N
**Longitude:** 97.6402°E

If you are looking for a meditative place of peace and beauty, look no further than the otherworldly Kyauk Ka Lat Monastery in Myanmar. Built on a small island in the middle of a lake, the highest pagoda is perched atop a gravity-defying pillar of rock. To reach it, cross the bridge and climb some steps to get toward the top.

The Buddhist monastery is an active one, so you will find monks and others praying and meditating here. The feeling of tranquility is simply blissful. In the morning, the island is often swirled in atmospheric mist, while sunsets here make magical photos.

▼ YANGON, MYANMAR
## 698. Visit Myanmar's Golden Pagoda
**When:** All year
**Latitude:** 16.8660°N
**Longitude:** 96.1951°E

Rising imposingly to a height of 325 ft (99 m) from Singuttara Hill, the Shwedagon Pagoda is one of the most breathtaking religious sights you'll see anywhere in the world. Dominating the Yangon skyline, it is a gold-plated destination for Buddhist pilgrims and missionaries—and it gives any visitor a sense of peace. Be sure to see it at sunrise or sunset for the most spectacular effect.

Myanmar's Golden Pagoda in Yangon

▶ BELIZE
## 699. See the flash of toucans in the wild

**When:** December to May
**Latitude:** 16.8535°N
**Longitude:** 88.2814°W

One of nature's more peculiar birds, toucans look as if their bill kept growing when the rest of them stopped. They are not difficult to spot in the wild, partly because of their bright-green bill and yellow chest, but also because they tend to stick together in noisy squawking groups. See them in Belize where they are the national bird.

A colorful toucan in the wild of Belize

BELIZE
## 700. Dive the Great Blue Hole

**When:** All year
**Latitude:** 17.3157°N
**Longitude:** 87.5348°W

Step from a diving boat into the clear waters of Lighthouse Reef before beginning a descent into the deep of the Great Blue Hole, one of the most spectacular dive sights in the world. As the depth gauge ticks over, so the scenery changes: 40 ft (12 m) … watch the air bubbles ascend sheer limestone walls in the clear, current-free water. At 60 ft (18 m) … spot silhouettes of Caribbean reef, bull, and hammerhead sharks. At 130 ft (40 m) … the descent slows as the Great Blue Hole opens out into a huge cavern dotted with ancient stalactites, like a huge underwater cathedral created millennia ago.

COCKSCOMB BASIN, BELIZE
## 701. Visit the world's only jaguar reserve

**When:** All year
**Latitude:** 16.7896°N
**Longitude:** 88.6144°W

The Cockscomb Basin Wildlife Sanctuary in Belize is unique: it's the only site anywhere dedicated to the preservation of the jaguar. Although you're not guaranteed to see one of these stealthy beasts, the resplendent jungle lands contain a wealth of fascinating flora and fauna either way.

ROATÁN, HONDURAS
## 702. Discover the curiosities of the subaqua world
**When:** January to August
**Latitude:** 16.3298°N **Longitude:** 86.5300°W

Learn to scuba dive and swim among the huge variety and complexity of the underwater world—there is no experience quite like it. It opens your eyes to a whole new world. The world of the coral reefs especially draw people back to scuba diving again and again. The reefs are brightly colored, diverse ecosystems, and across the planet, are estimated to be home to 4,000 species of fish, 700 species of coral, and thousands of other species of plants and animals.

Roatán is an island off Honduras that is less than 50 mi (81 km) long and 5 mi (8 km) wide. The vast majority of the island's tourism is set up for divers, and it's the perfect place to learn the sport. As a marine park, the reef here is protected and corals flourish. And with so much coral, species here thrive, too. More than 370 species of fish live on the reef, often traveling in huge schools. They come in all colors, with stripes and spots, and are everywhere.

Look beyond them, at the reef itself, and you'll find another layer of life: moray eels poke their noses out of crevices, lobsters' antennae give away their hiding spots under rocks, and tiny worms and mollusks add yet more color to the spectacle.

Reefs don't just support the smaller end of the food scale, and diving is about being in the presence of larger animals, too: rays that float past; turtles that hone into view; and, of course, sharks. Most sharks are fairly shy and won't bother humans at all. In Roatán they have Caribbean reef sharks, nurse sharks, hammerheads, and occasionally, whale sharks, all of which are fascinating to watch as they move stealthily through the deep.

The Caribbean is just one place to learn to dive. Other spots with equally impressive sea life that are well set up for beginners are Egypt, Israel, Australia's Great Barrier Reef, and Thailand.

Discovering the curiosities of the subaqua world off Roatán, Honduras

HANG SON DOONG, VIETNAM
703. Explore a vast underground cave system
**When:** All year
**Latitude:** 17.5911°N
**Longitude:** 106.2833°E

Plenty of people may have claustrophobic nightmares at the thought of caving—but stay aboveground and you miss a fascinating subterranean otherworld. Go underground in the world's biggest cave, in Phong Nha-Ke Bang National Park, and wonder at the river and huge stalagmites.

▼ DA NANG, VIETNAM
704. Have a Vietnamese feast on the side of the road
**When:** All year
**Latitude:** 16.0470°N
**Longitude:** 108.2062°E

The coastal city of Da Nang is modernizing fast, but it's still the best place to sample the country's succulent traditional cuisine. Sample its street food, which is particularly mouthwatering: with pleasing pho (noodles) and *xôi* (sticky rice) at the top of any list.

Vietnamese street food in Da Nang, Vietnam

FROM CHIANG MAI, NORTHWEST THAILAND
## 705. Use two wheels and get off Thailand's beaten track

**When:** November to February (cool); March to June (hot)
**Latitude:** 18.7061°N
**Longitude:** 98.9817°E

The combination of fabulous climate and captivating tropical scenery makes the wind-in-the-hair motorcycle journey around the legendary Mae Hong Son loop an eye-opening experience. Start in popular Chiang Mai for the 370 mi (596 km) round-trip, which takes in jungles, mist-covered mountains, and exhilarating riding.

▼ HOI AN, VIETNAM
## 706. Get a new tailored wardrobe in Vietnam

**When:** All year
**Latitude:** 15.8833°N
**Longitude:** 108.3333°E

The clothes-making industry dominates Hoi An's quaint streets, with tailors sewing anything from silk to leather. After your fittings, some will even take you—on the back of a moped through winding roads—to see your purchase in the making at a seamstress's home.

Tailored clothing stores in Hoi An, Vietnam

ZIPOLITE, MEXICO

707. Strip off on a nudist beach

**When:** All year
**Latitude:** 15.6630°N
**Longitude:** 96.5177°W

Do you dare to go bare? It's difficult to understand why there is such a difference between a skimpy bikini and your birthday suit, but there is. At a nudist beach, surrounded by other naked people, you'll realize that being naked isn't such a big deal, after all.

COBÁN, GUATEMALA
### 708. Get your caffeine fix in the place it's grown
**When:** All year
**Latitude:** 15.4833°N
**Longitude:** 90.3667°W

Learn all about coffee—growing it, selling it, making the perfect brew—on a plantation tour at a Chicoj plantation in Cobán. After you've had your caffeine fix, get your adrenaline rush on a tour of the plantation from above, by zip line.

OLD CITY OF SANA'A, YEMEN
### 709. Step back in time in one of the oldest cities
**When:** All year (although summer can be uncomfortably hot)
**Latitude:** 15.3520°N
**Longitude:** 44.2075°E

Looking like it stepped straight off a movie set, the gorgeous Yemeni city of Sana'a has been welcoming visitors for more than 2,500 years. Discover the distinctive and picturesque multistory mosques and houses that were all built before the eleventh century.

AMRAN GOVERNORATE, YEMEN
### 710. Go for a walk in the sky
**When:** All year (although summer can be uncomfortably hot)
**Latitude:** 16.1818°N
**Longitude:** 43.7071°E

Take a walk over the eye-popping Shaharah Bridge (or Bridge of Sighs)—but beware, it is not for the fainthearted. Built in the seventeenth century to connect two remote villages, this scarcely believable limestone arch traverses a 650 ft (198 m) deep canyon amid the looming al-Ahnum mountains.

▶ GUATEMALA
### 711. Marvel at the resplendent quetzal
**When:** October to April
**Latitude:** 15.2354°N
**Longitude:** 90.2350°W

With its long tail feathers, red chest, and bright-green plumage, it's easy to see why the quetzal became Guatemala's national bird. Less easy to see is the bird itself, which is in decline due to deforestation. Look for it in the natural reserve of Biotopo del Quetzal.

The resplendent quetzal, Guatemala

The beautiful Lake Atitlán in
Guatemala (see page 352)

# CHAPTER 5
# NORTHERN
# HEMISPHERE
from 15° north to 0° north

PARQUE NACIONAL CERRO VERDE, EL SALVADOR
## 712. Go trekking over extinct volcanoes
**When:** November to April
**Latitude:** 13.8310°N **Longitude:** 89.6421°W

Nature lovers must not miss the Parque Nacional Cerro Verde, a lush park that serves as an important migratory corridor. It harbors more than 120 species of bird and is also home to reptiles, amphibians, and dozens of species of insects. Meandering paths crisscross the park's 11,120 ac (4,500 ha), home to the Cerro Verde, Izalco, and Santa Ana volcanoes. If you are into trekking, the park's cool climate is ideal, and you'll find that the views from the summit of Santa Ana, with its spectacular emerald-green crater, are well worth the sweat.

▼ LAKE RETBA, SENEGAL
## 713. See a strawberry milkshake–colored lake
**When:** November to June for the most vivid colors
**Latitude:** 14.8388°N **Longitude:** 17.2341°W

Although it looks a little like there's been a chemical spill, the pretty pink color of Lake Retba is all natural. The lake is separated from the sea by a thin strip of dunes, and the waters are highly salty as a result. This makes them perfect for the red algae, which thrive in the waters and give them their distinctive hue. Dip your toes in the pink waters and marvel at the rose pigmentation.

The strawberry milkshake–colored Lake Retba, Senegal

CHICHICASTENANGO, GUATEMALA
## 714. Browse the markets in the mountains
**When:** All year (market days are Thursdays and Sundays)
**Latitude:** 14.9450°N **Longitude:** 91.1089°W

Known to the locals as "Chichi" (who has time to say Chichicastenango more than once?), this bright and buzzing mountaintop market town is jammed with Mayan textiles, crafts, and woodcarvings. When you've finished shopping, don't forget to explore the 400-year-old Iglesia de Santo Tomás.

▼ SAN ANDRÉS ITZAPA, GUATEMALA
## 715. Visit a sombrero-wearing "devilish" Mayan god
**When:** All year
**Latitude:** 14.6194°N **Longitude:** 90.8413°W

When Catholicism arrived in Latin America, it didn't replace all existing religious practices. In many parts of Guatemala, locals still invoke the powers of Maximón, the suit- and sombrero-wearing god, or perhaps saint. Visit his altars, which are festooned with cigars and rum.

The sombrero-wearing "devilish" Mayan god Maximón, in Guatemala

◄ START IN ANTIGUA, GUATEMALA

## 716. Unite former capitals in a journey across space and time

**When:** All year
**Latitude:** 14.5667°N **Longitude:** 90.7333°W

Visiting former capitals gives you more than simply a geographical experience—they offer a glimpse into a country's past while also showing how a country has changed and evolved.

Start in Antigua, the former capital of Guatemala and a UNESCO World Heritage site. It is like stepping back in time here: the Spanish colonial buildings that sit beneath three volcanoes are a mixture of old charm and grandiosity from another era.

Fez, in Morocco, is another former capital to get lost in. The old town is a warren of alleys: passageways that stumble out into squares and markets, all buzzing with people and life.

As the former capital of British India, Calcutta is a monument to colonial architecture and English-style gardens juxtaposed with the nitty-gritty of modern-day living for many of India's poorest citizens. As a result, the city today can charm and shock in the same breath.

Finally, another former capital with buckets of history, Turku in Finland is thought to be its oldest city, founded in the thirteenth century. Head to the open-air handicrafts museum of Luostarinmäki to see how the place looked in the eighteenth century.

DOGON COUNTRY, MALI

## 717. Trek into a world of charming architecture

**When:** November to February (to avoid the heat)
**Latitude:** 14.3489°N **Longitude:** 3.6091°W

In the heart of Mali, along the Bandiagara escarpment, you'll find Dogon Country (or Pays Dogon), where the Dogon people have lived for more than 1,000 years. A trek through the area takes four or five days, and the main attractions are the many picturesque Dogon villages. These are distinguishable by their clusters of granaries—mud buildings topped with thatched conical roofs—which often seem to be embedded on the cliff face, defying gravity. It's no surprise these villages became a UNESCO World Heritage Site in 1989.

DJENNÉ, MALI

## 718. Marvel at Mali's mud mosque

**When:** All year (but the cooler months of October to March are best)
**Latitude:** 13.9054°N
**Longitude:** 4.5560°W

The vast, imposing, mud-brick Great Mosque—the centerpiece of the ancient sub-Saharan city of Djenné—is stunning. Look closely at its studded walls: they require constant upkeep from an army of volunteers, constantly changing color under the sun.

Antigua, former capital of Guatemala

HO CHI MINH CITY TO HANOI, VIETNAM
## 719. Ride the *Reunification Express*
**When:** September to December and March to April
**Latitude:** 14.0583°N **Longitude:** 108.2772°E

For travelers and adventurers the *Reunification Express* represents the ultimate train ride. Vietnam's 1,073 mi (1,726 km) rail line stretches from Ho Chi Minh (formerly Saigon) to the capital, Hanoi, and is about experiencing the real Vietnam.

It was used by the US during the Vietnam War as a clear target for bombing while simultaneously cutting off supplies and weapons to the south. Following the war, the government worked to unify the two sides of the country, rebuilding the majority of the line's 1,334 bridges and 27 tunnels: the newly nicknamed *Reunification Express* made its first postwar journey on New Year's Eve, 1976.

Traveling on the *Express* is not about luxuriously plush surroundings, but the journey is an experience in itself and not just a means of getting from A to B.

The *Reunification Express* in Vietnam

VIETNAM
## 720. Create a masterpiece from sand
**When:** All year
**Latitude:** 14.0583°N
**Longitude:** 108.2772°E

The art of sand painting is a delightful Vietnamese tradition: using multicolored grains, it's possible to create some masterpieces with short life spans. Take one of numerous courses that guide beginners through creating their own.

HO CHI MINH TRAIL, VIETNAM
## 721. Cruise along the "Easy Rider Trail"
**When:** September to December and March to April
**Latitude:** 14.0583°N **Longitude:** 108.2772°E

The "Easy Rider Trail" is the more charismatic name of the Ho Chi Minh Trail, used as a supply route by the North Vietnamese during the Vietnam War. Under either name, this is a trail Vietnam style, with no official signposts or organized hints of a tourist route. But there are acres of luscious green rice fields, hamlets of a few dozen families cut off from the trappings of society, and the occasional evidence of the war left by the roadside as a spontaneous memorial. A word of warning: don't be fooled by the name—there is nothing easy about driving anything in Vietnam, but take a deep breath and it can be an exhilarating, if nail-biting, experience.

LAK LAKE, VIETNAM
## 722. Paddle in a dugout canoe
**When:** All year
**Latitude:** 12.4144°N
**Longitude:** 108.1851°E

There are few better ways to experience the sunrise than to watch it reflecting off the shimmering waters of Lak Lake, Vietnam, as you paddle in a dugout canoe, a traditional vessel hollowed from a tree trunk.

HO CHI MINH CITY, VIETNAM
## 723. Explore Vietnam's Cu Chi tunnels
**When:** All year
**Latitude:** 11.1437°N
**Longitude:** 106.4597°E

"The most bombed, shelled, gassed, defoliated, and generally devastated area in the history of warfare," according to one BBC journalist, the 75 mi (120 km) network of tunnels at Cu Chi is not for the fainthearted, and certainly not for the claustrophobic. So bear this in mind when you visit the pitch-black tunnels that are barely wide enough to crawl around in.

PHU QUOC ISLAND, VIETNAM
## 724. Go night fishing for squid
**When:** April to January
**Latitude:** 10.2899°N
**Longitude:** 103.9840°E

During squid season, the large shoals hovering around the bay after sunset guarantee the thrill of catching your own dinner. You'll be armed with fishing rods and rackets to ensure even the most inept fisherman is likely to catch two dozen squid, which are cooked and served immediately.

LAKE ATITLÁN, GUATEMALA
### 725. Be dazzled by a beautiful lake
**When:** All year
**Latitude:** 14.6907°N
**Longitude:** 91.2025°W

Lake Atitlán has drawn many superlatives from visitors over the years, and it really is majestically beautiful. Its deep, blue waters are surrounded by three volcanoes and a crenellated landscape full of peaks and valleys. Whether you stay at water level or hike up one of the volcanoes, the views you'll get will stay with you for a lifetime.

BANGKOK, THAILAND
### 726. Learn to give Thai head massages
**When:** All year
**Latitude:** 13.7563°N
**Longitude:** 100.5018°E

Thai head and neck massages are a great way to reduce stress and revitalize (especially for those who sit at a desk all day), so why not learn to be able to give this special gift to others? Intensive courses in Thailand can be completed in around five weeks—and can even lead to a new profession.

KANCHANABURI, THAILAND
### 727. Cross the bridge on the River Kwai
**When:** All year
**Latitude:** 14.0408°N
**Longitude:** 99.5037°E

A winner of seven Academy Awards, the 1957 movie *The Bridge on the River Kwai* was based on the experiences of around 60,000 Allied prisoners of war who were forced to work on constructing what became known as the "Death Railway." When you gaze upon the bridge (which was rebuilt after Allied bombing in 1945), you'll find it difficult to equate the suffering that occurred there with the peaceful, bucolic scene today.

BANGKOK, THAILAND
### 728. Meditate at a sacred Thai monastery
**When:** All year
**Latitude:** 13.7563°N
**Longitude:** 100.5018°W

Wat Phra Kaew is the hub of Thai Buddhism, and its Emerald Buddha—a meditating jade figurine—is one of its holiest religious symbols, deeply revered throughout the land. If you want some Zen bestowed on you, this is the place to go.

▶ SIEM REAP, CAMBODIA
### 729. Explore a long-lost Cambodian kingdom
**When:** All year
**Latitude:** 13.4120°N **Longitude:** 103.8646°E

Head out for an early-morning adventure in the Cambodian forest, and set foot among the beautifully preserved remains of the once-lost kingdom of the Khmer Empire—a vast complex of sandstone temples, including the majestic Angkor Wat.

Intended as a representation of the universe, the temples are covered with intricate carvings of mythological battles and the stirring of celestial oceans. Bas-reliefs of the gods and monsters—from Hindu and Buddhist mythologies—look down upon visiting mortals as you ascend narrow temple steps. Climb to the summit to watch the sunrise framed perfectly by one of the temple entrances.

The long-lost Cambodian kingdom of
Angkor Wat in Siem Reap, Cambodia

▼ COCOS ISLAND, COSTA RICA
## 730. Look up at hammerhead sharks
**When:** Best from June to October
**Latitude:** 5.5282°N
**Longitude:** 87.0574°W

What is the collective noun for hammerhead sharks—a toolshed of hammerheads? Who knows? But to dive down and look up at hundreds gathered above you in the sea off the remote Cocos Island is a truly spectacular sight.

COSTA RICA
## 731. Cross six hanging bridges in one day
**When:** All year
**Latitude:** 10.3026°N
**Longitude:** 84.7959°W

Do you have a head for heights? When you visit the Monteverde Cloud Forest Biological Reserve, you'll find six hanging bridges up in the forest canopy—and the longest is almost 1,000 ft (305 m) long. The forest also contains 2.5 percent of the world's biodiversity.

MANZANILLO, COSTA RICA
## 732. Gallop in the surf
**When:** All year (at sunset)
**Latitude:** 9.6298°N
**Longitude:** 82.6578°W

Even non-horse riders want to gallop a horse along a tropical beach, don't they? To feel the wind in their hair, to travel at full speed, but so naturally, and with the waves lapping at hoofs. Costa Rica has 800 mi (1,288 km) of coastline—pick the Caribbean end for a sunrise ride or the Pacific end for sunset.

Hammerhead sharks at Cocos Island, Costa Rica

CAYO GRANDE, VENEZUELA
**733.** Snorkel in solitude

**When:** November to April
**Latitude:** 11.7833°N
**Longitude:** 66.6167°W

Plenty of idyllic spots can lay reasonable claim to hosting the world's best snorkeling. Take a trip to this remote, yet accessible, chain of islands in the Caribbean, and you'll find it may just take the prize with its striking coral reef, sea grass beds, and lack of crowds. Bliss.

LALIBELA, ETHIOPIA
## 734. Wonder at the rock-hewn churches of Lalibela
**When:** January 7
**Latitude:** 12.0309°N **Longitude:** 39.0476°E

In one of the holiest towns in Ethiopia sits some of the world's most astonishing architecture. The eleven rock-hewn churches were hand-carved in the thirteenth century and are the largest monolithic statues on Earth.

It is an awe-inspiring site at any time of year; marvel at the churches that harbor old Christian paintings, artifacts, and religious paraphernalia. A guide will take you through a winding network of narrow tunnels that connect the buildings beneath the hundreds of other visitors above.

But visit during the Orthodox Christian Christmas, and you're in for a real treat. Thousands attend a twelve-hour-long Christmas mass on January 7. Hordes of priests and pilgrims gather, occupying every inch throughout the eleven structures, to pray, chant, and sing. Their booming voices reverberate off the high stone walls and echo throughout the complex in a hauntingly beautiful way.

Tourists at Biete Ghiorgis (House of St. George), Lalibela, Ethiopia

Carving out a route down an active volcano in Nicaragua

▲ NEAR MALPAISILLO, NICARAGUA
## 735. Carve a route down a volcano
**When:** All year
**Latitude:** 12.5078°N
**Longitude:** 86.7022°W

Adrenaline lovers can take a snowboard trip with a difference, down the black ash of an active volcano at Cerro Negro ("Black Hill") in Nicaragua. You can reach speeds of up to 60 mph (97 kph) on the nerve-tingling 1,600 ft (488 m) descent. Are you brave enough to board?

ETHIOPIA
## 736. Trek through the stunning Simien Mountains
**When:** November to March
**Latitude:** 13.1833°N **Longitude:** 38.0667°E

Move aside images of parched, barren Ethiopian lands and enter the Simien Mountains National Park. A gorgeous landscape of undulating lowlands and towering mountains, the Simiens are far from the preconceptions many have about this vast East African country. A trek through this range is rewarding on many levels: wildlife lovers can enjoy watching the 3,000-strong population of gelada baboons playing on the lush, green slopes, and those with a head for heights will be rewarded with astonishing views of the lowlands at every peak. At more than 13,120 ft (4,000 m) above sea level in places, the altitude makes any trek a challenge, but it's entirely worth the effort.

BOBO-DIOULASSO, BURKINA FASO
## 737. Learn the art and nuances of *djembe* drumming
**When:** All year
**Latitude:** 11.1649°N
**Longitude:** 4.3052°W

Originally, the *djembe* ("drum") was played by court musicians (known as "griots") at religious or important ceremonies. They accompanied it with storytelling as they passed on the oral history of past generations or celebrated a marriage or a birth. Although griots still perform this role all over West Africa, the *djembe* is now an instrument played by many musicians and has a surprising range of sounds. Although it might seem simple at first glance, playing a *djembe* well is a much more complex experience, so why not have a go yourself?

BLUE NILE GORGE, ETHIOPIA
## 738. Descend into Africa's Grand Canyon
**When:** All year
**Latitude:** 12.0000°N
**Longitude:** 37.2500°E

Take a trip on the road descending down to the Blue Nile Gorge, around 120 mi (190 km) outside of Addis Ababa in Ethiopia, for it is a dramatic drive. The gorge is almost as deep as the Grand Canyon, and the landscape here is far more lush and green than you might expect when you think of Ethiopia. The Blue Nile got its name from the color of the water tinged with minerals from the fertile highland soil.

▶ PHNOM PENH, CAMBODIA
## 739. Eat insects for lunch
**When:** All year
**Latitude:** 11.5500°N
**Longitude:** 104.9167°E

Not had the pleasure of a scorpion salad, a cricket cupcake, or a Bug Mac? How about a tarantula samosa or an ant spring roll? No? Then you need to get yourself to Cambodia's insect tapas bar, the aptly named Bugs Café in Phnom Penh. There's more to the menu than mere novelty factor, too—insects are packed with protein and billed as a sustainable solution to feeding our rapidly expanding global population.

Insects and tarantulas for lunch in Phnom Penh, Cambodia

▶ LA CIUDAD PERDIDA, SIERRA NEVADA DE SANTA MARTA, COLOMBIA
## 740. Become an explorer and discover a lost city
**When:** December to March (For a simpler hike in the dry season)
**Latitude:** 11.0382°N **Longitude:** 73.9252°W

In the Sierra Nevada, La Ciudad Perdida (Spanish for "the lost city") was "found" in 1972. Archaeologists identified the city as Teyuna, probably the central town of the Tairona people. It dates back to AD 800—predating Machu Picchu by around 650 years—and was probably abandoned when the conquistadores arrived.

The city consists of 169 terraces connected by roads paved with stone and interspersed with small circular plazas. There are staircases, canals, paths, houses, and storerooms to explore. And that is only what has been reclaimed from the tendrils of the jungle—there is much more still concealed behind its trees and vines. Be prepared to trek through dense undergrowth for a couple of days before you reach the 1,200 stone steps that lead up to the city.

COLOMBIA
## 741. Sleep in a hammock on a tropical beach
**When:** December to May or July and August (You don't want a hammock in the rainy season)
**Latitude:** 11.2882°N
**Longitude:** 74.1517°W

There is nothing quite so relaxing as lying in a hammock by the beach: the gentle swaying in the wind, the open air, the crash of the waves on the shore. In Tayrona National Natural Park in Colombia, you don't even have to take your own, as you can rent them there.

ADDIS ABABA, ETHIOPIA
## 742. Eat like a local in Addis Ababa
**When:** All year
**Latitude:** 9.0300°N
**Longitude:** 38.7400°E

Ethiopian food can be mind-boggling, so a tour with Go Addis in the capital is an excellent way to get your head around it. Stroll from café to restaurant with an Ethiopian guide and learn how to eat *injera* (a traditional flatbread) like a local.

GONDAR, ETHIOPIA
## 743. See the historic castles of Gondar
**When:** All year
**Latitude:** 12.6000°N
**Longitude:** 37.4667°E

This walled complex of ancient castles and palaces wouldn't look out of place in medieval Britain. Built by an emperor in the sixteenth and seventeenth centuries, a stroll around this enclosure offers an insight into the country's fascinating past.

EL TOTUMO, COLOMBIA
## 744. Float in the crater of a mud volcano
**When:** All year
**Latitude:** 10.7444°N
**Longitude:** 75.2414°W

It takes faith to step off the edge and into the "crater" of El Totumo mud volcano in northern Colombia. Your feet can't touch the bottom, but the consistency of the mud keeps you afloat—and provides a perfect skin treatment at the same time.

The lost city of La Cuidad Perdida in Sierra Nevada, Colombia

## 745. Circumnavigate the Caribbean by its beaches

**When:** Best in December to April to avoid rainy and hurricane seasons
**Latitude:** 10.6918°N **Longitude:** 61.2225°W

If you find it hard to choose one of the numerous Caribbean beaches for your vacation, why not just visit all of them?

To start, travel west along the coast of Venezuela and head north to Trinidad and Tobago with its very varied coastline. For the true, gleaming white sand and turquoise waters, head north to the islands of the Lesser Antilles: Grenada, Barbados, Saint Lucia, Dominica.

As the route curves westward, the slightly exclusive British Virgin Islands are a beach lover's paradise; then you head across to Central America, where you can either go north, taking in Turks and Caicos and the Bahamas, or the varied cultures of the Dominican Republic, Haiti, Cuba, and Jamaica.

When you're back on the mainland, head south down the coast and take in Mexico, Belize, and Honduras. When you get to Nicaragua's Caribbean coast, the roads aren't great, but once you're in Costa Rica, you could find it hard to leave its laid-back beaches.

In Panama, the Bocas del Toro Province region offers wonderful beaches and a plethora of islands to visit, too. Next, a visit to Colombia's Caribbean town of Cartagena de los Indios is more for the stunning architecture than its beaches.

And then it's the final leg of the beach tour, back into Venezuela, where the Isla de Margarita has beaches for everyone. Now you just have the task of choosing your favorite.

▶ COSTA RICA
## 746. See the wonderfully wobbly nose of a tapir
**When:** All year
**Latitude:** 10.6731°N
**Longitude:** 85.0150°W

Tapirs are shy animals that can sense people's presence and run before they are spotted. Find them at dawn and dusk, when they are most active, or catch them gathering to drink at Tapir Lake in Tenorio National Park.

The wonderfully wobbly nose of a Baird's tapir in Costa Rica

COSTA RICA
## 747. Spy on the slower-than-you'd-believe sloth
**When:** All year
**Latitude:** 9.3923°N
**Longitude:** 84.1370°W

Sloths can be hard to find in the wild, because they sleep for up to twenty hours a day—and when they are awake, they often just stay still. Try to spot the world's slowest mammal—they are almost comical to watch.

PORT OF SPAIN, TRINIDAD
## 748. Let your hair down at a pulsating party
**When:** February to March (the two days before Ash Wednesday)
**Latitude:** 10.6617°N
**Longitude:** 61.5194°W

The mother of all good times, in a corner of the world famous for its fiestas, is the Trinidad Carnival. Join in the riot of calypso, steel bands, and soca, all wrapped in extravagant costumes in the lead-up to Lent.

COLOMBIA
## 749. Travel on colorful public transport
**When:** All year
**Latitude:** 10.3910°N
**Longitude:** 75.4794°W

Forget sightseeing buses; the local buses in Cartagena de los Indios— and all over Colombia—come with brightly colored paintwork and blaring salsa music. It will feel like a party every journey—and all for just a handful of pesos.

CARTAGENA DE LOS INDIOS, COLOMBIA
750. Wander streets where great literature was born

**When:** All year
**Latitude:** 10.3910°N
**Longitude:** 75.4794°W

With its towering yellow dome, the cathedral in the heart of Cartagena de los Indios' old town is a distinctive and alluring sight. Below, the city's streets are full of colorful houses, arched arcades, intimate restaurants, and bustling market stalls—and there is a real sense that life is lived outside here. This is undoubtedly what drew Colombian novelist Gabriel García Márquez to the city: the stories unfolding on every street corner. Now the master is honored with a literary festival in the city each year—as if you needed any additional reason to visit the intriguing town.

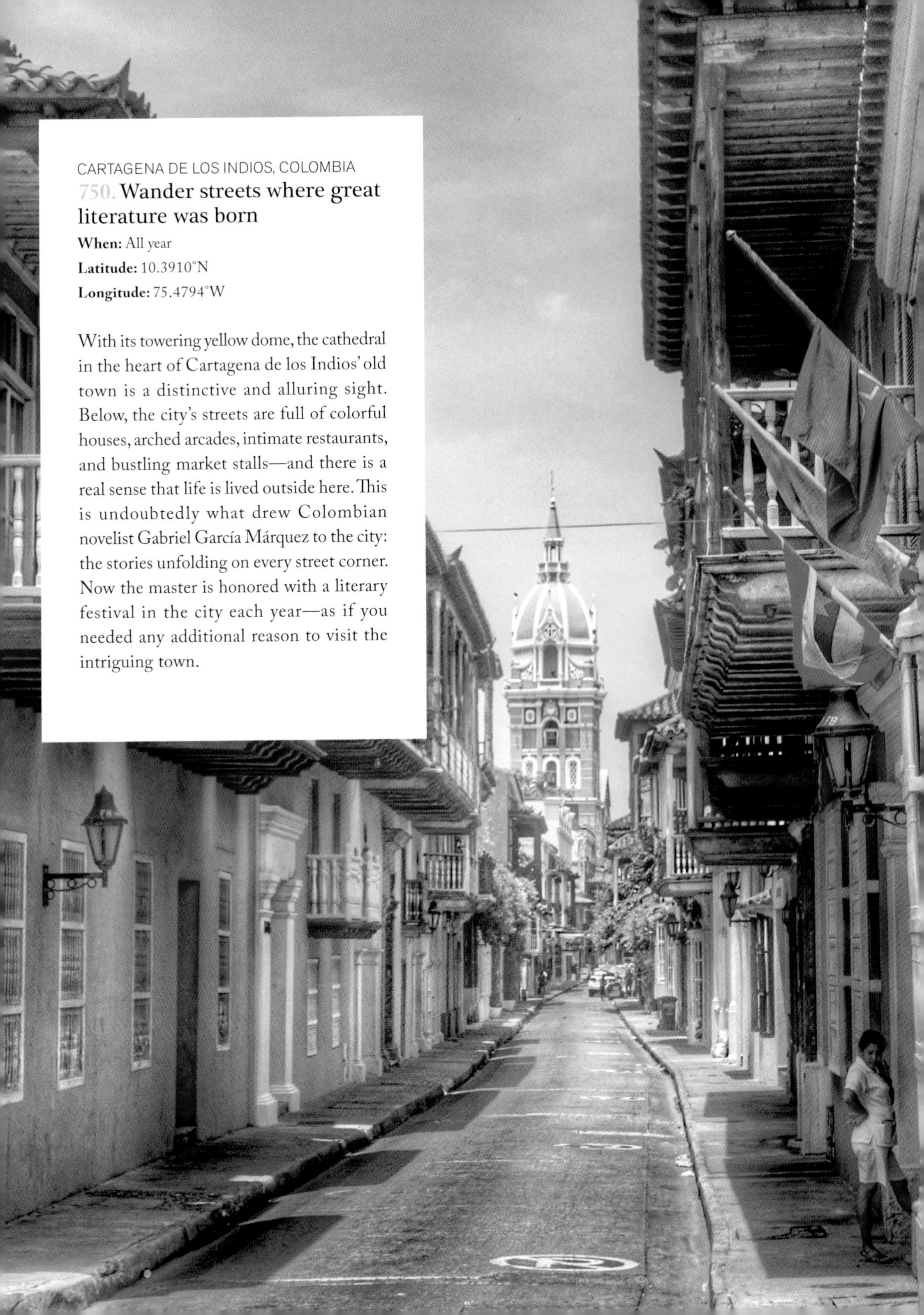

## 751. Be dazzled by magnificent temples

**When:** October to March
**Latitude:** 9.9252°N
**Longitude:** 78.1198°E

Feast your eyes upon the spectacular temples of the 2,500-year-old city of Madurai, where fourteen brightly colored towers dominate the skyline. The most striking is the 170 ft (52 m) tall, seventh-century Sri Meenakshi Amman, covered with thousands of painted sculptures of deities and mythical creatures.

MEKONG DELTA, LAOS
## 752. Watch the sunrise over the Mekong Delta
**When:** All year
**Latitude:** 10.0090°N
**Longitude:** 105.8240°E

Take a boat ride at sunrise on the Mekong Delta, a confluence of waterways known as the "River of Nine Dragons," whose waters flow from the mountains of Tibet all the way to the South China Sea via Laos, Cambodia, and Vietnam.

Before the heat and bustle of the day hits, hop aboard a long-tail boat and enjoy the serene sight of fishermen tossing their nets.

LA PAZ WATERFALL, COSTA RICA
## 753. Film the colorful frogs of Costa Rica
**When:** All year
**Latitude:** 10.1473°N
**Longitude:** 84.5318°W

Perhaps nothing else signifies Costa Rica as much as its huge range of fascinating frogs and toads: the nocturnal red-eyed tree frog, the blue jeans frog, glass frog, and poison dart frog (not actually a danger to humans). The easiest way to spy these treasures is at "frog gardens" situated all around the country, and once there, you can film your own mini-wildlife show of these colorful characters. Book onto a butterfly-and frog-tour, or try the ranarium at La Paz Waterfall, to learn about the lifestyles of these creatures.

VOLCÁN POÁS, COSTA RICA
## 754. Smell the sulfur of an active volcano
**When:** All year (but visit before noon when it clouds over)
**Latitude:** 10.1978°N
**Longitude:** 84.2306°W

Peer into the 1 mi (1.6 km) wide crater of Volcán Poás to see the bubbling, deep turquoise lake and occasional geyser as pressure builds up from the heat within the mountain. The last volcanic activity was 1910, so you should be safe from eruptions.

GEORGETOWN, GUYANA
## 755. Visit the world's least-visited country
**When:** All year
**Latitude:** 6.8013°N
**Longitude:** 58.1551°W

Officially the world's least-visited country, Guyana in South America is known for its wild interior of virgin rain forest. Unofficially—in that no figures are supplied—Nauru, off Australia's northeastern coast, holds the accolade, and you can walk around it in a day.

SRI LANKA
## 756. Dig a well for charity
**When:** All year
**Latitude:** 7.8730°N
**Longitude:** 80.7717°E

Helping an entire community through manual labor and protecting it against waterborne diseases as a result is one of the most fulfilling charitable contributions available. Many charities aim to help the sixth of humanity who lack access to safe water; Sri Lanka is a great place to start.

EQUATORIAL GUINEA, AFRICA
## 757. See how it feels to be in the doldrums
**When:** All year (weather dependent)
**Latitude:** 3.7504°N
**Longitude:** 8.7371°E

The doldrums isn't just a state of mind, it is also an area of the world—between 5°N and 5°S of the equator. In this area the wind can die for weeks at a time, which made it perilous for sailors in the days when wind power was everything. If you sail out into the doldrums now, just be sure you have an engine to get you back again.

**758.** Swim or dive with massive manta rays

**When:** All year
**Latitude:** 9.5557°N
**Longitude:** 138.1399°E

At Yap in Micronesia, manta rays can have wingspans of 20 ft (6 m) or more—that's as big as an elephant. They are incredibly graceful animals, and seeing them float into view is a memorable experience as you swim beside or dive below them.

ORINOCO DELTA, VENEZUELA
## 759. Enjoy a slower pace of life

**When:** All year (more mosses in the rainy season though,
May to June)
**Latitude:** 9.5500°N **Longitude:** 62.7000°W

A vast river delta of the Orinoco River, the fan-shaped
Orinoco Delta is home to the Warao people, who have
lived here for 8,500 years. Their houses stand on stilts
at the edge of the waterways, open to the elements and
topped with a thatched roof. Their name translates
as "people of canoes," and it's easy to see why—the
Warao spend a lot of time in their canoes fishing on
the tributaries, as well as hunting and gathering in
the forests.

When you visit the area, you can stay in houses
similar to the Warao and can spend time walking in
the jungle or exploring the river in a canoe. It's a relaxed
pace of life and one that is rewarded with fabulous
wildlife spotting. You might see giant otters, pink river
dolphins, spectacled caiman, and river turtles, while on
land, howler monkeys are usually heard before they are
seen. There are also sloths, capuchin monkeys, and a
huge and colorful array of birdlife.

With such a wealth of wildlife, a trip to the delta
can last for as many days as you can spare. The peace
and calm of living on the water soon starts to feel like
the right pace of life—and it doesn't take too long to
get used to the screams of the howler monkeys.

A slower pace of life on the
Orinoco Delta, Venezuela

◄ ALLEPPEY, KERALA, INDIA
## 760. Laze on the Indian backwater
**When:** September to March
**Latitude:** 9.4900°N **Longitude:** 76.3300°E

India's Alleppey, also known as Alappuzha and the "Venice of the East," is a crisscrossing network of canals reaching out into the backwater of the beautiful Kerala region. It is a serene series of lakes and lagoons, and the best way to explore is aboard a traditional houseboat; set sail for a couple of days and nights to really unwind and get used to the pace of life, and to truly soak in what is around you.

It is an exquisite way to travel and see life along the waterways—which can be surprisingly busy. Village life takes place along the banks of the waters: people washing themselves, their clothes, their dishes.

The wildlife here is not to be missed: crabs, frogs, turtles, otters, kingfishers, and cormorants. Endless lush vegetation growing along the banks gives everything a peaceful and glorious green hue.

Cruising along this backwater is to experience peace and beauty on an unrivaled scale.

KOH SURIN NATIONAL MARINE PARK, THAILAND
## 761. Glimpse a way of life that will soon be gone
**When:** November to April
**Latitude:** 9.4344°N **Longitude:** 97.8681°E

The nomadic Moken people, one of the rapidly disappearing sea-gypsy tribes scattered around the Mergui Archipelago off the coast of Thailand and Myanmar, eke out an increasingly fragile existence. Traditionally living on boats most of the year, Moken children can swim before they can walk and have underwater vision similar to that of dolphins. Increasingly, the remarkable Moken, who survive on fishing and foraging, live in stilted villages in the Koh Surin National Marine Park. Your visit will help to support the precarious local economy.

SOCOTRA ARCHIPELAGO, YEMEN
## 762. Discover dragon blood in a lost world
**When:** February to April
**Latitude:** 12.4634°N
**Longitude:** 53.8237°E

Looking like something from the set of *Star Wars*, the distinctive mushroom-like dragon blood tree is only found on an archipelago 250 mi (402 km) off the Yemeni coast. As if the shape of the trees wasn't enough to amaze you, when cut, it oozes a dark-red, blood-like resin, used in traditional medicine.

KOH PHANGAN, THAILAND
## 763. Party under a full moon in Koh Phangan
**When:** Full moon
**Latitude:** 9.7318°N
**Longitude:** 100.0135°E

Full moon parties have become something of a Thai hippie cliché, but they're well attended for a reason, and the original all-night good time—the party on Hat Rin beach, Koh Phangan—is still a semi-spiritual party with few equals. Be sure to visit the rest of the island, which is truly serene, too.

MOUNT MAYON, PHILIPPINES
## 764. Walk up a symmetrical volcano
**When:** February to April
**Latitude:** 13.2544°N
**Longitude:** 123.6850°E

No other volcano can aesthetically compare to Mount Mayon: it has the world's most symmetrical cone—a truly stunning sight—and is the Philippines' most active. Pass through forest, boulders, and grassland to be rewarded with breathtaking views from the summit.

Lazing on a Kerala houseboat on the Indian backwater

▼ THENMALA, KERALA, INDIA
### 765. Go all aflutter on a butterfly safari
**When:** All year
**Latitude:** 8.9500°N
**Longitude:** 77.0667°E

More than a hundred species of butterfly call the Butterfly Safari Park in Kerala, India, home, including many lesser-spotted beauties nestled among the 8 ac (3.5 ha) of tropical plants. Time a trip here with precision: some species live for as little as four days.

KERALA, INDIA
### 766. Learn to cook Keralan-style
**When:** November to March
**Latitude:** 9.9257°N
**Longitude:** 76.6717°E

Perched on a hill in Kerala's luscious countryside, the Pimenta Spice Garden is a perfect setting for cooking south Indian food. Owner Jacob takes you to shop for ingredients in the local market before a hands-on lesson in creating fragrant dishes with delicate Indian spices.

KERALA, INDIA
### 767. Watch a colorful Kathakali production
**When:** All year
**Latitude:** 10.8505°N
**Longitude:** 76.2711°E

Watch the eternal battle between good and evil played out before your eyes to a percussive beat in flamboyant Kathakali theater. Dramatic and brightly colored, the elaborate headdresses and bold costumes that developed in seventeenth-century Kerala are a photographer's delight.

The blue tiger butterfly in Kerala, India

PHANG NGA BAY, THAILAND
### 768. Kayak through stunning Thai caves
**When:** All year
**Latitude:** 8.4481°N
**Longitude:** 98.5116°E

Spot the famous "James Bond Island," weave through the lagoons and limestone-formed caves, observe eagles and kites soaring high above: a kayak trip around Phang Nga Bay is an out-of-this-world day out—and an easy introduction to kayaking for beginners, too.

KANHANGAD TO POOMPUHAR BEACH, SOUTH INDIA
### 769. Walk cross the Indian subcontinent
**When:** December to February
**Latitude:** 12.3094°N **Longitude:** 75.0961°E

India has been attracting spiritual adventurers and curious travelers for thousands of years. What better way to get under its skin than by going off the beaten track and making your own adventures as you travel on foot from the Arabian Sea to the Bay of Bengal?

A popular journey loosely tracks the course of the holy Kaveri River as it winds southeast from source to sea. Starting on the west coast at Kanhangad, the 500 mi (805 km) trek begins with a steady climb into the Western Ghats Mountains to find the starting point of the Kaveri at Bhagamandala. The water then travels underground, reappearing farther down the mountain, from where it can be followed to the Bay of Bengal.

Highlights of this trek include the Krishna Raja Sagar Dam, elaborate temples of Somanathapura, spectacular waterfalls at Shivasamudram, and mysterious Hogenakkal. You'll then pass through twisted gorges, lush countryside, and misty mountains before arriving at Srirangam, an island in the middle of the Kaveri that houses the awe-inspiring Sri Ranganatha Swamy, the largest temple complex in India.

After sensational Srirangam, strike for the coast and pretty Poompuhar Beach, where the Kaveri finishes its journey—and you finish yours—in the glittering Bay of Bengal.

SIGIRIYA, SRI LANKA

**770.** Climb up to a palace on top of a rock

**When:** All year
**Latitude:** 7.9563°N **Longitude:** 80.7601°E

From the surrounding area, Sigiriya ("Lion Rock" in Sinhalese) is a huge, flat-topped rock rising up 660 ft (200 m) from the surrounding countryside. On top of this rock lie the remains of a king's palace and extensive gardens that date back 1,600 years.

The palace is reached via numerous different staircases. The first of these start in gardens at the foot of the rock and lead you up to the Mirror Wall—a highly polished 600 ft (182 m) long wall that is thought could originally reflect the frescoes painted on the opposite rock face. Some of these are still visible today, their sheltered position protecting their vibrant colors and incredible detail.

The final ascent to the top is made up a staircase that once led into a lion's mouth, but now only the carved paws remain. This would have led the king and his entourage up to the palace complex, which consisted of many buildings set in lush gardens.

As with many ancient sites, it is partly the beauty of the location that drew the original inhabitants that draws visitors back today, but it is also to marvel at the incredible feats—and follies—of those who built palaces on the top of rocks.

Sigiriya palace at the top
of a rock, Sri Lanka

Takua Pa vegetarian festival in Phuket, Thailand

▲ PHUKET, THAILAND
## 771. Be inspired by vegetarian cuisine
**When:** October
**Latitude:** 7.8804°N
**Longitude:** 98.3922°E

With a vast worldwide population expansion inevitable—and meat farming using up far more resources than crop growth—vegetarianism may not be a choice in the future. Until then, why not dabble with a healthier lifestyle by going flesh-free for a week? Phuket's dazzling vegetarian festival provides some inspiring recipe ideas.

PHI PHI LEH ISLAND, THAILAND
## 772. Find the perfect beach ... from *The Beach*
**When:** All year
**Latitude:** 7.7461°N
**Longitude:** 98.7784°E

Anyone who has watched the Leonardo DiCaprio movie *The Beach* will know that plots don't always go as planned in paradise. Arrange a trip to the Phi Phi Island, where the blockbuster was filmed, for unsurpassable sands and rich, dense jungles.

SRI LANKA
## 773. Cruise among the clouds
**When:** January to April
**Latitude:** 7.4675°N
**Longitude:** 80.6234°E (Matale)

There is something rather magical about driving through the clouds amid the exotic flora and fauna of the mysterious Central Highlands of Sri Lanka. Look for bear monkeys, elephants, and leopards stalking the undergrowth in this otherworldly forest, which rises to a skykissing 8,200 ft (2,500 m).

KANDY, SRI LANKA
## 774. Join the quest for Buddha's tooth
**When:** Ten days, ending on the August full moon
**Latitude:** 7.2905°N **Longitude:** 80.6337°E

A reminder of how peculiar life's rich tapestry can sometimes be: hundreds of people jostling for the view of a gold box, on top of an elaborately decorated elephant, that may or may not contain a tooth once belonging to Buddha.

The Esala Perahera pilgrimage in Kandy is certainly unique. The legend runs that the deity was cremated in the fifth century BC, and one of his worshipers snatched a tooth from the funeral embers, which was smuggled to Sri Lanka. The king at the time, Megavanna, paraded it around, and a tradition was born.

A replica is used during the event, paraded round by a priest on elephant back, which is decorated in an elaborate silk costume. Other dapper pachyderms also join the march. It's astonishing to witness the fervor of the marching groups, banner carriers, fire jugglers, and loud whip carriers that add to the color and noise.

In the morning a priest plunges a sword in the Mahaweli River to denote the end of the ceremony, and trees are planted in Buddha's honor.

"MONKEY ISLAND", MALAYSIA
## 775. Learn to survive on a desert island
**When:** March to October
**Latitude:** 6.2941°N **Longitude:** 99.7113°E

If you've ever thought of getting away from it all—Robinson Crusoe style—this may be your dream come true. Just across the waters, off the coast of Malaysia, lies an isle that lives up to the true meaning of "desert island." Between resort-laden Langkawi and the private island of Rebak Besar, this little clump of sand and trees has been left unnamed, untamed, and unmanned—except for the cheeky monkeys from which it gets its nickname: "Monkey Island."

It's not an easy island to access, but ask around on Langkawi for a local with a boat to drop you on the invitingly empty shoreline for the day.

The ultimate castaway destination, the only man-made thing you'll find is a wooden chest at the back of the

beach in which to store your belongings out of reach of those mischievous monkeys, who won't hesitate to rummage for food. You can then hone your survival skills: with a little rope or some palm leaves, you can try your hand at making a shelter, or bring equipment to see what you can reel in to grill for lunch on an open fire. There is no greater reward than the fruits—or fish—of your own labor.

Of course, the best thing about being stranded here is the peace and quiet. It is the perfect back-to-basics getaway, where you can clear your mind of everyday worries and reset for the rest of your trip.

VENEZUELA
## 776. Spot a capybara in its natural habitat
**When:** All year
**Latitude:** 7.8817°N
**Longitude** 67.4687°W

Capybaras, the world's largest rodents, are more often than not seen basking in mud, having a little snooze. It's not surprising that they don't get up to much, as they reproduce about thirty times a day. You may even be able to nibble on one; capybara meat is a prized delicacy in Venezuela.

COLOMBIA
## 777. See the "river that ran away from paradise"
**When:** September to November
**Latitude:** 2.1817°N
**Longitude:** 73.7865°W

For a few months every year, between the wet and dry seasons, a plant on the floor of the Caño Cristales River in the Serranía de la Macarena turns a dramatic red. Capture the streaks of yellow sand, green algae, and blue water merging to become the "River of Five Colors."

SAN GIL, COLOMBIA
## 778. Abseil down a waterfall
**When:** All year
**Latitude:** 6.3797°N
**Longitude:** 73.1668°W

Once you've lowered yourself over the edge of the Juan Curi waterfall with just a harness around your waist and a rope gripped firmly in your hands, there's no going back. The waterfall splashes over you until, 230 ft (70 m) later, you're back on solid ground.

▶ ANGEL FALLS, VENEZUELA
## 779. Trek up to the world's highest waterfall
**When:** All year
**Latitude:** 5.9675°N **Longitude:** 62.5356°W

Deep in the heart of the Venezuelan rain forest is the world's highest waterfall: Angel Falls. It's not easy to get to—you first have to take a light aircraft to Canaima National Park, then take a boat upriver, and then hike up to the falls. When you get there, you need to look up, and up some more, as the waterfall plunges almost 2,500 ft (762 m) in a single chute from the top of the cliff into the Churun River. It's impressive, it's loud, and it's quite fun to have a swim in one of the freshwater pools right at the base of the falls.

The world's highest waterfall: Angel Falls in Venezuela

LIMÓN BAY, PANAMA

## 780. Experience the best water-borne engineering

**When:** All year
**Latitude:** 9.3459°N
**Longitude:** 79.9305°W

Built in the early twentieth century, the 50 mi (80 km) Panama Canal was an engineering masterstroke, creating a shortcut for ships between New York and California. Take a cruise and experience the ingenious lock system, which raises and lowers boats 85 ft (26 m) at a time to ensure safe passage.

ISLA GIBRALEÓN, PANAMA

## 781. Live like a Bear in Panama

**When:** All year (more fun in spring/summer)
**Latitude:** 8.5156°N
**Longitude:** 79.0462°W

Make the most of being outside by building a cozy, weatherproof den like the ones constructed on TV show *The Island with Bear Grylls*. Probably better to start in the backyard or a local national park than in the uninhabited Isla Gibraleón, mind you.

VOLCÁN BARÚ, PANAMA

## 782. See two different oceans from one spot

**When:** All year (weather permitting)
**Latitude:** 8.8088°N
**Longitude:** 82.5423°W

Volcán Barú, the highest point in Panama, is an inactive volcano that offers one of the world's most unique experiences—from the top on a clear day you can see both the Pacific Ocean in one direction and the Atlantic in the other.

GUATAPÉ, COLOMBIA

## 783. Scale the staircase in La Piedra del Peñol

**When:** All year
**Latitude:** 6.2311°N **Longitude:** 75.1535°W

Between the towns of Guatapé and Peñol in Colombia is a rock that towers 650 ft (200 m) over the surrounding flat countryside. Climb the 649 steps of the staircase that's built into a crevice in the rock for some epic views over the surrounding countryside.

DARIÉN GAP, BETWEEN PANAMA AND COLOMBIA

## 784. Walk from one continent to another

**When:** The dry season—December to April
**Latitude:** 7.9000°N **Longitude:** 77.4600°W

The Darién Gap connects Panama to Colombia, and it's possible to cross it on foot, but it's not for the fainthearted. It's a mass of jungle, swamps, mountains, snakes, scorpions, crocodiles … not to mention human undesirables in these lawless parts. You get the idea—everything that is bad for you is found here. So employ a local guide, stay safe, and expect three days of harsh trekking if you want to undertake this adventure of a lifetime.

GRAN SABANA, VENEZUELA

## 785. Climb a mountain with some of the world's oldest rock formations

**When:** All year

**Latitude:** 5.1517°N **Longitude:** 60.7571°W

Standing at 9,220 ft (2,810 m) high and 4 mi (8 km) across, Mount Roraima is the highest tabletop mountain in the Gran Sabana. This vast area is home to some of the world's oldest geological rock formations and the world's tallest waterfall, Angel Falls.

Climbing this giant mountain is a major highlight of any trip to the region. Intrepid trekkers can reach the summit on a five-night trek, sleeping in tents along the way. Hiking Mount Roraima will make for an unforgettable experience, largely thanks to the area's incredibly unique terrain. Species that exist nowhere else on Earth inhabit Roraima's wet, misty plateau, including tiny pebble toads that are thought to predate dinosaurs, nectar-feeding birds, and endemic carnivorous marsh pitchers and sundews that, over time, have adapted to the harsh terrain, learning to supplement their diet with insects. Where else on the planet can you witness such a sight?

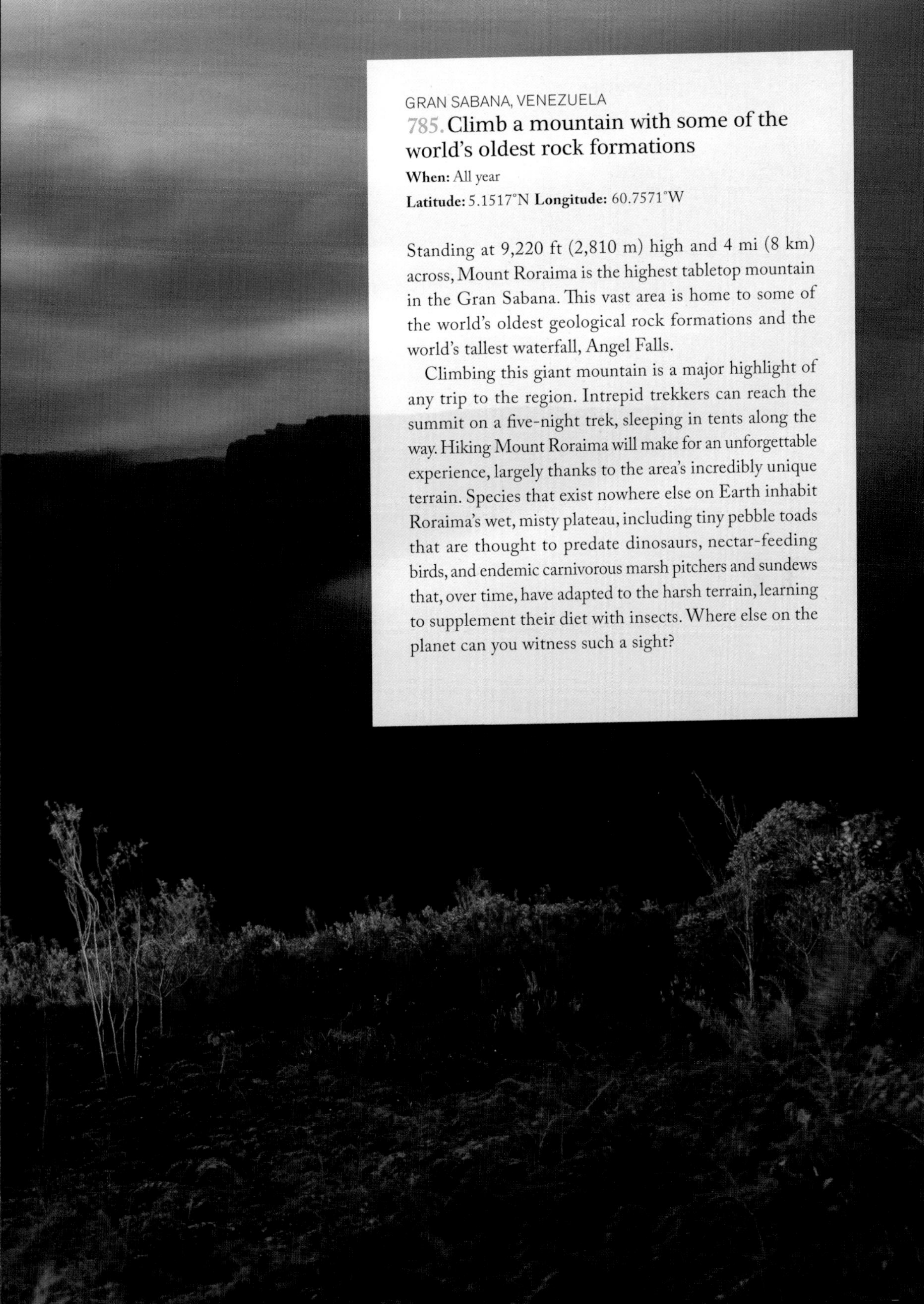

Brunei's Kampong Ayer water village
in Bandar Seri Begawan, Brunei

▲ BRUNEI
### 786. Pay a visit to a water village
**When:** All year
**Latitude:** 4.8827°N
**Longitude:** 114.9443°E

Kampong Ayer (or the "Water Village") is just like any other collection of homes, except it is built entirely on stilts and connected by a series of above water walkways. It is home to 40,000 people in the middle of Brunei's capital, Bandar Seri Begawan. Catch a speedy water taxi to whisk you to and fro.

THE MALDIVES
### 787. Dine at the bottom of the sea
**When:** All year
**Latitude:** 3.6164°N
**Longitude:** 72.7164°E

Ithaa, in the Maldives, is the world's first all-glass undersea restaurant. Enjoy top-rate food and amazing 180-degree underwater panoramic views filled with shoals of fish, sharks, and beautiful coral, 16 ft (5 m) below the surface of the sea.

THE MALDIVES
### 788. Sample luxury island living in a stilted home
**When:** December to April; May to November is best for diving/snorkeling
**Latitude:** 4.1755°N
**Longitude:** 73.5093°E (capital Malé)

Live like a superstar by staying in a cottage on stilts in an Indian Ocean paradise, complete with outdoor deck, plunge pools, and hammocks. Made up of 1,192 islands, the idyllic Maldives boast clear, warm water and white sandy beaches.

CHESOWANJA, KENYA
## 789. Learn to start a fire by rubbing sticks
**When:** All year
**Latitude:** 0.6321°N
**Longitude:** 36.0567°E

Our forebears learned to make fire possibly as long as 1.5 million years ago in Kenya. But how many of us could start a fire just using two sticks? Channel your inner paleontologist and teach yourself the ultimate in self-sufficiency.

LAKE BARINGO, KENYA
## 790. Be part of a bird-watching bonanza
**When:** October to April
**Latitude:** 0.6321°N
**Longitude:** 36.0567°E

Lush Lake Baringo hosts hippos and crocodiles, but it is the world's bird-watchers who flock to its shores, drawn by the incredible array of feathered friends who frequent this bountiful body of water. See how many of the 450 species of bird you spot in this ornithologist's paradise.

▼ LAKE TURKANA, KENYA
## 791. Take a dip with the locals at Lake Turkana
**When:** All year
**Latitude:** 3.5833°N
**Longitude:** 36.1167°E

The unusual "martian" landscape of Lake Turkana is as eerie as it is fascinating. It's home to some of the oldest human remains on Earth and some of the rarer Kenyan tribes. Swim in the azure waters for the perfect refreshment in this sweltering environment.

Flamingos at Lake Turkana, Kenya

BATU CAVES, MALAYSIA
### 792. Worship at the holiest of caves
**When:** All year
**Latitude:** 3.2365°N **Longitude:** 101.6816°E

Absolutely breathtaking for a number of reasons. Initially, it is the sheer scale and luminescence of the 140 ft (43 m) high, bright-gold Lord Murugan Statue that amazes. But as you travel through the Batu Caves site, the marvels just keep coming: after the flashy entrance, and the 272 steps to enter the caves themselves, you'll find Hindu statues, paintings, ornate shrines, stalagmites and stalactites. The place is packed with natural life, too: macaque monkeys, large spiders, and fruit bats.

As the most popular Hindu shrine outside India, it's always busy, but is particularly vibrant during festivals, when there are often parades and ceremonies.

PENANG, MALAYSIA
### 793. Enjoy the street art in George Town
**When:** All year
**Latitude:** 5.4167°N
**Longitude:** 100.3167°E

The latest craze in George Town? Posing for a photograph in front of quirky street art. You can spend hours scouring the city streets, hunting down wacky wrought-iron caricatures and interactive vignettes that are hidden in every nook and cranny of the city.

SABAH, BORNEO, MALAYSIA
### 794. Hang out with the distant relations
**When:** All year
**Latitude:** 5.5281°N
**Longitude:** 118.3045°E

One of mankind's closest cousins, the auburn-haired, potbellied orangutan makes for fascinating viewing. Observe these docile, entertaining, humanlike creatures in the wild—they are found only in Borneo and Sumatra, with by far the biggest concentration to be spied around the remote Kinabatangan River.

A path less traveled on the Jungle Railway in Malaysia

▲ MALAYSIA
## 795. Take the path less traveled on the Jungle Railway

**When:** March to October

**Latitude:** 2.5800°N **Longitude:** 102.6132°E

Snaking through the central part of Malaysia, the Jungle Railway line doesn't actually pass through any jungle at all. From its origin in Gemas, it traverses across farmland, forest, and kampong (small villages) on its 310 mi (500 km) route to Tumpat on the northeast coast.

Built by Tamil laborers in the early twentieth century, the Jungle Railway was originally used only for freight trains transporting tin and rubber across the country. But in 1938 it was opened to the public and has been operating as a passenger service ever since.

Carriages are basic, the trains are old and slow, delays are common, and tickets can be difficult to buy—but these are quirks that add to the line's character and authenticity as a truly local adventure. The line doesn't stop at major tourist destinations, but instead offers an excellent insight into everyday, rural life in Malaysia's lush countryside.

TAMAN NEGARA, MALAYSIA
## 796. Dive deep into ancient rain forest

**When:** All year

**Latitude:** 4.3920°N

**Longitude:** 102.4046°E

Reckoned to be the oldest rain forest on Earth, the Taman Negara National Park covers a huge swathe of Malaysia with impenetrable jungle. Inside lies priceless riches of flora and fauna: elephants, tigers, tapir, leopards, rhino, orchids, ferns, *Rafflesia arnoldii* (the world's largest flower), and many different insects. Take an overnight trek to get a proper idea of the scale of the place; expert guides point out the highlights along the way.

MALACCA, MALAYSIA
## 797. Visit the hybrid culture of Peranakan
**When:** All year
**Latitude:** 2.2061°N **Longitude:** 102.2471°E

No other country in Southeast Asia is as ethnically diverse as Malaysia. With three communities forming the backbone of society—Malay, Chinese, and Indian— the country is also home to one of the world's most unique communities: the Peranakan. The product of Chinese who settled in the peninsula and intermarried with Malays, Peranakan men are known as Baba, while the women are known as Nyonya. They assimilated and absorbed Malay influences while retaining Chinese beliefs and customs. Nowhere in the country does Peranakan culture come more alive than in Malacca, a UNESCO World Heritage site where quaint houses line the city's graceful historical core. Drop in to experience Baba-Nyonya culture at its most authentic.

▼ KENYA
## 798. Dance at tribal weddings in Kenya's northern wilderness
**When:** All year
**Latitude:** 2.0048°N **Longitude:** 37.4985°E

Weddings in northern Kenya are an almost weekly occurrence. Home to some of the country's most colorful tribes, an invite to one of these events is not to be turned down. Gorgeously decorated Rendille women wear colorful bracelets and necklaces, and the strong and handsome Samburu warriors don beaded headdresses adorned with feathers. Join hundreds of guests from surrounding villages who come to attend an evening dance. It often begins with drumming and singing traditional songs, and later turns into a hypnotic frenzy of chanting and jumping that's almost infectious.

Samburu warriors dancing in Kenya's northern wilderness

BAKO NATIONAL PARK, BORNEO
## 799. Monkey around in the rain forest
**When:** All year
**Latitude:** 1.7167°N **Longitude:** 110.4667°E

Bako National Park in Borneo is home to three types of monkey, including the rare and endangered proboscis, which is unique to the country. More than a hundred of them live here, making this place your best chance of seeing one in the wild. They are easy to identify, thanks to their huge—and frankly, rather ridiculous-looking—pendulous noses. To be in with the greatest chance of spotting them, head to the beach at low tide in the evening, as they come down from their homes in the headland above to forage in the mango tree swamps. Macaque monkeys are easier to spot— they are more common and pretty fearless, especially when it comes to trying to steal food. Silvered leaf monkeys also call Bako home.

The park comes to life at dusk, so for the most fulfilling experience, be sure to stay overnight in one of the bungalows.

LAGOS, NIGERIA
## 800. Dance at the New Afrika Shrine club
**When:** All year
**Latitude:** 6.6229°N
**Longitude:** 3.3591°W

As the home of Afrobeat legend Fela Kuti, the Shrine became the most famous nightclub in Africa. It closed after his death in 1997, but has since been reopened by his son, Femi, and established as a center for performing arts and funky music. Join in with the annual Felabration.

SARAWAK, BORNEO, MALAYSIA
## 801. Track down the world's biggest known flower
**When:** No set flowering season (although blooms more common during November to February)
**Latitude:** 1.6905°N **Longitude:** 109.8459°E

The *Rafflesia arnoldii* takes its name from Sir Thomas Stamford Raffles (governor of British Java 1811–15) and naturalist Joseph Arnold who, thanks to a Malay guide, "discovered" it in Sumatra in 1818. They must have pushed through the rain forest to find it, as that's where the "corpse flower" lurks, hosting on a vine, no stem, roots, or leaves to be seen, up to 40 in (1 m) in diameter. Its odorous fleshlike petals attract flies—and the humans who seek to track it down. Gaze upon it with your own eyes in rafflesia hot spots such as Gunung Gading National Park.

LAIKIPIA COUNTY, KENYA
## 802. Take a safari beyond the range of vehicles
**When:** January and February, and July to October
**Latitude:** 0.3771°N **Longitude:** 36.7884°E

Taking a camel safari allows you far greater freedom than traveling by jeep, and a much closer appreciation of your surroundings. The camels carry your camping equipment while you walk alongside, taking in the surroundings: high plains with streams and rivers that flow throughout most of the year. The area is home to around half of Kenya's black rhinos, several packs of wild dogs, and a growing herd of Grévy's zebras, giraffes, elephants, hippos, gazelles, ostriches, eagles, and chameleons. Keep your eyes peeled and truly enjoy experiencing the bush.

The perfect place for a cocktail: Raffles Hotel in Singapore

▲ SINGAPORE
### 803. Treat yourself to a cocktail at Raffles Hotel
**When:** All year
**Latitude:** 1.2949°N
**Longitude:** 103.8545°E

Raffles Hotel in Singapore was surely the epitome of glamour in its day. Everyone who was anyone came here, from Ernest Hemingway to Noel Coward, Liz Taylor to Ava Gardner. Enjoy a Singapore Sling in the Long Bar and see which celebrities drink there today.

PENANG, MALAYSIA
### 804. Eat street food in Penang
**When:** All year
**Latitude:** 5.4000°N
**Longitude:** 100.2333°E

Foodies will delight at the mouthwatering array of street food on offer in Penang, Southeast Asia's street food capital. The kaleidoscopic mix of cuisines reflects the country's multicultural heritage: Indian, Chinese, Malay, and Nyonya, a unique blend of Malay and Chinese cooking styles and ingredients. Try them all.

ECUADOR
### 805. Coax an orchid to flower
**When:** All year
**Latitude:** 0.0260°N
**Longitude:** 78.6324°W (El Pahuma Orchid Reserve)

Choose your plant well before cajoling an orchid into flower. Some flowers stick around for six months, while others last for only a few hours. There are 25,000 species of orchids, and at least 4,000 of them are found in Ecuador.

SINGAPORE
## 806. Glance into the future at the Gardens by the Bay
**When:** All year
**Latitude:** 1.3520°N **Longitude:** 103.8198°E

An architectural masterpiece and a feast for the imagination, Gardens by the Bay in Singapore lets you stare into the future of green cities. Spanning 250 ac (100 ha) of reclaimed land near Singapore's marina, visitors can drink in astonishing views of the city skyline from its Bay East Garden and marvel at the sheer range of tropical horticulture and garden artistry in the glorious Flower Dome and Cloud Forest. It's impossible not to feel vaguely sci-fi, and totally inspired about what mankind can achieve when it puts its mind to positive action.

OTAVALO, ECUADOR
## 807. Sell something made with your own hands
**When:** All year
**Latitude:** 0.2343°N **Longitude:** 78.2611°W

Otavalo in Ecuador is a riot of color: hats, sweaters, bags, shirts, scarves, blankets—anything that can be made out of wool, is. The local Otavalo people weave the wool themselves and make the products that are sold here. Take inspiration from them and make something that you can sell yourself; it's a powerful feeling to have a stranger part with money for something you've made. Find your nearest craft market now.

ECUADOR
## 808. Film a hummingbird
**When:** All year
**Latitude:** 0.5525°N
**Longitude:** 78.6115°W

Because hummingbirds hover in one place as they feed, they are ideal for capturing on camera—and exquisite to watch, too. Ecuador has 163 species of hummingbird, so find a feeder, set up a camera, and shoot.

Lions in Tanzania's Ngorongoro
Crater (see page 402)

# CHAPTER 6
# SOUTHERN HEMISPHERE

from 0° south to 15° south

# 809. Learn the art of capoeira

**When:** All year
**Latitude:** 14.2791°S **Longitude:** 38.9946°W

Capoeira, the martial art that combines a dazzling mixture of dance, acrobatics, music, and fighting, is quintessentially Brazilian. It arrived in Brazil with slaves brought over from Angola, and through oppression, developed into a violent form of combat—often with weapons—and was originally outlawed by the Brazilian state.

Now, though, it is popular all over the country, but nowhere more so than in Bahia. The moves of capoeira combine physical strength with flexibility and a delicate touch, all to a rhythmic beat provided by the *berimbau*—capoeira's captivating instrument that provides sound through the resonating of a single string.

There are numerous schools and *mestres*, or masters, throughout Brazil, but for a true immersion in capoeira's art and culture, head to Itacaré in Bahia—it will be the beginning of an addiction.

MINDO VALLEY, ECUADOR
## 810. Succumb to the addiction of bird-watching

**When:** All year
**Latitude:** 0.0487°S **Longitude:** 78.7752°W

There are many people who would say that bird-watching isn't for them. But put them in the cloud forests of Ecuador and even they will be pulling on their guide's sleeve, silently indicating a bird and asking for its name.

There are more than 1,600 species of bird in Ecuador, and while the whole country offers spectacular bird-watching opportunities, it is in the cloud forest of the Chocó region where you are treated to the highest concentration of species.

As soon as you start bird-watching in this area, it's easy to see why it can quickly become an obsession.

There's such an array of spectacular colors, but also amazing bills and tails to spy. With such amazing sights, bird-watchers inevitably get drawn into photographing these fast-moving subjects with telephoto lenses.

It's a beautiful hobby that takes you to wonderful parts of the world and gives a fascinating insight into nature's diversity. But be warned: it's not going to be cheap.

Crimson-rumped toucanet in Ecuador

GALÁPAGOS ISLANDS
## 811. Follow in the footsteps of Charles Darwin
**When:** All year
**Latitude:** 0.7500°S **Longitude:** 90.3167°W

On September 15, 1835, almost four years after setting off from the UK, Charles Darwin arrived in a little-known archipelago stranded some 559 mi (900 km) off the Ecuadorian coast and populated by a host of strange creatures. He spent five weeks researching on these inaccessible islands, which inspired his theory of evolution and—with the publication of *On the Origin of Species* in 1858—changed the world.

To follow in his footsteps on the Galápagos archipelago is to explore one of the most extraordinary wildlife destinations on Earth. The animals and birds—many of which are endemic—display little fear of humans, which enables you to have close-up encounters with them.

Depending on your itinerary and the time of year, you will encounter at close quarters giant tortoises ("galápagos" in Spanish), frigate birds, blue-footed boobies, and marine iguanas. There are also sea lions, penguins, Pacific green turtles, spotted eagle rays, and vast schools of hammerhead sharks, among many other species.

One of the most impressive sights, however, are the Darwin's finches, which are found on many of the islands. At first glance, they may seem underwhelming, but a closer look reveals that the birds on each island have beaks specially adapted to the local environment, an observation that played an important role in Darwin's theory of evolution by natural selection.

Marine iguana on Charles
Darwin's Galápagos Islands

▼ LAKE NAIVASHA, KENYA
## 812. See where the world is coming apart
**When:** All year
**Latitude:** 0.7754°S
**Longitude:** 36.3715°E

The Great Rift Valley in East Africa is where the Arabic and the African continental plates are gradually pulling away from each other—at a rate of less than an inch a year. Observe the steep sides of the Great Rift Valley dropping to its flat-bottomed valley, for they are a view as old as man.

NAIROBI TO MOMBASA, KENYA
## 813. Take a train journey while giraffe look on
**When:** All year
**Latitude:** 4.0500°S
**Longitude:** 39.6667°E

The Nairobi to Mombasa night train is a must-do Kenyan experience. Bed down in a first-class, two-berth cabin, then wake up to the breakfast bell and sip coffee in the dining car as you pass grazing giraffe in the national parks outside Mombasa.

NAIROBI, KENYA
## 814. Watch an egg hatch
**When:** All year
**Latitude:** 1.2920°S
**Longitude:** 36.8219°E

Witnessing new life come into the world should be on any to-do list and seeing a tiny bird tap its way out of its shell is perhaps the cutest way to experience it. The ostrich lays the largest egg of any bird, so visit Kenya's huge ostrich farms, which are the ideal place to meet these creatures.

Lake Naivasha in Kenya sits within the Great Rift Valley

▶ NAIROBI, KENYA
### 815. Pet a baby elephant in an orphanage
**When:** All year
**Latitude:** 1.2920°S
**Longitude:** 36.8219°E

A kind of orphanage for elephants and rhino, the David Sheldrick Wildlife Trust is dedicated to the protection of Africa's wilderness. Visit this heartwarming place to enjoy a close encounter you'll never forget with these majestic beasts.

A baby elephant at Nairobi's David Sheldrick Wildlife Trust in Nairobi, Kenya

SALVADOR, BRAZIL
### 816. Attend a candomblé ceremony
**When:** All year
**Latitude:** 12.9731°S
**Longitude:** 38.5099°W

Sitting in a room packed with devotees as priestesses become possessed by ancestor spirits is an experience that you won't forget in a hurry. During a candomblé ceremony, you'll watch practitioners enter a trancelike state to the sound of drumming music.

BELÉM, AMAZON, BRAZIL
### 817. Eat local Amazonian cuisine
**When:** All year
**Latitude:** 1.4558°S
**Longitude:** 48.5039°W

Foodies are up for a treat in the Brazilian Amazon: fish forms the basis of the region's cuisine, with exotic species such as pirarucu (weighing in at more than 440 lb; 200 kg!) featuring on the menu. Don't miss the *tacacá*, a shrimp soup that contains *jambu*, an anesthetizing plant that numbs the tongue.

MANAUS, BRAZIL
### 818. Fear the giant Amazonian ants
**When:** All year
**Latitude:** 3.0528°S
**Longitude:** 60.0151°W

They scuttle along the forest floor at incredible speeds, foraging for foods and prey that they inject with their strong venom, causing severe pain that can last up to forty-eight hours. Their appeal may not be immediate, but observing the comings and going of these giant creatures (some surpass 1–1.5 in; 3–4 cm in length) provides for a thrilling educational experience.

## 819. Swing over the edge of the world

**When:** All year
**Latitude:** 1.3964°S
**Longitude:** 78.4247°W

Casa del Arbol is a tree house in the mountains of Ecuador with an unusual installation—a swing hanging over the precipice. Below, a death-defying drop, while across, an amazing view of Tungurahua volcano rewards any adventurer brave enough to have a swing. Do you dare to have a go?

▶ ECUADOR
## 820. All aboard for a train ride

**When:** All year
**Latitude:** 1.8312°S **Longitude:** 78.1834°W (Ecuador)

There's something romantic about riding a train that is difficult to top. It's the sense of freedom and the chance to marvel at mankind's ingenuity for laying track in some of the most treacherous landscapes.

This is perhaps best exemplified by El Nariz del Diablo in Ecuador—which translates as "the Devil's Nose." After tracking a sequence of switchbacks cut through an avenue of volcanoes, the ride enters a truly hair-raising, death-defying stretch from Alausí to Sibambe. The steep Andean rock ascends to 6,562 ft (2,600 m), and you can appreciate the sheer drops by sitting on the roof with your legs dangling over the side—a small metal bar is the only thing between you and a plummet. Look out for the stone carving of old Beelzebub himself, chiseled out of the rock, and take layers of clothing, as temperatures change radically.

El Nariz del Diablo train ride in Ecuador

CUENCO, ECUADOR
## 821. Soak up a Colonial atmosphere

**When:** All year
**Latitude:** 2.8992°S
**Longitude:** 79.0153°W

Walk around the cobblestone streets in Cuenco, Ecuador, among the charming colonial steeples, rotundas, and arched windows of this UNESCO World Heritage site. It's like stepping back in time to experience a slower, more gentle, pace of life.

ECUADOR
## 822. Take one step to the other side of the world

**When:** All year
**Latitude:** 0.0000°
**Longitude:** 78.4544°W

In Ecuador (which is named after the equator) they have a park, Mitad del Mundo, with a monument to the dividing line of the world's hemispheres and a representation of the line painted on the ground. Modern measuring techniques show that their measurements are out by 787 ft (240 m). Cross the real thing at the nearby Intiñan Solar Museum.

MIRADOURO DA LUA, ANGOLA
## 823. Feel alien at a lunar landscape

**When:** All year
**Latitude:** 8.8803°S
**Longitude:** 13.1964°E

Drop someone in Miradouro da Lua and ask them to guess where they are, and they'd probably guess Arizona—or maybe even outer space (it translates as "viewpoint of the moon"). Watch the oddly eroded geological formation of Miradouro da Lua, close to Luanda, host psychedelic sunsets over the red rocks.

NAIROBI, KENYA
## 824. Get adventurous with your diet
**When:** All year
**Latitude:** 1.3291°S **Longitude:** 36.8013°E

It's always fun to eat like a local when you're traveling, but sometimes you need more than just an appetite: in some areas of the world you'll need a strong stomach and a serious sense of adventure.

The opportunity to try unusual foods around the globe is endless: whether you're eating deep-fried tarantulas in Cambodia, preserved eggs in China, or venomous ant larvae in Mexico. You can try putrid shark in Iceland, jellied moose nose in Canada, or Israeli chocolate-covered locusts.

In Kenya, all manner of unusual meats are served at the famous Carnivore Restaurant in Nairobi. It's all you can eat—waiters bring skewers of grilled meat from crocodile, to ox testicles and ostrich meatballs, until you lower the flag on your table—so come armed with an open mind and an empty stomach.

BAÑOS, ECUADOR
## 825. Freewheel on a downhill bike ride
**When:** All year
**Latitude:** 1.3928°S **Longitude:** 78.4269°W

The town of Baños in Ecuador has many attractions. It is set in a valley between lush forested hills, and as its name suggests, it is known for its waters—locals have been bathing in the hot springs here for years. The hills around are full of waterfalls, and the best way to see these is on an (almost) all-downhill bike ride. There is a 40 mi (64 km) road from Baños to Puyo, which drops 3,000 ft (914 m) in elevation and takes in twelve waterfalls, including the Devil's Cauldron. Here, water tumbles ferociously between two walls of a canyon, and if you don't mind getting a little splashed, you can get behind the water and into a cave to enjoy a magnificent view out from behind the thunderous veil. When you're ready to head back to Baños, don't worry about the uphill cycle; hail a local bus and stow your bike on the roof.

▶ VOLCANOES NATIONAL PARK RWANDA, RWANDA
## 826. Join a mountain gorilla family in the wild
**When:** All year
**Latitude:** 1.5098°S
**Longitude:** 29.4875°E

Unleash an inner Attenborough with a guided mountain gorilla trek through Volcanoes National Park Rwanda—a vast, cloudy range of peaks that was immortalized in the Sigourney Weaver movie *Gorillas in the Mist*. There are nearly 400 of the animals in the Rwandan section of the park (which also covers Uganda and the Democratic Republic of Congo), and you're almost guaranteed to "encounter" a silverback (along with babies, if you're lucky). It's an experience that really does leave you with unforgettable memories.

NGORONGORO CRATER, TANZANIA
## 827. Go wild in Africa's own Garden of Eden
**When:** June to September is best;
April and May is wet, but has fewer visitors
**Latitude:** 3.1740°S **Longitude:** 35.5639°E

Occupied by humans for more than 3 million years, the vast, fertile Ngorongoro Crater is home to a huge array of wildlife, including lions, zebras, wildebeest, and rhinoceros. It is a UNESCO World Heritage site, and you will find few better places on the planet in which to go on a safari.

A mountain gorilla in the wild, in
Volcanoes National Park, Rwanda

JEMBRANA, BALI, INDONESIA
### 828. Enjoy buffalo racing—and a fashion show
**When:** July to November
**Latitude:** 8.3000°S **Longitude:** 114.6667°E

If there is one thing perhaps more amusing than the annual buffalo races in Jembrana, it has to be the fashion shows—which are, of course, performed by the buffalo. Dressed with ornaments from hoof to horn, they take part in best-dressed competitions: if you haven't seen a buffalo looking unimpressed in a headdress, you haven't lived.

The serious action, however, is in the races themselves, known as Makepung. Jockeys ride traditional wooden plows pulled by a pair of buffalo to compete for the coveted Governor's Cup. Races usually take place on Sundays—early in the morning before the heat affects the beasts' performances. Soak up the festive atmosphere, with the skill and machismo of the riders, and the colorful dressings and painted horns of the beast, enhanced with music and entertainment.

INDONESIA
### 829. Taste a cup of *kopi luwak*
**When:** All year
**Latitude:** 0.5897°S
**Longitude:** 101.3431°E

The most expensive cup of coffee in the world—at $100 a cup—is nicknamed "cat poop coffee" for good reason. Produced from beans eaten and digested by the cat-like civet, the creature's feces is collected, cleaned, and roasted. When you have a brew, be mindful that free-range civets produce the best-quality coffee.

YOGYAKARTA, JAVA, INDONESIA
### 830. Make your own batik
**When:** All year
**Latitude:** 7.8014°S
**Longitude:** 110.3644°E

"Batik" is a term that originated in the Indonesian island of Java to describe the traditional method of using dye and wax to color and pattern cloth. Learn the art in Yogyakarta, famous for producing the cloth and selling vast swathes of it at Beringharjo market.

INDONESIA
### 831. Munch on the world's smelliest fruit
**When:** All year
**Latitude:** 0.7892°S
**Longitude:** 113.9213°E

To say durians are an acquired taste is an understatement: the odor of this green spiky fruit has been compared to sewage or rotting flesh. Enthusiasts say that if you can get over the stink, they have a pleasant, custardy taste. Give one a go as a Southeast Asian rite of passage.

INDONESIA
### 832. Spot kingfishers in a jungle pond
**When:** All year
**Latitude:** 0.7892°S
**Longitude:** 113.9213°E

One of nature's most beautiful birds, the brightly colored kingfisher can be spotted all over the globe. Indonesia, though, has a scope and variety of these marvels—including the delicate forest kingfisher. Flock to see them feed by jungle ponds.

▼ STONE TOWN, ZANZIBAR, TANZANIA

## 833. Get lost in the winding streets of Stone Town

**When:** All year

**Latitude:** 6.1622°S **Longitude:** 39.1921°E

Stone Town in Zanzibar is a wonderful maze of narrow, winding streets, dating back to the late 1800s, when streets didn't need to be wide enough for cars. Constructing buildings close together like this meant the heat of the sun's rays couldn't get in, yet the cooling breeze from the sea could blow through.

Getting lost in the town's streets is one of the best ways to soak up the unique atmosphere of Stone Town. Stroll from one impressive wooden studded door to the next, stumble upon shops full of spices and artifacts on Gizenga Street, and enjoy the small vignettes of life that pass you by—children on their way to school, donkeys, and motorbikes.

ZANZIBAR, TANZANIA

## 834. Skewer an octopus for dinner

**When:** All year (at low tide)

**Latitude:** 6.3159°S

**Longitude:** 39.5446°E

They are clever beasts, octopi. They crawl into holes on a rock and pull stones over the opening to hide themselves. At low tide, when the rocks are on show, pit your wits against theirs to catch one for your dinner.

The winding streets of Stone Town in Zanzibar, Tanzania

▼ MOUNT MERU, TANZANIA
## 835. Watch the sun rise over Mount Kilimanjaro
**When:** June to February
**Latitude:** 3.2392°S **Longitude:** 36.7627°E

The three-day climb may seem rather lax at first, but the third day is when the fun (or pain) really begins. You won't have much sleep, as you set off in the early hours—we're talking 1 a.m.—to reach Mount Meru's summit for sunrise, along the narrow ridge of the crater rim. Tanzania's second-highest mountain, Mount Meru, is often treated as an acclimatization trip before trekking up Mount Kilimanjaro, although the spectacular views from the top make it equally as rewarding. From here you can watch the sun rise and bathe Mount Kilimanjaro in gentle hues of red, orange, and pink.

GALÁPAGOS ISLANDS
## 836. Witness the dance of the blue-footed booby
**When:** Spring
**Latitude:** 0.6518°S
**Longitude:** 90.4056°W

Sometimes nature is awe-inspiring; sometimes it's just plain funny. Watch the blue-footed booby—a clumsy-looking bird that does indeed have blue feet—putting on a highly entertaining display of boogieing in an attempt to attract a mate.

The sun rising over Mount Kilimanjaro in Tanzania

ARUSHA, TANZANIA
## 837. Watch a chameleon change color
**When:** All year
**Latitude:** 3.2088°S
**Longitude:** 36.7157°E

Tanzania conjures up images of wild game and safaris yet it also harbors the world's second-richest chameleon diversity after Madagascar. Get up close with these extraordinary creatures for a thrilling experience as you observe how they mimic the movement of branches, move their eyes 360 degrees, and extend their sticky tongues to gobble up their prey.

DEMOCRATIC REPUBLIC OF CONGO
## 838. Spot rare birds on a Congolese "safari"
**When:** June to August are likely to be the coolest, driest months
**Latitude:** 1.0554°S
**Longitude:** 23.3645°E (Ikela township)

Recently rediscovered in the lowland forests of the Democratic Republic of Congo, the spectacularly plumed Congo peafowl has been described as the most elusive bird on Earth. Embark on a camping and hiking expedition in the area for the chance to spot one of these rare beauties that were presumed extinct for eighty years.

▶ FERNANDO DE NORONHA, BRAZIL

## 839. Find heaven on Earth off the coast of Brazil

**When:** All year

**Latitude:** 6.5181°S **Longitude:** 49.8624°W

Fernando de Noronha is a surreally beautiful archipelago found just more than 200 mi (322 km) off the Brazilian coast. It has been designated a UNESCO World Heritage site because of its delicate and vitally important ecosystem.

Many people visit to view the rich marine life—snorkelers and divers can regularly frolic with sea turtles, spotted and spinner dolphins, short-finned whales, and many other species—and the beaches are totally unspoiled. On land, there is world-class hiking.

Most choose to stay in the tiny capital, Vila dos Remedios, which has pleasant rococo houses, or at Porto de Santo Antonio, the only harbor.

The downside? Due to its fragility, visitor numbers are seriously restricted. Those who do go must pay an environmental tax. It's also expensive, thanks to its remoteness and desirability. Oh, and there are mosquitoes. Lots and lots of mosquitoes. Get over that, and this might just be paradise found!

MANAUS, BRAZIL

## 840. Cruise on the mighty Amazon River

**When:** All year

**Latitude:** 3.0528°S **Longitude:** 60.0151°W

One of the world's mightiest river systems, the Amazon covers half of Brazil; a fifth of the planet's freshwater is found here. With approximately 49,710 mi (80,000 km) of the river being navigable, it's best to explore the Amazon by boat.

Head out on a private riverboat cruise with a small vessel that will penetrate the river system's waterways and channels. The vessels are equipped with cozy rustic cabins and private facilities, as well as communal areas where you can socialize with a dozen or so other travelers. These journeys offer spectacular jungle scenery and excellent wildlife-spotting opportunities.

The Amazon is one of the most biodiverse regions on Earth, with about 10 percent of known species living in the rain forest. You'll be able to hop onto smaller rowing boats and head deep into the depths of the rain forest along small canals, observing fauna and flora from up close.

Heaven on Earth at Fernando de Noronha, off the coast of Brazil

## 841. Enjoy the peace on a traffic-free island

**When:** All year
**Latitude:** 8.3500°S **Longitude:** 116.0600°E

Like three little thought bubbles rising from the island of Lombok in Indonesia, the Gili Islands are sand-fringed dots of peace. No traffic is allowed on the islands, so no fumes or engine noise will disturb your stay.

INDONESIA

## 842. See the world's largest lizard

**When:** All year
**Latitude:** 8.5433°S
**Longitude:** 119.4894°E

Komodo dragons were discovered only a hundred years ago, and today, there's just one place in the world you can see them: the Komodo National Park in Indonesia. Catch a glimpse of these giant lizards at this UNESCO World Heritage site collection of islands that are home to nearly 6,000 of them.

MARQUESAS ISLANDS, FRENCH POLYNESIA

## 843. Sail to the edge of the world

**When:** April to September
**Latitude:** 8.8605°S **Longitude:** 140.1421°W (Nuku Hiva Island)

If remote, almost comically beautiful, jagged volcanic landscapes are what you are after, then a trip by boat into the world's most far-flung island chain will fulfill every fantasy. More than 850 mi (1,368 km) northeast of Tahiti, and some 3,000 mi (4,828 km) from the nearest continental landmass of Mexico, the picture-postcard Marquesas Islands are a tropical paradise writ large.

They are located in French Polynesia, in the southern Pacific Ocean, and traveling to the Marquesas is not a trip to be taken lightly—it's seen as something of a rite of passage for blue-water sailors (those who partake in long-distance ocean sailing). The most popular way to get there is from Mexico and the Galápagos Islands, while some freighter companies offer an informal cruising option for passengers.

PAPUA NEW GUINEA
## 844. See dance displays by birds of paradise
**When:** All year
**Latitude:** 5.8667°S
**Longitude:** 144.2167°E

Deep in the rain forest of Papua New Guinea, you can spy birds of paradise putting on the most spectacular dance displays in the hope of attracting a mate—because strutting your stuff and busting moves are an essential part of any modern courtship.

▼ PAPUA NEW GUINEA
## 845. Get haunted by the ghostly Asaro Mudmen
**When:** All year
**Latitude:** 9.4438°S
**Longitude:** 147.1802°E

Few countries have preserved their traditions and sense of "otherness" as well as Papua New Guinea, and the bizarre, vaguely terrifying dancing of the Asaro Mudmen is certainly one such example. Watch, if you dare, the ghostly figures, white from mud, wearing huge clay heads set with grotesque grins, and carrying sharpened hunting spears, as they taunt and haunt spectators with their unforgettable rhythms.

The ghostly Asaro Mudmen of Papua New Guinea

MADIDI NATIONAL PARK, BOLIVIA
## 846. Swim with pink river dolphins
**When:** May to October
**Latitude:** 14.4422°S (at Rurrenabaque, gateway to Madidi National Park)
**Longitude:** 67.5283°W

Perhaps the most surprising inhabitants of the meandering, tea-colored waterways of Madidi National Park are *bufeos*, pink freshwater dolphins. You can observe them from the boat on the Amazon, but the best way to get a sense of these bright and playful creatures is to swim alongside them.

LAKE MALAWI, MALAWI
## 847. Hang out at a unique music festival
**When:** September to October
**Latitude:** 11.8817°S
**Longitude:** 34.1694°E

The Lake of Stars music festival is set on a beach on Lake Malawi with perfect soft white sand and turquoise-blue water. By night the beach is the dance floor until dawn, when the sun rises magnificently over the lake. Enjoy a great lineup of Afro and European music.

LAKE MALAWI, MALAWI
## 848. Waterski on the immense Lake Malawi
**When:** All year
**Latitude:** 11.6701°S
**Longitude:** 34.6856°E

The gigantic Lake Malawi is a haven for water sports, and perhaps the greatest place anywhere to waterski, with warm, freshwater in idyllic surroundings. If high speeds aren't for you, there are kayaking, snorkeling, or boat trip options to choose from instead.

SAMOA
## 849. See a sunrise before the rest of the world
**When:** All year
**Latitude:** 13.4993°S
**Longitude:** 172.7872°W

It's hard to beat a sunrise in Samoa, one of the postcard-perfect treasure islands of the South Pacific: with crystal clear waters, miles of sand, and waterfall-packed, rain forest interiors, this is many people's idea of heaven. Another reason to go is that you can be at the first place on Earth to see the dawn of a new day—and a new year, too.

▶ ZAMBIA
## 850. Watch a fruit bat migration
**When:** October to December
**Latitude:** 12.5833°S
**Longitude:** 30.2000°E

Every year, 10 million tiny fruit bats descend on this small patch of forest in the Kasanka National Park. Marvel at the spectacle of them leaving and returning to their roost as their numbers turn the sky black.

Fruit bats in Kasanka National Park, Zambia

SERENGETI, TANZANIA
## 851. Watch the great wildebeest migration
**When:** July to October
**Latitude:** 6.3690°S
**Longitude:** 34.8888°E

The great Serengeti migration is one of Africa's blockbuster moments: on these open plains, more than a million wildebeest and 200,000 zebra race for life across 150,000 sq mi (388,498 sq km) of territory to the Maasai Mara. The best place to view them is probably from the Seronera River Valley, where spotters can stay in a variety of camps—from highly luxurious to very basic—and tours rush out to witness the literal stampede at its peak, as well as picking out lions and other big game.

PELOURINHO DISTRICT, SALVADOR, BRAZIL
## 852. Drink in the color of the Pelourinho
**When:** All year (or carnival for the true party lovers)
**Latitude:** 12.9731°S
**Longitude:** 38.5099°W

The colonial buildings of Salvador's Pelourinho district are painted green, yellow, red, pink, blue, orange … and that's just one side of the street. There are streets and streets of buildings, all nestled in among numerous elegant churches with tall bell towers and baroque archways. The area is a riot of color and culture—many of the buildings house music and dance schools or capoeira centers. Join the party every Tuesday night, when the cobbled streets fill with live music and dancing.

▶ MACHU PICCHU, PERU
## 853. Walk an ancient Incan trail to Machu Picchu
**When:** All year
**Latitude:** 13.1631°S **Longitude:** 72.5450°W

There can't be many people who visit Peru without visiting Machu Picchu, and there's a good reason for that. Perched high up in the Andes, the setting alone of these Incan ruins is epic, and the insight they give to an ancient civilization, fascinating.

The site can be visited as a day trip from Cuzco, but anyone who can walk through the mountains to get here instead is well-advised to do so. The trek takes four days, and many parts of the route follow an original Inca trail—at times even with original Incan features such as a paved path underfoot, steps cut into the rock, and even a couple of tunnels.

The highlight of the trek has to be the moment you first see Machu Picchu. This is from a point known as the Sun Gate, and many walkers get up early to be here for when the sun rises and reveals Machu Picchu on the clearing below, ready to be discovered by them.

PERU
## 854. Know your alpacas, guanacos, llamas, vicuñas
**When:** All year
**Latitude:** 14.7502°S
**Longitude:** 74.3822°W

It is always useful (or at least impressive) to be an expert in something nonlocal to you. Visit Pampas Galeras National Reserve in Peru to learn how to spot the long ears of the llama, the squashed face of the alpaca, and know that the deerlike vicuña (Peru's national animal) and the larger guanacos live wild.

Ancient Incan trails lead to the magnificent Machu Picchu

AUSTRALIA
## 855. Spot crocs in the Northern Territory
**When:** All year
**Latitude:** 13.0922°S
**Longitude:** 132.3937°E

Kakadu National Park in Australia's Northern Territory is absolutely gigantic—about half the size of Switzerland—and is home to the aptly named Alligator Rivers Region, which contains a number of endangered species. Spot the star attraction: estuarine and saltwater crocodiles, often growing up to 6 ft (2 m) long.

CHRISTMAS ISLAND, AUSTRALIA
## 856. Wonder at wildlife: crab or climbing cat?
**When:** All year (but October to November is the annual migration)
**Latitude:** 10.4475°S
**Longitude:** 105.6904°E

In the weird and wonderful wildlife stakes, it's hard to look past the coconut crabs of Australia's Christmas Island. Watch these crustaceans—the size of small cats and with a leg span of more than 30 in (76 cm)—as they climb trees and crack coconuts.

SACSAYHUAMAN, PERU
## 857. Worship the Incan sun god
**When:** June 24
**Latitude:** 13.5050°S
**Longitude:** 71.9801°W

A citadel first established around AD 900, Sacsayhuaman (meaning "satisfied falcon") is a hugely significant Incan site, and the megalithic venue is still home to the remarkable Festival of the Sun on the summer solstice. Witness a theatrical display for the sun god Inti, involving llamas, marches, music, and folk dance.

TIPÓN, NEAR CUZCO, PERU
## 858. Eat like the locals— try guinea pig in Peru
**When:** All year
**Latitude:** 13.5708°S
**Longitude:** 71.7831°W

One man's meat is another's household pet, they say. In Peru, guinea pig—or *cuy*—is a staple part of the diet. Easily raised, roaming free in people's kitchens, they are then generally barbecued on a spit and some say it tastes a little like chicken. Try it in Tipón, near Cuzco, which is famous for its *cuyerias*.

HUACACHINA, PERU
## 859. Race around the desert in a dune buggy
**When:** All year
**Latitude:** 14.0875°S
**Longitude:** 75.7633°W

Get into Mad Max's frame of mind—minus the heavy weaponry, please—and thunder about the sand dunes of Huacachina for a few hours in a buggy. Once parked, you can enjoy exquisite sunsets, sand-boarding, and the mystical oasis party town of Huacachina itself.

PERU
## 860. See a macaw in the wild
**When:** All year
**Latitude:** 12.5825°S
**Longitude:** 69.1933°W

With their striking colorful plumage, macaws are some of the Amazon's most brilliant birds. Head to the best place to see them: at the world's largest clay lick in the Peruvian Amazonian. The birds supplement their diet with clay, flocking here early in the morning, forming an incredible spectacle of colors.

The mysterious Nazca Lines in Peru

PERU
## 861. Appreciate the mystery of the Nazca Lines
**When:** All year
**Latitude:** 14.7390°S **Longitude:** 75.1300°W

At ground level in the Nazca Desert, you will find nothing remarkable about the ground. But fly over it in a small aircraft, and suddenly, the desert is full of images: a giant spider, a condor, and hundreds of perfectly straight lines and geometric shapes.

The lines were put there by the Nazca people between 200 BC and AD 600. They were made by brushing away the top layer of stones to reveal the contrasting light-colored sand beneath. In the dry and windless desert, this sand has formed a crust and resisted erosion over the years, leaving the lines still visible today.

Why they were put there, and how the Nazca people drew such huge forms before modern flight was invented, has proved a mystery. One study suggests that the straight lines have some astrological bearing; others think they were connected to pilgrimage routes. Extraterrestrial visits to Earth have also been suggested.

Why the images were created is likely to remain one of life's mysteries. To find your own solution, you'll just have to fly over the lines yourself and see if you can add anything to the theories of the scientists.

Uluru (or Ayers Rock) in Australia's
Northern Territory (see page 435)

# CHAPTER 7
# SOUTHERN HEMISPHERE

from 15° south to 30° south

An Andean condor soaring high above the Colca Canyon in Peru

▲ COLCA CANYON, PERU
### 862. Watch Andean condors soar high above

**When:** All year (best at dawn)
**Latitude:** 15.6093°S
**Longitude:** 72.0896°W

Catch the majestic sight of a condor as it sweeps up and past the edge of the canyon. Its 10 ft (3 m) wingspan is immense—it's the largest flying bird of the western hemisphere—and it's easy to see why this regal bird holds such an esteemed place in Andean folklore.

RAROTONGA, COOK ISLANDS
### 863. Sway along to South Pacific music

**When:** April or May
**Latitude:** 21.2292°S
**Longitude:** 159.7763°W

There are plenty of reasons to visit the lovely Cook Islands and its sapphire blue lagoon, but while there, make sure you see some authentic South Pacific dancing. The Island Dance Festival in Rarotonga showcases this traditional art form at its very best.

CHIRUNDU, ZAMBIA
### 864. Safari by canoe along the Zambezi

**When:** All year
**Latitude:** 16.0271°S
**Longitude:** 28.8509°E

Most safaris tend not to involve ever getting off the back of a jeep or bus, so to really connect with the natural world, why not paddle along one of the great African rivers? Canoe safaris on the Zambezi take you through an unspoiled wilderness, where you can witness wildlife along the way. Four-day trips from Chirundu to Mana Pools National Park are particularly recommended.

LAKE TITICACA, BOLIVIA
## 865. Step on a floating island
**When:** All year
**Latitude:** 15.9254°S
**Longitude:** 69.3354°W

The floating islands in Lake Titicaca are home to the Uros people. They make the islands out of reeds, which grow in the lake and need constant replacing and refreshing. Feel the islands bob with every footstep you take, which also makes them sink a little.

POTOSÍ, BOLIVIA
## 866. Crawl through a silver mine
**When:** All year
**Latitude:** 19.5722°S
**Longitude:** 65.7550°W

It is not pleasant to go inside the mine at Potosí, but if you do, you'll find it humbling. The air is thick and hot, the tunnels are narrow, and the experience is extremely claustrophobic. It's no surprise miners take down offerings of cigarettes and alcohol to appease the god of this underworld, El Tío.

LA PAZ TO EL ALTO, BOLIVIA
## 867. Get "high" in a Bolivian cable car
**When:** All year
**Latitude:** 16.4897°S
**Longitude:** 68.1193°W

Bolivia's residents are the only commuters in the world to travel mainly by cable car. At a vertigo-inducing 13,000 ft (3,962 m) above sea level, the Mi Teleférico service links La Paz to El Alto. Ride it to experience spectacular panoramas as well as a thrilling ten-minute trip.

▶ AREQUIPA, PERU
## 868. Stumble upon serenity at Santa Catalina
**When:** All year
**Latitude:** 16.4090°S **Longitude:** 71.5375°W

Step through the gates of the Santa Catalina Monastery in Arequipa and you step into a town within a town. It is a peaceful haven of arches, fountains, courtyards, and gardens. Narrow streets of rich ochers and bright blues lead from chapels to living quarters and laundries to patios in this quiet monastery, which covers a whole city block. Wander through it and soak up the calmness of the nuns and the simplicity of their lives.

Serenity at Santa Catalina Monastery in Arequipa, Peru

▶ BAHIA, BRAZIL
## 869. Drink straight from a coconut

**When:** All year
**Latitude:** 16.4871°S
**Longitude:** 39.0789°W (Arraial d'Ajuda)

To truly enjoy drinking a coconut straight from the shell, you need to be on a beach, and it needs to be hot. That way, you get to experience just how remarkably refreshing this nectar of nature is. It's also an excellent hangover cure.

A refreshing drink straight from a coconut in Bahia, Brazil

LA PAZ TO COROICO, BOLIVIA
## 870. Ride the "world's most dangerous road"

**When:** All year
**Latitude:** 16.4897°S
**Longitude:** 68.1193°W (La Paz)

Known as the "road of death," this 43 mi (69 km) dirt track that descends 11,500 ft (3,505 m) between La Paz and Coroico attracts thrillseekers galore. Sliced into the mountainside, it features sheer drops, landslides, poor visibility, and casualties aplenty. Go on a guided mountain-biking trip to experience it in the least reckless way.

LA PAZ, BOLIVIA
## 871. Shop at the Witches' Market in La Paz

**When:** All year
**Latitude:** 16.5000°S
**Longitude:** 68.1500°W

Drop into the tiny stores of the Witches' Market, which are stocked with weird and wonderful potions, powders, amulets, incense, statuettes, and ingredients such as dried llama fetuses and coca leaves. They are overseen by indigenous Aymara women, known as "witches," who claim to cure ailments and provide good-luck talismans.

BOLIVIA
## 872. Explore the Jesuit Missions of Chiquitos

**When:** All year
**Latitude:** 17.3500°S
**Longitude:** 63.5833°W (at San Javier)

Scattered across the remote, dusty Chiquitos region are six of the finest colonial-era churches in Latin America. Immaculately restored and jointly declared a UNESCO World Heritage site, they are the remnants of a series of pioneering sixteenth- and seventeenth-century Jesuit settlements that transformed this part of eastern Bolivia. Be sure to visit the oldest-surviving Jesuit Mission town of San Javier.

873. Swim in a paradise lagoon

**When:** All year

**Latitude:** 16.5064°S **Longitude:** 151.7494°W

Bora Bora is a French Polynesian island surrounded by a lagoon and barrier reef. Swim, snorkel, scuba dive, or find any other way to get wet among the incredible fish, sharks, stingrays, and other sea life.

TIWANAKU, BOLIVIA
## 874. Discover some of Earth's oldest ruins
**When:** All year
**Latitude:** 16.5542°S
**Longitude:** 68.6782°W

Home to some of the planet's earliest civilizations, South America holds a treasure trove of ancient ruins that mark critical early stages of human development.

Believed to have been inhabited from around 1500 BC, the extraordinary city of Tiwanaku predates the legendary Incan remains at Peru's Machu Picchu. The capital of a powerful early empire that ruled over huge swathes of the southern Andes around Lake Titicaca, it was rediscovered by the Spanish in the sixteenth century.

The plundered remains of this ancient city have been partially excavated under the watchful eye of UNESCO. Explore these mouthwatering archaeological treasures, including ruined palaces, carved monoliths, and temples, as well as mysterious pyramids.

Some of Earth's oldest ruins in Tiwanaku, Bolivia

The edge of Victoria Falls, Zambia

▲ DEVIL'S POOL, VICTORIA FALLS, ZAMBIA
### 875. Lie on the edge of Victoria Falls
**When:** Mid-August to mid-January
**Latitude:** 17.9244°S **Longitude:** 25.8559°E

Victoria Falls on the Zambezi River crash down a
350 ft (107 m) drop. Surely nobody would be foolish
enough to venture into the river above the falls, right?
Wrong! On the Zambian side of the river, when water
levels drop low enough, the natural rock wall at the
edge of the waterfall is close enough to the surface to
create a pool that the brave can venture into. Known
as the Devil's Pool, it is not for the fainthearted. To
reach it, you need to walk a rocky route and swim in
the Zambezi before launching yourself into water that
appears to flow straight over the edge of the cliff. The
pull of the water can be felt around you as it heads
onward and over in the ultimate infinity pool while
that natural rock wall makes it safe for people.

TRANCOSO TO ARRAIAL D'AJUDA, BRAZIL
### 876. Walk all day on the beach
**When:** All year (at low tide)
**Latitude:** 16.5906°S **Longitude:** 39.0958°W

In the early days of life in Trancoso, the place was so
remote it was only possible to reach by a daylong walk
along the beach. Today, at low tide, it is still possible
to walk along the beach from the small town to
neighboring Arraial d'Ajuda 9 mi (15 km) away.

Trancoso is famed for its rustic charm and pristine
beaches, so you'll find walking alongside the emerald
sea an absolute pleasure, despite the odd bit of clambering
over rocks and wading.

The best named of Madagascan wildlife is the aye-aye

▲ MADAGASCAR
## 877. See the best named of Madagascan wildlife

**When:** All year (after dusk)
**Latitude:** 18.7669°S
**Longitude:** 46.8691°E

A bit scrawny and batlike with big ears and wide-set round eyes, aye-ayes shouldn't really be cute, but somehow they are. This nocturnal primate is only found in Madagascar, and if you're lucky enough to spot one, you'll find it employs a unique method of foraging for food. It taps on trees, listening to the echo until it finds a chamber, then it chews a small hole in the wood through which it inserts its long, bony middle finger to get grubs out.

MANGOKY RIVER, MADAGASCAR
## 878. Explore the wilderness of Madagascar's Mangoky River

**When:** April to November (dry season)
**Latitude:** 21.5857°S **Longitude:** 43.7220°E

The island nation of Madagascar is unlike anywhere else on Earth. Cut off from the southeastern coast of Africa by the Indian Ocean, this remoteness makes the vast island a hot spot of biodiversity. An estimated 90 percent of the wildlife on Madagascar exists nowhere else on our planet.

When you get here, head for the island's west coast and explore via the waterways—they offer the best routes through this beguiling wildlife wonderland. Rafting down the largely tranquil Mangoky River is a genuine journey into the wild, as this 350 mi (563 km) river flows from the central highlands to the Mozambique Channel, then out into the Indian Ocean. You'll pass baobab forests overlooked by sandstone cliffs, while the occasional scuttling among the tree branches tells you the country's lemurs are keeping an inquisitive eye on you.

MENABE, MADAGASCAR
## 879. Wonder at the world turned upside down
**When:** All year
**Latitude:** 20.2508°S
**Longitude:** 44.4183°E

The eerie Avenue of the Baobabs, best seen at dawn or dusk, is home to a large collection of the eponymous "upside-down" trees. Note how the stunted branches at the top resemble a root system, and you'll see why legend suggests the trees kept running away so were planted the wrong way around.

KUNENE REGION, NAMIBIA
## 880. Meet the Himba people of Namibia
**When:** April to May
**Latitude:** 18.0556°S
**Longitude:** 13.8406°E

In the northwestern Kunene region of Namibia lives one of the world's most photographed tribes: the Himba. Known for their red-brown painted skin, elaborate hairstyles, and seminaked traditional dress, they've been pictured on magazine covers and featured in documentaries all over the world. You can meet the Himba on an organized village visit from the region's capital, Opuwo, to learn more about their traditional way of life.

NAMIBIA
## 881. Climb the world's biggest sand dune
**When:** April to May
**Latitude:** 24.5464°S
**Longitude:** 15.3297°E

The world's tallest sand dune, Dune 7, is 1,256 ft (383 m) high and sits in the world's oldest desert in Namibia. Scale its orange sands, shaped by winds from the Atlantic, at dawn and watch the sun rise over an otherworldly terrain.

PRINCIPALITY OF HUTT RIVER, WESTERN AUSTRALIA
## 882. Found your own micronation
**When:** All year
**Latitude:** 28.0910°S **Longitude:** 114.4489°E

Covering only 29 sq mi (75 sq km)—and attracting 40,000 visitors a year—the Principality of Hutt River was founded in 1970 by farmer Leonard Casley (who now calls himself Prince Leonard I of Hutt), who fell out with the Australian government over wheat quotas. Though no country officially recognizes this micronation, it does feature on Google Maps.

Founding a micronation is a growing trend—there are now probably more than a hundred, and they can be found across the world. They do, though, seem to be inexplicably popular in Australia, where Aeterna Lucina, Empire of Atlantium, the Grand Duchy of Avram, and Independent State of Rainbow Creek have all been founded. Anyone seeking to launch their own micronation could do worse than ask Leonard I of Hutt for advice.

COOBER PEDY, SOUTH AUSTRALIA
## 883. Find your own gemstone in the desert
**When:** All year
**Latitude:** 29.0111°S
**Longitude:** 134.7556°E

To find yourself an opal in Coober Pedy, just turn up and dig—that was how the first opal was found here, by a fourteen-year-old boy in 1915. Some opals are said to lie as little as 8 in (20 cm) below the desert surface, and some have even been found lying on the surface itself.

Freshly caught piranha in the Pantanal, Brazil

▲ PANTANAL, BRAZIL
## 884. Dine on freshly caught piranha

**When:** All year (though the best time to visit is the May to September dry season)
**Latitude:** 19.0089°S (at Corumbá)
**Longitude:** 57.6528°W

Covering an area larger than France, the Pantanal is the world's largest freshwater wetland, rich in wildlife such as spectacled caiman, jaguars, and giant armadillos. One of the most enjoyable activities in this region is fishing for piranha—so drop your line and then barbecue your catch for lunch.

MOREMI GAME RESERVE, OKAVANGO DELTA, BOTSWANA
## 885. Explore the last Eden on Earth

**When:** July to September is best
**Latitude:** 19.1667°S **Longitude:** 23.1667°E

Africa's Okavango Delta often gets called "the last Eden on Earth," because as one of the largest wetland wildernesses in the world, it offers uninterrupted wildlife and sweeping landscapes reminiscent of a time before man trod these shores.

The most unusual thing about the delta is that it is in the heart of the desert—after flowing hundreds of miles, the river spills out into the surrounds, creating a lush and idiosyncratic wilderness in a sea of sand. It lies in the Kalahari Desert and creates a very unusual ecosystem that hosts a varied array of life.

You can find all sorts of creatures here calling this strange place home: from tiny insects to the largest concentration of elephants in Africa, mixed with aquatic and desert-adapted animals.

Visit in July through to September, following the floods, when hundreds of thousands of animals gather together on this huge oasis to escape the baking desert, to see it in all its magnificence.

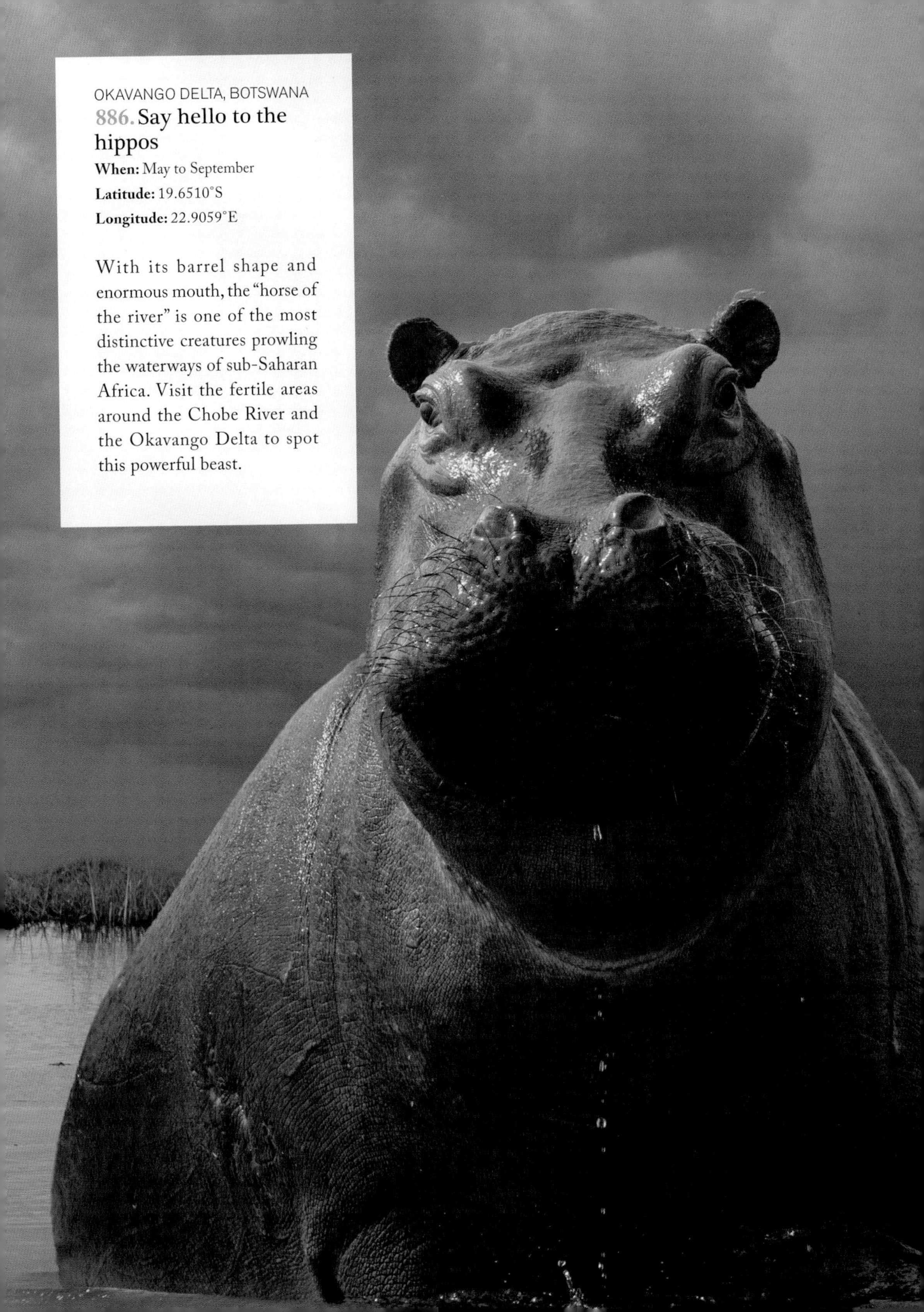

OKAVANGO DELTA, BOTSWANA

## 886. Say hello to the hippos

**When:** May to September

**Latitude:** 19.6510°S

**Longitude:** 22.9059°E

With its barrel shape and enormous mouth, the "horse of the river" is one of the most distinctive creatures prowling the waterways of sub-Saharan Africa. Visit the fertile areas around the Chobe River and the Okavango Delta to spot this powerful beast.

## 887. Visit Namibia's dramatic Skeleton Coast

**When:** All year

**Latitude:** 20.0000°S **Longitude:** 13.3333°E

Namibia's Skeleton Coast is one of the most evocatively named areas of Africa. It has also been called "the Gates of Hell" by Portuguese sailors, and "the Land God made in Anger" by the local bushmen. By all accounts, then, a hostile place.

But for all that, it is a place of delicate beauty. The dunes roll along the coastline in varying degrees of gold to red. There are rivers that cross the desert, bringing with them green oases, waterholes for wildlife, and a focal point for bird-watchers. And skeletons of numerous ships (more than a thousand) that have been wrecked on these shores provide desolate, but intriguing, points of interest. The reason behind the many shipwrecks is partly because of rocks and currents out at sea, but also because of the all-enveloping sea fogs. One of the most famous of the shipwrecks is the *Eduard Bohlen*, a German ship that ran aground in 1909. Originally stranded at sea, the desert sands have gradually encroached on the ocean, and the rusting hull is now 1,500 ft (457 m) from any water, surreally stranded in the sand.

Despite its size and supposed barrenness, this desert is also home to a surprising amount of wildlife. Take a safari into one of the desert's riverbeds for the chance to see the elephants, oryx, giraffes, hyenas, and Namibia's rare desert lions.

SALAR DE UYUNI, BOLIVIA
## 888. Cross the world's biggest salt flat
**When:** All year (best in dry winter season: May to October)
**Latitude:** 20.1431°S (Isla del Pescado) **Longitude:** 67.8075°W

In the deep southwest of Bolivia, you'll find the largest salt flat in the world, the Salar de Uyuni. Spanning some 3,475 sq mi (9,000 sq km), and flanked by towering mountains and smoldering volcanoes, this shimmering expanse was once the deepest extent of an enormous lake that covered the region until 12,000 years ago.

Set off from the bleak town of Uyuni on a multiday jeep trip across the Salar de Uyuni and through the surrounding region to explore some of the area's most popular sights: Isla del Pescado ("Fish Island"), covered with giant cacti; blood-red and emerald-green lakes within the Eduardo Avaroa Andean Fauna National Reserve; Sol de Mañana geyser; and rock formations on the Pampa Siloli.

The best time to visit is in the dry winter season (May to October), though it can be very cold during this period. Few people make the journey in the rainy, summer season, but if you do, you'll witness a magical sight: when huge sections of the salt flat flood, they are transformed into vast mirrors that perfectly reflect the sky and the surrounding mountains.

▶ MAURITIUS
## 889. Gaze at Mauritius' cloak of many colors
**When:** All year
**Latitude:** 20.4251°S
**Longitude:** 57.3917°E

Feast your eyes upon the colored earth of Chamarel, a vision so bizarre, it feels almost like an optical illusion. Rolling dunes of rainbow-colored earth in the Rivière Noire District of Mauritius have been formed by the weathering of volcanic rock, and the minerals within it, creating a mind-bending brown, red, purple, violet, blue, green, and yellow backdrop.

SALAR DE UYUNI, BOLIVIA
## 890. See all six species of flamingo
**When:** All year
**Latitude:** 20.1338°S
**Longitude:** 67.4891°W

Fortunately, three flamingo species—the Chilean, Andean, and James's flamingos—live in South America and you can see them all on the Salar de Uyuni salt flats. Catch two more species—the greater and the lesser—in Africa, while the final one is native to the Caribbean and Mexico.

JUST OUTSIDE POTOSÍ, BOLIVIA
## 891. Spend a night at an old hacienda
**When:** All year
**Latitude:** 19.5500°S
**Longitude:** 65.8500°W

Located in a fertile valley just outside Potosí, and dating back to 1557, Hacienda de Cayara is a living museum. Marvel at the highlights, which include a beautiful colonial-era chapel, a 6,000-book library, and an array of relics, from a 500-year-old suit of armor to Stone Age weapons.

QUEENSLAND, AUSTRALIA
## 892. Spot one of nature's most timid creatures
**When:** May to August
**Latitude:** 21.1078°S
**Longitude:** 148.5422°E (Eungella)

When scientists first examined a platypus, they thought somebody was playing a trick on them, so unlikely did the creature look. Were they right? A visit to Broken River offers the chance to peek at these unlikely looking mammals and see for yourself.

Mauritius' cloak of many colors
in the Rivière Noire District

Whale sharks are the planet's largest fish, Australia

▲ NINGALOO REEF, AUSTRALIA

### 893. Swim with the planet's largest fish

**When:** March to September
**Latitude:** 21.9331°S
**Longitude:** 114.1281°E

Sail out onto Ningaloo Reef in search of whale sharks. These gentle giants (some 39 ft; 12 m long) don't mind people swimming alongside, snorkel in mouth, and mesmerized by the graceful flip of their massive tails. Check out their spots—no two have the same pattern.

QUEENSLAND, AUSTRALIA

### 894. Gather your thoughts in peace

**When:** All year (but May to September is best)
**Latitude:** 16.1700°S
**Longitude:** 145.4185°E

Looking for a spot of peaceful reflection? Take a stroll through the 150 million-year-old Daintree Rainforest in tropical far-north Queensland. Its hundreds of miles of tracks and countless deserted beaches offer plenty of chances to ponder amid the sounds of wildlife.

GREAT BARRIER REEF, AUSTRALIA

### 895. Go diving at the Great Barrier Reef

**When:** All year
**Latitude:** 16.4472°S
**Longitude:** 145.8173°E

The largest coral reef system anywhere, the Great Barrier Reef supports an astronomic array of sea life. Experience it in the most fun way: rent some diving gear and get up close and personal with its kaleidoscope of colorful species.

SOUTH AFRICA
## 896. Run with the wild dogs of Kruger
**When:** All year
**Latitude:** 24.7562°S
**Longitude:** 31.8107°E

The African wild dog is one of the continent's most endangered mammals, but it's still found on the plains of places like Kruger National Park, which are attempting to conserve it. They're wily, scrappy animals: seeing—and hearing—a pack in action is a real thrill.

TO SALTA, ARGENTINA
## 897. Go on a road trip with your child
**When:** All year
**Latitude:** 24.7821°S
**Longitude:** 65.4231°W

There's no better way to bond with a son or daughter than on a road trip and there are few road trips finer than exploring Argentina. Investigate its wild northwest with magical landscapes, tradition, gaucho villages, and some roads that will truly test anyone's nerves.

ATACAMA DESERT, CHILE
## 898. Put your name among the stars
**When:** All year
**Latitude:** 24.6272°S
**Longitude:** 70.4042°W

Boasting some of the world's finest stargazing opportunities, the Atacama Desert is home to numerous astronomy centers, including Paranal Observatory with its famous "Very Large Telescope." Once you've spotted your dream constellation, numerous online organizations offer the chance to (unofficially) name it.

NORTHERN TERRITORY, AUSTRALIA
## 899. Escape the crowds in Australia's Red Centre
**When:** All year (but May to September is cooler)
**Latitude:** 24.2498°S
**Longitude:** 131.5118°E

Less well known than its famous neighbors Uluru (Ayers Rock) and Kata Tjuta (Olgas), the remote and beautiful Kings Canyon area has been home to the local Aboriginal people for 20,000 years. Take on the challenging 3.7 mi (6 km) rim walk that offers unmatched panoramic views.

NORTHERN TERRITORY, AUSTRALIA
## 900. Eat under the stars at Uluru
**When:** All year (though around the new moon is best)
**Latitude:** 25.3450°S
**Longitude:** 131.0361°E

This is dinner in a million-starred restaurant. Soak up the atmosphere with the Sounds of Silence dinner, in a secret location overlooking Uluru at sunset, with champagne and a dinner of bush tucker (think kangaroo and crocodile) as the Milky Way emerges overhead.

NORTH QUEENSLAND, AUSTRALIA
## 901. Walk inside tunnels where lava once flowed
**When:** All year
**Latitude:** 18.2011°S
**Longitude:** 144.5961°E

Lava isn't just something that you can walk on and over; at the Undara Lava Tubes in North Queensland, you can walk in it. The tubes were formed when molten lava cooled on the outside and formed a crust, leaving some wonderful, long tunnels in which you can explore.

RIO DE JANEIRO, BRAZIL
### 902. Wonder at Brazil's architecture
**When:** All year
**Latitude:** 22.9090°S
**Longitude:** 43.1766°W

The outside of the Theatro Municipal in Rio de Janeiro is a treat for the senses, with its fabulously eclectic architecture. Expect to see domed blue cupolas, intricate mosaics, gold adornments, and great columns—an altogether lovely ensemble.

RIO DE JANEIRO, BRAZIL
### 903. Feel the epic scale of Rio's Jesus
**When:** All year
**Latitude:** 22.9524°S
**Longitude:** 43.2114°W

*Christ the Redeemer* at the top of the Corcovado Mountain in Rio de Janeiro is an internationally recognized view. Yet get up close, and the true scale and pure whiteness of the sculpture is revealed—there is even a minichapel in its base.

RIO DE JANEIRO, BRAZIL
### 904. See a big band put on a big concert
**When:** Last time was 2006—keep your eyes peeled for the next big thing
**Latitude:** 22.9698°S
**Longitude:** 43.1869°W

No concert can quite match The Rolling Stones performance on Copacabana Beach in Rio de Janeiro when 2 million people came to watch. Never mind that the front few rows only would have been able to see anything; it's about being part of an epic night. Look out for the next big event here.

NITERÓI, RIO DE JANEIRO, BRAZIL
### 905. Step inside a legendary Niemeyer landmark
**When:** All year
**Latitude:** 22.9078°S
**Longitude:** 43.1259°W

Inspired by the female form, Brazilian architect Oscar Niemeyer is famous for his striking buildings. His signature curved Museum of Contemporary Art, perched like a space rocket overlooking the ocean, takes the breath away. Take a trip to the landmark, and you'll also enjoy spectacular views.

The temple of soccer: Maracanã Stadium in Rio de Janeiro, Brazil

▲ RIO DE JANEIRO, BRAZIL
## 906. Cheer a match at the temple of soccer
**When:** All year
**Latitude:** 22.9122°S
**Longitude:** 43.2302°W

When the Maracanã Stadium comes to life, you'll understand why soccer matches played here are considered to be the most exciting in the world. Experience the electric atmosphere, a feast for all the senses—particularly during big championship games or local derbies.

RIO DE JANEIRO, BRAZIL
## 907. Play volleyball on the beaches of Rio
**When:** All year
**Latitude:** 22.9847°S
**Longitude:** 43.1986°W

They might have played beach volleyball in Hawaii and France before Brazil, but there's no denying that the beaches of Rio de Janeiro are now its spiritual home. There's always a game on the go here and plenty of schools to help hone your technique, so go along and join in the action.

NANUYA LEVU ISLAND, FIJI
## 908. Jump into a lake in your birthday suit
**When:** All Year
**Latitude:** 16.9667°S
**Longitude:** 177.3833°E

To be fair, you don't need to be on a deserted island to go skinny-dipping; just be a little bit away from the public gaze. The freedom of swimming without any clothes on is hard to beat—there's something so pure and life-affirming about it, so why not take the plunge?

PARATY, BRAZIL
## 909. Stand on water and paddle
**When:** May to December (to avoid the rainy season)
**Latitude:** 23.2201°S
**Longitude:** 44.7205°W

It looks like an ancient skill, and it probably is, but stand-up paddle boarding (or S.U.P.) is a relatively new addition to the activities available at many coastal beauty spots. There's less hanging around than in surfing and more calmness than kayaking. Try the sport in the still waters of Paraty—it gives the option of traveling around a coastline while keeping an eye out for underwater sea life at the same time.

BRAZIL
## 910. Monkey about with the pygmy marmoset
**When:** All year
**Latitude:** 22.9068°S
**Longitude:** 43.1728°W

This ridiculously cute little mammal weighs less than 3.5 oz (100 g) and is found in the rain forests of the Amazon basin in Brazil. Holding the world's smallest monkey on your fingertip, given the chance, is a real privilege.

BONITO, BRAZIL
## 911. Take a long, lazy snorkel ride
**When:** All year
**Latitude:** 21.1286°S
**Longitude:** 56.4929°W

Nestled in the southwestern corner of Brazil's Mato Grosso do Sul, Bonito is the fulcrum of ecotourism for the area. Partake in a lazy snorkel ride in the pristine waters of Rio Olha d'Água, the highlight of the area.

BRAZIL
## 912. Overcome arachnophobia
**When:** All year
**Latitude:** 22.9068°S
**Longitude:** 43.1728°W

Anyone who wants to become a properly seasoned traveler needs to get over the fact that there are some seriously big critters out there. Holding one of the largest spiders about, the tarantula, under expert guidance is a direct way to confront this fear. Spider-packed Brazil is the arachnid capital and a good place to put this to the test.

▶ RIO DE JANEIRO, BRAZIL
## 913. Be a guest at the party of parties
**When:** February to March (before Lent)
**Latitude:** 22.9068°S
**Longitude:** 43.1729°W

Carnival defines Rio like nothing, and nowhere, else. A five-day celebration leading into the Christian festival of Lent, the streets are alive with the sound of samba as 2 million people come out to play. The highlight is the Rio Samba Parade, but you can join the party that goes on everywhere.

Carnival is the party of parties, Rio de Janeiro, Brazil

◄ SOUTH AFRICA

## 914. Tick off the Big Five in South Africa

**When:** All year
**Latitude:** 24.8167°S
**Longitude:** 26.2167°E

Climb aboard a jeep in Madikwe Game Reserve and keep those eyes peeled—for lions slumbering or stalking prey; elephants emerging from the bush, trunks swinging; or hippos lounging in water holes. Look out for buffalo in the floodplains and never stop scanning for a leopard, notoriously the hardest to spot.

The leopard and elephant are two of the Big Five in South Africa

---

◄ SOUTH AFRICA

## 915. Gaze through "God's Window"

**When:** All year
**Latitude:** 24.5911°S
**Longitude:** 30.8128°E

They call it "God's Window," and the legendary viewing point over Blyde River Canyon in the Drakensberg Mountains lives up to its moniker. Overlooking a lush, green, mountainous reserve, it's a remarkable piece of geology. When you visit, choose from hiking, swimming, and biking activities—or do them all.

DRAKENSBERG, SOUTH AFRICA

## 916. Trek across remote South Africa

**When:** All year
**Latitude:** 28.9233°S
**Longitude:** 29.1339°E

Walk the North Drakensberg Traverse for an amply rewarding challenge. It's 40 mi (64 km) of strenuous, remote, mountain-edge trekking that offers amazing views across mystical rising spires, stunning wildlife, and the odd bushmen rock painting.

KOSI BAY, SOUTH AFRICA

## 917. Fear the real-life Jaws

**When:** All year
**Latitude:** 25.8463°S
**Longitude:** 28.3023°E

Seeing a shark's fin cutting through the water is a sight to terrify and excite in equal measure, and it's not uncommon in Kosi Bay—a series of four pristine linked lakes. Explore the area in a 4x4.

Blyde River Canyon in the Drakensberg Mountains, South Africa

Flowers in Atacama Desert, Chile

▲ ATACAMA DESERT, CHILE
## 918. Pick flowers in the desert

**When:** September to November
(for flowers)
**Latitude:** 23.8634°S
**Longitude:** 69.1328°W

The driest place on Earth—parts of it have not seen rain in 400 years—the arid Atacama Desert hosts fascinating adobe villages and hypnotic scenery. If and when the rains do come, the desert bursts into unlikely, vibrant life, carpeted with thousands of pink and orange flowers. Don't miss the spectacle.

ARGENTINA
## 919. Board the "Train to the Clouds"

**When:** All year
**Latitude:** 24.7821°S
**Longitude:** 65.4231°W

Most rail trips are simply a matter of getting from A to B. The ride from Salta to San Antonio de los Cobres in Argentina is quite different: it's a high-altitude, high-adrenaline journey on the "Train to the Clouds." Take the journey that's perhaps the nearest thing to flying without leaving terra firma.

QUEENSLAND, AUSTRALIA
## 920. Drive down a really, really long beach

**When:** All year
**Latitude:** 25.2663°S
**Longitude:** 153.1561°E

How do you even start to imagine a beach that is 75 mi (121 km) long? But that is the extent of the sandy coastline of Fraser Island in Australia's Queensland. Rent a 4x4 and drive on the beach; it just keeps going and going.

FREEDOM TRAIL, DURBAN TO CAPE TOWN, SOUTH AFRICA
## 921. Pedal your way across Africa

**When:** All year, but most comfortable in spring (March to May) and fall (September to October)
**Latitude:** 29.6006°S **Longitude:** 30.3794°E (Pietermaritzburg)

It is hard to imagine a cycling route that packs in more natural highs than the Freedom Trail that meanders 1,460 mi (2,350 km) between South Africa's east and west coasts, climbing and falling 23 mi (37 km) along the way. Starting in Pietermaritzburg by the Indian Ocean, the route travels through immense, unspoiled wilderness areas, over six mountain ranges, across national parks and nature reserves before hitting the Atlantic coast, outside Cape Town.

Mountain bikes are the order of the day, and completing the entire course is no mean feat. Riding, and sometimes walking and carrying your bike, for six to eight hours a day, it will take about twenty-seven days, with accommodation available along the way.

The truly committed can attempt the annual Freedom Challenge Race Across South Africa, which is held in midwinter. Riders battle through sometimes freezing conditions without the aid of any GPS navigation or other support. Slightly less serious—or crazy—saddle jockeys can break the course down and tackle it in sections. Or just pop in for a nice day's riding before heading off to enjoy another of South Africa's incredible range of attractions.

Pedaling across Africa at Cape Town, South Africa

RICHTERSVELD NATIONAL PARK, NAMIBIA

## 922. Follow in the footsteps of dragons

**When:** May to September

**Latitude:** 28.0643°S **Longitude:** 17.1905°E

If there is an ounce of spirit in your soul, Namibia's yawning Fish River Canyon was created by the lash of a dragon's tail. If science is your preference, then water erosion and a collapse of the valley floor some 500 million years ago account for what locals describe as being second in size only to Arizona's Grand Canyon. Whichever explanation you prefer, there is no doubting that the 100 mi (161 km) long, 1,800 ft (549 m) deep rift is a sight to behold.

## 923. Go on a flower safari

**When:** Blooming season is from July to September
**Latitude:** 29.6655°S
**Longitude:** 17.8880°E

Dry and dusty Namaqualand becomes a defiant ocean of jewel-like colors when the first rains arrive. Stay in the town of Springbok to behold this riotous bloom-fest, from where regular flower updates are shared during high season (July to September). Wild daisies are the dominant floral force here, with orchids, *vygies*, and succulents dotted in between.

◄ KWAZULU-NATAL, SOUTH AFRICA
## 924. Dive or swim with the sardine run

**When:** May to July
**Latitude:** 28.5305°S
**Longitude:** 30.8958°E

One of the sea's great migrations: every year in early summer, millions of silver sardines travel north from South Africa's Cape Point. Scuba dive or snorkel among the shoal off the rugged shores of KwaZulu-Natal for a once-in-a-lifetime thrill.

Diving with the sardine run in KwaZulu-Natal, South Africa

▲ EASTER ISLAND, CHILE
925. Watch the sunrise
on Easter Island
**When:** All year
**Latitude:** 27.1167°S
**Longitude:** 109.3667°W

In the middle of the Pacific Ocean, 1,398 mi (2,250 km) from its closest inhabited neighbor, Easter Island is one of the remotest places on Earth. Known to locals as Rapa Nui, this tiny island gave birth to a fascinating culture, the most beguiling result of which are the moai—monolithic stone statues. Be sure to catch the unforgettable sight of watching the sunrise behind Ahu Tongariki, a row of fifteen colossal moai on the northeastern edge of the island.

SAN PEDRO DE ATACAMA, CHILE
926. See the sunset in
Chile's Valle de la Luna
**When:** All year
**Latitude:** 22.9087°S
**Longitude:** 68.1997°W

There's no doubt how Chile's Valle de la Luna got its name—the sudden peaks and large craters of this part of the Atacama Desert are distinctly lunar. View them at sunset when they are transformed into rich reds and golds, best seen from the height of a sand dune.

SALTA, ARGENTINA
927. Visit the world's
largest Turrell Skyspace
**When:** All year (closed Mondays; during rainy season (December to March) the Skyspace may be out of service)
**Latitude:** 25.5132°S
**Longitude:** 66.3925°W

Looking at the sky through one of artist James Turrell's Skyspaces can be like seeing it for the very first time. At the Colomé Winery and James Turrell Museum—one of Argentina's oldest wineries and his biggest Skyspace to date—the sky appears truly immense, a forever-changing blue. Drink it in with a glass or two of the bodega's delicious, high-altitude wine.

The sunrise on Easter Island, Chile

Iguazú Falls in Argentina

ARGENTINA TO CHILE
## 928. Cross the Andes on horseback
**When:** Summer
**Latitude:** 27.7882°S **Longitude:** 64.2739°W (Argentine start point)

One of the great South American adventures, the spectacular Andes is best seen in the way that the pioneers and smugglers of yesteryear did: on horseback. Numerous companies offer excursions—running from Chile to Argentina or vice versa over a week to ten days. The pace is steady and reasonably comfortable (although rookies might get a bit saddlesore).

The old pioneer trail over the Puelo Valley is an adventure into the Patagonian wilderness, with pristine lakes, lush forests, and fresh mountain air all clearing the mind. Elsewhere, you'll find swaying Argentine pampas grass on huge open plains, still-smoking volcanoes, dense rain forests, and snow-tipped peaks. It's hard to think of a trip that covers more variable territory.

It's a perfect way to immerse yourself in local culture: you'll get to stay in local pioneer rustic houses, and be treated to a tasty *asado* ("barbecue") after a day's trekking.

▲ IGUAZÚ FALLS, ARGENTINA
## 929. Walk behind a waterfall
**When:** All year
**Latitude:** 25.6867°S
**Longitude:** 54.4447°W

Iguazú Falls in Argentina are utterly awe-inspiring, with more than 250 cascades of water to rival Niagara and Victoria. Follow the walkways that bring you up close and personal to the torrent of foaming water, taking you below, above, and even behind these magnificent waterfalls.

Torres del Paine National Park in Chile
(see page 471)

# CHAPTER 8
# SOUTHERN HEMISPHERE

from 30° south to 90° south

▼ WESTERN AUSTRALIA
## 930. See wildflowers turn the ground yellow
**When:** July to September
**Latitude:** 30.4326°S
**Longitude:** 115.4378°E

Travel through Western Australia in springtime for carpets of wildflowers as far as the eye can see. Roadside verges are turned into a riot of yellows, pinks, and whites during this annual spectacle of nature.

NEW SOUTH WALES, AUSTRALIA
## 931. Sing opera on top of a bus in the outback
**When:** All year
**Latitude:** 31.8841°S
**Longitude:** 141.2177°E

Pay homage to one of cinema's greatest movie scenes when Guy Pearce sings opera in a giant silver stiletto on top of the bus in *The Adventures of Priscilla, Queen of the Desert*. The tune is "Sempre Libera" from *La Traviata*—silver jumpsuit is optional.

HERMANUS, SOUTH AFRICA
## 932. Watch whales by moonlight
**When:** August to November
**Latitude:** 34.4092°S
**Longitude:** 19.2504°E

Witness 60 ton (54,431 kg) southern right whales throw themselves out of the water, sticking their tails up and slapping the water in enjoyably dramatic fashion at Hermanus, South Africa's whale-watching capital. It's a common sight from dry land and especially enigmatic by moonlight.

Wildflowers turn the ground yellow in Badgingarra National Park, Australia

Ostriches along South Africa's Garden Route

MOSSEL BAY TO STORMS RIVER, SOUTH AFRICA
## 933. Drive South Africa's Garden Route

**When:** All year (but particularly May to December)
**Latitude:** 34.4092°S **Longitude:** 19.2504°E (starting in Hermanus)

Stretching 150 mi (241 km) from Mossel Bay in the Western Cape to Storms River in the east, South Africa's Garden Route is a floral paradise complete with the perfect temperate climate; majestic wildlife; and white, sandy shorelines. You can navigate the route in a day, but the beauty of this drive lies in what can be discovered by taking the time to stop.

Working west to east, although not technically part of the Garden Route, Hermanus provides the opportunity for whale watching. Gansbaai is another essential addition, where you can cage dive with great white sharks. Take a detour inland to Oudtshoorn, "the ostrich capital of the world," to the Cango Caves, which offer a challenging introduction to caving.

Knysna boasts the charms of a thriving waterfront, a town brewery, and an elephant sanctuary. Robberg Nature Reserve near Plettenberg Bay has challenging but beautiful hiking trails, while Plettenberg itself is a great place in which to simply relax and savor everything seen en route. As a final stop off, there are a number of safari parks near Port Elizabeth.

NEW SOUTH WALES, AUSTRALIA
934. Stroll in a sculpture park in the outback
**When:** All year
**Latitude:** 31.9559°S
**Longitude:** 141.4651°E

Art is everywhere. And that's certainly the case at Broken Hill in New South Wales. See how the sandstone sculptures in the desert here highlight the skyline and lend a new perspective to the views.

SYDNEY, AUSTRALIA
935. Go inside Australia's most famous exterior
**When:** All year
**Latitude:** 33.8571°S
**Longitude:** 151.2152°E

Sydney Opera House is such a hugely significant architectural venue that everyone who visits Oz needs to see it—but it's sometimes easy to forget that inside, plenty of world-class culture is going on, too. Look out for visiting ballet and opera companies, orchestras, musical theater, gigs, and talks.

COQUIMBO, CHILE
936. Stroke the world's softest fur
**When:** All year
**Latitude:** 31.5458°S
**Longitude:** 71.1022°W

Some animals have to be felt to be believed, and the softness of a chinchilla is one of them. These Andean rodents grow sixty hairs per follicle, giving them their luxurious coat. See them at Reserva Nacional Las Chinchillas in Chile, but don't stroke a wild one.

TIERRA DEL FUEGO, CHILE
937. Sail a tall ship around Cape Horn
**When:** All year
**Latitude:** 55.9817°S
**Longitude:** 67.2695°W

Cape Horn is the stuff of maritime myth: a milestone on clipper trade routes, its winds, currents, and icebergs make the waters hazardous. It's still seen as a major yachting challenge, so do it in a tall ship—with a good captain!—for the most romantic way to follow famous trails.

SAN ALFONSO DEL MAR, ALGARROBO, CHILE
938. Teach someone to swim
**When:** All year
**Latitude:** 33.3496°S **Longitude:** 71.6523°W

While most learn to swim in a slightly decaying local swimming pool with barely tepid water, what better place to spread the joy of the freedom of the water than the biggest swimming pool in the world? San Alfonso del Mar in Algarrobo, Chile, is 3,324 ft (1,013 m) long, or the length of twenty Olympic-size swimming pools laid end to end. Filled with 66 million gallons of sea water, pumped in from the Pacific Ocean (before being filtered and treated), the crystal clear waters make this an enviable location for a first foray into teaching.

**939.** Travel by funicular
in historic Valparaiso

**When:** All year
**Latitude:** 33.0472°S
**Longitude:** 71.6127°W

There is something iconic about
the funiculars in Valparaiso, Chile's
coastal town of steep hills and
colorful houses. They were built
because other forms of transport
couldn't get up the steep hillsides.
Jump on board to discover a great
insight into many parts of the town.

One of Pablo Neruda's unique houses: Casa de Isla Negra in Chile

▲ CASA DE ISLA NEGRA, CHILE
### 940. Visit Pablo Neruda's unique houses
**When:** All year
**Latitude:** 33.4429°S
**Longitude:** 71.6838°W

To the Chilean people, Pablo Neruda is more than just their most famous poet—he's a national hero. Explore his three houses in Chile, which are packed full of slightly wonderful eccentric objects that show Neruda's great passion for life.

CHILE
### 941. Navigate the fjords of southern Chile
**When:** All year
**Latitude:** 52.1667°S
**Longitude:** 74.6667°W

Viewed from above, the southern coast of Chile is a crumbling mass of islands falling away from the mainland. Experience it at sea level and adventure through beautiful fjords and lakes, past vivid green islands and spectacular glaciers.

PATAGONIA, CHILE
### 942. Race to the "end of the world"
**When:** All year
**Latitude:** 31.4092°S
**Longitude:** 70.5437°W

The Patagonian Expedition Race takes teams of four across the astonishing southern Patagonian landscape—trekking, climbing, kayaking, biking, and navigating over hundreds of miles, often without seeing another human. Taking around a week to complete, it's considered "the last wild race." Are you ready to take it on?

SANTIAGO, CHILE
## 943. Build a home for a stranger
**When:** All year
**Latitude:** 33.4566°S
**Longitude:** 70.5978°W

Nearly 10 percent of Chile's population live in poor-quality housing, and the nation is prone to being hit by natural disasters, so the Chilean government's partnership with Habitat for Humanity has become an important way of working with communities and families to provide housing solutions. Take part in a build as voluntary labor—it is certainly rewarding and good for the soul—but it's also great fun, a nice way to bond with other travelers, and to truly get to know some small, welcoming communities.

SANTIAGO, CHILE
## 944. Play chess in Chile
**When:** All year
**Latitude:** 33.4379°S
**Longitude:** 70.6504°W

The Chess Club of Santiago meets on the stage at the eastern side of the Plaza de Armas most afternoons, and if you want to join in, you just have to go up and ask. Be warned—standards are high, and play is fast. If your match is over quicker than you can say "queen to king's rook five," there are plenty of other attractions going on in this always busy square, home to soapbox speakers, performance artists, and shoeshiners.

PUCÓN, CHILE
## 945. Toboggan down a volcano
**When:** June to December
**Latitude:** 39.4208°S
**Longitude:** 71.9391°W

Perfectly conical, snowcapped, and sometimes even sporting a plume of smoke, Volcán Villarrica outside Pucón in Chile is almost a parody of a volcano. After the long and arduous climb up, you'll be rewarded with incredible views—but it's the sledding back down that will be the highlight of your trip.

▶ AUSTRALIA AND WORLDWIDE
## 946. Learn to hula-hoop
**When:** All year
**Latitude:** 33.8674°S
**Longitude:** 151.2069°E

Many will have tried this popular pastime as a kid—the fad started in Australia during the 1950s—but few ever mastered it. Revisit it for a number of reasons: it's fun, it's incredibly good exercise, and Sydney runs some fantastic dance-style classes where you can reconnect with your inner child.

Hula-hooping in Sydney, Australia

PALM BEACH, SYDNEY, AUSTRALIA
## 947. Have a barbie on a beach
**When:** October to March
**Latitude:** 33.5965°S
**Longitude:** 151.3241°E

Indulge in a barbecue on a beach for the epitome of the simple life made delicious. And when it's also a public barbecue, as they generously supply on beaches in Australia, the simple life gets even simpler.

WESTERN AUSTRALIA
## 948. Chill on the beach with kangaroos
**When:** All year (best in summer)
**Latitude:** 33.9944°S
**Longitude:** 122.2325°E

Is there anything more quintessentially Australian than a kangaroo lolling on a white sand beach? For the ultimate Aussie selfie, it has to be Lucky Bay, in Cape Le Grand National Park, on the idyllic south coast of Western Australia. Here, a troop of kangaroos has colonized the pure white sands—and the animals are docile enough to practically pose for photographs.

SYDNEY, AUSTRALIA
## 949. Surf the Bondi Beach
**When:** All year
**Latitude:** 33.8910°S
**Longitude:** 151.2777°E

There are few names in surfing as iconic as Bondi Beach, and this utterly stunning setting has brilliant breakers, bronzed beach bodies, and buzzing bars. Go by ferry from central Sydney for an extra thrill.

CAPE TOWN, SOUTH AFRICA
## 950. Eat lunch on Table Mountain

**When:** All year
**Latitude:** 33.9628°S
**Longitude:** 18.4098°E

Picnicking on top of flat-topped Table Mountain, overlooking Cape Town in South Africa, is a must-do. Either catch the cable car or hike up for a couple of hours to dine on what must surely be the world's biggest lunch table.

SOUTH AFRICA
## 951. Follow ancient elephant tracks mixed with art

**When:** All year (but September for a guided tour)
**Latitude:** 34.0333°S **Longitude:** 23.2000°E

Around 200 years ago, the elephants of the Knysna forests, near South Africa's Garden Route National Park, were free to roam on ancient migration paths. You can walk the route they might once have taken—and hopefully will take again—along the 249 mi (400 km) Eden to Addo Corridor Initiative, taking in land art as you go.

This conservation corridor first took form in 2006. The idea was to create a series of five corridors between major conservation areas to form a route all the way from the indigenous forest of the Garden of Eden on the coast up to Addo Elephant National Park.

The best way to appreciate the route is to join an eighteen-day guided Great Corridor Hike, which takes place each September. There are rich rewards: this is the most biodiverse corridor on the planet, which also traverses seven mountain ranges, cuts through six national parks and nature reserves, and crosses two rivers.

The hike requires physical and mental stamina, but there are ready-made camps and cooked meals at the end of each day. There are also experts on hand to explain the flora and fauna.

While hiking the Eden to Addo Corridor, you can also bear witness to the beginnings of South Africa's first ever land art route designed to create conservational landmarks and talking points along the way. You'll come across stone elephants, *Aartmoeders*, an experience which is particularly poignant and celebrates the corridor of conservation between the Garden Route National Park and the Robberg Nature Reserve, and the right to roam of those Knysna elephants.

An elephant on the Eden to Addo
Corridor Initiative in South Africa

▼ ARGENTINA
## 952. Take in seven scenic lakes in Patagonia

**When:** All year
**Latitude:** 40.1572°S
**Longitude:** 71.3524°W

Driving the Seven Lakes route is the best way to discover the astounding natural beauty of Patagonia. Start in San Martín de Los Andes and drive it in a day—or bicycle it over three or four days to really enjoy everything the 60 mi (97 km) route has to offer.

NEUQUÉN, PATAGONIA, ARGENTINA
## 953. Go dinosaur hunting in a real-life Jurassic Park

**When:** All year
**Latitude:** 38.9459°S
**Longitude:** 68.0731°W

This is a mind-blowing pilgrimage for dinosaur fans. Discoveries have included a virtually complete 100-million-year-old Giganotosaurus skeleton and some well-preserved footprints, as well as the first dinosaur eggs ever to be found. Travel is tricky without your own car, although there are tours from Neuquén. Have a go and see what you might uncover.

WELLINGTON, NEW ZEALAND
## 954. Hang on to your hat in "windy Wellington"

**When:** All year
**Latitude:** 41.2889°S
**Longitude:** 174.7772°E

No, not Chicago, but Wellington in New Zealand is actually the windiest city in the world, as well as being the most southerly capital. The wind here averages 18 mph (29 kph) over the year, at one time reaching a record high of 154 mph (248 kph). Be prepared for a buffeting.

The seven scenic lakes in Patagonia, Argentina

SAN ANTONIO DE ARECO, ARGENTINA
## 955. Ride with the gauchos on a traditional Argentine *estancia*
**When:** All year
**Latitude:** 34.2500°S
**Longitude:** 59.4667°W

From the wilds of Patagonia to the pancake-flat pampas grasslands, the moors and hills of the Central Sierras to the steamy expanses of the north, Argentina's vast *estancias* ("ranches") are patrolled by *gauchos* ("cowboys"), perhaps the country's most romantic, heroic, and mythologized figures. Join these expert horsemen on a ride for a memorable experience, especially so when it ends with a hearty beef or lamb *asado* ("barbecue").

GAIMAN, PATAGONIA, ARGENTINA
## 956. Sample Welsh tea in Patagonia
**When:** All year
**Latitude:** 43.2895°S **Longitude:** 65.4920°W

In 1865 some 153 Welsh men, women, and children set off from the UK and landed in northeastern Patagonia to found a new colony. Despite several decades of hardship, the Welsh community settled and eventually flourished. Today, many people speak Welsh, several annual *eisteddfodau* ("cultural festivals") are held, and the region is littered with well-preserved Welsh chapels. The biggest tourist attraction, however, is the Welsh high teas, served in cute *casas de té* ("teahouses") in Gaiman, the most archetypal Welsh-Patagonian town. Expect a copious selection of homemade cakes and scones, accompanied by pots of tea (or coffee).

BUENOS AIRES, ARGENTINA
## 957. Learn the passionate dance of tango
**When:** All year
**Latitude:** 34.6033°S
**Longitude:** 58.3817°W

Born in the Argentine capital in the late nineteenth century—with African, European, and indigenous influences—the sultry, passionate tango swiftly became an integral part of the national identity. There are nightly tango shows in the city, but taking a class is a must, so get your dancing shoes on.

BUENOS AIRES, ARGENTINA
## 958. Search out the world's best steak
**When:** All year
**Latitude:** 34.6033°S
**Longitude:** 58.3817°W

Buenos Aires was built on the back of the beef industry and is jam-packed with first-class *parrillas* ("steakhouses"); serving flavorsome, succulent, and simply massive steaks. Try the *bife de chorizo* ("sirloin"); the *ojo de bife* ("rib eye"); or the *tira de asado* ("short ribs").

BUENOS AIRES, ARGENTINA
## 959. Design your own tomb
**When:** All year
**Latitude:** 34.6036°S
**Longitude:** 58.3815°W

La Recoleta in Buenos Aires is perhaps the most famous cemetery in the Americas: a virtual city, full to the brim of imaginative gravestones. Why not get inspired and try to design an original headstone for yourself? There's no better way to remind people of your bucket-list brilliance after you've actually kicked one … .

START IN BUENOS AIRES, ARGENTINA

### 960. Take a revolutionary ride across South America

**When:** All year

**Latitude:** 34.6037°S **Longitude:** 58.3816°W (Buenos Aires)

Before playing his part as iconic revolutionary leader, charismatic Che Guevara tackled a monumental nine-month motorcycle odyssey that has become the stuff of legend and was immortalized in the 2004 movie *The Motorcycle Diaries*. Following in his wheel tracks across the Andes remains a rite of passage for many enthusiasts of two-wheeled travel.

You will head out of the Argentinian capital via beach resort Miramar, before the route heads inland through the country's spectacular lake district, throbbing past glacial lakes and forests, all the while towered over by the snow-capped peaks of the Andes. It is a truly exhilarating ride, overlooked by the incredible mountain backdrop of the imperious Andes.

Don't miss the world's largest open-pit copper mine at Chuquicamata in northern Chile, where Guevara's political consciousness began to take hold, before heading into Peru to see the Inca Trail and the cosmopolitan capital of Lima. The route then winds through the Amazon rain forest via Colombia and Venezuela.

Taking in open roads, breathtaking scenery, and unforgettable experiences right across the continent of South America, Guevara's epic ride is just as memorable and packed with adventure today as it was in the early 1950s. Get your motor running.

A revolutionary ride across
South America, from
Argentina to Venezuela

KLEINBAAI, SOUTH AFRICA
## 961. Cage dive with great white sharks
**When:** All year
**Latitude:** 34.6150°S
**Longitude:** 19.3530°E

One for the plucky: even though you're safely housed inside a cage, the image of those movie-famous great white teeth just a few feet away will live long in the memory—while the trip will also separate myth from reality when it comes to these extraordinary predators.

START WITH CANBERRA, AUSTRALIA
## 962. Take a tour of unexpected capital cities
**When:** All year
**Latitude:** 35.3075°S
**Longitude:** 149.1244°E

Anyone who is a fan of pub quizzes will know there are some capital cities that stump competitors every time—those of Australia, Turkey, Switzerland, Canada, Brazil, and Morocco, to name some of the most common stumbling blocks. Can you name them? Find them on a map? Then why not visit them, too? (For the record, they are Canberra—not Sydney; Ankara—not Istanbul; Bern—not Zürich; Ottawa—not Toronto; Brasília—not Rio de Janeiro; and Rabat—not Marrakech.)

◀ CAPE REINGA TO STIRLING POINT, NEW ZEALAND
## 963. Drive the length of New Zealand
**When:** All year
**Latitude:** 34.4287°S **Longitude:** 172.6804°E (northernmost point)

If there's a more bewitchingly beautiful country to traverse behind the wheel of a car, it's yet to be found. State Highway 1—a 1,274 mi (2,050 km) road—runs the entire length of the country from Cape Reinga in the north to Stirling Point in the south.

What's along the way? Cape Reinga itself is wild and rugged (see entry no. 979 on page 474); the drive to Auckland is magical, and the city itself—New Zealand's largest—is one of the finest anywhere. Farther south is culture-rich Hamilton, and the country's largest lake, Taupo. After the stunning estuary of Porirua comes the capital, Wellington, with a fabulous arts scene.

Over the Cook Strait to the South Island, things really open up, with grand, cinematic countryside. Blenheim has boat cruising and fine wines, while dolphins and whale watching are to be found in Kaikoura, before you reach grand Christchurch. The east coast is wonderful as it winds through Timaru, Oamaru, Dunedin, and Gore. Invercargill is the southernmost city, and there, the road ends. From the warmth of the people to the quality of food and wines, New Zealand is a nonstop marvel.

COROMANDEL, NEW ZEALAND
## 964. Dig your own spa pool
**When:** All year
**Latitude:** 36.7612°S
**Longitude:** 175.4981°E

In New Zealand's Coromandel, you can literally dig your own tub. Grab a spade and create a spa pool two hours either side of high tide on the aptly named Hot Water Beach—then relax in the natural spring water that pours in from underground fissures. With temperatures of up to 147°F (64°C), it's a unique beach experience.

Driving the length of New Zealand from Cape Reinga to Stirling Point

Albatross near Otago, New Zealand

BAY OF ISLANDS, NORTH ISLAND, NEW ZEALAND

## 965. Sail around New Zealand's beautiful Bay of Islands

**When:** All year (but November to February is best)
**Latitude:** 35.2807°S **Longitude:** 174.0910°E (Paihia)

It would almost be rude to visit New Zealand and not go sailing somewhere. The bewitching Bay of Islands—crammed with 144 dots of land, dozens of coves, and all enveloped by inviting, clear, azure waters—is the perfect place to start. Helped by a temperate, subtropical climate, the watery delights of the Bay of Islands have made the area one of New Zealand's prime attractions. Whether you charter a yacht, take a relaxed guided cruise, a G-force-inducing jet boat, or the more energetic option of a sea kayak, getting out on the water is the area's raison d'être. Scuba diving, snorkeling, and swimming with dolphins are also popular pastimes.

Gliding about on the water is such a pleasure, and lack of light pollution also make night sailing a treat.

▲ OTAGO, NEW ZEALAND

## 966. Watch albatross near Otago

**When:** All year
**Latitude:** 45.8337°S
**Longitude:** 170.6152°E

The rugged Taiaroa Head—overlooking Otago Harbour—is home to a colony of northern royal albatross, the only such example on inhabited mainland. See these majestic creatures in flight where the colony has been carefully nurtured and raised by the nearby Royal Albatross Centre.

▼ KANGAROO ISLAND, AUSTRALIA
## 967. Become at one with nature on Kangaroo Island

**When:** All year
**Latitude:** 35.7752°S **Longitude:** 137.2142°E

Most people heading Down Under want to see kangaroos, koalas, and wallabies, so why not go the whole hog and visit the none-more-Aussie venue of Kangaroo Island? Situated 70 mi (113 km) off Adelaide, this very special slice of Australia has several nature reserves. Perhaps most popular is the Flinders Chase National Park, on the western strip of the island. Here, kangaroos and wallabies bounce freely alongside brushtail opossums, bandicoots, fur seals, platypus, and wild koalas. There is also significant birdlife here, including colonies of little penguins and the endangered fairy tern and stone curlew.

For close-up encounters—including cuddling a koala or kangaroo, getting wrapped in a snake or cradling an opossum, horseback riding, or popping a parrot on your shoulder—try Paul's Place Wildlife Sanctuary, set on Stokes Bay.

NEW SOUTH WALES, AUSTRALIA
## 968. Learn to play a tune on a banjo

**When:** All year (but January for the big country music festival)
**Latitude:** 31.0911°S
**Longitude:** 150.9304°E

Tamworth in New South Wales is the center of Australia's country music scene and therefore the only place to go to master playing the banjo. Learn to play "Waltzing Matilda" here—it's a skill everybody should aspire to.

The friendly inhabitants of Kangaroo Island, Australia

▶ WAITOMO, NEW ZEALAND
**969.** Visit a real-life fairy-tale grotto
**When:** All year
**Latitude:** 38.2609°S
**Longitude:** 175.1036°E

Waitomo Glowworm Caves look like something from a fairy-tale stage set: view thousands upon thousands of these magical living lights that adorn the cave and cast a beautiful glow across the rock formations as you ride below them on a boat. Perfection.

NEW ZEALAND AND COOK ISLES
**970.** Celebrate New Year's Eve twice in one day
**When:** December 31
**Latitude:** 36.8406°S
**Longitude:** 174.7400°E

New Zealand is one of the first places to celebrate each new year, while the Cook Islands, on the opposite side of the international date line, is one of the last. The two are just a four-hour flight apart, so celebrate first in Auckland and then in Avarua.

A real-life fairy-tale grotto: Waitomo Glowworm Caves, New Zealand

TORRES DEL PAINE NATIONAL PARK, CHILE

## 971. Wander in the wilderness at the end of the world

**When:** October to April (although avoid January and February to avoid the crowds)

**Latitude:** 50.9423°S **Longitude:** 73.4068°W

While national parks in every country offer vast wildernesses and beautiful views, few do so with quite the captivating magic of Chile's Torres del Paine National Park in the very south of the country. The park covers almost 1,000 sq mi (2,590 sq km), and the views over rugged landscapes and turquoise lakes are epic in scale. It's a wilderness, but one that is well set up for trekkers whether you want to hike for a week on a circular route around the whole park, or just for a couple of nights, taking in the most captivating views the park has to offer.

The park is named after the three dramatic towering spires of rock at its center—the tallest of which is 9,350 ft (2,850 m). The north tower offers magnificent climbing for those with the right experience—although with a five-hour trek just to reach its base, you need to be prepared to carry a lot of gear. It has been known for climbers to climb all three of the towers in one expedition—but only four times in history.

Fortunately, you don't have to climb to the top of the Torres to get magnificent views: the view from the road is unforgettable. You'll see the dramatic forms of the Torres rise behind the turquoise waters of Lago Nordenskjöld. It's a view that will repeat itself again and again, with different lakes and different angles as you hike through the park, but it's one you will never tire of. It's a place that suits all manner of visitors—especially those in search of unforgettable views of a dramatic Patagonian landscape.

---

QUEENSTOWN, NEW ZEALAND

## 972. Zoom along on an exciting jet-boat ride

**When:** All year

**Latitude:** 44.9140°S

**Longitude:** 168.6822°E

Famed as the ultimate jet-boat experience, the ride at Shotover Canyon sees the vessel reach breathtaking speeds of up to 85 mph (137 kph) and has been thrilling visitors since 1965. When not screaming with excitement, you will marvel at this unspoiled canyon paradise.

---

LAKE TEKAPO, NEW ZEALAND

## 973. Place yourself in the middle of a postcard

**When:** All year (October to April for hiking; May to September for skiing)

**Latitude:** 43.8837°S

**Longitude:** 170.5327°E

Imagine a picture-perfect glacial lake, with rolling hills backed by snowcapped mountains, turquoise water, and a cute church perched on the edge. That imaginary spot is realized at Lake Tekapo in New Zealand's stunning South Island. For added value, the lake is in the middle of the world's largest International Dark Sky Reserve, offering unrivaled opportunities for stargazing.

---

QUEENSTOWN, NEW ZEALAND

## 974. Bungee jump where the extreme sport began

**When:** All year

**Latitude:** 45.0090°S

**Longitude:** 168.8990°E

Unsurprisingly, it's not that long since people started attaching elastic to their feet and throwing themselves off tall structures for fun. Take the leap at the place it all began: bungee jumping kicked off in New Zealand in the 1980s, and the Kawarau Gorge Suspension Bridge in the South Island became the world's first permanent commercial bungee site.

A seaplane on Lake Taupo, New Zealand

▲ LAKE TAUPO, NORTH ISLAND, NEW ZEALAND

## 975. Take flight in a seaplane

**When:** All year
**Latitude:** 38.7931°S
**Longitude:** 175.9713°E

Is it a boat? Is it a plane? Well, it's a bit of both. A flight on a seaplane is just you, the pilot, and one other passenger stepping on board a single-engine propeller plane as it bobs on the waters of Lake Taupo. Flying this way feels like a proper adventure: below, you'll see a wild frontier of turquoise waters, snowcapped volcanic craters, craggy mountains, and pristine forests. Hop aboard for the exhilaration of taking off and landing on a lake set in a caldera.

TAUMATA, NORTH ISLAND, NEW ZEALAND

## 976. Visit the place with the longest name in the world

**When:** All year
**Latitude:** 40.3460°S
**Longitude:** 176.5402°E

Taumatawhakatangihangakoauauotamateaturipukaka-pikimaungahoronukupokaiwhenuakitanatahu is the full Maori name for the hill in the Hawke's Bay region of New Zealand. Listed in the *Guinness World Records* as the world's longest place name, roughly translated it means: "the place where Tamatea, the man with the big knees, who slid, climbed, and swallowed mountains, known as 'land eater,' played his flute to his loved one." It's worth visiting purely for a photograph next to the impressively long sign.

TONGARIRO ALPINE CROSSING, NORTH ISLAND, NEW ZEALAND
## 977. Trek New Zealand's best one-day hike
**When:** All year (but you'll need crampons in winter)
**Latitude:** 39.1447°S **Longitude:** 175.5814°E

Who wouldn't want to complete a one-day, 12 mi (19 km) trek that takes in two volcanic craters and lakes by the names of Emerald Lakes and Blue Lake? This beautiful trek through the striking volcanic landscape of Tongariro National Park in the North Island is often called the best day-hike in New Zealand.

Any route that takes in an ascent known as the Devil's Staircase comes with its challenges, but the higher you go, the greater the views. You can look down inside Red Crater at the otherworldly volcanic formations and across the countless peaks of the Oturere Valley. From the top, you look down on the Blue and Emerald Lakes, which truly live up to their names, before walking right by them and down into forest that marks the end of your epic hike.

▶ ROBBEN ISLAND, CAPE TOWN, SOUTH AFRICA
## 978. Visit the most well-known prison in history
**When:** All year
**Latitude:** 33.8076°S **Longitude:** 18.3712°E

It's just a small outcrop of rock off the coast of Cape Town, but Robben Island looms large in South African history. This was the key prison during the shameful apartheid era, and three former inmates went on to become prime ministers: Jacob Zuma, Kgalema Motlanthe, and—most famous of all—Nelson Mandela. Take a trip to the island, which is now a UNESCO World Heritage Site with a fascinating museum. Tours are given extra resonance and gravitas due to the fact that they are conducted by former prisoners.

The most well-known prison in history: Robben Island in Cape Town, South Africa

CAPE REINGA, NEW ZEALAND

**979.** Watch two oceans
collide and dance

**When:** All year

**Latitude:** 34.4287°S

**Longitude:** 172.6804°E

Situated at the north end of the
North Island of New Zealand, this
wild spot is where the Tasman Sea
meets the Pacific Ocean. The Maori
call it the "leaping-off place of
spirits," and it's thrilling to view
the unsettled waters caused by the
tidal race from the lighthouse.

The original kiwis on Kapiti Island, New Zealand

▲ KAPITI ISLAND, NEW ZEALAND
## 980. Meet the original kiwis

**When:** All year
**Latitude:** 40.8516°S
**Longitude:** 174.9158°E

Situated off the North Island of New Zealand, Kapiti Island offers the unique opportunity to see kiwis and other endangered, flightless birds in their natural habitat. Stay overnight in luxury tents or cabins to see these feathered creatures in their ideal habitat, which is totally free of predators.

QUEENSTOWN, NEW ZEALAND
## 981. Discover the thrill of canyoning

**When:** October to April
**Latitude:** 45.0311°S
**Longitude:** 168.6625°E

Canyoning is the term given to exploring canyons by any means necessary—climbing, jumping, ziplining, abseiling—for anyone who loves messing about in the water, on rocks, and in steep, unforgiving, ruggedly beautiful gorges. Get adventurous with this exhilarating sport.

KAIKOURA, NEW ZEALAND
## 982. Swim with seals

**When:** All year
**Latitude:** 42.4212°S
**Longitude:** 173.7098°E

Snorkel with New Zealand fur seals in the shallow waters of the Kaikoura Peninsula. They are a friendly, playful, and inquisitive breed that are free and untamed, but seem to genuinely enjoy the human interaction.

▶ TASMANIA, AUSTRALIA
## 983. Pedal through a Tasmanian paradise
**When:** All year
**Latitude:** 42.8819°S
**Longitude:** 147.3238°E

Bicycle around the east coast of this Aussie isle on gentle, meandering roads that command barely believable views, and stop offs for tours of several national parks. You can also take an exotic guided day trip to the Green Islands in this classic bicycle-friendly destination.

Pedaling through a Tasmanian paradise, Australia

SYDNEY, AUSTRALIA
## 984. See the biggest blockbuster ever
**When:** All year
**Latitude:** 33.8674°S
**Longitude:** 151.2069°E

IMAX is an immersive, exciting way to see a movie—especially a mindless, all-action blockbuster, it has to be said. Watch one on the biggest IMAX screen on Earth, at Sydney's Darling Harbour—it's 117x97 ft (35.7x29.7 m).

MOERAKI, SOUTH ISLAND, NEW ZEALAND
## 985. Take a selfie with the mysterious Moeraki boulders
**When:** All year
**Latitude:** 45.3630°S **Longitude:** 170.8488°E

Scattered haphazardly on the beach of New Zealand's South Island are numerous spherical boulders. They look a bit like enormous eggs or massive marbles, but are in fact natural rock formations. Measuring up to 10 ft (3 m) in diameter, with some weighing several tons, these unusual rocks were formed of sea-floor sediment some 60 million years ago. They make a remarkable backdrop for an original selfie, so get out your camera and selfie stick, and start snapping!

WESTLAND TAI POUTINI NATIONAL PARK, SOUTH ISLAND, NEW ZEALAND
## 986. Trek across a glacier
**When:** All year
**Latitude:** 43.4645°S
**Longitude:** 170.0176°E

Ten minutes by helicopter is all it takes for the transition from the lushly forested foothills of New Zealand's Southern Alps to the white, bluish-gray of the Fox Glacier. This vast tongue of solid ice fills a valley that is so steep it pushes the glacier down to meet the temperate rain forest below, making Fox one of the most accessible glaciers on Earth.

Once you touch down on the ice, crampons are attached, wet weather and safety gear is put in place, and then it's time to step out into this craggy white landscape. The misty mountaintop looms above as you lock into a harness and abseil into a crevasse, or wriggle your way into a pristine blue-ice cave for a closer look. All the while waterfalls provide the sound of rushing water (your soundtrack for this ice adventure) as they send crystal clear glacial water cascading down the surrounding gray rock walls.

CHRISTCHURCH, NEW ZEALAND
## 987. Traverse the Alps by train
**When:** All year
**Latitude:** 43.5320°S
**Longitude:** 172.6362°E

Anyone who has seen *The Lord of the Rings* can account for New Zealand's scenic credentials, and the TranzAlpine train is probably the most beautiful rail route on Earth. Jump aboard for the four-and-a-half-hour journey from Christchurch to Greymouth through the misty Alps and glorious glaciers.

▶ CHRISTCHURCH, NEW ZEALAND
## 988. Step out into thin air
**When:** All year (avoid windy days)
**Latitude:** 43.5321°S
**Longitude:** 172.6362°E

Slacklining has brought tightrope walking down to a level that most of us could contemplate—a few feet off the ground. It involves focusing so strongly on your balance that proponents liken it to active meditation—stepping out into a space where feet don't usually tread. Take the challenge, and once you have mastered the basics, step it up a gear and go high-lining above great canyons such as the Gap in Porters Pass near Christchurch.

Stepping out into thin air at the Gap in Porters Pass, New Zealand

MILFORD SOUND, SOUTH ISLAND, NEW ZEALAND

**989.** Gasp at the "eighth wonder of the world"

**When:** All year

**Latitude:** 44.6716°S  **Longitude:** 167.9256°E

A fjord to rival any in Scandinavia, to say Milford Sound has gotten rave reviews would be understating the point. Gaze upon the bays and waterfalls that Rudyard Kipling judged the "eighth wonder of the world." It's a truly beautiful setting.

▶ DUNEDIN, NEW ZEALAND
## 990. Gather up some Manuka honey

**When:** All year
**Latitude:** 45.8787°S
**Longitude:** 170.5027°E

Manuka honey is rated as something of a miracle food—it's rich, healthy, and most importantly, delicious. Head along to places such as Dunedin's Blueskin Bay that run "hive tours," where you can get suited up and collect spread for your toast, direct from the source.

Gathering some Manuka honey at Blueskin Bay in Dunedin, New Zealand

START AT MATAMATA, NORTH ISLAND, NEW ZEALAND
## 991. Take a trip to Middle Earth

**When:** All year
**Latitude:** 37.8575°S **Longitude:** 175.6797°E

The Hobbiton Movie Set at Matamata isn't the only draw for *The Lord of the Rings* fans coming to New Zealand—more than 150 locations throughout the country were used in the movie trilogy. Hobbiton itself lies a two-hour drive south of Auckland in the Waikato region. Take a guided tour of the movie set, and you'll visit the Shire, with its beautifully detailed hobbit homes, including Bilbo Baggins' very own Bag End.

With its dramatic peaks contrasting with lush valleys, New Zealand's scenery is stunning, and it is easy to see why it was chosen as the embodiment of Middle Earth. Head south from Matamata to other major locations that include Wellington (Kaitoke Regional Park became Rivendell), Nelson, Canterbury, Mackenzie Country (for the epic battle of Pelennor Fields), Southern Lakes, and Fiordland (Fangorn Forest).

DUNEDIN, NEW ZEALAND
## 992. Stagger up one of the steepest streets

**When:** All year
**Latitude:** 45.8492°S
**Longitude:** 170.5342°E

The short, straight Baldwin Street in Dunedin is made of concrete—it is so steep, tarmac might melt in summer and pour down it. Partake in the annual Baldwin Street Gutbuster, which sees competitors race to the top. Or saunter up it at your own pace at any time of year.

PATAGONIA, ARGENTINA
## 993. Reflect on a magnificent ancient ice river

**When:** October to March
**Latitude:** 50.4691°S **Longitude:** 73.0311°W

See one of the few remaining advancing glaciers in the world and be awestruck by the power and majesty of its glittering blue ice. A walking circuit takes you to some outstanding viewpoints, while tour companies offer the chance to trek on the ice itself.

ARGENTINA
## 994. Drink whiskey chilled with glacial ice

**When:** November to April
**Latitude:** 50.4691°S
**Longitude:** 73.0311°W

The ice from a glacier isn't like the ice cubes in your freezer. It is crystal clear—and it tastes that way, too. Drop some in a tumbler with a dram of whiskey for the ultimate Scotch on the rocks.

▼ USHUAIA, TIERRA DEL FUEGO, ARGENTINA
## 995. Visit the penguin capital of the world

**When:** November to March
**Latitude:** 54.8000°S **Longitude:** 68.3000°W

Fans of the black-and-white waddling bird need to make their way to Argentina to be in with a chance to see the most species they can in one hit—a cruise from Ushuaia in Tierra del Fuego will land you with a chance to see seven of the world's seventeen types of penguin. November through to March is prime penguin-spotting time—the warm period, when the birds spend more time on shore to breed and raise their young.

The penguin capital of the world: Ushuaia in Argentina

PETERMANN ISLAND, ANTARCTICA
## 996. Swim beneath the ice
**When:** February to March
**Latitude:** 65.1667°S **Longitude:** 64.1667°W

When you need to arrive at your vacation destination with a letter of permission from your doctor, as well as your international diving certificate and diving logbook, you know you are in for something special. And certainly, polar diving is not for the fainthearted—or inexperienced (you will need to be familiar with cold-water diving and have taken part in at least thirty dry-suit dives). But your reward will be a dive unrivaled anywhere in the world, among extraordinary ice formations that create spectacular hues of changing light and every shade of blue.

Incredible marine life, such as giant woodlice-like isopods, thirty-four-armed starfish, and bloodless fish inhabit one of the last truly unspoiled waters of the world. You may be able to dive with leopard seals and penguins, although be warned: you may also witness the former feed upon the latter.

▶ SYDNEY, AUSTRALIA
## 997. Strip for art's sake
**When:** Follow Spencer Tunick to find out his future plans
**Latitude:** 33.8568°S
**Longitude:** 151.2153°E

Doesn't everybody secretly want to strip in public? Okay, perhaps not. But for those who do, to be part of a Spencer Tunick installation is to be part of a wonderful art piece that celebrates the human form and the world it's in. Five thousand people posed at the Sydney Opera House in 2010.

VICTORIA, AUSTRALIA
## 998. Drive the Great Ocean Road
**When:** All year
**Latitude:** 38.6805°S **Longitude:** 143.3914°E

The journey along Australia's dramatic southern coastline really is picture perfect. Known as the more prosaic B100, there are spectacular views that demand attention right along the 150 mi (241 km) of this road trip. The best direction to travel is from east to west; since Australians drive on the left-hand side of the road, it means you'll be traveling on the side closest to the ocean.

From Torquay, surfers can journey to Bells Beach, to catch a wave on this popular surf beach. Stop at Lorne during May to September, and you can watch female southern right whales and their calves. From Apollo Bay, the B100 turns inland and ocean views are replaced by those of the lush temperate rain forest of Great Otway National Park.

One detour worth making is where the Bass Strait collides with the Southern Ocean, an unforgiving place for seafarers, known as the shipwreck coast. And no one can leave the road without viewing the 12 Apostles, colossal limestone structures that rise 130 ft (40 m) above the tempestuous Southern Ocean.

Beyond the 12 Apostles lies the eighteenth-century bluestone town of Port Fairy. From there, the westward finish lies at Allansford, near Warrnambool, where you return to city life.

ACROSS AUSTRALIA
## 999. Let the train take the strain Down Under

**When:** All year
**Latitude:** 34.9214°S **Longitude:** 138.5970°E (Adelaide railway station)

Long-distance rail travel Down Under is a very laid-back affair, and you'll get to savor magnificent views, glorious sunrises and sunsets, and the hypnotic thrum of wheels on track. There are two great railway journeys to undertake in Australia.

The country's original long-distance train, *The Ghan*, plies 1,851 mi (2,979 km) from tropical Darwin, through the heart of the country's mysterious Red Centre, and the pastoral plains and wine country of South Australia, before coming to rest in Adelaide.

The Indian Pacific links Sydney and Perth, traveling from the Pacific Ocean to the Indian Ocean (and back).

It covers more than 2,700 mi (4,345 km), much of it following the vast and eerie Nullarbor Plain, named from the Latin *"null arbor,"* meaning "no trees." You can stop at the gold-mining area of Kalgoorlie, the ghost town of Cook, and Broken Hill, famous for its silver mines. Traveling by rail Down Under is a magical way to observe this ancient and fascinating land at a steady pace.

Sydney Opera House in Australia was the location of the 2010 Spencer Tunick large-scale nude shoot

## 1,000. Set foot on Antarctica
**When:** October to March
**Latitude:** 55.0991°S **Longitude:** 69.2747°W

The Antarctic is Earth's last great proper wilderness. If you really want to get away from it all, this is the place; it can be done as part of a trip to South America.

Why come? To see the unique wildlife, spectacularly untouched scenery, and to soak up the history of explorers who have been here before. Small expedition ships tend to run through the warmer months (October to March, before the ice begins to set again), while the very intrepid can even fly up the region's mountains for some extreme skiing—or push on to the South Pole. Punta Arenas is probably Chile's easiest point to jump into the area: from this southernmost populated center, a boat trip into Antarctica proper takes just a week.

Seeing penguins, whales, dolphins, sea lions, seals, and albatross is almost guaranteed. Cruises from King George Island head out to numerous other islands, and short hikes can be undertaken. Knowledgeable tour guides can educate about the region's biology, glaciology, and oceanography. There's no sky like an Antarctic one, either: a thousand shades of blue and white, tinted azure. Extremely unforgettable.

# INDEX

# CONTRIBUTORS

### TIM BARNETT

A big fan of the sometimes under-appreciated mountains and valleys of Wales, Tim makes his living writing about sports and travel and combines the two by working at major sporting events around the world whenever the opportunity arises. Recent trips have taken him to Australia, Azerbaijan, China, Italy, Norway, and Russia, as well as his native UK. While he has ticked off a fair few of the journeys in this book, he still has a long way to go—literally and metaphorically—before completing the full 1,000. Any trip involving camping, hiking, and fire is likely to get his attention.

### MICHAELA BUSHELL

Michaela has been a writer and editor for the best part of two decades. She has written about superheroes, supply chains, and shopping. Her work has taken her driving across the sandy Saharan desert in Africa, searching for the elusive Loch Ness monster in Scotland, and celebrating the glorious cherry blossom in Japan. As part of her travels, Michaela has ridden camels in Cairo, elephants in Asia, and tuk-tuks in Thailand. She got married in France, climbed a volcano on her honeymoon, and now lives in South London with her husband, son, and daughter.

### KIKI DEERE

Kiki Deere is a travel writer raised bilingually in London and Turin, who writes regularly for a number of print and online travel publications, including Lonely Planet online and UK broadsheets. She has completed numerous guidebook writing assignments for major travel titles, including Rough Guides and Dorling Kindersley. Her work has taken her to far-flung corners of the globe, from the Brazilian Amazon to Batanes, the remotest province of the Philippines. Being half Italian, she is an avid foodie. Kiki tweets about her travels @kikideere.

### SONYA PATEL ELLIS

Sonya is a writer, editor, artist, and founder of the Herbarium Project, a platform for conversations about links between nature, art, books, science, and culture. She shares her passion through events, workshops, writing projects, talks, and exhibitions, including recent collaborations with the Garden Museum and the British Library. Her published work includes *Nature Tales: Encounters with Britain's Wildlife*, features for the *Sunday Times Travel Magazine*, and regular articles for her online publication, *Herbier* magazine.

### LOTTIE GROSS

Lottie is a travel writer, editor, digital journalist, and social media specialist. She's been documenting her travels since 2012, when she spent two months making short films in Kenya, and is currently the web editor on RoughGuides.com, writing, editing, and commissioning content. Lottie has also placed stories in *National Geographic Traveller*, Mashable.com, *SUITCASE* magazine, and UK newspapers the *Guardian* and the *Observer*. She is a desert dweller at heart, having fallen for the bleak landscapes of the Kenyan, Namibian, and Rajasthani deserts on her travels.

### WILL JEFFREYS

Will is a writer, father, and someone who likes looking for the out of the ordinary. Having traveled through Europe and Latin America in his teens and twenties, his limited funds now find him exploring closer to home in person and to the farther reaches of the globe through dusty vinyl. He hopes, one day, to take his children to revisit some of his fondest memories: dancing at an impromptu fiesta in Salvador, jumping off jade waterfalls in Venezuela, and riding a tandem bicycle on a wet day in Cornwall.

## TESS LAMACRAFT

Tess is a freelance editor, writer, and mother of two, who lives in London. She has written for national newspapers and magazines, including *Family Traveller*, *Woman's Own*, *Good Living*, and UK newspaper the *Daily Mirror*. She's been on safari in Africa, climbed Mount Vesuvius in Italy, ridden a camel across the Moroccan desert, and gone diving in Egypt. She still has hundreds of things to do on her own bucket list, but while she contemplates those, one of her favorite pastimes is rambling along London's South Bank on a sunny day.

## SHAFIK MEGHJI

Shafik is a travel writer, journalist, and guidebook author based in South London. He has cowritten more than thirty Rough Guides to Argentina, Australia, Bolivia, Chile, India, Laos, Mexico, and other destinations. Shafik writes regularly for publications around the world, including the *Guardian*, *South China Morning Post*, and the *Huffington Post*. His writing has been published in several anthologies, and he appears regularly on talkRADIO. Shafik is a member of the British Guild of Travel Writers and a fellow of the Royal Geographical Society.

## NICK MOORE

Nick is a sports and music journalist who has worked for *FourFourTwo*, the *Independent*, the *Times*, *Q*, and the International Olympic Committee. He is the author of several books, including *The Rough Guide to Cult Football* and *Daft Names Directory*. Nick also plays the drums for cult Welsh psychedelic rock group Howl Griff. Originally from Lancashire, England, he lives on a houseboat in West Byfleet, England, with his girlfriend, two sons, and two cats.

## HELEN MORGAN

Helen Morgan is a writer and managing editor who lives in Reading in the UK with her husband and two children. During her career as a travel writer, she has traced Ingmar Bergman's Swedish heritage, basked in the medieval cityscape of Sienna's Piazza del Campo, and been floored by the heat and solitude of Death Valley. Also a keen movie fan, on her bucket list of places still to experience is the Tikal National Park in Guatemala, otherwise known as the Massassi Outpost on the fourth moon of Yavin (*Star Wars: Episode IV—A New Hope*). Although her children would prefer to go to Lapland.

## HELEN OCHYRA

Helen is a travel writer, editor, and broadcaster who is based in London but spends about half her time on the road. She loves uncovering hidden corners of discovered destinations, and although sometimes tempted to keep the best ones to herself, she loves sharing these in her articles, guidebooks, and videos. Helen writes for a wide range of newspapers, magazines, and websites and has also written guidebooks to Australia, New Zealand, and Spain. You can follow Helen's travels on Twitter and Instagram @helenochyra.

## CHRISTIAN SADLER

Christian is an editor, writer, and content creator who has commissioned and contributed to numerous travel campaigns that have appeared in print and online in UK newspapers the *Guardian* and the *Observer*. He has been lucky enough to travel all over the world, and his list of must-visit places would include the Basque Country in Spain, Thailand, and Vietnam. Although based in London, he would consider swapping his current home and taking his family to sample life in either Melbourne or New York.

PAUL SIMPSON

Paul is an award-winning journalist who has contributed to a variety of publications, from *Wanderlust* to *Q* and the *Financial Times*. In 1994, he was launch editor of *FourFourTwo*, the world's biggest soccer magazine. He is also the author of the critically acclaimed *The Rough Guide to Elvis*, *The Rough Guide to Westerns*, *Movie Lists: 397 Ways to Pick a DVD*, and coauthor, with Uli Hesse, of *Who Invented the Stepover?* His favorite travel journey is the vaporetto ride from Fondamente Nove to Burano in Italy, followed closely by the train to Takayama in Japan, and the coastal walk from Whitstable to Seasalter in England.

KATH STATHERS

Kath is a writer and editor who lives in London with her partner and two children. Her career as a travel writer has taken her everywhere, from Iceland to the deserts of Dubai, and her work has appeared in national UK newspapers, including the *Times* and the *Guardian*, as well as a number of magazines. She is never happier than when on a new adventure, whether it's going to the top of the Sagrada Família in the center of Barcelona (which she recently ticked off her bucket list) or exploring the wildernesses of South America. Still on her to-do list are to see the northern lights and to learn how to surf.

# IMAGE CREDITS

t = top, b = bottom, l = left, r = right, m = middle

**4 Corners:** Maurizio Rellini/SIME 70; Olimpio Fantuz/SIME 150–1; Jacques Boussaroque/Onlyfrance/Sime 152; Bruno Cossa/SIME 306–7; Richard Taylor 332; Guido Cozzi 342; Roberto Rinaldi/SIME 355; Beniamino Pisati 405; Richard Taylor 460–1

**Alamy:** age fotostock 40–1; Bildarchiv Monheim GmbH 106; Glasshouse Images 116; wanderluster 120; Nino Marcutti 154–5; MELBA PHOTO AGENCY 159; Janos Csernoch 164; Luca Quadrio 171; BLM Photo 175; Zoonar GmbH 312; J. T. Lewis 338–9; Alan Novelli 398; Robert Wyatt 452; Danita Delimont 456; Gábor Kovács 462; David Wall 468; Hideo Kurihara 472; epa european pressphoto agency b.v. 483

**Getty:** Jordan Siemens front cover; Cameron Davidson 12; Joe Klementovich 18; Silvia Otte 19; Peter Mather 28–9; Ron Crabtree 32–3; Sylvain Sonnet 34; Donar 46–7; Cultura RM Exclusive/Philip Lee Harvey 48; Philippe Jacquemart/EyeEm 49; www.tonnaja.com 54–5; Michelle McMahon 60–1; Sjoerd van der Wal 67; Soo Hon Keong 68; Sergio Pitamitz 69; Michael Steele 71; EMMANUEL DUNAND 72; Keith Hursthouse 73t; CARL DE SOUZA 75; Dark Horse 80; Damien Davis, Cricklade 82–3; Ken Gillham/robertharding 87; Matt Cardy 92; Borut Trdina 98–9; Jeff Kravitz 101; GREG BAKER 104; Christian Kober 119; New York Daily News Archive 121, 188; ullstein bild 123; aetb 124; Robert Boesch 127; AGF 131; Cultura RM Exclusive/WALTER ZERLA 135; DuKai photographer 137; Romina Amato/Red Bull 138–9; Papics55 141; Alexander Rieber/EyeEm 142; Paul Williams—Funkystock 143; Bruno De Hogues 144; Nadia Isakova 149; Neil Emmerson/robertharding 178; Ray Laskowitz 179; RADEK MICA 181; Christopher Pillitz 182; DON EMMERT 183; Seth K. Hughes 185; Bettmann 186; Tom Nebbia 187; Education Images 191; Scott Stulberg 192–3; Alessandro Miccoli/EyeEm 195; Murat Taner 198; Pete Turner 199; Bill Hatcher 200; AJ Wilhelm 205; Alan Tobey 208–9; Westend61 210; Istvan Kadar Photography 211; Shaheer Shahid 214; Johnny Greig 216; photography is a play with light 219; Lauren Bentley Photography 222; ROSLAN RAHMAN 223; Bkamprath 228; The Asahi Shimbun 230, 234–5; Tristan Brown 236; Feifei Cui-Paoluzzo 237; flocu 243; Allen J. Schaben 248; Rei Tsugamine 250–1; Kevin Schafer/Minden Pictures 256; Martin Moos 257; TJ Blackwell 266; Anne Dirkse 270; Stanislaw Pytel 272–3; Bob Sacha 275; Edward Slater 277; Leisa Tyler 282–3; Punnawit Suwuttananun 284–5; Courtesy of 286–7; De Agostini/G. De Vecchi 288–9; Ira Block 292; Jim Zuckerman 296; Christophe Boisvieux 298; Amos Chapple 300; Jason Edwards 303; Ross Woodhall 305; Frank Bienewald 308; WIN-Initiative 309; John Warburton-Lee 310; Ephotocorp 311; Felisha Carrasco/EyeEm 315; Adria Photography 321; Mint Images—Frans Lanting 324, 337; G. Brad Lewis 325; Viaggiare 326; Michael S. Lewis 334; Norbert Eisele-Hein 335; Pham Le Huong Son 340; Jeremy Woodhouse 344–5; Dave Wilson, WebArtz Photography 348; Alvaro Faraco 358; NZSteve 359; LucyMaynard144 366–7; Tim Draper 372; ManuMNair 374; Natthawat 378; Marcelo Andre 382–3; Anup Shah 386; Tui De Roy/Minden Pictures 395; Jami Tarris 399; Filmuphigh.com 406–7; Michele Falzone 408–9; Dallas Stribley 410; Fabian von Poser 412–13; Atlantide Phototravel 424; Pete Oxford 426; Lost Horizon Images 429; Paul Souders 430–1; Ary Diesendruck 439; Vincent Grafhorst/Minden Pictures 444–5; Alexander Safonov 446–7; traumlichtfabrik 448; Ignacio Palacios 450–1; Dirk Bleyer 453; Ed Norton 457; Gerhard Zwerger-Schoner 466; Blaine Harrington III 473; Mark Meredith 474; Tui De Roy 475; Andrew Bain 476; Anthony Maw 481; David Doubilet 484–5

**iStock:** Kalypso World Photography 6–7; yulkapopkova back cover, 21; George Clerk 44, 77; DeadDuck 51; bulentumut 52; Joel Carillet 53; meshaphoto 59; Maciej Bledowski 63; Alexander Ishchenko 84; Saro17 back cover, 102–3; Leminuit 107; Razvan 110–11; bluejayphoto 115; kalasek 117; andrearoad 122; USO 148; MaFelipe 162–3; Marje 173; f9photos 246; alvaher 255; Meinzahn 294; arthit somsakul 302; lena_serditova 318–19; suttipon 336; DavorLovincic 356–7; Christian Wheatley 362–3; jakkapan21 422; VV-pics 423; Konstik 433; Diriye 441t; alfnqn 442; PeopleImages.com back cover, 443; Kseniya Ragozina 455; LazingBee 480

**National Geographic Creative:** DAVID EDWARDS 105; RALPH LEE HOPKINS 245; XPACIFICA 253; PATRICK MCFEELEY 316; DAVID LIITTSCHWAGER 328; RAUL TOUZON 333; STEVE WINTER 343; Frans Lanting 364, 388; MARK COSSLETT 380; JOE SCHERSCHEL 469; PAUL ZAHL 470

**Rex Features:** Everett Collection/REX/Shutterstock 76, 244

**Shutterstock:** Enfi 190; LUISMARTIN 194; Roy Firth 226; oneinchpunch 247; givaga 376–7; Pascal zum Felde 387; KalypsoWorldPhotography 401; upslim 438; Dudarev Mikhail back cover, spine

**Also:** www.pauledmundson.com back cover, 8–9, 14–15, 36, 146–7, 170; www.reubenkrabbe.com 11, 97, 136; Chris Burkard 16–17, 23, 26–7, 64–5, 88–9, 100, 184; Photo by Guillaume Dutilh @ photoxplorer.com 22, 375; Asaf Kliger www.icehotel.com 24; www.chrishigginsphoto.com 31; ljcphoto.co.uk 38–9; www.wildernessprints.com 57; www.alpine-photography.com 62; www.dumitrutira.com 73b; Paulo del Valle back cover, 78, 112, 133, 134, 145, 176, 212, 217, 221, 261, 274, 276, 299, 437, 478–9; Instagram @andreanoni_15 86; www.paulkporterphotography.com 90–1; www.gillallcock.com 94; juanjerezphotos.com back cover, 108–9; www.valthorens.com 113; © MaxCoquard www.bestjobers.com 114, 161, 322–3; www.thecambrianadelboden.com 126; www.cloud9adventure.com 128–9; Łukasz Kasperek 140, 384; www.oliviaohlen.com 156–7, 233; www.brendansadventures.com 166–7, 201, 224–5, 268–9, 304, 331, 341, 400, 415, 420, 421, 428; www.davidoliete.com 169, 260, 262–3; Matthew Gee 196–7, 259, 265; @dani.daher back cover, 202–3; www.tentsile.com 204; www.instagram.com/king_roberto back cover, 43, 206–7, 239; Megan Perkins 241; GARY HE/INSIDER IMAGES 254; www.simonjpierce.com 278–9, 354, 434; www.tommiandlyndell.wix.com/ourtravels 281, 293, 361, 365, 396–7; www.parahawking.com back cover, 291; Jumeirah 301; www.alexblairphotography.co.uk 329, 392–3, 417, 449, 464–5; www.instagram.com/marinebalmette 346; Jorge Lara/Mister Menu's Lake Atilan Foodie Tour 347; Rusty Goodall 350; www.instagram.com/dhalsmith 353; Brad Holland 369; https://500px.com/asayeghr 370–1; Lorna Buchanan-Jardine 385; © RAFFLES SINGAPORE WWW.RAFFLES.COM 390; Michael Lorentz, Safarious 391, 441b; www.instagram.com/giovanicordioli 394, 436; Chris Whittier 403; www.laurenjadehill.com 411; @KS Imagery/facebook 418–19; Jeffrey Sweers 425; www.lucastefanutti.com back cover, 440, 459; Lauren Azor 458; www.bengingold.com 477

While every effort has been made to credit photographers, Quintet Publishing would like to apologize should there have been any omissions or errors, and would be pleased to make the appropriate correction for future editions of the book.